FIVE THOUSAND AMERICAN FAMILIES—

PATTERNS OF ECONOMIC PROGRESS

VOLUME V

Components of Change in Family Well-Being
and Other Analyses of the First Eight Years
of the Panel Study of Income Dynamics

Edited by Greg J. Duncan and James N. Morgan

With Contributions by Richard D. Coe, Martin David, Greg J. Duncan,
C. Russell Hill, Daniel Hill, Martha S. Hill, Saul Hoffman, John W. Holmes,
James N. Morgan, and Arland Thornton

Conducted Under Contracts with the Office of Economic Opportunity
(Responsibility for this project has been transferred to the Office of the
Assistant Secretary for Planning and Evaluation, Department of
Health, Education, and Welfare)

SURVEY RESEARCH CENTER
INSTITUTE FOR SOCIAL RESEARCH
THE UNIVERSITY OF MICHIGAN

ISR Code No. 3916

Five Thousand American Families—Patterns of Economic Progress, Volume V
Library of Congress Catalog Card No. 74-62002
ISBN 0-87944-211-5 paperbound
ISBN 0-87944-212-3 clothbound

Published by the Institute for Social Research
The University of Michigan, Ann Arbor, Michigan 48106

Published 1977
Printed in the United States of America

CONTENTS

V

Preface

This volume contains analyses of data from the first eight waves of the Panel Study of Income Dynamics. Past analysis has shown that family composition changes, labor force participation decisions, and changes in earnings all contribute to the fluctuations in economic status experienced by our panel members. In the first part of this volume, we attempt to evaluate the relative importance of these events and decisions for various groups of panel individuals. The second part deals with a variety of loosely related topics: the relationship between macroeconomic growth and family income; how family background, education, and attitudes affect earnings level and change; and the patterns of year-to-year change in earnings. Other chapters cover fertility patterns, labor force participation decisions of wives, and the determinants of participation in the food stamps program. As in previous volumes, we summarize work of other researchers who are using the panel data. We also have three short, descriptive chapters which update past research or present information on some of the questions that are new to the eighth wave.

Amazingly, our staff has remained largely unchanged and sane. Joan Brinser continues to care for our respondents and our English. Beverly Harris and Paula Pelletier manage the increasingly long and complicated data set. Charles Stallman supervises the data editors; Tecla Loup, the coders. Wanda Lemon and Barbara Browne perform countless clerical tasks skillfully. Priscilla Hildebrandt and Anne Sears do so many different things that they defy any occupational classification, three-digit or otherwise. Mary Corcoran has joined our analysis staff this year. Richard Coe, Daniel Hill, Martha Hill, and Saul Hoffman help analyze the data, plan for the future waves of the study and somehow are finding time to complete their dissertations. After several years of looking after and caring for the panel study within HEW, Jonathan Lane has left government service for journalism. We wish him well and welcome his successor at HEW, Gordon Goodfellow.

We extend our thanks to Linda Stafford, who edited this volume, and to Doug

Truax and the staff of SRC's Publishing Division.

We are greatly indebted to the following individuals for their kindness in reading early drafts of this volume which incorporates many but not all of their suggestions: W. H. Locke Anderson, Frank M. Andrews, William Birdsall, Angus Campbell, and Harold Levinson of The University of Michigan; Robert Ferber, The University of Illinois; Paul Glick, Bureau of the Census; Arthur Goldberger, The University of Wisconsin; Zvi Griliches, Harvard University; C. Russell Hill, The University of South Carolina; Jonathan P. Lane, The U. S. Department of Health, Education and Welfare; Gilbert Nestel, The Ohio State University; Janet Peskin, The U. S. Department of Health, Education and Welfare; and Paul Taubman, The University of Pennsylvania.

Greg J. Duncan
James N. Morgan

Ann Arbor

PART I

COMPONENTS OF CHANGE IN FAMILY WELL-BEING

Chapter 1

AN OVERVIEW OF PART I FINDINGS

Greg J. Duncan and James N. Morgan

Introduction

Social scientists have, in recent years, learned a great deal about the determinants of various components of family well-being. While this understanding is far from complete, we now have a large number of empirical studies—some which use data from the Panel Study of Income Dynamics—of the ways in which earnings, labor force participation, labor supply, and fertility are affected by such factors as education, work experience, race, sex, and family background.

Our understanding of *change* in economic status, however, is still quite primitive. A primary reason for this empirical "underdevelopment" has been the lack of longitudinal observations of a representative sample of individuals. In the absence of data of this kind, most of the commonly held notions about change in economic status have been drawn from the analysis of cross-sectional data, but there are obvious limits to the propriety of dynamic inferences from static (cross-sectional) data. As a result, it is probably fair to say that social science has thus far failed to discover even the basic empirical dimensions of change in economic status, let alone begun to understand the processes by which these changes take place.

The analyses presented in the first four chapters of this volume focus directly on the description of changes in economic status experienced by different subgroups of the population. The Panel Study of Income Dynamics is well-suited for this kind of analysis, since it has followed a representative national sample of families for eight consecutive years from 1968 to 1975.[1] The panel study data include annual measures of the components of economic status and show incredibly diverse changes in the well-being of panel families over the eight-year period.

Previous volumes in this series have presented some preliminary material on the nature of change in economic status, and these earlier findings provide the focus for much of the analysis which follows. A comparison of the economic status of individuals in 1967 and 1972, measured by the ratio of family income to estimated family needs in each of the two years, was presented in Volume III.[2] Only a quarter of the individuals in the study remained in the same relative

---

[1] Because the study follows all *members* of the original sample of families, it retains its representativeness over time. Income is reported for the years prior to each interviewing year (i.e., 1967-1974).

[2] "Family income" and "needs" are defined in the Glossary.

income/needs position in both years. Less than half of the persons even in the lowest income/needs decile in 1967 were in the same economic position in 1972. Analysis also demonstrated that the composition of the low-income population itself was highly volatile; over the first six years of the study, only 2 percent of all sample individuals fell into the poverty group (income less than needs) every year, but over one-fifth fell below the poverty level during at least one of the panel years.[3]

Attempts to explain change in economic status and in its main component--the earnings of the head of the family--were, for the most part, unsuccessful. The conventional independent variables which satisfactorily explained the *level* of economic status in cross-sectional analyses did not explain *change* in status nearly as well. A series of attitudinal and behavioral measures were also tested and failed to show a significant relationship. It was concluded that there was "a great deal of heterogeneity and a great deal of change that has little to do with the gradual increase in earnings that is so often the focus of theoretical analyses."[4]

One factor which did appear to be strongly related to change in economic status was change in family composition. Volume IV of this series examined this relationship in detail and documented not only the pervasiveness of family composition change, but also its effects on changes in economic well-being. A particularly strong relationship was found between change in marital status and economic status for both married women and women who began the panel period as single heads of families.

Purpose

When economic status is measured by total family income relative to a family needs standard, then change in economic status may be seen to result from changes in the various components of income and also from changes in the composition of the family. The components of total family income are the wage rates and work hours of family members, and transfer and capital income; the needs standard accounts for the number, age, and sex of family members.

In the first four chapters of this volume we attempt to account for the *variability* of change among individuals--not just central tendencies--in several

---

[3]Lane and Morgan (1975), p. 34.

[4]Morgan (1974), p. 75.

measures of economic change. Our measure of the variability is the *variance*[5] of
the change measures, which we allocate (1) among additive components of the
change measures and (2) among different subgroups of the population. Thus, we
hope to provide a broad perspective on the relative importance of changes in
family composition, in the labor force participation of all family members, in
wages and work hours for those continuously in the labor force, and in transfer
and capital income.

Our analysis of the components of change is largely descriptive. We show,
for example, the relative importance of family composition changes and labor
force participation decisions, but we have not attempted a theoretical explanation of these changes and decisions. Because of the descriptive nature of the
analysis, the correspondence between what accounts for changes in family economic
well-being and what ought to be the focus of research and public policy is by no
means direct. Some components of family income and family composition changes
which make a large relative contribution to the explanation of change in economic
status may be expected and planned for or may be unlikely to be altered by public
policy. Policy decisions need to be based on analysis of the causal models of
the changes and decisions that are described here, and this descriptive analysis
points out the potentially most important components of change in economic well-
being whose determinants deserve investigation and also identifies the components
which are the least important.[6]

The reader may object to this analysis of change because it combines such
obvious and dramatic events as entering or leaving the labor force with things
which have been of more theoretical interest to economists such as unemployment
or changes in earnings. A causal analysis surely requires looking separately at
these disparate sources of change in status. But our purpose is to put all the
various analytic studies into some perspective, particularly since it is not
always true that the changes we have assumed to be determined by individual

---

[5]We use the conventional, statistical definition of variance, i.e.,

$$\frac{\sum_{i=1}^{n} (Y_i - \bar{Y})^2}{n - 1}$$

where Y is the change measure, the subscript i refers to the ith individual,
and n is the total number of individuals. (See Appendix 1.1.)

[6]It should be kept in mind, however, that components which account for little
of total *change* may constitute a large fraction of income *level*. Information on
the level of the components is given in Appendix A.

choices or affected by public policy are really any more discretionary or subject to influence than other events. Indeed, decisions such as when to start a new household or when to retire may be more under an individual's control than his promotions or his unemployment, and they may also be affected by public policies, intentionally or not.

Method

To study change one must have an unchanging unit of analysis. Families are not suitable since family members may marry, divorce, split off, or join other families; only individuals remain identifiable year after year. Individuals can be classified according to their relationship to the head of the family at a point in time. Their economic status during any year is simply that of whatever family they belong to at that time.

Following the procedure described in Volume IV, we conducted our analysis separately for the following groups of individuals, classified by their relationship to the head of the household in 1968:[7]

1. Married male household heads.
2. Wives of household heads.
3. Unmarried (i.e., single, widowed, divorced) male household heads.
4. Unmarried female household heads.
5. Sons, aged 10-29 in 1968.
6. Daughters, aged 10-29 in 1968.
7. Children, aged 1-9 in 1968.

The general pattern of analysis was as depicted in Figure 1.1, although the analysis for each group of individuals had its own minor differences. Each individual in the sample was associated with a level of family income/needs reported in the first and eighth years of the study. The interpersonal variance in change of income/needs was first decomposed into parts associated with changes in income and with changes in needs.[8] Since the changes in these two components

---

[7]Less than 2 percent of sample individuals were children over 30 years of age or some other relative of the household head (e.g., grandchildren, brothers, nieces, etc.). These individuals have been excluded from this analysis. In nuclear families, the husband is defined to be the household head.

In addition, we have departed from the purely descriptive and assessment-oriented mode by looking separately at blacks and at the low-income population. And for the married men, we looked separately at the middle-aged group only to see what accounts for most of the change during the middle years when entering or leaving the labor force is rare.

[8]See the appendix to this chapter for algebraic detail.

6

Figure 1.1

COMPONENTS OF CHANGE IN TOTAL FAMILY INCOME/NEEDS, 1967-1974

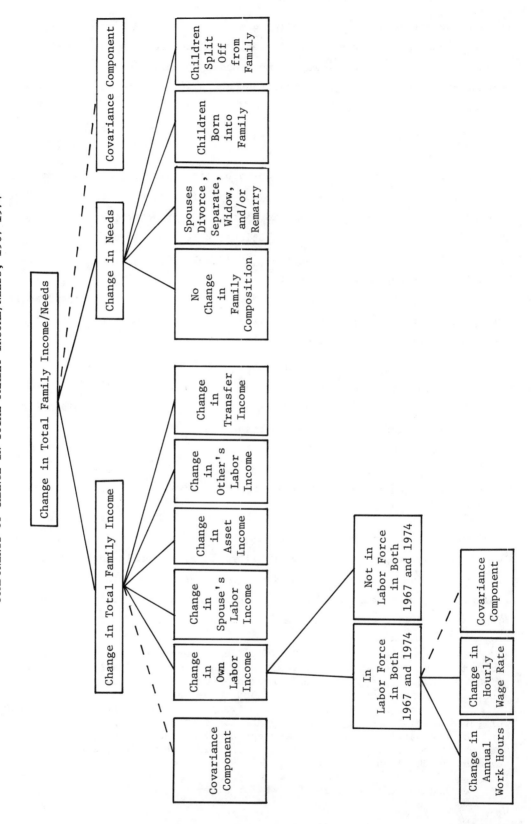

are not completely independent of one another, it was expected that there would be some covariation that could not be uniquely allocated to the two components separately.

The second stage in the analysis involved accounting for changes in the income and needs components. Because changes in family income are composed of changes in the several additive *types* of income (e.g., labor, transfer, and asset income), the variance of change in income is made up of the sum of the variance of change in each component and covariance terms for each pair of income components. The variance of changes in family needs, on the other hand, cannot be decomposed neatly into a set of additive components. It can, however, be allocated among *subgroups of individuals* that experience different types of family composition change.[9]

A third analysis stage took the variance of change in the labor incomes of a set of individuals and allocated it among subgroups according to change in labor force status. Some income changes were brought about by retirement or extensive unemployment, while others were due to changes in hourly wage rates and (smaller) variations in work hours. This stage revealed the relative importance of changes in labor force participation in producing changes in labor income.

A final analysis was performed for individuals in the labor force in both the first and last years of the study. Since labor income is the product of hourly earnings and annual hours, it is possible to decompose the variance of change in labor income into the variance of change in hours, hourly earnings, and a covariance term.

A very brief summary of the findings and their policy implications is given in the final section of this chapter. The following section summarizes the results of Chapters 2-4 in greater detail.

Summary of Results

Changes in Income/Needs

The initial analysis stage allocates the variance of change in economic status (total family income relative to needs) into parts associated with the variance of change in *income* (in constant dollars) and with variance in change in *needs*. The results of this analysis for several subgroups of sample individuals are presented in Table 1.1 and can be summarized quite succinctly: For all groups in the sample, changes in family income were much more important in

---

[9]Components of variance accounted for by subgroups add up to the total variance without any covariance terms.

Table 1.1

COMPONENTS OF THE VARIANCE OF LOG CHANGES IN
TOTAL FAMILY INCOME/NEEDS, 1967–1974
(Various Groups of Sample Individuals)

Subgroup	Weighted Percentage of Population	ℓn Change in Total Family Income	ℓn Change in Needs
Married Male Household Heads in 1968	21.2%*	83.2%	16.8%
Wives of Household Heads in 1968	22.9*	85.9	14.1
Unmarried Male Household Heads	1.7	87.5	12.5
Unmarried Female Household Heads	6.2	85.2	14.8
Sons of Household Heads, Age 10–29 in 1968	13.8	78.7	21.3
Daughters of Household Heads, Age 10–29 in 1968	12.2	79.7	20.3
Children of Household Heads, Age 1–9 in 1968	22.1	85.7	14.3

Note: The natural logarithm of the change in income/needs is equal to the log of the change in income minus the log of the change in needs. The *variance* of the log change in income/needs, therefore, equals the variance of the log of change in income plus the variance of the log of change in need minus two times the covariance. In this table the variances have been scaled to add to 100.0 percent in order to facilitate comparisons between groups. The unscaled variances and covariances for children age 1–9 in 1968 are given in the appendix to this chapter and in the appropriate chapters for the other groups.

In the above calculations, incomes have been deflated by the increase in the Consumer Price Index since 1967.

*
There are more former wives than former husbands left in the panel because of differential mortality and other panel losses.

accounting for change in economic status than were changes in needs.[10] The
importance of income changes was remarkably uniform across the various subgroups,
accounting for a low of three-quarters of the variance of the change in income/
needs for those who were initially sons and daughters of household heads in 1968
and for almost nine-tenths of the variance for the initially unmarried male
household heads. Since changes in family needs came about primarily from family
composition changes (and, to a lesser extent, from changes in the ages of family
members), we can conclude that changes in family composition did not account for
a major fraction of the change in family economic well-being by operating through
changing family needs. They may, however, have been more amenable to the will
and decisions of the individual, and they affected family income as well as
needs. The extent to which family composition changes affect family income
alone, however, is a separate issue to which we now turn.

Changes in Income

Since changes in family income so dominated changes in the income/needs
ratios, it is crucial to determine how much each of its components contributed
to its importance. This analysis is summarized in Table 1.2 for the various
subgroups of individuals. In contrast to the results for income/needs, the
relative importance of the separate income components varied considerably across
the subgroups.

As might be expected, the variance of change in the labor income of the
male adults was very important for most sample individuals. More than three-
fifths of the variance of change in the total *family* income of husbands, wives,
and young children was accounted for by changes in the husband's (father's)
labor income. The importance of labor income for those who began the panel
period as unmarried household heads was similar in magnitude.

Since the earnings and labor force participation patterns of women are
important subjects, it is helpful to put into perspective the relative importance of changes in the incomes of wives and female household heads. As
Table 1.2 shows, the variance of labor income changes of these women were much
less important than those of the men; and, for certain groups of individuals,
these changes were also less important than changes in asset income or in the
income of other family members. A look at the components of change in the fam-

---

[10]As explained in the appendix to this chapter, the variance of the natural
logarithm of change in income/needs equals the sum of the variance in log change
in income plus the variance of log change in needs plus a covariance term. To
simplify this summary of results, the covariance term is allocated to the income
and needs components in proportion to the size of the variance of the components.

Table 1.2

COMPONENTS OF THE VARIANCE OF CHANGE IN TOTAL FAMILY INCOME, 1967-1974
(Various Subgroups of Sample Individuals)

Subgroup	Weighted Percentage of Population	Change in Own Labor Income	Change in Spouse's Labor Income	Change in Transfer Income	Change in Others' Income	Change in Asset Income	Change in Father's Labor Income	Change in Mother's Labor Income
Married Male Household Heads in 1968	21.2%	61.2%	10.7%	4.8%	8.6%	14.7%	*	*
Wives of Household Heads in 1968	22.9	8.4	65.2	4.5	8.1	13.2	*	*
Unmarried Male Household Heads	1.7	69.7	7.8	4.7	11.0	6.8	*	*
Unmarried Female Household Heads	6.2	23.3	43.4	8.4	20.2	4.7	*	*
Sons of Household Heads, Age 10-29 in 1968	13.8	15.1†	3.0†	2.2	10.3	*	69.4†	
Daughters of Household Heads, Age 10-29 in 1968	12.2	6.5†	19.1†	2.2	6.7	*	65.5†	
Children of Household Heads, Age 1-9 in 1968	22.1	*	*	3.2	9.9	16.0	63.1	7.8

Note: The variances have been scaled to add to 100.0 percent in order to facilitate comparisons between groups. The unscaled variances and covariances are given in the appendix for children age 1-9 and in the appropriate chapters for other groups.

Incomes have been deflated by the increase in the Consumer Price Index since 1967.

*Component not included.

†Includes asset income.

ily income of young children, for example, shows that while the variance of
change in the father's labor income accounted for 63.1 percent of the variance
of change in total family income, variance of the *mother's* earnings accounted
for only 7.8 percent. The latter fraction was smaller than that for asset income (16.0 percent) or for the income of other family members (9.9 percent).
The relative importance of changes in the wife's labor income to the husband's
family income (10.7 percent) and to the family income of the wife herself (8.4
percent) were quite similar to the importance of the mother's earnings to the
family income of the children. Although movements into and out of the labor
force were more frequent for women than for men, the variance of change in
labor income associated with the wife's work experiences was very small relative
to those of the husband.

The situation of female heads of households was quite different. Although
only about one-seventh of these female heads married during the eight panel
years, the 1974 labor incomes of the husbands of those who did marry were large
enough to make the variance of change in *spouse's* income account for a larger
fraction of variance of change in total family income than variance in the female head's *own* labor income. It may also be surprising that changes in the
incomes of *other* family members (e.g., children and other relatives) accounted
for almost as much of the variance in the total family income of households
initially headed by a female as changes in the female head's own labor income.

A final interesting subgroup is composed of individuals who were the sons
or daughters in the initial panel year. For them, changes in parental income
dominated the change in economic status. This income fell from a high figure
to zero for many of those who had split off by the eighth year. The variance
of change in their own labor income was considerably larger for the sons than
the daughters, while the variance of change in spouse's income (which rose from
zero to a high figure for the many who split off and married) was much more
important for daughters than for sons.

Thus, a clear contrast between the male and female members of the panel
emerged from these results. For men, changes in the level of their family income were closely tied to their own experiences in the labor market. For the
women members of the panel--whether they began as wives, household heads, or
daughters--changes in the level of their family money income were much less
closely tied to their own labor market experiences and were primarily determined by the family composition changes which they underwent, particularly
marriages or divorces. The question remains as to how much control women have
over changes in family composition, the earnings of others, and even their own

earnings. Job discrimination, family stability, and the assignment of family responsibilities all affect this.

Changes in Labor Income

The variance of change in the earnings of the male adult dominated the variance of change in total family income for many of the individuals in our sample. But these variations themselves were composed of changes in hourly earnings, work hours, and labor force participation (which may have been due to retirement or extensive unemployment) and even family composition changes. To assess the relative importance of these components, we focused next on the make-up of specific components such as changes in annual earnings.

As we mentioned above, 63.1 percent of the variance in the total family income of the young children in the sample resulted from the variance of change in their father's labor income. Some of these changes came about because a divorce or separation dropped the father's contribution to family income from an initially high level when the father was present to zero when he was absent. In other cases, a mother remarried and the father's (or, in this case, new step-father's) income rose from zero to a high figure. The frequency of these kinds of family composition changes and their relative importance to change in economic status are shown in Table 1.3. Although more than three-quarters of the young children in the sample had a father in both the first and last panel years and the average change in the father's real labor income exceeded $1,500, the fraction of the total variation in the father's labor income accounted for by this group barely exceeded 60 percent. Children who lost a father through divorce or death constituted less than one-tenth of the total group of children, but the fraction of variance in the father's labor income explained by this group exceeded 20 percent. Another group of children which accounted for about one-seventh of the total variance of change in the father's labor income consisted of those who had a father in the initial panel year, lost him through divorce or death, and acquired a stepfather. Their stepfathers earned, on average, $3,000 more than their original fathers did eight years earlier.

This analysis of the young children in the sample shows that even though the variance of change in the father's income was considerably more important than other components of the family income, it was not only the change in the father's wage rate, hours of work, or even labor force participation that deserved attention. The frequency and impact of certain family composition changes combined to account for a considerable fraction of changes in the economic status of children.

Table 1.3

CHANGE IN FATHER'S LABOR INCOME BY CHANGE IN FATHER, 1967-1974
(All Children Age 1-9 in 1968)

Status of Father	Number of Observations	Weighted Proportion of Observations	Mean Change in Father's Labor Income	Fraction of Variance of Change in Father's Labor Income Explained by Subgroup
Father Not Present in Either 1968 or 1974	583	7.1%	$ 0	0.2%
Father Present in Both 1968 and 1975	2,210	76.0	1,568	60.3
Father Present in 1968 But Not Present in 1975	363	9.5	-6,438	20.4
Father Not Present in 1968, (Step)Father Present in 1975	138	2.8	6,638	4.4
Father Present in 1968, Stepfather Present in 1975	122	4.6	3,090	14.8
TOTAL	3,416	100.0%	$ 906	100.0%

Note: Income figures have been deflated by the increase in the Consumer Price
       Index since 1967.

MTR #7136

Labor Force Participation Decisions

Changes in an individual's own labor income can come about both from movements into and out of the labor force and, for those continuously in the labor
force, from variations in work hours and hourly earnings. The relative importance of labor force participation decisions in explaining income changes depends
upon their frequency and the size of the resulting earnings changes. Table 1.4
summarizes the importance of movements into and out of the labor force for sample
individuals who in 1968 were married men, wives, or unmarried female household
heads.[11]

As might be expected, most (81.6 percent) of the married men were in the
labor force in both the first and eighth years of the panel, and this group
accounted for a large fraction (79.9 percent) of the variance of change in labor
income. About one-tenth of these men left the labor force (primarily due to
retirement) and the loss in labor income that they experienced accounted for most
of the remaining one-fifth of the variance in labor income. Some of these decreases, of course, were counterbalanced by increases in transfer income from
pensions and Social Security income.[12]

The pattern for the two groups of women shown in Table 1.4 is quite different. Fewer than one-third of the initial wives were in the labor force both
years and this group accounted for less than one-third of the total variance of
change in wives' labor income. The patterns of the initially unmarried female
heads were more like those of the married men, although fewer than half of them
were working in both the first and last year, and changes in their incomes accounted for about one-half of the total variance.

Movements into and out of the labor force, then, were much more frequent
and important for these women than for the husbands. About one-quarter of the
wives and female heads changed their labor force status, and they accounted for
more than half of the variance of change in the labor incomes of their respective
groups.

Changes in Work Hours and Wages

The path from changes in our global measure of economic status--total family
income/needs--to changes in hourly earnings and work hours for those continuously

---

[11]The initially unmarried male household heads constitute a very small subsample of adults and are omitted from these summary tables. Complete results for
them are given in Chapter 3.

[12]In the second chapter, part of the analysis is repeated for husbands in the
age range 25-45. Even though this removes the effects of retirement, the importance of changes in labor income relative to changes in other components remained
roughly the same.

Table 1.4

COMPONENTS OF CHANGE IN LABOR INCOME BY CHANGE IN LABOR FORCE STATUS, 1967-1974
(Married Males, Wives, and Unmarried Female Household Heads)

Population Subgroup

Change in Labor Force Status	Married Male Heads of Households in 1968 (n=2209)		Wives of Household Heads in 1968 (n=2365)		Unmarried Female Household Heads (n=974)	
	Weighted Percent of Observations	Percent of Variation in Change in Labor Income Explained by Subgroup	Weighted Percent of Observations	Percent of Variation in Change in Labor Income Explained by Subgroup	Weighted Percent of Observations	Percent of Variation in Change in Labor Income Explained by Subgroup
Always in: In Labor Force in Both 1967 and 1974	81.6%	79.9%	27.4%	31.1%	44.9%	49.9%
Left: In Labor Force in 1967, Out by 1974	10.8	18.1	12.7	33.4	18.5	39.1
Entered: Out of Labor Force in 1967, in by 1974	1.1	1.9	16.1	33.8	5.2	11.0
Never in: Out of Labor Force in Both 1967 and 1974	6.5	0.0	43.7	1.7	31.4	0.1
TOTAL	100.0%	100.0%	99.9%	100.0%	100.0%	100.1%

Note: Incomes have been deflated by the increase in the Consumer Price Index since 1967.

An individual is defined as in the labor force in a year if he/she worked at least 250 hours.

in the labor force was quite long. Changes in needs, family composition, transfer and capital income, income of other family members, and labor force status
all accounted for some of the variance in the overall measure. The role of
changes in wage and work hours was extremely small for wives, quite small for
female heads of households, and somewhat larger for husbands. While it is not
possible to calculate precisely a single figure that represents the importance of
these changes, it can be noted that even for husbands--the group for whom wage
and work hours changes were most important--changes in earnings for those working
in both the first and eighth years accounted for about 80 percent of the variance
of change in labor income for all husbands; the variance of change in labor income, in turn, accounted for just over 60 percent of the variance in total family
income; and the variance of change in family income comprised about 85 percent of
the variance of family income/needs.[13] For the wives and female heads, most of
the corresponding percentages were much lower.

With this in mind, we now turn to the relative importance of changes in wage
rate and work hours in explaining labor income changes for those who worked in
the beginning and ending years of the panel. We began this analysis with the
fact that the natural logarithm of the percentage change in earnings equals the
sum of the log change in annual work hours and log change in hourly wage rate.
The variance of log change in earnings equals the sum of the variance of log
changes in the two components.[14] The relative sizes of the variance of hours
and wage rates is shown in Table 1.5 separately for 1968 husbands, wives, and
female heads of households. Although changes in work hours were comparatively
less important for men than for the two groups of women, the variance of change
in hours was surprisingly high among all groups. For the women, the variance of
the log change in work hours accounted for more of the variance of log change in
annual income than did the variance of change in wage rates.[15] For men, hours
accounted for about three-fourths as much of the variance of log change in labor
income as wage rates.

---

[13]These fractions can't just be multiplied to get an overall fraction because
of switches from income to log income and because of covariance terms associated
with the components.

[14]As with the other decompositions into subcomponents, there is also a covariance term. In this summary chapter, we allocate covariances in proportion to the
size of the variance of the components.

[15]Remember that individuals who either entered or left the labor force have
been omitted from these calculations; only changes for those who worked at least
250 hours in both years are involved here.

Table 1.5

COMPONENTS OF THE VARIANCE OF LOG CHANGE IN
INDIVIDUALS' OWN LABOR INCOME, 1967-1974
(Married Males, Wives, and Unmarried Female Household Heads
Who Were in the Labor Force in Both 1967 and 1974)

	Fraction of Variance of ℓn Change in Labor Income Explained by Component		
Component	Married Male Heads of House- holds in 1968 (n=1821)	Wives of Household Heads in 1968 (n=660)	Unmarried Female Household Heads (n=412)
ℓn Change in Hourly Wage Rate	57.4%	42.9%	46.8%
ℓn Change in Annual Work Hours	42.6	57.1	53.2
TOTAL	100.0%	100.0%	100.0%

Note: Wage rates have been deflated by the increase in the Consumer Price Index since 1967.

In this table, the variances have been scaled to add to 100.0 percent in order to facilitate comparison between groups. The unscaled variances and covariances are given in the appropriate chapters.

Results for Blacks and the Poor

The results presented thus far have been based on analyses of the entire sample of individuals (which is representative of the entire population of the United States). We repeated the analysis separately for blacks and for the following nested subgroups: (1) the "target population" (i.e., individuals in families in the bottom income/needs quintile for at least one of the eight years), (2) the initially poor, and (3) those among the initially poor who had climbed above the poverty line by the eighth year of the panel. Most of the patterns for these subgroups are quite similar to those already discussed, and so we highlight only the differences:

The economic well-being of black women was much less closely tied to marital decisions than that of white women. Because earnings of black men were substantially lower than those of white men, divorce caused a much smaller drop in the family income of black wives, and marriage or remarriage led to much smaller increases.

Incomes of black families were affected more than those of whites by the incomes of their children and, more important, by the earnings of other relatives of the husband and wife. For black female household heads, changes in the incomes of those other family members were even more important than changes in their own earnings or income changes brought about by marriage. To gain an understanding of the changes in the economic well-being of black families, it is crucial to study the patterns of economic help among relatives.

For the families that were below the poverty line at the beginning of the panel period, earned income of the head and others was much more important than transfer income in lifting them over the poverty line.

Conclusions and Implications

Changes in economic well-being are pervasive and result from the interaction of many forces. In this analysis, we have defined an individual's economic status by total family income relative to needs. Changes in status can come about from events that range from the dramatic--such as divorce or disability, to the more mundane--such as taking a second job; labor force participation decisions, wage changes, and children leaving home lie somewhere in between. These events had varying importance to different classes of individuals in our panel. Divorce and remarriage decisions were critical to the individuals who were wives, female household heads, or young children in the first year of the panel study, while they had relatively little effect on husbands or unmarried male household heads. Changes in the labor force participation of wives were surprisingly unimportant for the economic well-being of other family members involved. This was not so much because these changes in labor force participation were so infrequent but rather because the changes in earnings that they brought about were often smaller than changes in other components of income. Indeed, the changes in the earned incomes of children and, especially for black families, other relatives were often more important than changes in the wife's earnings. As might be expected, changes in the earned income of the husbands were more important than any other component for most sample individuals. Some of these changes were due to decisions about labor force participation (such as retirement), but a surprisingly large fraction resulted from changes in the work hours of those continuously in the labor force.

The implications of these past events for the future, and for public policy, can only be drawn uncertainly. Events which have accounted for much of the total variance of change may have been normal life-cycle occurrences, unaffected by possible changes in any public or private policy. Events which have accounted for little of the variance in the past may or may not be changeable. A case in point is that the earnings of women and black men accounted for little change because they were relatively smaller than the earnings of white men. If earnings differences between races or sexes become smaller, the relative importance of the income components may change accordingly. With these caveats in mind, we now turn to some possible policy implications of our analysis.

Since various types of family composition changes bring about dramatic and often detrimental changes in well-being, it is important that policy makers be aware of the implications of their policies on the composition of families. The analysis of composition changes presented in Volume IV found that economic factors do play a role in these changes. Low-income couples living in states paying higher levels of Aid to Families with Dependent Children (AFDC) were considerably more likely to get divorced. Women with high actual or potential earnings were more likely to get divorced and less likely to marry. Economic incentives that are built into tax, income maintenance, and subsidy programs may have similar effects.

Analysts of the family should be aware of the fact that the concept and very definition of a family becomes less clear as time passes. Barely one-quarter of the individuals in our sample were in families where no composition changes occurred over the eight-year period, and about the same number were in families where there was a change in either the household head or wife. Clearly, the longer the time period the more useful it is to choose the *individual* rather than the *family* as the unit of analysis.

The finding that changes in work hours were almost as important as changes in wage rates in producing changes in labor incomes points up the need to determine the extent to which changes in work hours are involuntary. Previous analysis using the panel data has found that fully one-third of the male heads of households were unemployed at some point in the first five years of the panel, and over one-fifth were out of work for at least *one month* during that time. And each year we find that almost one-fifth of the employed heads of households we interview are unable to work as much as they would like. These facts suggest that many work hours changes are not freely chosen and further suggest a possible role for policies that would enable those wanting more work to get it or at least ease the financial burdens that accompany large involuntary decreases in work hours.

Related to the importance of changes in work hours is the relative unimportance of changes in wage rates. Although wage rates are the object of voluminous research and costly manpower programs, our analysis has found that wage rate changes accounted for only a small fraction of the total changes in family well-being.

One surprising finding is that changes in the incomes of family members other than the head and wife mattered more than changes in the wife's earnings. Some of these incomes were earned by the children entering the labor market for the first time, while some came from the earnings of other relatives moving in and out of the household. The incomes of these other family members were particularly important for black families. Clearly, the role of other family members deserves more attention from researchers interested in the economic well-being of families. Do their earnings or even presence in the household respond to fluctuations in the earnings of the head of the family, or to administrative treatment of the "household" for income maintenance programs and tax administration? If definitions of "need" or of "taxable income" are based on the household or family, they inevitably subject decisions about household arrangements to economic incentives or disincentives. Arrangements that bring additional people into the family may increase the stability of the household's economic well-being and increase its level by pooling resources.

Finally, transfer incomes such as Social Security, AFDC, unemployment benefits—often thought of as a major defense against adversity—are relatively unimportant components of change in family well-being, although they do have the expected negative covariance with other components. Not all transfer incomes respond to short-run changes in family incomes or needs, and those which do are sufficiently small and limited to leave a great deal of instability in the combined family income.

References

Lane, Jonathan and Morgan, James N. "Patterns of Change in Economic Status and
   Family Structure." In Five Thousand American Families--Patterns of Economic
   Progress. Volume III. Edited by Greg J. Duncan and James N. Morgan.
   Ann Arbor: Institute for Social Research, 1975.

Morgan, James N. "Change in Global Measures." In James N. Morgan et al. Five
   Thousand American Families--Patterns of Economic Progress. Volume I.
   Ann Arbor: Institute for Social Research, 1974.

APPENDIX 1.1

The Algebra of Components of Variance

The analysis of the first four chapters in this volume are based on the decomposition of the variance of change in several measures of economic status. The variance of a change measure can be decomposed in two distinct ways: (1) among different subgroups of the population and (2) among additive components of the measure. The algebra of these two types of decomposition is described in this appendix.

Allocating Variance Among Population Subgroups

Any quantitative measure available for individuals in a population can be used to characterize subgroups in the population. In this volume, we are interested in variability, not just central tendencies, and we want to be able to say how much of the total variability each subgroup accounts for. A group can contribute disproportionately to the overall variability if its members are more heterogeneous than members of other groups or if its average is widely different from the overall average. Where there is only one level of grouping, a one-way analysis of variance components is possible using the following identity:

$$\sum_{i=1}^{N_1+N_2} (y_i-\bar{y})^2 = N_1(\bar{y}_1-\bar{y})^2 + N_2(y_2-\bar{y})^2 + \sum_{i=1}^{N_1} (y_{i1}-\bar{y}_1)^2 + \sum_{i=1}^{N_2} (y_{i2}-\bar{y}_2)^2$$

Explanation:

	Accounted for by:			
Total Variance =	Difference of Group 1 mean from grand mean (and size of Group 1)	+ Difference of Group 2 mean from grand mean (and size of Group 2)	+ Variance of Group 1 Members around their group mean	+ Variance of Group 2 Members around their group mean
=	"explained" by membership in Group 1	+ "explained" by membership in Group 2	+ "unexplained" variance in Group 1	+ "unexplained" variance in Group 2

If one were interested in explanation, the two explained components would be pooled to estimate the explanatory power (Eta^2) of knowing which of the two subgroups individuals are in. But we are interested in "where the action is"; namely, how much of the variance--explained or unexplained--is attributable to each group, whether it is due to overall deviation from the average or its members' greater variability around its own average level. A group can account for much of the variance if it is large, deviant, or very heterogeneous.

The fact that our measure is not a static measure but one of *change* between 1967 and 1974 makes the emphasis on contribution to overall variance even more important, since a group can have an average change of zero but be so large and heterogeneous that it accounts for a great deal of the variance in patterns of change.

Allocating the Variance of a Variable Among Additive Components of That Variable

A second kind of decomposition is possible when a measure is made up of additive components. If $Y = Z + W$, then

(1) $VAR(Y) = VAR(Z) + VAR(W) + 2COV(Z,W)$

And if $Y = Z - W$, we have:

(2) $VAR(Y) = VAR(Z) + VAR(W) - 2COV(Z,W)$

Thus the variance of a sum can be more or less than the sum of the variances of the components, depending on the sign of the covariance and on whether the covariance enters positively or negatively--that is, whether it is the sum or the difference of the components.

When there are more than two components, there is a covariance term for each pair. When, as in our case, we are dealing with a measure of change, the

covariances are interesting revelations of offsetting or reinforcing patterns
of change in components.

One final complication: Two of our three examinations of components of
change involved components that multiply rather than add--hours times dollars
per hour equals earnings, and income times (1/Needs) equals income/needs. In
this case, in order to use the decomposition formulas (1) and (2), we must convert to logarithms, which transforms the product into a sum. But the absolute
change in a measure can be zero or negative, and the ℓn of zero is minus in-
finity. So we must also switch from absolute changes (1974 minus 1967) to ratios
(1974/1967), which means that we are decomposing the ℓn of the *relative* change
in the product into the ℓn of the relative change in each term and the ℓn of the
covariance of the two changes.

In the case of Income/Needs we have:

$$\ell n \ \frac{\text{Income } 74/\text{Needs } 74}{\text{Income } 67/\text{Needs } 67} = \ell n \ \frac{\text{Income } 74}{\text{Income } 67} - \ell n \ \frac{\text{Needs } 74}{\text{Needs } 67}$$

The decomposition of variance, then, is:

$$\text{Variance } [\ell n \ \frac{(\text{Income}/\text{Needs } 74)}{(\text{Income}/\text{Needs } 67)}] = \text{Variance } [\ell n (\frac{\text{Income } 74}{\text{Income } 67}) - \ell n (\frac{\text{Needs } 74}{\text{Needs } 67})] =$$

$$\text{Variance } [\ell n \ (\frac{\text{Income } 74}{\text{Income } 67})] + \text{Variance } [\ell n \ (\frac{\text{Needs } 74}{\text{Needs } 67})]$$

$$- \ 2 \ \text{Covariance } ([\ell n \ (\frac{\text{Income } 74}{\text{Income } 67})], \ [\ell n \ (\frac{\text{Needs } 74}{\text{Needs } 67})]) \ .$$

The two main components of variance of change in income/needs will add to
more than the total when there is a *positive* correlation between changes in
income and changes in needs, since a positive correlation would maintain the
negative sign preceding the covariance term.

In the case of hours and hourly earnings we have:

$$\ell n \ (\frac{\text{Labor Income } 74}{\text{Labor Income } 67}) = \ell n \ (\frac{\text{Hours x \$/Hour } 74}{\text{Hours x \$/Hour } 67})$$

$$= \ell n \ (\frac{\text{Hours } 74}{\text{Hours } 67}) + \ell n \ (\frac{\$/\text{Hour } 74}{\$/\text{Hour } 67})$$

$$\text{Variance } [\ln(\frac{\text{Labor Income 74}}{\text{Labor Income 67}})] = \text{Variance } [\ln(\frac{\text{Hours 74}}{\text{Hours 67}}) + \ln(\frac{\$/\text{Hour 74}}{\$/\text{Hour 67}})]$$

$$= \text{Variance } [\ln(\frac{\text{Hours 74}}{\text{Hours 67}})] +$$

$$\text{Variance } [\ln(\frac{\$/\text{Hour 74}}{\$/\text{Hour 67}})] +$$

$$2 \text{ Covariance } ([\ln(\frac{\text{Hours 74}}{\text{Hours 67}})], [\ln(\frac{\$/\text{Hour 74}}{\$/\text{Hour 67}})]).$$

The two main components of variance of change in labor income add to less than the total when there is a positive correlation between changes in wage rate and changes in hours worked.

Figure A1.1a

ANALYSIS OF THE VARIANCE OF THE LOG CHANGE
IN REAL TOTAL FAMILY INCOME/NEEDS, 1967-1974
(Children, Age 1-9 in 1968)

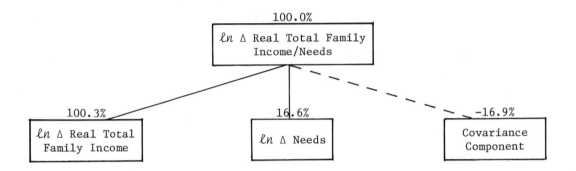

Number of Observations: 3,416

Note: The natural logarithm of the change in income/needs is equal to the log
of the change in income minus the log of the change in needs. The *variance* of the log change in income/needs is equal to the variance of the
log change in income plus the variance of the log change in needs minus
two times the covariance. Hence, a positive covariance leads to a negative covariance component.

MTR #7136

Figure A1.1b

ANALYSIS OF THE VARIANCE OF CHANGE IN
REAL TOTAL FAMILY INCOME, 1967-1974
(Children, Age 1-9 in 1968)

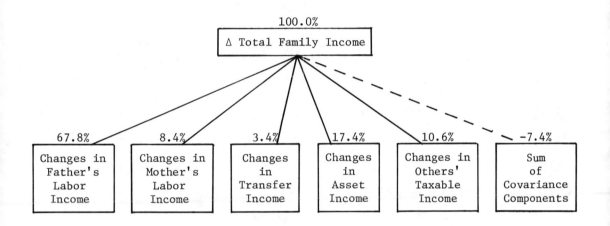

Number of Observations: 3,416

Note: The variance of change in total family income equals the sum of (1) vari-
       ance of change in father's labor income, (2) variance of change in moth-
       er's labor income, (3) variance of change in transfer income, (4) vari-
       ance of change in asset income, (5) variance of change in others taxable
       income and (6) the sum of the covariance components (i.e., the sum of two
       times the variance between change in each pair of income sources).

MTR #7136

Table A1.1a

MEANS AND STANDARD DEVIATIONS OF COMPONENTS OF
CHANGE IN REAL TOTAL FAMILY INCOME, 1967-1974
(Children Age 1-9 in 1968)

Income Change Component	Mean Change 1967-1974	Standard Deviation of Change
Change in Father's Labor Income	$ 895	$5,572
Change in Mother's Labor Income	761	1,965
Change in Transfer Income	296	1,250
Change in Asset Income	456	2,809
Change in Other's Taxable Income	678	2,205
TOTAL	$3,086	$6,769

Number of Observations: 3,416

Note: 1974 income figures have been deflated by the increase in the Consumer
Price Index since 1967.

Chapter 2

HUSBANDS AND WIVES

Daniel Hill and Saul Hoffman

Introduction

This chapter examines the eight-year change in economic status among individuals who were married as of the first year of the panel study (1968). We present
the means and standard deviations of change, as well as the decomposition of the
total variance of change in economic status into its components, following the
procedure outlined in Chapter 1. Each of these measures highlights a different
element of change and, together, it is hoped they suggest the dimensions of change
in economic status and the relative importance of its various sources. Section I
examines change among all initially married men, while Section II focuses on
their 1968 wives.

Analysis

I. CHANGES IN ECONOMIC STATUS AMONG THE INITIALLY MARRIED MEN

Changes in Income/Needs

Does an individual's economic status remain relatively constant over time or
is there widespread change in economic standing? If we answer that question by
considering panel members' income/needs decile positions in 1967 and again in
1974, it is clear that change in status is not only quite common but often quite
dramatic as well. Table 2.1 summarizes the eight-year changes in income/needs
deciles for all the initially married men in the panel and for those who began in
the lowest decile. Overall, less than a quarter of the men were in the same decile position in both 1967 and 1974, about 30 percent changed by one decile and
about 45 percent shifted by two deciles or more. Those in the lowest decile in
1967 also experienced a great deal of change in economic status. Although about
44 percent were still in the lowest decile in 1974, 28 percent had moved up one
decile and another 28 percent had moved up two deciles or more.[1]

The actual mean change in income/needs during the panel period, shown in
Table 2.2, was .63. On average, total family income rose in real terms by $1,835,
while needs declined by about $130. The huge variability in the distribution of
these changes is suggested by the sizes of the standard deviations. For change
in income/needs the standard deviation was almost five times as large as the
mean, while the standard deviation of change in family income was three and one-

---

[1]See Table A2.1a for the complete distribution of 1974 income/needs decile position by 1967 decile position.

Table 2.1

CHANGE IN INCOME/NEEDS DECILE POSITION, 1967-1974
(Married Men in 1968)

Change in Decile Position	All	Lowest Decile, 1967
Fell Two Deciles or More	21.9%	--
Fell One Decile	13.5	--
No Change	23.7	44.2
Increased One Decile	17.9	27.5
Increased Two Deciles of More	23.0	28.2
TOTAL	100.0%	100.0%

Number of Observations: 2,209

Note: The deciles were constructed from the distribution of income/needs for
the entire sample of families. Consequently, more or less than 10 percent of any subgroup can fall into any one decile.

See Appendix Table A2.1a for the complete distribution of 1974 income/
needs decile by 1967 income/needs decile.

Table 2.2

MEANS AND STANDARD DEVIATIONS OF COMPONENTS OF
CHANGE IN REAL TOTAL FAMILY MONEY INCOME/NEEDS, 1967–1974
(Married Men in 1968)

Income/Needs Change Component	Mean Change	Standard Deviation of Change
Change in Total Family Income	$ 1,835	$6,748
Change in Needs	- 129	1,089
Change in Income/Needs	.63	3.0

Number of Observations: 2,209

Note: Income and Income/Needs have been deflated by the increase in the Consumer Price Index since 1967.

Table 2.3

MEANS AND STANDARD DEVIATIONS OF COMPONENTS OF CHANGE
IN REAL TOTAL FAMILY INCOME, 1967–1974
(Married Men in 1968)

	Mean Change	Standard Deviation of Change
Change in Husband's Labor Income	$ 396	$5,525
Change in Wife's Labor Income	140	2,320
Change in Head's and Wife's Capital Income	395	2,701
Change in Transfer Income	518	1,549
Change in Others' Taxable Income	379	2,081
TOTAL CHANGE	$1,828	$6,747

Number of Observations: 2,209

Note: 1974 Income has been deflated by the increase in the Consumer Price Index since 1967.

MTR #7508

half times its mean value.

We began by decomposing the variance of the eight-year change in income/
needs into its two components, variance of change in income and variance of
change in needs (see Figure 2.1).[2] As Figure 2.1 clearly shows, changes in income accounted for the largest share of the total variation. Note that the covariance between change in income and change in needs was positive (although the
covariance component was negative). Since needs can change only gradually
through aging or more suddenly through changes in family composition, the covariance term suggests that change in needs may have had an important effect on
changes in economic status by also affecting income. This issue will be considered in more detail later in this chapter.

Changes in Income

For the initially married men, the mean change in real family income from
1967 to 1974 was more than $1,800. That change can be decomposed into five addi-
tive terms: (1) change in the labor income of the head and (2) of the spouse,
(3) change in capital income, (4) change in transfer income, and (5) change in
the taxable income of other household members. Table 2.3 presents the means and
standard deviations of change in these components.

The mean changes were, for the most part, relatively moderate. The largest
mean change was in transfer income (over $500), with change in the husband's la-
bor income, the income of others, and the capital income of the head and wife all
averaging just under $400. While it may seem surprising to find that average
change in head's and wife's labor income was less than one-third of the total
change, the explanation is straightforward. The mean changes included not only
the positive changes commonly associated with regular labor force participation,
but also large negative changes. For example, some men may have retired by 1974,
while others whose wives were working in 1967 may have become divorced or widowed.
In either case, a large drop in the labor income of the head or the spouse would
have resulted. The diversity of this change in labor income is suggested by the
standard deviations given in Table 2.3. The standard deviation of change in the
head's labor earnings was more than $5,500, while for their wives it was just
over $2,300. And for total change in family income, the standard deviation was
more than $6,700--about three and one-half times the mean change.

If we consider the same components in terms of their respective contributions to total variation rather than average change, we come to somewhat differ-

---

[2]This required transforming all the measures by taking the logarithm of the
ratio of 1974 to 1967 income and needs.

34

Figure 2.1

COMPONENTS OF THE VARIANCE OF THE LOG CHANGE
IN REAL TOTAL FAMILY INCOME/NEEDS, 1967-1974
(Married Men in 1968)

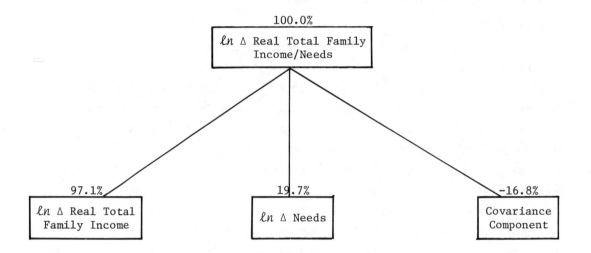

Number of Observations: 2,209

Note: The natural logarithm of the change in income/needs is equal to the log
        of the change in income minus the log of the change in needs. The vari-
        ance of the log change in income/needs is equal to the variance of the
        log of change in income plus the variance of the log of change in needs
        minus two times the covariance. Hence, a positive covariance leads to
        a negative covariance component. (See the appendix to Chapter 1 for
        details on this procedure.)

MTR #7508

ent conclusions regarding the relative importance of the components as Figure 2.2
illustrates. Change in the head's labor income accounted for over two-thirds of
the total variation even though its mean change was relatively small. In contrast, changes in transfer income and in others' income accounted for only 15
percent of the total variance, although they amounted to half the mean change.
The different results here reflect the fact that positive and negative changes
offset each other in the calculation of mean changes, but not in the computation
of variances. Clearly, there was much more variation in labor earnings than in
the other components of family income.

Changes in Labor Force Status

As noted above, the mean change in the labor income of husbands and wives
reflects the net effect of groups of individuals who experienced rather different
changes. Most husbands worked throughout the period, but some retired or were
disabled, others joined the labor force during the period, and still others
worked in neither 1967 nor 1974. We would expect large differences in change in
labor income and in the average amount of variability in income changes among
these groups.

These changes in the head's labor income are given in Table 2.4 for four
subgroups, classified according to their changes in labor force status. Both
mean changes in labor income and the percentage contribution of each subgroup to
the total variation of change in labor income are shown. The largest group, over
80 percent of the sample, worked in both 1967 and 1974; their real labor incomes
rose, on average, by nearly $1,200 during the period. The most dramatic changes
in earnings were experienced by those whose labor force status changed. The
small group who entered the labor force during the period had a mean increase of
over $5,800, while for the larger group of men who were no longer working in 1974
labor income declined by an average of nearly $5,700. For about three-quarters
of the men in this last group, the decline represented normal planned retirement
from work. For the others the decline in work hours and the accompanying drop in
earnings were due to disability or extended unemployment and were probably not anticipated. The two groups which accounted for most of the variance were those
who left the labor force and those who worked in both years. In particular,
those no longer working accounted for a disproportionately large share of the
total variance relative to their population size. Those out of the labor force
in both years accounted for virtually none of the variance, while those who
worked in both years accounted for a proportion of the variance which was approximately equal to their sample size.

Changes in the labor income of the wife can be analyzed similarly, with the

36

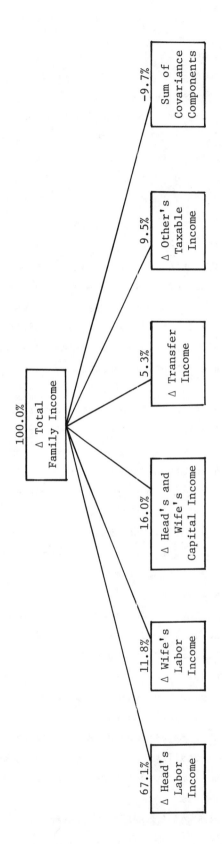

Figure 2.2

COMPONENTS OF THE VARIANCE OF CHANGE
IN REAL TOTAL FAMILY INCOME, 1967-1974
(Married Men in 1968)

Number of Observations: 2,209

Note: The variance of change in total family income equals the sum of the variance of change in each of the five
income sources shown above plus the sum of the covariance components (i.e., the sum of two times the covariance between changes in each pair of income sources).

MTR #7508

Table 2.4

CHANGE IN HUSBANDS' LABOR INCOME
BY CHANGE IN LABOR FORCE STATUS, 1967-1974
(Married Men in 1968)

Change in Labor Force Status	Number of Observations	Weighted Proportion of Observations	Mean Change in Labor Income	Percentage Contribution to Total Variance in Change in Labor Income
Out of Labor Force in both 1967 and 1974	133	6.5%	$- 5	0.1%
Entered Labor Force by 1974	29	1.1	5,842	1.9
Left Labor Force by 1974	226	10.8	-5.695	18.1
In Labor Force in both 1967 and 1974	1,821	81.6	1,170	79.9
TOTAL	2,209	100.0%	$ 396	100.0%

Note: 1974 Income has been deflated by the increase in the Consumer Price Index since 1967.

An individual is defined as in the labor force if he worked at least 250 hours during the year.

Table 2.5

CHANGE IN SPOUSE'S LABOR INCOME
BY CHANGE IN LABOR FORCE OR MARITAL STATUS, 1967-1974
(Married Men in 1968)

Change in Labor Force or Marital Status	Number of Observations	Weighted Proportion of Observations	Mean Change in Labor Income	Percentage Contribution to Total Variance in Change in Labor Income
Out of Labor Force in both 1967 and 1974	844	39.4%	$ 8	0.9%
Entered Labor Force by 1974	323	13.7	2,578	26.6
Left Labor Force by 1974	238	11.5	-2,262	25.5
In Labor Force in both 1967 and 1974	515	22.9	759	23.3
No Wife in 1975	179	7.2	-1,475	10.2
New Wife in 1975	110	5.3	984	13.4
TOTAL	2,209	100.0%	$ 168	100.0%

Note: 1974 Income has been deflated by the increase in the Consumer Price Index since 1967.

An individual is defined as in the labor force if she worked at least 250 hours during the year.

added possibilities that in 1975 there may have been no wife or there may have
been a different wife. These changes are presented in Table 2.5 and they suggest
that changes in the labor force status of the 1968 wives were both common and
dramatic in their effects on family income. The wives in about 60 percent of the
households maintained the same labor force status in both 1967 and 1974; about a
quarter of the wives changed labor force status (slightly more entered than
left), and in another 12.5 percent of the families there was a change in marital
status. As would be expected, mean changes in earnings varied significantly
among these subgroups. The most important subgroups in accounting for the total
variance of change were those who worked in both years and those with a change
in labor force status. These latter two groups and the two groups with marital
status change—those with no wife in 1975 and those with a different wife—all
accounted for a large share, relative to their group size, of the total variance
in spouse's income.

Changes in Hours and Wages

For those men who worked in both 1967 and 1974, the variance in the logarithmic change in labor earnings can be decomposed further into the variances in
the logarithmic changes in work hours and hourly wages and into a covariance
term. This decomposition is shown in Figure 2.3. Although changes in wage rates
dominated changes in hours in accounting for the total variance of change in labor earnings, the effect of changes in hours was surprisingly large. If most
men worked regular (40-hour) work weeks year after year, then the effect of
change in hours would have been essentially zero. However, not only was a 40-
hour week far from universal, but change in annual hours over the eight-year
period was substantial as well. The average absolute change in hours for these
men—all of whom worked at least 250 hours in both 1967 and 1974—was over 500.
And as Table 2.6 shows, this mean change in hours was not due just to large
changes for men with initially low or high hours. Change was pervasive in all
1967 hours categories, much of it across more than one category (at least 350
hours). Job change was one obvious cause of changes in hours, but sickness, unemployment, overtime, strikes, and second jobs were also likely to be important.

Changes in Needs

We noted at the beginning of this section that changes in family needs accounted for a relatively small portion (about 20 percent) of the total variance
of change in income/needs, but that these needs changes also influenced change
in economic status by affecting change in income. Table 2.7 examines both of
these effects in greater detail. Note first that change in the composition of
families was, indeed, common. More than two-thirds of all families experienced

Table 2.6

ANNUAL WORK HOURS IN 1974 BY ANNUAL WORK HOURS IN 1967
(Married Men in 1968)

1967 Hours	Weighted Percentage of Observations (1967)	1974 Hours							
		0-1499	1500-1849	1850-2149	2150-2499	2500-2999	3000-3499	3500+	Total
0-1499	5.5%	35.7%	12.4%	14.7%	14.1%	13.5%	5.9%	3.7%	100.0%
1500-1849	7.0	16.7	26.1	31.7	15.1	4.8	3.0	2.6	100.0
1850-2149	29.0	10.1	10.5	49.5	18.1	7.8	2.4	1.6	100.0
2150-2499	23.7	8.7	10.7	28.2	28.6	16.1	5.8	1.8	100.0
2500-2999	19.3	5.0	8.5	20.7	27.4	23.3	9.6	5.6	100.0
3000-3499	9.4	8.1	2.5	17.3	15.3	30.2	18.0	8.6	100.0
3500+	6.0	7.4	7.6	11.9	9.7	17.1	23.1	23.2	100.0
	100.0%								

Number of Observations: 2,209

MTR #7508

Figure 2.3

COMPONENTS OF THE VARIANCE OF THE LOG
CHANGE IN OWN LABOR INCOME, 1967–1974
(Married Men in 1968 Who Were in the
Labor Force in both 1967 and 1974)

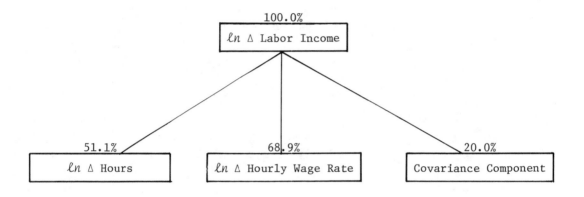

Number of Observations: 1,821

Note: The variance of the natural logarithm of change in annual labor income
equals the sum of (1) the variance of ℓn change in hours, (2) the variance of ℓn change in hourly wage rate, and (3) the covariance component
(equal to $2 \cdot COV(\ell n \ \Delta$ hours, $\ell n \ \Delta$ wage rate)).

some change, including almost 10 percent who were divorced or separated during the period. The most common changes were those associated with the life cycle of the family—children being born and older children leaving the parental home. Changes in needs varied among the family composition subgroups in a predictable fashion: needs increased most for those who had a baby during the period and decreased most for those who were divorced or separated (especially when change involved children), for those who were widowed, and for those families where an older child left home. One group which accounted for a disproportionately large share of the total variance was that of married men with children who were divorced as of 1975; although they were only 3.1 percent of all families, their fraction of the total variance was 12.1 percent.

The effects of changes in family composition on changes in family income are also evident in Table 2.7. The groups of households headed by men who were married throughout the period (groups 1, 6, 7, 8, and 9) all had mean increases in income of $2,000 or more, while those families headed by men who were no longer married by 1975 (groups 2, 3, and 4) all suffered substantial decreases in earnings. Indeed, the only marital status change which led to an increase in family income was being first widowed or divorced and then remarried. It seems clear that family income was, in many families, composed of the earnings of both husband and wife and that the most dramatic determinants of change in family income were those things which affected the number of income earners in a family.

Finally, these changes in income and in needs jointly determined change in income/needs. Families with splitoffs had the largest change in income/needs since needs fell substantially as income rose. Other large mean increases were experienced by those who remarried and by men with children who were divorced or separated as of 1975. For household heads who remarried this change was due primarily to a large increase in income, while for divorced or separated men the change in needs was primarily responsible. A comparison of the change in income/needs for divorced or separated men—both those with and without children prior to the divorce or separation—shows most clearly the importance of change in needs in accounting for change in overall economic status. Both groups of men had virtually identical changes in family income (a decrease of about $800). But, since needs dropped much more for the men with children (because the children generally stayed with their mothers) than for those without children, the change in income/needs for the former group was quite large, while income/needs for the second group remained essentially unchanged.

The Analysis of Subgroups

Did the pattern of change in economic status differ for various subgroups

42

Table 2.7

CHANGE IN INCOME, NEEDS, AND INCOME/NEEDS
BY TYPE OF FAMILY COMPOSITION CHANGE, 1967–1974
(Married Men in 1968)

Family Composition Change	Number of Observations	Weighted Percentage of Observations	Mean Δ Income/ Needs	Mean Δ Income	Mean Δ Needs	Percentage Contribution to Total Variance in Δ Income/Needs	
						Due to Change in Income	Due to Change in Needs
1) No Change	690	36.2%	.08	$ 1,218	$ 222	34.2%	8.7%
2) Widowed	59	2.7	.20	-1,203	- 803	3.8	6.4
3) Divorced/Separated: Family Size Fell by More than One	90	3.1	.93	- 786	-1,540	4.4	12.1
4) Divorced/Separated: Family Size Fell by One	30	1.4	-.01	- 800	- 209	1.6	0.2
5) Divorced or Widowed and Remarried	110	4.4	.82	2,917	37	7.1	9.4
6) Child Born, 1968–1975	479	19.5	.41	3,197	641	21.5	21.0
7) Split off	653	29.0	1.48	2,063	953	21.2	39.6
8) Other Increases in Family Size	68	2.5	.49	3,119	600	5.1	2.2
9) Other Decreases in Family Size	30	1.2	.77	2,680	- 263	1.1	0.3
TOTAL	2,209	100.0%	.63	$ 1,835	$- 129	100.0%	100.0%

Note: 1974 Income and Income/Needs have been delfated by the increase in the Consumer Price Index since 1967.

MTR #7508

within our population of initially married men? To consider that question we
looked at five major subgroups: (1) prime-aged males (age 25-45 in 1968); (2)
blacks; (3) those who fell into the bottom quintile of the income/needs distribution at least once during the eight-year period (the "target population"); (4)
those who fell below the official poverty line in 1967 (the "initially poor");
and (5) those among the fourth group who were no longer in poverty by 1974 (the
"climbers-out"). Note that the last three groups are nested, so that each successive group is a subset of the preceding group. We do not present a complete
decomposition for these groups, but rather focus on the major components of
change in economic status.

The components of the variance of change in income/needs are summarized in
Table 2.8. In general, the same pattern held for each of the subgroups: change
in family income was the most important component of variance in income/needs.
The only group which differed from the others was black families, where change
in needs was relatively more important than for the other groups. The covariance
between change in income and change in needs, however, varied significantly among
the groups. The large positive covariance terms for blacks, for the initially
poor families, and for those who climbed out of poverty suggests the importance
for these groups of changes in family composition (which affect needs) and corresponding changes in income as the number of income earners differed. For example, less than a quarter of all black families headed by a male had no changes
in family composition during the eight-year period, compared to nearly 40 percent
for white families. More than twice as many black families as white families increased their family size by moving in with (or taking in) friends or relatives.
At the same time, a greater percentage of black families (14 percent compared to
7 percent for whites) had decreases in family size due to divorce, separation or
becoming widowed.

The importance of family composition and changes in family composition for
these five subgroups is also apparent in the decomposition of change in family
income into its additive components. Mean changes for each of the components are
given in Table 2.9, while the components of the total variance are shown in Table
2.10.

As we noted previously, changes in the head's labor income, the family's
nonlabor income, and the income of others were approximately equal for all married male heads of households. Among the subgroups, however, the relative importance of these components varied substantially. Black families, those who
were initially poor, and those who climbed out of poverty all had large mean increases in the income of others, ranging from about $560 for blacks to over

Table 2.8

COMPONENTS OF THE VARIANCE OF LOG
CHANGE IN REAL FAMILY INCOME/NEEDS, 1967-1974
(Married Men in 1968)

Group	Number of Observations	Changes in Real Income	Changes in Needs	Sum of Covariance Component
All	2,198	83.2%	16.8%	16.3%
Males, Aged 25-45 in 1968	1,183	78.0	22.0	17.2
Blacks	553	78.1	21.9	32.4
Target Population	848	89.5	10.5	8.7
Initially Poor	278	85.5	14.5	31.4
Climbers-Out	132	83.4	16.6	46.6

Note: The variances have been scaled to add to 100.0 percent in order to facilitate comparisons between groups. The actual fraction of variance accounted for by each component can be computed by multiplying the scaled variances by the sum of the covariance components plus one.

MTR #7508

Table 2.9

MEAN CHANGES IN COMPONENTS OF CHANGE IN REAL INCOME, 1967-1974
(Married Men in 1968)

Group	Number of Observations	Total Change	=	Δ Head's Labor Income	+	Δ Wife's Labor Income	+	Δ Transfer Income	+	Δ Nonlabor Income	+	Δ Other Income
All	2,209	$1,828		$ 396		$140		$518		$395		$379
Males, Aged 25-45 in 1968	1,183	3,412		1,637		312		146		582		649
Blacks	553	1,407		189		206		384		67		562
Target Population	848	718		- 232		19		518		58		355
Initially Poor	278	2,565		759		277		458		336		730
Climbers-Out	132	3,599		1,232		435		416		485		1,030

Table 2.10

COMPONENTS OF THE VARIANCE OF CHANGE IN REAL INCOME, 1967–1974
(Married Men in 1968)

Group	Number of Observations	Percentage Contribution to Total Variance					
		Δ Head's Labor Income	Δ Wife's Labor Income	Δ Transfer Income	Δ Nonlabor Income	Δ Other Income	Sum of Covariance
All	2,198	61.2%	10.7%	4.8%	14.7%	8.6%	- 9.8%
Males, Aged 25–45 in 1968	1,183	61.1	12.8	1.6	16.4	8.1	- 1.2
Blacks	553	47.6	22.0	5.2	5.7	19.4	-16.6
Target Population	848	56.3	10.9	7.5	16.4	12.1	- 3.2
Initially Poor	278	50.8	12.1	12.9	24.8	30.7	-31.3
Climbers-Out	132	58.1	14.6	10.2	32.3	37.5	-52.7

Note: The variances have been scaled to add to 100.0 percent in order to facilitate comparisons between groups. The actual fraction of variance accounted for by each component can be computed by multiplying the scaled variances by the covariance plus one.

$1,000 for the climbers-out. Changes in the head's labor income were greatest for the prime-aged males and for the initial poverty population and were also well above average for the climbers-out; but these changes were only about half as great for black families. Finally, average changes in transfer income were similar for all of the groups except the prime-aged males whose transfer income increased less than $150.

The components of variance show a similar pattern of effects. Change in the head's labor income accounted for the largest share of variance for all of the groups, but the relative importance of some of the other components differed among the groups. Overall, changes in others' income accounted for less than 10 percent of the total variance in income, but the corresponding percentage was nearly 20 percent for blacks, 30 percent for the initial poverty population, and over 35 percent for those who climbed out of poverty. For blacks, change in the head's labor income accounted for relatively less of the total variance, but change in the wife's labor income accounted for relatively more. This increased importance of the wife's income for blacks reflected, in part, their higher divorce and separation rates. Changes in transfer income and changes in nonlabor income were relatively more important for the initially poor and for those who climbed out of poverty. Finally, the components of variance for the prime-aged males were quite similar to those for all married men.

II. CHANGES IN ECONOMIC STATUS AMONG THE INITIALLY MARRIED WOMEN

Changes in Income/Needs

Change in economic status, in terms of income to needs, was just as prevalent for married women as Table 2.1 showed it to be for married men. Table 2.11 shows the percentages of women who began the panel period as wives and the amount and direction of change in relative economic status they experienced over the panel period. The first column of figures refers to the entire population of these women and shows that less than a quarter (23.6 percent) of them experienced no change in relative economic status over the eight years of the panel study. Almost half of the women experienced changes of two or more deciles in relative economic status, with the proportion experiencing declines (24.6 percent) being nearly equal to that experiencing increases (21.4 percent). The small remaining group of women had only minor changes in relative economic status (changed by one decile), with slightly more increases in well-being (17.0 percent) than declines (13.4 percent).

The second column of numbers in Table 2.11 presents similar measures of change for that subgroup of the entire population which began the panel period

Table 2.11

CHANGE IN INCOME/NEEDS DECILE POSITION, 1967-1974
(Married Women in 1968)

Change in Decile Position	All	Lowest Decile, 1967
Fell Two or More Deciles	24.6%	0.0%
Fell One Decile	13.4	0.0
No Change	23.6	43.1
Increased One Decile	17.0	26.2
Increased Two Deciles or More	21.4	30.7
TOTAL	100.0%	100.0%

Number of Observations: 2,209

Note: The deciles were constructed from the distribution of income/needs for the entire sample of families. Consequently, more or less than 10 percent of that subgroup can fall into any one decile.

See Appendix Table A2.1b for the complete distribution of 1974 income/needs decile by 1967 income/needs decile.

in the lowest income/needs decile. By definition, none of these women could experience declines in relative economic status since they were already in the lowest decile of well-being. The only place to move was up--and more than half of
them did just that, many of them enjoying substantial increases. It should be
noted, however, that nearly half of the women who began poor remained trapped in
poverty (43.1 percent).

Since change in well-being has proved to be quite prevalent, it is of interest to examine the sources of this change. Table 2.12 presents the means and
standard deviations of the change in the two components of our measure of economic well-being over the eight-year panel period. Total real family income increased on average by $1,511 for the group of individuals who began the panel
period as wives, while the family needs standard declined by an average of $159.
As is indicated below, the increased real family income is a manifestation of
increased labor income of major wage earners, predominately the husband, while
the decline in needs is a reflection of the loss from the household of individuals with large needs, mostly older children who left the parental household during the panel period to establish their own households. The net result of these
changes in income and needs for wives was that our measure of economic well-
being, income/needs, increased by an average of only .45, which is two-tenths of
a unit less than the increase for their husbands.

That the standard deviation of change in well-being and its components (see
the last column of figures in Table 2.12) was large compared to the mean
changes indicates that there was substantial variation across individuals in
these changes. For instance, the large standard deviation of change in income/
needs indicates that the modest average increase in income/needs was the result
of a great many individual cases with very large increases in this measure being
nearly offset by a large number of cases with very large decreases.[3]

As outlined in Appendix 1.1, our measure of change in economic well-being
for wives, as well as for husbands, can be decomposed into that portion resulting from change in income and that from change in needs by examining the relation of the variance in the logarithms of the ratio of eighth-year and first-
year incomes and needs to the logarithm of the overall ratio. The results of
this decomposition are shown in Figure 2.4. As is the case for all the groups
examined in this analysis, change in income for individuals who began the panel

---

[3]It should be noted that the standard deviation of change in income/needs for
wives (2.28) was considerably smaller than the corresponding number for husbands
(3.01). This might be due to the fact that more husbands experienced significant increases in income/needs than did wives (see Tables A2.1a and A2.1b).

Table 2.12

MEANS AND STANDARD DEVIATIONS OF COMPONENTS OF
CHANGE IN REAL TOTAL FAMILY INCOME/NEEDS, 1967-1974
(Married Women in 1968)

Income/Needs Change Component	Mean Change	Standard Deviation of Change
Change in Total Family Income	$ 1,511	$7,165
Change in Needs	- 159	1,066
Change in Income/Needs	0.45	2.28

Number of Observations: 2,355

Note: 1974 Income and Income/Needs figures have been deflated by the increase
in the Consumer Price Index since 1967.

Table 2.13

MEANS AND STANDARD DEVIATIONS OF COMPONENTS OF CHANGE
IN REAL TOTAL FAMILY INCOME, 1967-1974
(Married Women in 1968)

	Mean Change	Standard Deviation of Change
Change in Husband's Labor Income	$- 184	$6,141
Change in Wife's Labor Income	333	2,203
Change in Asset Income	350	2,768
Change in Transfer Income	600	1,618
Change in Other's Taxable Income	412	2,160
TOTAL CHANGE	$ 1,511	$7,167

Number of Observations: 2,355

Note: 1974 Income figures have been devlated by the increase in the Consumer
Price Index since 1967.

Figure 2.4

COMPONENTS OF THE VARIANCE OF THE LOG CHANGE
IN REAL TOTAL FAMILY INCOME/NEEDS, 1967–1974
(Married Women in 1968)

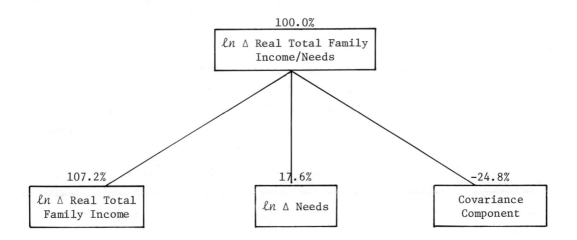

Number of Observations: 2,355

Note: The natural logarithm of the change in income/needs is equal to the log
of the change in income minus the log of the change in needs. The variance of the log change in income/needs is equal to the variance of the
log of change in income plus the variance of the log of change in needs
minus two times the covariance. Hence, a positive covariance leads to
a negative covariance component. (See the appendix to Chapter 1 for
details on this procedure.)

MTR #2171

period as wives overwhelmingly dominated change in needs in its importance in explaining change in well-being. Indeed, for wives the variation in income component *exceeded* the aggregate variation by more than seven percentage points, whereas variation in needs accounted for less than one-fifth (17.6 percent) of the total variance in economic standing. The reason that well-offness is more than explained by its components is that there is a large positive correlation between change in income and change in needs for these women. Large decreases in the needs standard--resulting, for instance, from the loss of a husband--were generally associated with large declines in money income. That this correlation (and, hence, the overexplanation of variance in income/needs by its components) was stronger for wives than for husbands is merely an indication that husbands generally earned much more than wives, while husbands' contributions to overall family needs was only slightly greater.

Changes in Income

Table 2.13 gives the means and standard deviations of change in family money income and its components for individuals beginning the panel as wives. The mean change in money income for wives was $1,511, which was some $300 less than for the initially married men. This difference was due, in part, to the fact that among the panel members who lost a spouse (through death or marital disruption), the wives were more likely than the husbands to have lost a spouse *with money income*. Consistent with this is the fact that the standard deviation of family money income for wives was over $7,100 while the corresponding figure for husbands was only $6,700.

Also consistent with the fact that wives were more apt to lose a spouse with substantial labor earnings was the fact that the average "spouse's" income for the initially married women declined by almost $200 (see Table 2.13). Referring back to Table 2.3, we see that the average income of the initially married men *increased* by nearly $400. Thus, since the differences in these populations of husbands are those created by marital disruptions, we must conclude that divorce and separation led to large declines in spouse's income for women despite the fact that a substantial number of women acquired new husbands. It should also be noted that remarriage rates for women were substantially lower than for men.

Another interesting difference between the mean changes in income for the initially married women and men was that mean change in the wives' *own* labor income was more than twice as large as the mean change for husbands in their *spouse's* labor income ($333 versus $140). This would indicate that women who experienced marital disruption were more likely than stably married women to increase their work hours over the period, or that they enjoyed much greater than average increases in wages than their stably married counterparts, or both.[4]

For wives, as was found for the husbands, the standard deviations of the components of change in money income were sufficiently high to indicate that there was quite a bit of individual variation within these components despite the rather modest mean changes. Figure 2.5 utilizes these standard deviations to partition the overall variance in change in money income into the same five exhaustive components used in Section I of this chapter.

The relative sizes of the components of variance of change in total family money income for wives shown in Figure 2.5 are virtually identical to those shown in Figure 2.2 for husbands. In both cases the changes in husband's labor income accounted for over 70 percent of the total variance in family income while changes in the wife's labor income accounted for about 10 percent. Change in capital income was approximately one and one-half times as important as change in the wife's labor income (14.9 percent versus 9.5 percent) or about equal to the sum of the contributions of change in transfer income (5.1 percent) and change in others' taxable income (9.1 percent). It should be noted, however, that much of this capital income was comprised of the asset portion of individually-owned small businesses and farms. Small businesses were particularly hard hit by the recession which occurred toward the end of the panel period, while farmers benefited from dramatically increasing world demand for food. Hence, the rather large contribution to total variance in income/needs made by change in capital income was likely to have been exaggerated by fluctuations in the business climate during the eight-year period.

Since change in husband's labor income was so important in accounting for change in total family real income for the women who began the panel period as wives, it is interesting to see to what extent the former was the result of change in marital status. Table 2.14 lists the mean change in husband's labor income and the amount of its variance which can be accounted for by changes in marital status. The top row of figures represents those women who remained stably married throughout the panel period. The majority of the initially married women (81.6 percent) were in this group and they accounted for more than 70 percent of the variance of change in husband's labor income. The second group were women who lost a husband through marital disruption or death and did not remarry (14.9 percent of the weighted sample). On average, the families of these women lost nearly $5,000 in husband's labor income, and this family composition change accounted for nearly 16 percent of the variance in husband's labor income.

---

[4]This is exactly what was found in the analyses described in Volume IV of this series. See Hoffman and Holmes (1976), pp. 34-36.

Table 2.14

CHANGE IN HUSBAND'S LABOR INCOME
BY CHANGE IN MARITAL STATUS, 1967-1974
(Married Women in 1968)

Change in Marital Status	Number of Observations	Weighted Proportion of Observations	Mean Change in Husband's Labor Income	Fraction of Variance of Change in Husband's Labor Income Explained by Subgroup
No Change in Husband	1,913	81.6%	472	71.4%
Lost Husband, Did Not Remarry	368	14.9	-4,794	15.8
Lost Husband, Remarried	74	3.5	3,818	12.8
TOTAL	2,355	100.0%	- 196	100.0%

Table 2.15

CHANGE IN LABOR INCOME
BY CHANGE IN LABOR FORCE STATUS, 1968-1974
(Married Women in 1968)

Change in Labor Force Status	Number of Observations	Weighted Proportion of Observations	Mean Change of Labor Income	Fraction of Variance of Change in Labor Income Explained by Subgroup
Out of Labor Force in both 1967 and 1974	998	43.8%	$ 6	1.7%
Entered Labor Force in 1974	416	16.1	2,689	33.8
Left Labor Force by 1974	291	12.7	-2,623	33.4
In Labor Force in both 1967 and 1974	650	27.4	852	31.1
TOTAL	2,355	100.0%	$ 336	100.0%

Note: 1974 Income figures have been deflated by the increase in the Consumer Price Index since 1967.

An individual is defined as in the labor force if she worked at least 250 hours during the year.

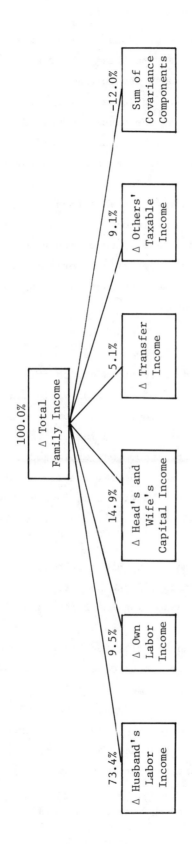

Figure 2.5

COMPONENTS OF THE VARIANCE OF CHANGE
IN REAL TOTAL FAMILY INCOME, 1967-1974
(Married Women in 1968)

Number of Observations: 2,355

Note: The variance of change in total family income equals the sum of (1) variance of change in husband's labor
       income, (2) variance of change in own labor income, (3) variance of change in head's and wife's capital
       income, (4) variance of change in transfer income, (5) variance of change in others' taxable income, and
       (6) the sum of the covariance components (i.e., the sum of two times the covariance between changes in
       each pair of income sources).

MTR #2171

This is an interesting result which tells us that the spouse's labor income for the women who remained stably married throughout the eight-year period were almost as variable as those for women who became divorced.

The most interesting results in Table 2.14 are for those women who lost a husband and then remarried during the panel period. While they represented only 3.5 percent of the initially married women, the variance of change in spouse's labor income for this group accounted for nearly 13 percent of the total variance in husband's labor earnings. The major reason they explain such a relatively large fraction of the total variance is that these women experienced much more *diverse* changes in husband's labor income than did any of the other groups. The variance of change in husband's labor income (not shown in Table 2.14) was over six times as great for women who remarried after a marital dissolution as for those who did not. On average, new husbands were considerably better bread-winners than were the former husbands.

Changes in Labor Force Status

One interesting difference between husbands and wives appeared when change in labor income was decomposed in accordance with change in labor force status, as in Table 2.15. More than half of the total variation in wives' labor income can be explained by labor force turnover (33.8 percent for those entering the labor force and 33.4 percent for those leaving the labor force). Only 20 percent of the change in husbands' labor income was explained by such a turnover, and most of that was due to retirement. Hence, the timing of labor force participation was much more important for the wife than for the husband in explaining changes in earnings contributions to family economic well-being.

Changes in Hours and Wages

The change in labor income of the 650 initially married women who were in the labor force in both 1967 and 1973 can be attributed to changes in hours worked or changes in wages by examining the relationships of the variance in the logarithmic change in earnings, hours, and wages for both years (see Figure 2.6). In contrast to the corresponding results for husbands presented in Figure 2.3, changes in hours were more important than changes in wages for wives in explaining the labor income change, the former accounting for 53 percent of the total variation in change in labor income and the latter explaining less than 40 percent. The fact that changes in wages were much less important for wives than for husbands may be a reflection of the fact that age-earnings profiles for women (especially married women) were flatter than those for men (especially married men).

Another interesting comparison between the results for wives and husbands is

Figure 2.6

COMPONENTS OF THE VARIANCE OF THE LOG
CHANGE IN OWN LABOR INCOME, 1967–1974
(Married Women in 1968 Who Were in the
Labor Force in both 1967 and 1974)

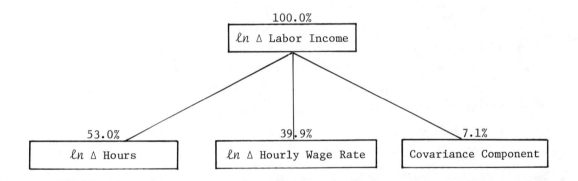

Number of Observations: 2,355

Note: The variance of the natural logarithm of change in annual labor income
        equals the sum of (1) the variance of ℓn change in hours, (2) the vari-
        ance of ℓn change in hourly wage rate, and (3) the covariance component
        (equal to $2 \cdot \mathrm{COV}(\ell n \; \Delta \; \text{hours}, \; \ell n \; \Delta \; \text{wage rate})$).

MTR #2171

that changes in hours and wages *more* than explained change in labor income for husbands (indicating a negative correlation between changes in hours and changes in wages) while they *less* than explained labor earnings for wives (meaning the correlation was positive). Hence, for husbands larger than average increases in wages were associated with larger than average decreases in hours, while the reverse was true for wives. While it is impossible to say with certainty without examining the structural equations underlying this implicit labor market result, the above findings are consistent with the hypothesis that (1) for men the supply side relationship dominates demand, and the resulting negative correlation is a manifestation of the classical backward bending supply curve; and (2) demand considerations dominate for wives, and the positive correlation is a reflection of the fact that employers are only willing to hire part-time women if they can get them at lower wages. Thus, women who change from part-time to full-time work would receive a greater than average increase.

As a crude test of this proposition, Tables 2.16 and 2.17 present the mean change in real wage by change in work fraction for wives and husbands in the work force in both 1967 and 1974. As the first and second columns of the two tables indicate, change in work fraction was much more common for wives than for husbands. Nearly a quarter of the wives experienced such changes while fewer than 10 percent of the husbands changed their work fractions. The notion that the backward bending supply curve dominates for men is supported by the fact that the husbands who reduced their work fractions received a $1.76 average increase in hourly earnings, while those who increased their work fractions had an average increase of only 12 cents per hour. The conjecture that women are penalized in terms of wages for working part time and that this is responsible for the positive correlation of change in hours and change in wages received only mixed support from the results on mean changes in wages presented in Table 2.16. While the wives who changed from part-time to full-time hours experienced larger than average increases in hourly wages ($0.89), so did those wives who changed from full time to part time ($0.75). As we noted above, the proper testing of these conjectures requires the identification and estimation of the underlying structural equations of labor supply and demand, a task which is beyond the scope of this paper.

Changes in Needs

We have alluded several times to the fact that, for the panel members who were married women in 1968, certain types of family composition change were responsible, at least in part, for the patterns of change in economic well-being and its components. Table 2.18 (which corresponds to Table 2.7 for husbands)

Table 2.16

MEAN CHANGE IN REAL WAGES
BY CHANGE IN WORK FRACTION
(Wives Employed in both 1967 and 1974)

Change in Work Fraction*	Number of Observations	Weighted Percent of Observations	Mean Change in Real Wage
Became Full Time	60	10.7%	$0.89
Became Part Time	68	11.7	0.75
No Change	413	77.5	0.44
TOTAL**	541	100.0%	$0.52

Table 2.17

MEAN CHANGE IN REAL WAGES
BY CHANGE IN WORK FRACTION
(Husbands Employed in both 1967 and 1974)

Change in Work Fraction*	Number of Observations	Weighted Percent of Observations	Mean Change in Real Wage
Became Full Time	34	2.0%	$0.12
Became Part Time	82	4.9	1.76
No Change	1,566	93.1	0.79
TOTAL	1,682	100.0%	$0.82

* Full time is defined here as working 34 or more hours per week on the individual's main job.

** The number of observations here is less than reported earlier because cases with missing data on hours per week were deleted.

MTR #2171

lists for the initially married women the types of family composition changes
which were most prevalent, their frequency of occurrence, and the changes in economic well-being and its components with which they are associated. Of course,
the same proportions of husbands and wives were in families where no change in
composition occurred (one-third), and the number of children born and children
leaving stable parental homes was, of course, the same for both groups. However,
nearly three times as many wives as husbands (8.2 percent versus 2.7 percent) became widowed over the eight-year period, and the wives were three and a half
times more likely to be left with the responsibility for supporting children following divorce or separation. Among couples who became divorced, the women were
35 percent less likely to remarry.

Marital dissolution generally resulted in declines in economic well-being
for wives since declines in family needs were more than offset by declines in
family income. This was particularly true for the divorced women whose family
size declined by more than one; this group suffered the severest declines in in-
come/needs (-.58 units) since the real family income declined by more than $5,000
while needs declined by less than $2,000. However, because losing a spouse
through death was much more prevalent than any other type of marital disruption,
it was the most important of these changes in explaining overall variations in
income (14.6 percent) and needs (16.5 percent). Even more important in this
sense were changes in the number of children in the household. For the families
where a child was born during the panel period, income increased by more than
$3,000 while needs increased by little more than $600. The increased income for
this group was probably a manifestation of the fact that these households had
relatively young husbands who were at an age where earnings increased most rapidly. In any event, the variance in income for this group accounted for over 17
percent of the variance in income for all families, while the variance in needs
(resulting mostly from the birth and aging of children) accounted for more than
20 percent of the total variance in needs for all families.

Families where children left the household experienced some of the greatest
increases in overall economic well-being (1.22 units) of all the subgroups listed.
This resulted not only from a needs decrease of nearly $1,000, but also from in-
creases in family income. The large decline in needs for this group, in conjunction with the relatively large proportion of families experiencing this type of
family composition change (26.8 percent of the sample), explains why these changes
were so important in accounting for such a large proportion (over one-third) of
the overall variance in family needs.

The family composition change with the most interesting results was made by

Table 2.18

CHANGE IN INCOME, NEEDS, AND INCOME/NEEDS
BY TYPE OF FAMILY COMPOSITION CHANGE, 1967-1974
(Married Women in 1968)

Family Composition Change	Number of Observations	Weighted Percentage of Observations	Mean Δ Income/ Needs	Mean Δ Income	Mean Δ Needs	Percentage Contribution to Total Variance in Δ Income/Needs	
						Due to Change in Income	Due to Change in Needs
No Change	687	33.3%	0.05%	$1,219	$ 223	25.6%	10.1%
Widowed	171	8.2	-0.32	-2,372	- 863	14.6	16.5
Divorced/Separated: Family Size Fell by More than One	75	2.2	-0.58	-5,300	-1,773	6.2	6.9
Divorced/Separated: Family Size Fell by One	109	4.0	-0.35	-2,085	- 231	6.4	3.1
Divorced or Widowed and Remarried	74	3.4	1.69	6,735	474	7.0	4.4
Child Born	479	18.1	0.40	3,197	641	17.2	21.2
Splitoff	653	26.8	1.22	2,063	- 953	16.0	34.7
Other Increases in Family Size	67	2.3	0.44	3,079	606	3.8	2.3
Other Decreases in Family Size	40	1.7	1.09	4,037	- 288	3.3	1.0
TOTAL	2,355	100.0%	0.45	$1,512	$- 158	100.0%	100.0%

Note: 1974 Income and Income/Needs have been deflated by the increase in the Consumer Price Index since 1967.

women who divorced and subsequently remarried. Their income/needs increased by
an average of more than one and one-half units due to a very large average increase in real family income ($6,735). We found earlier that among this group,
the spouse's labor income increased by an average of nearly $4,000 and accounted
for less than two-thirds of total increase in family money income. Undoubtedly,
the remainder was accounted for by increases in transfer income and the wife's
own labor income.

The Analysis of Subgroups

Table 2.19 shows the relative importance of the variance of change in income/
needs in explaining the variance of change in economic well-being for the same
set of subgroups analyzed in Section I. At first glance one is struck by the remarkable similarity in the pattern of the proportions of variance explained by
the components across these groups. Closer observation, however, does reveal
some differences. The most interesting of these involves the bottom three subgroups which comprise a "nesting" set. That is, the initially poor are a subset
of the target population, and the climbers-out are a subset of those who were
initially poor. As one reads down the columns labeled "change in needs" and "sum
of covariances," one sees that the figures in each column progressively (albeit
modestly) increase. The increase in the importance in needs suggests that, as we
focus more closely on those individuals who were poor but who managed to move out,
family composition became an important determinant of change in well-being. Furthermore, the steady increases in the covariance terms indicate that the types of
family composition change taking place were increasingly those which involved individuals with sizable incomes as well as needs. The data in Tables 2.20 and
2.21, which show mean changes in the components of income and their relative importance in explaining variance in family income, provide support for this conclusion. The last column of Table 2.20 and the next-to-last column of Table 2.21
concern the contribution of other household members to family money income. In
each instance the figures increase from the target population through the initially poor to those who climbed out of poverty. Although much of this increased income of others was due to increases for those already in the household, it is
apparent that among the poor "doubling-up" of income receivers did take place and
that it was a somewhat effective means of coping with, or even overcoming, economic adversity.

Another interesting difference among the subgroups was that for blacks,
where changes in the wife's labor income accounted for nearly 20 percent of the
variance of change in total family income. For all other groups, this source
of change accounted for less than 10 percent of the variance in family income.

Table 2.19

COMPONENTS OF THE VARIANCE OF LOG
CHANGE IN REAL FAMILY INCOME/NEEDS, 1967-1974
(Married Women in 1968)

Group	Number of Observations	Percentage Contribution to Total Variance		
		Changes in Real Income	Changes in Needs	Sum of Covariance Compoment
All	2,355	85.9%	14.1%	24.8%
Blacks	587	85.4	14.6	21.1
Target Population	991	90.7	9.3	16.9
Initially Poor	310	90.2	9.8	27.9
Climbers-Out	184	85.4	14.2	46.5

Note: The variances have been scaled to add to 100.0 percent in order to facilitate comparisons between groups. The actual fraction of variance accounted for by each component can be computed by multiplying the scaled variances by the sum of the covariance components plus one.

MTR #2170

Table 2.20

MEAN CHANGES IN COMPONENTS OF CHANGE IN REAL INCOME, 1967-1974

(Married Women in 1968)

Group	Number of Observations	Total Change	=	Δ Wife's Labor Income	+	Δ Husband's Labor Income	+	Δ Transfer Income	+	Δ Nonlabor Income	+	Δ Other Income
All	2,355	$1,511		$ 333		$- 184		$ 600		$ 350		$ 412
Blacks	587	929		495		- 787		544		56		622
Target Population	991	349		235		- 950		593		95		349
Initially Poor	310	2,637		406		560		579		235		852
Climbers-Out	184	3,762		599		1,018		576		352		1,216

Note: The variances have been scaled to add to 100.0 percent in order to facilitate comparisons between groups. The actual fraction of the variance accounted for by each component can be computed by multiplying the scaled variances by the sum of the covariance components plus one.

MTR # 2170

Table 2.21

COMPONENTS OF THE VARIANCE OF CHANGE IN REAL INCOME, 1967-1974

(Married Women in 1968)

Group	Observations	Percentage Contribution to Total Variance					
		Δ Wife's Labor Income	Δ Husband's Labor Income	Δ Transfer Income	Δ Nonlabor Income	Δ Other Income	Sum of Covariance Component
All	2,355	8.4%	65.2%	4.5%	13.2%	8.1%	12.7%
Black	587	18.7	54.3	5.6	4.7	16.7	43.6
Target Population	991	7.6	62.0	6.1	15.7	8.7	0.2
Initially Poor	310	9.3	43.3	9.4	12.6	25.4	12.3
Climbers-Out	184	9.2	43.0	8.3	13.7	25.8	28.2

Note: The variances have been scaled to add to 100.0 percent in order to facilitate comparisons between groups. The actual fraction of the variance accounted for by each component can be computed by multiplying the scaled variances by the sum of the covariance components plus one.

As was found among the initially poor and women whose families climbed out of poverty, change in the incomes of other household members was quite important for black wives, accounting for 16.7 percent of the variance of change in their family income as opposed to 8.1 percent for the entire population of wives.

Summary

In explaining the eight-year change in family economic well-being for men who were husbands in 1968, change in real family money income dominated change in family needs. Nearly 70 percent of the total variance of change in family money income was accounted for by changes in the husband's own labor income, while only 12 percent could be attributed to changes in the wife's labor income. These figures were virtually unaffected when the population was restricted to men who were between the ages of 25 and 45 in 1968; this restriction changed only the relative importance of transfer income, which declined as a result of eliminating variations in retirement-related transfers.

For married men who were in the work force in both 1967 and 1974, changes in wages were somewhat more important than changes in hours in explaining the variance of change in labor income, and these two components were found to move in opposite directions.

For women who began the panel period as wives, changes in real family money income dominated changes in needs in explaining eight-year change in the variance of economic well-being. Approximately 70 percent of the variance in family income resulted from changes in the spouse's labor income, while changes in the wife's labor income accounted for almost 20 percent of the total variance of change in family income.

For those initially married women who were in the work force in both 1967 and 1974, it was found that change in hours was more important than change in wages in explaining variance of change in labor income and that these components were positively correlated. This is exactly the opposite result of that found for husbands. Furthermore, labor market exit and entry was found to be much more important for wives than for husbands in explaining the variance of change in the wife's own labor income.

References

Hoffman, Saul and Holmes, John W. "Husbands, Wives, and Divorce." In Five Thousand American Families--Patterns of Economic Progress. Volume IV. Edited by Greg J. Duncan and James N. Morgan. Ann Arbor: Institute for Social Research, 1976.

APPENDIX 2.1

Table A2.1a

1974 FAMILY INCOME/NEEDS DECILE BY 1967 FAMILY INCOME/NEEDS DECILE
(Married Men in 1968)

1967 Income/Needs Decile	1974 Income/Needs Decile										
	Lowest Tenth	Second	Third	Fourth	Fifth	Sixth	Seventh	Eighth	Ninth	Highest Tenth	Total
Lowest Tenth	2.2	1.4	0.4	0.2	0.2	---	0.2	0.2	0.1	---	4.9
Second	1.2	1.3	1.1	0.6	0.4	0.2	0.2	0.4	---	0.2	5.7
Third	1.1	1.2	1.9	1.5	0.9	0.7	0.3	0.3	0.3	0.2	8.6
Fourth	0.5	1.0	1.2	1.6	1.8	1.1	1.1	0.8	0.5	0.3	9.8
Fifth	0.4	0.6	0.6	1.4	2.1	2.2	1.2	1.0	1.0	0.6	11.0
Sixth	0.1	0.5	0.9	1.6	1.6	1.5	1.9	2.2	1.1	0.7	12.2
Seventh	0.2	0.4	0.4	0.8	1.3	1.5	1.8	1.8	1.9	1.5	11.5
Eighth	0.2	0.2	0.6	0.6	1.2	1.6	1.7	2.0	2.4	1.7	12.3
Ninth	0.1	0.1	0.2	0.4	0.8	1.0	0.6	1.9	3.4	3.8	12.4
Highest Tenth	0.1	0.2	0.2	0.3	0.6	0.8	0.9	0.9	1.8	5.9	11.7
TOTAL	6.1	6.8	7.5	9.0	11.0	10.6	10.0	11.6	12.5	14.9	100.0

Note: The deciles were constructed from the distribution of income/needs for the entire sample of families. For any subgroup, more or less than 10 percent of that subgroup can fall into any one decile.

Table A2.1b

1974 FAMILY INCOME/NEEDS DECILE BY 1967 FAMILY INCOME/NEEDS DECILE

(Married Women in 1968)

1967 Income/Needs Decile	1974 Income/Needs Decile										
	Lowest Tenth	Second	Third	Fourth	Fifth	Sixth	Seventh	Eighth	Ninth	Highest Tenth	Total
Lowest Tenth	2.4	1.5	0.6	0.3	0.2	0.1	0.2	0.1	0.1	0.1	5.5
Second	1.6	1.5	1.3	0.6	0.3	0.2	0.2	0.4	0.0	0.2	6.2
Third	1.3	1.4	2.2	1.7	0.9	0.7	0.3	0.3	0.3	0.2	9.2
Fourth	0.7	1.1	1.3	1.7	1.6	1.1	1.2	0.7	0.6	0.2	10.1
Fifth	0.5	1.0	0.9	1.3	2.0	2.1	1.1	0.6	1.0	0.5	11.0
Sixth	0.3	0.5	1.0	1.8	1.4	1.6	1.6	2.2	0.9	0.5	11.8
Seventh	0.2	0.4	0.7	0.8	1.6	1.3	1.9	1.5	1.6	1.3	11.1
Eighth	0.2	0.1	0.8	0.7	1.1	1.3	1.8	1.8	2.2	1.6	11.7
Ninth	0.2	0.1	0.1	0.6	0.8	1.0	0.6	1.8	3.3	3.5	12.1
Highest Tenth	0.2	0.3	0.1	0.4	0.6	1.0	0.9	0.9	1.7	5.4	11.5
TOTAL	7.5	7.8	9.0	9.9	10.7	10.3	9.7	10.2	11.6	13.42	100.0

Note: The deciles are constructed from the distribution of income/needs for the entire sample of families. For any subgroup, such as wives, more or less than 10 percent of that subgroup wll fall into any one decile.

MTR #2295

Chapter 3

UNMARRIED HEADS OF HOUSEHOLDS

Richard D. Coe and John W. Holmes

Introduction

Analysis based on the first seven years of the Panel Study of Income
Dynamics (1968-1974) and reported in Volume IV of this series found that family
composition changes among initially unmarried household heads were quite frequent
and, for women, were associated with substantial changes in economic status.
This link between family composition change and economic well-being was particularly evident among those women who married (or remarried) during the panel
period. Even after adjusting for the effects of demographic variables, the group
of women who married experienced three times the percentage increase in income/
needs of those who remained unmarried.[1]

In this chapter, we discuss in greater detail the changes in economic status
of the households headed by persons who were unmarried at the beginning of the
panel period (1968) and the relationship of these economic changes to changes in
family composition. First, we present some descriptive data on the initial
marital status, age distribution, and change in economic status of unmarried
heads of households. The last two sections use the analysis procedure outlined
in Chapter 1 as the basis for assessing the extent to which various components of
well-being contribute to the variability of change in household economic status
over an eight-year period. In Section II, we consider briefly the experiences of
initially unmarried male heads of households. This is followed in Section III by
a more detailed analysis of their female counterparts.

Analysis

I. DEMOGRAPHIC CHARACTERISTICS OF UNMARRIED HEADS OF HOUSEHOLDS

Prior to considering the eight-year change in economic well-being for
initially unmarried heads of households, it is useful to present some descriptive
data for this diverse population. As shown in Table 3.1, in the first year of
the panel slightly more than three-quarters of these households were headed by
women.[2] The distribution of unmarried heads of households by 1968 marital status
indicated a differential grouping between men and women. Twice as many men as

---

[1]Duncan (1976), p. 89.

[2]These proportions also reflect differential nonresponse rates between men and
women since 1968.

Table 3.1

SEX AND MARITAL STATUS OF UNMARRIED HEADS OF HOUSEHOLDS IN 1968

Sex	Number of Observations	Weighted Percentage*
Male		
White	125	18.4%
Nonwhite	66	3.9
Subtotal	191	22.3
Female		
White	429	61.3
Nonwhite	545	16.4
Subtotal	974	77.7
TOTAL	1165	100.0%

Marital Status	Men White	Men Nonwhite	Women White	Women Nonwhite
Single	54.2%	26.0%	21.7%	13.7%
Widowed	18.5	17.2	54.4	33.8
Divorced	17.2	19.6	18.0	19.1
Separated	7.4	37.2	5.3	31.2
Other or NA	2.7	--	0.6	2.2
TOTAL	100.0%	100.0%	100.0%	100.0%

*Since low-income families and blacks were initially oversampled, sample estimates were weighted to make the combined sample representative of the U.S. population.

Table 3.2

AGE DISTRIBUTION OF UNMARRIED HEADS OF HOUSEHOLDS IN 1968

Age	Men White	Men Nonwhite	Women White	Women Nonwhite
< 25	21.7%	3.4%	8.0%	6.8%
25-34	11.6	19.4	10.6	19.3
35-44	12.9	16.8	12.5	23.6
45-54	13.5	34.4	18.1	21.9
55-64	17.0	10.3	26.0	11.8
65 +	23.3	15.7	24.8	16.6
TOTAL	100.0%	100.0%	100.0%	100.0%

women were single,[3] while a substantially higher percentage of the women reported
being widowed. Indeed, among whites, three times as many women as men were
widowed. Although the proportions of men and women who were divorced were similar among both whites and nonwhites, there was a substantial racial difference
in the proportion of unmarried heads of households who were separated as of 1968;
while only slightly more than 5 percent of the whites were separated, a third of
the nonwhites reported being separated.

The age composition of white unmarried heads of households was skewed
toward the older age brackets compared to nonwhites, especially for women (see
Table 3.2). Nearly one out of every four whites was older than age 65 in 1968;
only 15 percent of the nonwhites were 65 or older.

II. UNMARRIED MALE HEADS OF HOUSEHOLDS

Changes in Relative Level of Economic Well-Being

The changes in relative economic status experienced by initially unmarried
male heads of households over the eight-year period are illustrated in Table 3.3.
There was considerable variability in the relative level of economic well-being
of these men, as defined by family money income/needs deciles in 1967 and 1974.
Only 29.6 percent remained in the same income/needs decile in both 1967 and 1974.
Almost one-half (45.9 percent) moved by two or more deciles, with the increases
and decreases being evenly divided.

Changes in Income/Needs

The decomposition of the logarithm of the ratio of the level of family income/
needs in 1974 to the level in 1967 into its two components--the logarithm of the
percentage changes in income and in needs over the eight-year period--is shown in
Figure 3.1. As can be seen, change in household income accounted for most of the
variance of change in family income/needs. Hence, it would seem likely that the
factors most important to an understanding of the dynamics of family economic well-
being are those which affect money income rather than needs, as there are commonly
other income earners in the family. The percentage of the variance of change in
income/needs accounted for by the two components was more than 100 percent because of their positive intercorrelation. (See Table A3.2a for the correlations
coefficients of the variables used in this section.)

Changes in Income

Total family money income can be exhaustively decomposed into five components: (1) the individual's own labor income, (2) spouse's labor income,

---

[3]By single we mean the respondent was never married.

Table 3.3

CHANGE IN INCOME/NEEDS DECILE POSITION, 1967-1974
(Unmarried Male Heads of Households in 1968)

Change in Decile Position	All	Bottom Decile, 1967
Fell Two or More Deciles	23.4%	--
Fell One Decile	10.0	--
No Change	29.6	44.1
Increased One Decile	14.7	16.9
Increased Two or More Deciles	22.5	39.7
TOTAL	100.2%	100.7%

Number of Observations: 191

NOTE: The deciles were constructed from the distribution of income/ needs ratios for the entire sample of *families*. Consequently, more or less than 10 percent of any subgroup can fall into any one decile.

See Table A3.1a for the complete distribution of 1974 income/needs deciles by 1967 income/needs deciles for unmarried men.

MTR #6081

Figure 3.1

COMPONENTS OF THE VARIANCE OF THE LOG CHANGE
IN REAL TOTAL FAMILY INCOME/NEEDS, 1967-1974
(Unmarried Male Heads of Households in 1968)

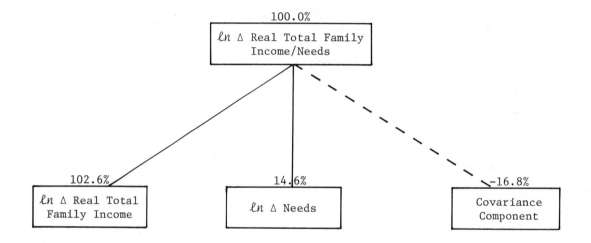

Number of Observations: 191

NOTE: The natural logarithm of the change in income/needs is equal to the log
of the change in income minus the log of the change in needs. Thus, the
variance of the log change in income/needs is equal to the variance of
the log of change in income plus the variance of the log of change in
needs minus two times the covariance. Hence, a *positive* covariance leads
to a *negative* covariance component. (See the appendix to Chapter 1 for
details on this procedure.)

MTR #7300

(3) head's and spouse's capital income, (4) transfer income, and (5) other household members' taxable income. Before considering the extent to which changes in these components accounted for the variance of change in total family income, it is useful to look at the mean changes in these components over the eight-year period. After adjusting for the interim inflation since 1967, family money income of these initially unmarried heads increased by $1,399 from 1967 to 1974 (see Table 3.4). However, their own labor income declined, on the average, by $95 in real terms. Nearly half the mean increase in real family income resulted from change in spouse's labor income (approximately 27 percent were married in 1975). The remainder of the increase in real family income was evenly divided between changes in transfer income and in head's and spouse's capital income. It should be noted, however, that change in the household head's own labor income had a much higher variability than any of the other components. Thus, although its *mean* change was small relative to the mean change in family income, it still accounted for a significant proportion of the *variance* of change in real family income.

Figure 3.2 shows the relative importance of the components of the variance of change in real family money income. Similar to the findings reported for husbands in Chapter 2, change in the household head's own labor income was the predominant explanation for change in total household income, accounting for nearly 94 percent of the total variance. The variance of change in the earnings of other family members (14.8 percent) was slightly more important than either variance of spouse's labor income (10.5 percent) or head's and spouse's capital income (9.2 percent). Among the five additive components of household income, change in transfer income (6.3 percent) was the least important. The correlations among the components of change in family income (detailed in Table A3.1a) were mostly negative offsetting movements--that is why the main component changes account for more than 100 percent of the variance.

Changes in Own Labor Income

Some of the association between changes in the head's labor income and the changes in total family income undoubtedly stemmed from normal life-cycle occurrences. In Table 3.2 we saw that among white unmarried male heads of households 40 percent were older than age 55 in 1968 and slightly less than 22 percent were under age 25. Using 250 hours as the threshold for being in the labor market, four groups were defined on the basis of the head's annual work hours in 1967 and 1974: those who entered, left, were always in, or were never in the labor force. As Table 3.5 shows, panel members who entered the labor force after 1967 experienced large positive changes in labor income and, hence, in total family income; those who left the labor force experienced large negative changes.

Table 3.4

MEANS AND STANDARD DEVIATIONS OF COMPONENTS OF CHANGE IN
TOTAL FAMILY REAL MONEY INCOME, 1967-1974
(Unmarried Male Heads of Households in 1968)

Income Change Component	Mean Change	Standard Deviation of Change
Change in Head's Labor Income	$ -95	$5,235
Change in Spouse's Labor Income	693	1,753
Change in Head's and Spouse's Capital Income	394	1,639
Change in Transfer Income	430	1,357
Change in Others' Taxable Income	-23	2,083
TOTAL	$1,399	$5,408

Number of Observations: 191

NOTE: 1974 income figures have been deflated by the increase in the
Consumer Price Index since 1967.

MTR #6080

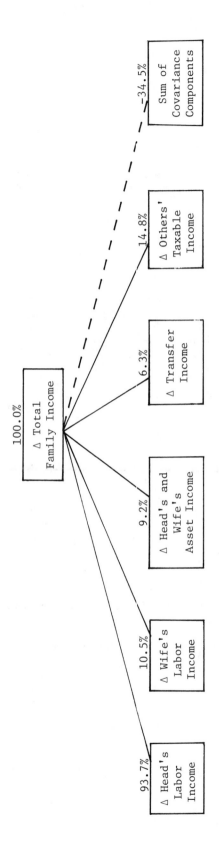

Figure 3.2

COMPONENTS OF THE VARIANCE OF CHANGE
IN REAL TOTAL FAMILY INCOME, 1967-1974
(Unmarried Male Heads of Households in 1968)

Number of Observations: 191

NOTE: The variance of the change in total family real income equals the sum of: (1) the variance of change in
wife's labor income, (2) the variance of change in head's and wife's asset income, (3) the variance of
change in head's labor income, (4) the variance of change in the taxable income of others in the family,
(5) the variance of change in family transfer income, and (6) the sum of the covariance components (two
times the covariance between each pair of income sources).

MTR #6080

Table 3.5

CHANGE IN LABOR INCOME BY CHANGE IN LABOR FORCE STATUS, 1967–1974
(Unmarried Male Heads of Households in 1968)

Change in Labor Force Status	Number of Observations	Weighted Percent of Observations	Mean Change in Labor Income	Percent of Variance of Change in Labor Income Accounted for by Subgroup
Out of Labor Force Both Years	24	17.3%	$ -7	0.0%
Entered Labor Force by 1974	9	4.0	6,457	7.9
Left Labor Force by 1974	26	15.4	-6,133	42.2
In Labor Force Both Years	132	63.3	940	50.0
TOTAL	191	100.0%	$ -95	100.1%

NOTE: 1974 income figures have been deflated by the increase in the Consumer Price Index since 1967.

An individual is defined as in the labor force in a given year if her work hours for that year were 250 or more.

MTR #6081

These groups also accounted for a disproportionately large percentage of the variance of change in the head's own labor income. Although male heads of households who entered or left the labor market represented only 20 percent of the population, they accounted for 50 percent of the variance of change in head's labor income. In contrast, the much larger group of individuals who worked in both 1967 and 1974 accounted for the remaining 50 percent of the total variance.

To examine the contribution of annual hours worked and hourly earnings in accounting for the variability in head's labor income, we again used logarithms to isolate the two components. We restricted the population to initially unmarried male heads of households who had at least 250 annual work hours in both 1967 and 1974. As Figure 3.3 shows, the variance of change in annual hours worked was slightly more important than that for wage rates in accounting for the variance of change in head's labor income.

In sum, we have found that for unmarried male heads of households, change in family income accounted for most of the variability of change in household economic well-being, measured by income/needs. After separating change in family income into its components, we found that changes in the household head's own earnings were most important in explaining the variability of the changes which occurred in household income. On the other hand, for the men who were in the labor force at both the beginning and end of the panel period, changes in *hourly* earnings accounted for only about one-half of the variance of change in annual earnings. Furthermore, changes in the labor income of these men accounted for only one-half of the variance of changes in the earnings of *all* initially unmarried male heads of households. It would appear, then, that a substantial array of changes other than wage rate changes remains to be investigated as possible sources of poverty, or ways out of it.

III. UNMARRIED FEMALE HEADS OF HOUSEHOLDS

Introduction

Female heads of households occupy a unique position in a society characterized by a male-dominated labor market and a social structure in which the nuclear family predominates. Recognizing this, one might expect that their patterns of change in economic well-being would be markedly different from those of male heads of households and wives of male heads. In particular, the fortunes of this group may be more sensitive to the experiences of other members of the family and to changes in the composition of their households than to their own labor efforts. Indeed, previous work in this series has provided evidence on this point; in Volume IV it was reported that "Marital status change was the

Figure 3.3

COMPONENTS OF THE VARIANCE OF CHANGE IN HEAD'S LABOR INCOME
(Unmarried Male Heads of Households in 1968 Who Were
in the Labor Force in both 1967 and 1974)

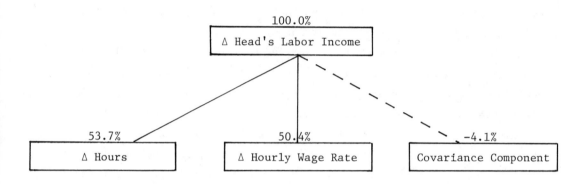

NOTE: The variance of the natural logarithm of change in annual labor income
        equals the sum of: (1) the variance of the log of the change in annual
        hours, (2) the variance of the log of the change in average hourly wage
        rate, and (3) the covariance component (which equals two times the covari-
        ance of log change in hours and log change in wage rate).

MTR #6080

most important predictor of change in the economic status for (unmarried) women."[4]

In this section we attempt to outline the dimensions of change in the economic well-being of unmarried women who were heads of households in 1968. Changes occurring in the eight-year period between 1967 and 1974, the principal components of such change, and their contribution to the variability in the change in economic well-being are the major subjects addressed. Particular attention is devoted to the effects of family composition change on the economic well-being of female heads of households. It should be noted that the presentation in this section is purely descriptive and, as such, can only suggest the possible causal forces in operation. This point should be kept in mind especially during the discussion of the effects of family composition change on economic well-being, for it is certainly possible that changes in well-being could be a cause rather than a result of family composition change.

Changes in the Level of Economic Well-Being

In the eight-year period between 1967 and 1974 there was substantial change in the relative economic position of women who were heads of households in 1968. As shown in Table 3.6, only 25.4 percent of these women were in the same income/ needs decile in 1974 as they were in 1967. For many, the change in economic status was substantial, as a full 40 percent moved at least two deciles during the eight-year period. A slight majority of this latter group experienced an increase in their relative economic status, but the number suffering a sharp decline was large, equaling 17.8 percent of the entire sample. It is encouraging to note, however, that one-half of the women who were in the bottom decile in 1967 had managed to move out by 1974. Unfortunately, the gains for these women were more than offset by a decline in the relative economic status of other women, as 19.5 percent of the sample were in the bottom decile in 1974 compared to 19.0 percent in 1967 (see Table A3.2b).

Since the measure of an individual's level of well-being is composed of two components (family money income and an estimated level of family needs), changes in either (or both) result in changes in the absolute level of economic well-being of the individual. As shown in Table 3.7, for female heads of households in 1968 the mean change in the income/needs ratio over the eight years was .50, an increase of 25.6 percent. Most of this increase resulted from an increase in family real money income, which rose an average $1,405. Complementing this increase was a slight decline in family needs, down an average of $46. Thus, both

---

[4]Duncan (1976), p. 86.

Table 3.6

CHANGE IN INCOME/NEEDS DECILE POSITION, 1967–1974
(Unmarried Female Heads of Households in 1968)

Change in Decile Position	All	Bottom Decile, 1967
Fell Two or More Deciles	17.8%	--
Fell One Decile	18.0	--
No Change	25.4	48.9
Increased One Decile	16.7	27.4
Increased Two or More Deciles	22.3	23.2
TOTAL	100.2%	99.5%

Number of Observations: 974

NOTE: The deciles were constructed from the distribution of income/
       needs ratios for the entire sample of *families*. Consequently,
       more or less than 10 percent of any subgroup can fall into any
       one decile.

       See Table A3.1b for the complete distribution of 1974 income/needs
       deciles by 1967 income/needs deciles for unmarried women.

MTR #6081

Table 3.7

MEANS AND STANDARD DEVIATIONS OF COMPONENTS OF CHANGE
IN TOTAL FAMILY REAL MONEY INCOME/NEEDS, 1967-1974
(Unmarried Female Heads of Households in 1968)

Income/Needs Change Component	Mean Change	Standard Deviation of Change
Change in Total Family Money Income	$1,405	$4,687
Change in Needs	$ -46	$1,022
Change in Income/Needs	0.50	1.63

Number of Observations: 974

NOTE: 1974 money income has been deflated by the increase in the Consumer
Price Index since 1967. The needs standard is based on 1967 prices.

MTR #7300, 7308, 7320

components of the measure of well-being operated, on the average, to improve the economic position of the original female heads of households.

These mean changes in economic well-being, however, can hide substantial variations in the situations of individual families. Mean changes average out the effects of positive and negative changes. In order to get a fuller picture of the extent of change in the level of well-being of female heads of households, we next turn our attention to the variability of this change.

As explained in the methodological appendix to Chapter 1, the variance of the change in economic well-being can be decomposed into the variance of its two components, income and needs, plus a covariance term. As shown in Figure 3.4, the variance of the change in total family money income was the dominant contributor to the variance of the change in economic well-being, while the variance of the change in needs played a relatively minor role. It is interesting to note that the covariance component for this group was substantially larger than for male household heads or for wives. This would indicate that for female heads of households changes in income and changes in needs were more highly associated (positively) than for other groups of individuals. (See Table A3.2b for the correlation coefficients of the variables used in this section.) Since changes in needs result almost solely from changes in the composition of the family,[5] we can surmise that changes in the family income of these women were strongly associated with family composition change. We will examine this point in more detail later in this chapter when we look explicitly at the effects of family composition change.

Changes in Family Money Income

Since changes in family money income clearly dominated in determining change in economic well-being of female heads of households, a closer examination of changes in family money income is in order. Family money income is the sum of five separate components: (1) the labor income of the woman, (2) the labor income of her spouse (if she was married in 1975), (3) the asset income of these two, (4) the taxable income of other members of the family, and (5) the transfer income of the family. As mentioned above, total family real money income increased from 1967 to 1974 by an average of $1,405. Somewhat surprisingly, this increase is virtually identical to the increase experienced by unmarried male heads of households. Most of this mean increase came from an increase in the spouse's labor income, from zero in 1967 to an average of $1,103 in 1974 (Table 3.8). This increase, of course, resulted from some of the original female heads becoming married. On the other hand, the labor income of the women themselves

---

[5]Needs can also change as existing family members grow older.

Figure 3.4

COMPONENTS OF THE VARIANCE OF CHANGE IN
REAL TOTAL FAMILY INCOME/NEEDS, 1967-1974
(Unmarried Female Heads of Households in 1968)

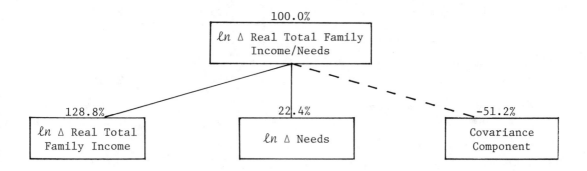

Number of Observations: 974

NOTE: The natural logarithm of the change in income/needs is equal to the log of
        the change in income minus the log of the change in needs. Thus, the
        variance of the log change in income/needs is equal to the variance of the
        log of change in income plus the variance of the log of change in needs
        minus two times the covariance. Hence, a *positive* covariance leads to a
        negative covariance component.

MTR #7300

Table 3.8

MEANS AND STANDARD DEVIATIONS OF COMPONENTS OF CHANGE
IN TOTAL FAMILY REAL MONEY INCOME, 1967–1974
(Unmarried Female Heads of Households in 1968)

Income Change Component	Mean Change	Standard Deviation of Change
Change in Own Labor Income	$ -125	$2,693
Change in Spouse's Labor Income	1,103	3,678
Change in Taxable Income of Others	182	2,510
Change in Asset Income of Head and Wife	66	1,200
Change in Family Transfer Income	179	1,619
Change Total Family Income	$1,405	$4,687

Number of Observations: 974

NOTE: 1974 income figures have been deflated by the increase in the
Consumer Price Index since 1967.

MTR #7300

decreased by an average of $125 over the eight-year period. Most of this de-
crease, it will be seen (Table 3.9), can be attributed to women who retired from
the labor force. This average decrease is in sharp contrast to the $333 *increase*
in labor income experienced by the initially married women in the panel.

Change in family transfer income, which rose by an average of $179, also
contributed to the mean increase in the family money income of these individuals.
However, when compared to figures for other subgroups of the total sample, this
increase is quite small. Family transfer income increased an average of $518
for husbands, $600 for wives, and $430 for unmarried men. This result is somewhat surprising, as the years 1967 to 1974 were a period of expansion in public
transfer programs aimed primarily at female-headed households, most notably the
AFDC program.

Examining the components of the variance of the change in family money income (Figure 3.5), we see that the change in the spouse's labor income was by
far the major contributor, accounting for roughly twice as much of the variance
as any other single component of income. This result differs substantially from
that for male heads of households and provides further evidence that the labor
market experience of males is far more crucial for changes in their level of
well-being than it is for females, whose changes are dominated by family composition change.

The variance of the change in the woman's own labor income and of the change
in the taxable income of other members of the family were the other major contributors to the variance of the change in family money income. The importance
of the woman's own labor income is somewhat unexpected, given its small mean
change, indicating that there was considerable variability among individuals in
this component of income. It is interesting to contrast the relative importance
of this component of income for wives and for female heads. While the mean
change was substantially larger for wives (in absolute value), the contribution
to the variance of the change in total family money was much less important for
wives than for female heads. The explanation is straightforward. Even though a
wife may experience a larger increase in labor income than a female head, in
general it will have a much smaller effect on changes in total family money income because of the domination by changes in the husband's earnings. On the
other hand, if a female head does not become married (only 14.4 percent did),
the change in her labor income, although smaller in absolute size, will exert a
much greater effect on total family money income, which does not include any income from a husband.

Changes in the asset income of the woman and her spouse and changes in

Table 3.9

CHANGE IN THE LABOR INCOME
BY CHANGE IN LABOR FORCE STATUS, 1967–1974
(Unmarried Female Heads of Households in 1968)

Change in Labor Force Status	Number of Observations	Weighted Percent of Observations	Mean Change in Labor Income	Percent of Variance of Change in Labor Income Accounted for by Subgroup
Out of Labor Both Years	315	31.4%	$ -8	0.1%
Entered Labor Force by 1974	76	5.2	3,092	11.0
Left Labor Force by 1974	171	18.5	-3,164	39.1
In Labor Force Both Years	412	44.9	675	49.9
TOTAL	974	100.0%	$ -125	100.0%

NOTE: 1974 income figures have been deflated by the increase in the Consumer Price Index since 1967.

An individual is defined as in the labor force in a given year if her work hours for that year were 250 or more.

MTR #7306

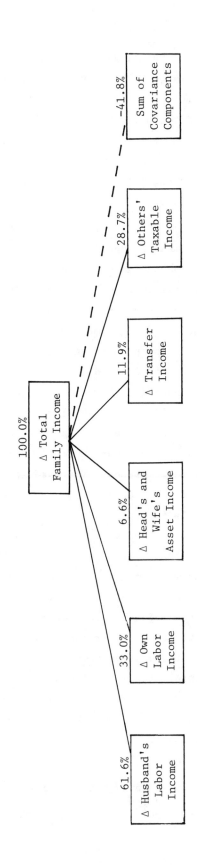

Figure 3.5

COMPONENTS OF THE VARIANCE OF CHANGE
IN REAL TOTAL FAMILY INCOME, 1967-1974
(Unmarried Female Heads of Households in 1968)

100.0%

Δ Total
Family Income

61.6%

Δ Husband's
Labor
Income

33.0%

Δ Own
Labor
Income

6.6%

Δ Head's and
Wife's
Asset Income

11.9%

Δ Transfer
Income

28.7%

Δ Others'
Taxable
Income

−41.8%

Sum of
Covariance
Components

Number of Observations: 974

NOTE: The variance of the change in real total family income equals the sum of: (1) the variance of the change in husband's labor income, (2) the variance of the change in own labor income, (3) the variance of the change in head's and wife's asset income, (4) the variance of the change in transfer income, (5) the variance of the change in the taxable income of others in the family, and (6) the sum of the covariance components (two times the covariance between each pair of income sources).

MTR #7300

family transfer income contributed relatively little to the variance of the
change in family money income. Indeed, these women fared poorly with respect to
changes in asset income when compared to other groups of individuals. Their mean
increase was substantially smaller ($66, compared to at least $350 for husbands,
wives, and unmarried men), and the variance of the change in asset income was the
least important component of the variance in the change in total income for
female heads, while it was the second most important component for both husbands
and wives.

Changes in Own Labor Income

As seen above, although the mean change in the real labor income of 1968
female heads over the subsequent eight years was relatively small, there was
considerable variability in that change among the sample individuals. One would
expect that one of the primary sources of this variability would be differences
in the labor force status of these women. Some may have entered the labor force,
others may have left, resulting in sharp increases and decreases in labor income.
Additional variability could come from individuals who remained in the labor
force experiencing differential changes in hours worked and/or average wage rates.
One would expect little change and little variability in the labor income of
individuals who were not in the labor force in either of the two years.[6]

Table 3.9 shows the mean change in labor income of female heads of households by changes in their labor force status. The majority of these women experienced no change in their labor force status--31.4 percent were out of the labor
force in both 1967 and 1974, while 44.9 percent were in the labor force in both
years. Those who were out both years had virtually no change in their labor income. Those who remained in the labor force averaged a $675 increase in real
labor income. But the really dramatic changes in labor income occurred for those
who either entered or left the labor force. Only 5 percent of the female heads
in 1968 entered the labor force by 1974, and they averaged an increase of $3,092
in labor income. By far the more common experience was that of women leaving the
labor force--almost one-third of those women who were in the labor force in 1967
had left by 1974; this group represented one-fifth of the entire population.
This shift in labor force status was accompanied by a substantial decrease
($3,164) in labor income.

In looking at the contribution of each of these groups to the variance of

---

[6]Since an individual is defined as being out of the labor force if she
worked less than 250 hours during the year (rather than no hours), small changes
in labor income are possible for those not in the labor force in either year.

the change in labor income, as shown in Figure 3.6, these results are reinforced. By far the most important groups in accounting for the variance of the change in own labor income were those who remained in the labor force (accounting for one-half of the total variance) and those who left the labor force (accounting for 40 percent of the total variance). This latter group is particularly significant, for their contribution to the total variance was disproportionately large compared to their sample size. The group that was out of the labor force in both years, although constituting one-third of the sample, contributed nothing to the overall variance due to the fact that the change in their labor income was relatively small (in relation to the overall mean) and varied little. For those who entered the labor force, although their change in labor income was large and exhibited considerable variance, their contribution to the total variance was nevertheless relatively small as a result of the small fraction of the sample which they comprised.

Given the importance of leaving the labor force, it is of interest to see how much of the variance can be accounted for by the normal life-cycle pattern of old age and retirement, and how much resulted from other factors. Figure 3.6 shows that two-thirds of the variance accounted for by those leaving the labor force can be attributed to those unmarried women who were over the age of 64 in 1975 or who reported themselves as retired. Becoming married or leaving the labor force for reasons other than retirement were relatively unimportant events in contributing to the variance of labor income accounted for by female heads of households who left the labor market.

For those women who were in the labor force in both years, a change in labor income could result from a change in hours and/or a change in wages. Figure 3.7 shows the relative contribution of each of these components to the variance of the change in the labor income of these women. As can be seen, the variability of the change in hours and of the change in wages were about equally important in contributing to the variance of the change in labor income.

Changes in Economic Well-Being and Family Composition Change

The results presented thus far strongly suggest that family composition change, particularly marriage, was the dominant determinant of changes in the level of economic well-being of unmarried female heads of households. In order to examine this proposition more closely, we will now look at changes in the level of economic well-being according to the different types of family composition change which these women experienced during the eight-year panel period.

Changes in the composition of a family can be expected to result in changes in the level of both family income and family needs, the two components of the

94

Figure 3.6

COMPONENTS OF THE VARIANCE OF CHANGE IN OWN LABOR INCOME, 1967-1974
(Unmarried Female Heads of Households in 1968)

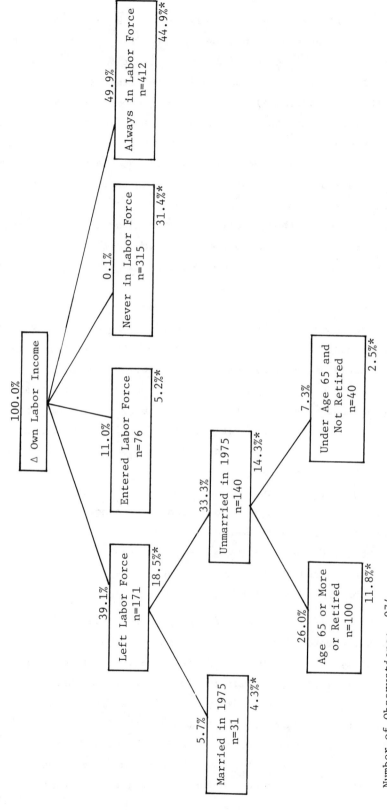

Number of Observations: 974

*Weighted percent of observations in cell.

MTR #7306, 7312, 7313

Figure 3.7

COMPONENTS OF THE VARIANCE OF THE LOG
CHANGE IN OWN LABOR INCOME, 1967-1974
(Unmarried Female Heads of Households in 1968 Who Were
in the Labor Force in Both 1967 and 1974)

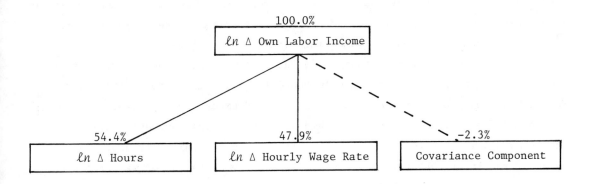

Number of Observations: 974

NOTE: The variance of the natural logarithm of change in annual labor income
equals the sum of: (1) the variance of the log of the change in annual
hours, (2) the variance of the log of the change in average hourly wage
rate, and (3) the covariance component (which equals two times the covariance of log change in hours and log change in wage rate).

MTR #7300

measure of an individual's level of economic well-being. Since the estimate of
a family's needs level is based on the size and age-sex structure of the family,
changes in the members of a family will, by definition, cause changes in the
estimate of needs. Family composition change can also result in changes in
family money income, as a new income earner is gained or an old one lost. Thus
we might expect that the aggregate changes in economic well-being reported earlier
would hide substantial differences among individuals who experienced different
family composition changes.

As Table 3.10 indicates, changes in the members of the families headed
initially by an unmarried woman were common; more than half of these families experienced some composition change during the eight-year period. The most frequent changes were marriage and children leaving home. Fourteen percent of these
female heads in 1968 were married as of 1975. Seventeen percent did not marry
but had children leave home at some time during the panel period. Table 3.10
also confirms the expectation that different family composition changes lead to
considerable differences in changes in economic well-being. Most strikingly,
female heads who were married in 1975 experienced exceptionally large increases
in economic well-being. This occurred despite higher than average increases in
family needs, which were overwhelmingly offset by gains in family money income.
We shall see later that the mean increase in family money income was accounted
for almost entirely by the husband's labor income. Also of interest is the fact
that female-headed families which decreased in size, although suffering a loss
in family money income, still experienced a higher than average increase in well-
being, as the reduction in family needs due to individuals leaving the family
more than offset the loss in income. These groups no doubt accounted for the
large positive covariance between change in income and change in needs. Further
emphasizing the importance of family composition change for this group of individuals is the fact that the women who experienced no change in family members
had virtually no change in their average level of well-being over the eight
years.

The last two columns of Table 3.10 show the proportions of the total variance of the change in income and the change in needs accounted for by each of
the family composition change subgroups. The effect of marriage again dominated
in contributing to the variance of the change in total income. Although the
women who were married as of 1975 constituted only 14.4 percent of the sample,
they accounted for 37.9 percent of the variance of the change in income. Other
groups which accounted for a substantial portion of the total variance were
families in which children left home and those that experienced no change in fam-

Table 3.10

MEAN CHANGE AND COMPONENTS OF THE VARIANCE OF THE CHANGE IN INCOME/NEEDS
BY FAMILY COMPOSITION CHANGE, 1967-1974
(Unmarried Female Heads of Households in 1968)

Family Composition Change	Number of Observations	Weighted Percent of Observations	Mean Change in Income/Needs	Mean Change in Income	Mean Change in Needs	Percent of* Variance of Change in Income Accounted for by Subgroup	Percent of* Variance of Change in Needs Accounted for by Subgroup
No Change in Family Members	338	45.2%	0.06	$ 101	$ 4	23.6%	3.1%
Married, Then Widowed, Divorced or Separated	37	4.1	0.52	1,625	-167	3.8	4.4
Married, Child Under Seven in Family	57	5.9	2.42	10,111	1,410	26.5	15.6
Married, No Child Under Seven in Family	68	8.5	1.43	5,897	653	11.4	11.6
Unmarried, Child Under Seven in Family	128	5.0	0.28	1,791	367	4.2	6.7
Family Size Decreased, with Children Moving Out	206	17.0	0.71	-179	-1,171	20.8	41.8
Family Size Decreased, with No Children Moving Out	42	4.2	0.62	-163	-904	3.3	7.1
Other Changes in Family Composition	98	10.1	0.28	1,475	395	6.4	9.8
TOTAL	974	100.0%	0.50	$1,405	$ -46	100.0%	100.1%

*These change variables are in log form.

MTR #7308, 7320, 7311

ily members. The contribution of the latter group to the variance of the change
in income resulted primarily from its large size (45.2 percent of the sample).

Changes in Family Money Income and Family Composition Change

As seen above, women who married experienced exceptionally large increases,
on the average, in total family real money income. Table 3.11 confirms the expectation that this increase resulted almost entirely from the labor income of
the newly acquired husband. It should also be noted that these women also
experienced the largest average increases in asset income, a large part of which
would also be expected to result from the new husbands.

But the women who were married as of 1975 were not the only ones to experience substantial mean increases in income. For the women who were not married
but had large increases in income, these increases resulted primarily from increases in the taxable income of other members of the family. The point that
stands out from the findings for each of these subgroups is that for *no* group
that had large average increases in family income did the increase result from an
increase in the labor income of the woman who was the head of the family in 1968.
These results suggest that the increases in family money income which these individuals experienced were not due to their own advancement in the labor market,
but rather to their relationship with others who were in the labor market.

Black Female Heads of Households in 1968

It was our hypothesis that black female heads of households, living in a
male-dominated *and* a white-dominated society, would be subjected to radically
different social and economic forces. In this section, we attempt to describe
how these forces influence the pattern of changes in economic well-being of
black females who were heads of households in 1968, emphasizing those results
which differ from those found for all female household heads.

Black women comprised 18.7 percent of the entire sample of unmarried female
heads of households in 1968. As shown in Table 3.12, the average level of income/
needs for this group increased less than for the entire group, .29 compared to
.50. This smaller average increase occurred because of a smaller average increase in family money income ($1,039 compared to $1,405), as the level of family
needs of black females decreased by virtually the same amount as for the entire
sample of female heads. However, the variability of the change in needs was
somewhat more important for blacks in contributing to the variance of the change
in well-being as compared to the variability of the change in family money income.
This would indicate that black females were subject to more family composition
change (as also evidenced by the fact that only 27.4 percent of black females
were in families which had no change in family members; see Table 3.13) and, con-

Table 3.11

MEAN CHANGES IN THE COMPONENTS OF INCOME BY FAMILY COMPOSITION CHANGE
(Unmarried Female Heads of Households in 1968)

Family Composition Change	Number of Observations	Weighted Percent of Observations	Change in Total Income	Change in Own Labor Income	Change in Spouse's Labor Income	Change in Others' Taxable Income	Change in Family Transfer Income	Change in Asset Income of Head and Spouse
No Change in Family Members	338	45.2%	$ 101	$ 313	$ 0	$ -58	$566	$-94
Married, Then Widowed, Divorced, or Separated	37	4.1	1,625	-1,043	0	2,093	482	92
Married, Child Under Seven in Family	57	5.9	10,111	-83	10,377	-476	-119	412
Married, No Child Under Seven in Family	68	8.5	5,897	-156	5,842	-237	-92	540
Unmarried, Child Under Seven in Family	128	5.0	1,791	-161	0	1,645	288	18
Family Size Decreased, With Children Moving Out	206	17.0	-179	524	0	-196	-656	148
Family Size Decreased, With No Children Moving Out	42	4.2	-163	101	0	171	-470	35
Other Changes in Family Composition	98	10.1	1,475	-76	0	1,131	348	71
TOTAL	974	100.0%	$1,405	$ -125	$1,103	$ 182	$179	$ 66

NOTE: 1974 income figures have been deflated by the increase in the Consumer Price Index since 1967.

MTR #7311, 7321

Table 3.12

MEANS, STANDARD DEVIATIONS, AND CONTRIBUTION TO THE VARIANCE OF COMPONENTS
OF CHANGE IN TOTAL FAMILY REAL MONEY INCOME/NEEDS, 1967-1974
(Unmarried Black Female Heads of Households in 1968)

Income/Needs Change Component	Mean Change	Standard Deviation	Contribution to the Variance of the Change in Income/Needs*
Change in Total Family Money Income	$1,039	$3,081	110.4%
Change in Needs	$ -49	$1,417	27.4%
Change in Income/Needs	.29	.90	--

Number of Observations: 526

*The decomposition of the variance of the change in income/needs was done in
 logarithmic form. See appendix to Chapter 1.

NOTE: 1974 money income has been deflated by the increase in the Consumer Price
       Index since 1967. The needs standard is based on 1967 prices.

MTR #7320, 7300, 7308

Table 3.13

MEAN CHANGES IN THE COMPONENTS OF INCOME BY FAMILY COMPOSITION CHANGE
(Unmarried Black Female Heads of Households in 1968)

Family Composition Change	Number of Observations	Weighted Percent of Observations	Change in Total Income	Change in Own Labor Income	Change in Spouse's Labor Income	Change in Others' Taxable Income	Change in Family Transfer Income	Change in Asset Income of Head and Spouse
No Change in Family Members	130	27.4%	$ 642	$ 65	$ 0	$ 70	$ 508	$ 2
Married, Then Widowed, Divorced, or Separated	20	4.1	-1,477	-2,673	0	190	1,000	6
Married, Child Under Seven in Family	25	3.5	3,522	-615	5,989	-2,577	800	-76
Married, No Child Under Seven in Family	27	5.3	6,199	1,969	4,561	-471	50	90
Unmarried, Child Under Seven in Family	113	16.6	1,259	23	0	721	512	3
Family Size Decreased, With Children Moving Out	131	22.8	140	315	0	198	-381	7
Family Size Decreased, With No Children Moving Out	28	8.1	231	-255	0	447	-132	170
Other Changes in Family Composition	52	12.0	1,694	-10	0	857	734	112
TOTAL	526	100.0%	$1,039	$ 44	$ 466	$ 210	$ 288	$ 31

NOTE: 1974 income figures have been deflated by the increase in the Consumer Price Index since 1967.

MTR #7318

sequently, greater increases and decreases in family needs.

But the truly striking difference between blacks and the entire sample was in the change in the components of income. Looking first at the aggregate mean changes, the point that stands out is the large difference in the change in spouse's income (Table 3.13). For black female heads of households in 1968, this component of income increased by an average of only $466 from 1967 to 1974, compared to an increase for the entire sample of $1,103. Part of this smaller increase can be attributed to the lower propensity of black females to marry--only 9 percent of the black female heads were married in 1975, compared to 14.4 percent of all female heads. But even for those black women who did marry, the increase in their spouse's income was substantially less than that for the entire sample. For example, for those black women who married and (presumably) gave birth during the panel period, their husbands' incomes averaged $5,989 in 1974, compared to an average of $10,377 for all women who married and gave birth. For black women who married and did not give birth, the difference was not as great ($4,561 compared to $5,842) but was still substantial. These results suggest a further disadvantage faced by black women due to their race. If it is indeed true that the primary path by which women improve their economic well-being is through the addition of an income-earning husband, then the discrimination faced by black men in the labor market may operate to close that path of improvement to black women.

It is also of interest to note the difference between the change in black women's own labor income and that of the entire sample. The average labor income of black women increased by $44, a sharp contrast to the $125 *decrease* for the entire sample. Comparing the labor force participation patterns of blacks and the entire sample (Table 3.14), it can be seen that this increase resulted from a higher percentage of black women entering the labor force (10.1 percent compared to 5.2 percent for the entire sample) and from a higher average increase in the labor income of black women who remained in the labor force ($923 versus $675). In addition, black women who dropped out of the labor force experienced a smaller absolute decline in labor income ($2,090 compared to $3,164), probably as a consequence of the fact that black women occupy lower paying jobs, on the average, and thus have less to lose.

When the contribution of the components of income to the variance of the change in family income is examined (Figure 3.8), the differential importance of the labor income of black females is further emphasized, especially in comparison to the contribution of spouse's labor income. While the variance of the change in spouse's labor income was of overwhelming importance in contributing to the variance of the change in total family money for the entire sample, it ranked

Table 3.14

MEAN CHANGE IN THE LABOR INCOME
BY CHANGE IN LABOR FORCE STATUS, 1967–1974
(Unmarried Black Female Heads of Households in 1968)

Change in Labor Force Status	Number of Observations	Weighted Percent of Observations	Mean Change in Labor Income	Percent of Variance of Change in Labor Income Accounted for by Subgroup
Out of Labor Force Both Years	170	32.8%	$ -25	0.0%
Entered Labor Force by 1974	53	10.1	2,370	17.2
Left Labor Force by 1974	97	23.7	-2,090	51.6
In Labor Force Both Years	206	33.5	923	31.0
TOTAL	526	100.0%	$ 44	99.8%

NOTE: 1974 income figures have been deflated by the increase in the Consumer Price Index since 1967.

An individual is defined as in the labor force in a given year if her work hours for that year were 250 or more.

MTR #7306

104

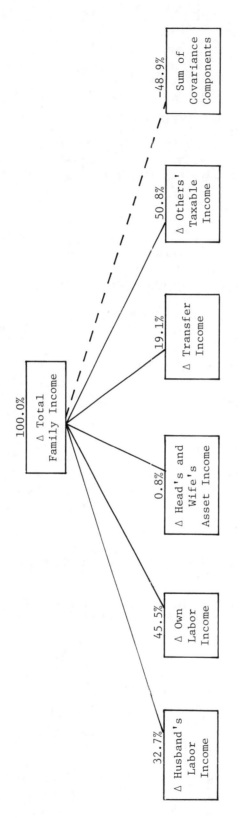

Figure 3.8

COMPONENTS OF THE VARIANCE OF CHANGE
IN FAMILY INCOME, 1967-1974
(Unmarried Black Female Heads of Households in 1968)

NOTE: The variance of the change in total family real money income equals the sum of: (1) the variance of the change in husband's labor income, (2) the variance of the change in own labor income, (3) the variance of the change in head's and wife's asset income, (4) the variance of the change in family transfer income, (5) the variance of the change in the taxable income of others in the family, and (6) the sum of the covariance components (two times the covariance between each pair of income sources).

MTR #7300

third in importance for black females, behind both others' taxable income and own labor income. These results indicate that the change in total family money income of black women was much more closely associated with their own labor force experience than it was for white women, and much less strongly associated with marriage.

The last column of Table 3.14 shows the contribution to the variance of the change in own labor income by different subgroups of the sample, classified according to change in labor force status. When compared to Table 3.9, it is clear that the labor income of black women was more influenced by changes in labor market status, that is, by entering and leaving the market, than was true for the entire sample. For blacks, these changes accounted for two-thirds of the variance of the change in their own labor income, while only accounting for one-half the variance for the entire sample. Especially significant for black women was the effect of leaving the labor force, which alone accounted for one-half of the variance.

However, the change in total family money income for black women was still highly sensitive to changes in the income of people other than themselves, as shown by the large contribution to the variance of the change in total income accounted for by changes in the taxable income of other members of the family. This component was the largest contributor for black women, indicating that both family composition change, by increasing or reducing the number of income receivers, and the labor market experiences of other members who remain in the family were more important determinants of the change in total family money income of black women than for nonblack women.

Other Subgroups of Unmarried Female Heads of Households in 1968

Thus far we have examined the results of changes in economic well-being for all unmarried female heads of households in 1968 and for black female heads of households. We now briefly turn our attention to three other subgroups of female heads—those who were in the bottom quintile of the distribution of income/needs in any of the eight panel years (the "target population"), those who were poor in 1967 (the "initially poor"), and those who were poor in 1967 but not in 1974 (the "climbers-out" of poverty). The results are presented in Tables 3.15, 3.16, and 3.17.

One point to note from these results is the high incidence of poverty experienced by families headed by a woman. Fifty-six percent of all unmarried female heads of households in 1968 were below the poverty level during at least one of the eight years between 1967 and 1974. Fully one-fifth (21.1 percent) were poor in the initial year 1967; however, 67.3 percent of the initially poor

106

Table 3.15

COMPONENTS OF THE VARIANCE OF CHANGE IN INCOME/NEEDS, 1967-1974
(Different Populations of Unmarried Female Heads of Households in 1968)

Group	Number of Observations	Weighted Percent	Percentage of Contribution to Total Variance of Change in Income/Needs*		
			Change in Income*	Change in Needs*	Covariance Component
All	974	100.0%	85.2%	14.8%	51.2%
Black	526	18.7	80.1	19.9	37.8
Target Population	737	56.4	86.7	13.3	47.3
Initially Poor	374	21.1	87.5	12.5	58.0
Climbers-Out	210	14.2	86.9	13.1	64.4

*These variables are in logarithmic form.

NOTE: The variances have been scaled to add to 100.0 percent in order to facilitate comparisons between groups.

MTR #7300

Table 3.16

COMPONENTS OF THE VARIANCE OF CHANGE IN TOTAL FAMILY MONEY INCOME
(Different Populations of Unmarried Female Heads of Households in 1968)

Group	Number of Observations	Weighted Percent of Observations	Percentage Contribution to Total Variance of Change in Family Money Income					
			Change in Own Labor Income	Change in Spouse's Labor Income	Change in Others' Taxable Income	Change in Family Transfer Income	Change in Capital Income of Head and Wife	Sum of Covariance Components
All	974	100.0%	23.3%	43.4%	20.2%	8.4%	4.7%	41.8%
Blacks	562	18.7	30.6	22.0	34.1	12.8	0.5	48.9
Target Population	737	56.4	16.9	42.7	30.2	8.2	1.9	23.1
Initially Poor	374	21.1	18.1	54.7	16.3	10.4	0.4	-0.2
Climbers-Out	210	14.2	17.5	57.8	15.9	8.3	0.4	11.8

NOTE: The variances have been scaled to 100.0 percent in order to facilitate comparisons between groups.

1974 income figures have been deflated by the increase in the Consumer Price Index since 1974.

Table 3.17

MEAN CHANGES IN COMPONENTS OF FAMILY MONEY INCOME

(Different Populations of Unmarried Female Heads of Households in 1968)

Group	Number of Observations	Weighted Percent of Observations	Change in Family Money Income	Change in Own Labor Income	Change in Spouse's Labor Income	Change in Others' Taxable Income	Change in Family Transfer Income	Change in Capital Income of Head and Wife
All	974	100.0%	$1,405	$-125	$1,103	$182	$179	$66
Blacks	526	18.7	1,039	44	466	210	288	31
Target Population	737	56.4	1,233	-15	861	239	139	9
Initially Poor	374	21.1	1,952	568	838	441	81	23
Climbers-Out	210	14.2	2,932	852	1,235	677	136	31

NOTE: 1974 income figures have been deflated by the increase in the Consumer Price Index since 1974.

MTR #7300

women had climbed out of poverty by 1974.

The relative importance of changes in needs and changes in income in contributing to the total variance in the change in income/needs was very similar among these three subgroups (Table 3.15), a result which corresponds to that found for other groups of individuals. Similarly, the relative contribution of the different components of income to the variance of the change in total income was roughly the same (Table 3.16), except perhaps for the change in others' taxable income for the target population, which was larger than for the other subgroups. This may indicate that these individuals cope with temporary poverty by moving in with (or accepting) other income earners, or that other members of the family enter the labor market to provide funds in emergency situations. Looking at the mean changes in the income components (Table 3.17), one can see that those individuals who moved out of poverty had larger increases in virtually all the components than did the other two subgroups, with the increase in the spouse's labor income being the largest contributor to the increase in family income. What does stand out is that the increase in transfer income (such as welfare or Social Security) was one of the *smallest* contributors, indicating that the labor market is still the primary vehicle by which families move out of poverty.

Summary

The major results of the analysis of unmarried heads of household in 1968 are:

For both unmarried men and unmarried women heads of households in 1968, there was considerable change in the relative level of economic well-being, as only approximately one-quarter of these individuals were in the same income/needs decile in 1974 as they were in 1968.

For both groups, change in total family income was much more important than change in needs in determining the change in the absolute level of economic well-being.

For both men and women, the mean change in spouse's labor income accounted for the major portion of the mean increase in total family money income.

For men, the variation of the change in own labor income was the dominant component in accounting for the *variance* of the change in total family income. For women, on the other hand, the variance of the change in *spouse's* labor income was the dominant component.

For both men and women who were in the labor force in both 1967 and 1974, the variances of the change in hours worked and of the change in wage rate were equally important in accounting for the variance of the change in own labor income.

The mean increase in family transfer income was smaller for 1968 female heads of households than any other group analyzed.

Changes in family composition were common for female-headed households, and such changes were often associated with large changes in the level of economic well-being of the family. In particular, women who were married in 1974 experienced exceptionally large increases in economic well-being, largely as a result of the labor income of the newly acquired husband.

For the women who did not marry but still experienced substantial increases in total family income, these increases were primarily the result of increases in the labor income of other family members.

Black female heads of households had smaller increases in their level of economic well-being than did the entire sample of female heads. This smaller increase was mainly due to smaller increases in spouse's labor income. This phenomenon is partly attributable to the fact that fewer of the black women married, but it was also a result of husbands of black women who did marry having much lower labor incomes than the husbands of the entire sample of females who were married in 1974.

For black female heads of households, the importance of the variance of the change in spouse's labor income in accounting for the variance of the change in total family income was much lower than for the entire sample of female heads. The variance of the change in *other's* taxable income was the dominant factor for black female heads.

References

Duncan, Greg J. "Unmarried Heads of Households and Marriage." In Five Thousand American Families--Patterns of Economic Progress, Volume IV. Edited by Greg J. Duncan and James N. Morgan. Ann Arbor: Institute for Social Research, 1976.

APPENDIX 3.1

Table A3.1a

1974 FAMILY INCOME/NEEDS DECILE BY 1967 FAMILY INCOME/NEEDS DECILE
(Unmarried Male Heads of Households in 1968)

1967 Income/Needs Decile	1974 Income/Needs Deciles										
	Lowest Tenth	Second	Third	Fourth	Fifth	Sixth	Seventh	Eighth	Ninth	Highest Tenth	Total
Lowest Tenth	6.0	2.3	0.8	0.3	0.1	0.0	1.2	2.2	0.8	0.0	13.6
Second	2.0	3.5	2.9	0.4	0.0	0.0	0.0	0.4	0.4	0.5	10.0
Third	0.3	1.9	2.2	1.4	1.0	0.5	0.4	1.5	1.4	0.0	10.5
Fourth	2.0	1.3	1.5	1.0	1.6	0.0	1.3	1.4	1.0	0.0	11.1
Fifth	0.0	0.9	0.0	2.2	2.0	0.0	0.7	0.0	0.9	0.0	6.6
Sixth	0.0	0.2	0.9	0.0	0.0	0.5	0.7	0.0	0.9	0.0	3.2
Seventh	0.5	0.0	0.8	1.4	0.0	0.0	1.0	1.2	0.9	0.0	5.8
Eighth	0.0	0.8	0.8	1.6	0.0	0.0	0.9	1.1	1.4	3.5	10.0
Ninth	0.0	1.6	0.0	0.0	0.1	0.4	1.7	0.8	3.8	3.2	11.7
Highest Tenth	0.0	0.0	0.7	0.0	1.4	0.9	2.0	3.1	0.7	8.5	17.4
TOTAL	10.7	12.4	10.5	8.3	6.2	2.3	9.9	11.7	12.2	15.7	100.0

Number of Cases = 191

Rank Correlation (Kendall's Tau-B) = .47

NOTE: The deciles were constructed from the distribution of income/needs ratios for the entire sample of *families*. Consequently, more or less than 10 percent of any subgroup can fall into any one decile.

MTR #6081

Table A3.1b

1974 FAMILY INCOME/NEEDS DECILE BY 1967 FAMILY INCOME/NEEDS DECILE
(Unmarried Female Heads of Households in 1968)

1967 Income/Needs Decile	1974 Income/Needs Decile										
	Lowest Tenth	Second	Third	Fourth	Fifth	Sixth	Seventh	Eighth	Ninth	Highest Tenth	Total
Lowest Tenth	9.3	5.2	2.1	0.9	0.8	0.2	0.0	0.1	0.2	0.1	19.0
Second	7.0	4.1	3.5	0.8	0.9	0.7	0.8	0.1	0.0	0.3	18.2
Third	1.6	2.9	2.0	1.6	2.1	0.4	0.8	0.2	0.7	0.2	12.4
Fourth	0.9	1.3	2.0	0.8	1.2	1.2	1.0	0.8	0.1	0.0	9.4
Fifth	0.3	0.5	1.4	0.8	1.2	0.4	0.8	1.0	1.1	0.5	8.0
Sixth	0.0	0.3	0.7	1.1	0.8	0.4	1.7	0.5	0.5	0.1	6.1
Seventh	0.2	0.9	1.2	1.0	0.3	1.3	1.5	1.1	0.6	0.8	8.9
Eighth	0.2	0.3	0.4	0.0	0.0	1.0	0.8	1.0	0.7	0.9	5.3
Ninth	0.0	0.0	0.2	0.5	0.3	0.3	0.5	0.7	2.2	1.3	5.9
Highest Tenth	0.0	0.0	0.3	0.0	0.2	0.4	0.8	0.7	1.7	2.9	6.9
TOTAL	19.5	15.4	13.7	7.6	7.8	6.4	8.5	6.2	7.8	7.0	100.0

Number of Cases = 974

Rank Correlation (Kendall's Tau-B) = .56

NOTE: The deciles were constructed from the distribution of income/needs ratios for the entire sample of *families*. Consequently, more or less than 10 percent of any subgroup can fall into any one decile.

MTR #6081

APPENDIX 3.2

Table A3.2a

CORRELATIONS AMONG COMPONENTS OF CHANGE IN FAMILY INCOME/NEEDS
(Unmarried Male Heads of Households in 1968)

	1	2	3	4	5	6
1 Change Income/Needs*	1.00					
2 Change Family Income*	.93	1.00				
3 Change Needs*	-.16	.22	1.00			
1 Change Family Income	1.00					
2 Change Head's Labor Income	.78	1.00				
3 Change Wife's Labor Income	.40	.04	1.00			
4 Change Head's and Wife's Asset Income	.21	-.12	.06	1.00		
5 Change Transfer Income	-.38	-.64	.00	-.01	1.00	
6 Change Others' Taxable Income	.37	-.02	.03	.00	-.03	1.00
1 Change Head's Labor Income*	1.00					
2 Change Head's Hourly Earnings*	.68	1.00				
3 Change Head's Annual Work Hours*	.71	-.04	1.00			

*Variable expressed in logarithms.

NOTE: 1974 income figures are deflated by the increase in the Consumer Price Index since 1967.

MTR #6080

114

Table A3.2b

CORRELATIONS AMONG COMPONENTS OF CHANGE IN FAMILY INCOME/NEEDS, 1967-1974
(Unmarried Female Heads of Households in 1968)

	1	2	3	4	5	6
1 Change Income/Needs*	1.00					
2 Change Family Income*	.91	1.00				
3 Change Needs*	.07	.48	1.00			
1 Change Family Income	1.00					
2 Change Own Labor Income	.37	1.00				
3 Change Spouse's Labor Income	.66	-.10	1.00			
4 Change Taxable Income of Others	.44	.00	-.03	1.00		
5 Change Family Transfer Income	-.15	-.42	-.17	-.19	1.00	
6 Change Head and Wife's Asset Income	.32	.07	.06	-.01	-.06	1.00
1 Change Own Labor Income*	1.00					
2 Change Wage Rate*	.68	1.00				
3 Change Annual Work Hours	.72	-.02	1.00			

*Variables expressed in logarithms.

NOTE: 1974 income figures are deflated by the increase in the Consumer Price Index since 1967.

MTR #7300

APPENDIX 3.3

Description of the Family Composition Change Categories

The family composition change categories were priority coded so that a
family was placed in the first category which matched the changes which the
family underwent over the eight-year period from 1968 to 1975. A description
of the categories, in order of priority, follows.

1. No Change in Family Members. Families in this category had the same
members in the family in *each* of the eight years between 1968 and 1975. Therefore, while every family in this category would have the same members in 1975
as in 1968, it is possible that some families with the same members in each of
these two years would *not* be in this category. This could occur, for example,
if an original family member left for two years but rejoined the family by 1975.

2. Married, Then Widowed, Divorced, or Separated. This category consists
of families headed in 1968 by an unmarried women who married at some time during
the eight-year period but who was the head of the household in 1975. It is
possible that the original female head married more than once over the eight
years.

3. Married, Child under Seven in the Family. This category consists of
families in which the original female head married at some time in the eight-
year period, and was married in 1975. In addition, there was in 1975 at least
one child under seven years of age in the family, presumably indicating that
the woman gave birth, although this is not necessarily the case. It is possible
that the original female head married a husband with a small child, or that the
couple adopted a child or took in a young relative (nephew, etc.).

4. Married, No Child under Seven in the Family. This category is identical
to the above category, except that in 1975 there was no child under seven years
of age in the family.

5. Unmarried, Child under Seven in the Family. This category consists of

families in which the original female head did not marry at any time during the eight-year period and in which there was a child under seven in 1975. Presumably this would indicate that the woman gave birth, but it could also occur if a relative or friend with a child under seven moved in with the original female head.

6. <u>Family Size Decreased, with Children Moving Out</u>. This category consists of families which had fewer members in 1975 than in 1968, and at least one child moved out during the eight-year period. The child moving out, however, did not necessarily have to be a member of the household in 1968.

7. <u>Family Size Decreased, with no Children Moving Out</u>. This category consists of families which had fewer members in 1975 than in 1968, but had no children leave the household during the eight-year period.

8. <u>Other Changes in Family Composition</u>. This is a miscellaneous category for families which did not fulfill the requirements for classification in any of the above seven categories.

Chapter 4

SONS AND DAUGHTERS

Martha S. Hill

Introduction

Older children, as they approach adulthood and begin to exert some control over their lives, are faced with many important decisions. Among these decisions are those concerning commitments to the labor force, to starting one's own household (splitting off), and to establishing a family life of one's own in terms of marriage and children.

Commitments with respect to these decisions can change substantially during early adult years, as evidenced by the actions of the population considered in this chapter. This population consists of those persons who were sons and daughters in the original panel families and who were aged 10-29 in the initial year of the study (1968). By the final year (1975), about 50 percent of these sons and daughters had entered the labor force, over 50 percent had become splitoffs,[1] about 40 percent had married, and over 20 percent had married and become parents themselves. For young adults, changes of this kind are likely to entail drastic changes in economic well-being.

Analysis

Changes in the economic well-being of these sons and daughters over the eight-year period of the panel study are the focal point of this chapter. Although this discussion centers on the individual, an individual's level of economic well-being is so closely linked to that of his family that it must be measured in terms of change in the economic well-being of their families. Economic well-

---

[1] A splitoff is a member of an original sample family who was living with that family or only temporarily away from it in 1968 when the study began and who subsequently moved out either to get married or to start his or her own household. (The term "own household" means anywhere the splitoff lives other than in institutional housing.) Splitoffs could be husbands, wives, children, grandparents—any type of family member. However, in the context of this chapter, the term "splitoff" refers only to children who have formed households separate from those of their parental families.

Moving out of the original family's home is not a necessary nor a sufficient condition for becoming a splitoff. Children who married and continued living in the parental dwelling but in a clearly separate unit of the dwelling were classified as splitoffs. College students who left the parental dwelling were classified as splitoffs only if they were either: (1) living in off-campus housing and were clearly self-supporting or (2) married and living in married student housing. Children who left the parental dwelling to become members of the armed forces were only classified as splitoffs if they were married and living in married housing provided by the military.

being is measured by the ratio of total family money income relative to a needs standard that is adjusted for family size and the age-sex composition of the family.

In this analysis, change in the family money income/needs of the sons and daughters is separated into its components in order to compare the relative contribution of the parts to the whole. Due to the possibility that the contribution of the components may vary with the sex of the child, observations on sons and daughters are discussed separately.[2]

It is useful to begin by obtaining some idea of the extent of change in the economic well-being of this population, as indicated by movement between income/needs deciles. Tables 4.1 and 4.2 describe the extent of such movement between 1967 and 1974 for sons and daughters, respectively. These tables are strikingly similar and indicate extensive movement between deciles for both sons and daughters; less than 20 percent of the entire group experienced no change in family income/needs decile, although this percentage was higher for those who began the panel period in either the lowest or highest income deciles. Most of the change in deciles was in an upward direction, with about 50 percent of sons and daughters moving up by at least one income/needs decile over the eight-year period. The extent of upward movement is somewhat surprising considering the extent of new household formation (splitting off) by these young people. (Splitting off entails the loss of parents' income and, by 1975, 53.2 percent of the sons and 58.4 percent of the daughters were splitoffs.)

Changes in Income/Needs

Where did most of this change in family income/needs originate? As a first step in answering this question, consider the basic components of the family income/needs measure. This measure, by definition, is composed of two parts—family income and family needs. Changes in either or both of these components result in change in family income/needs, unless by chance a change in income is exactly offset by a change in needs. The magnitude of these changes for sons and daughters are shown in Tables 4.3 and 4.4 respectively. As in the previous set of figures, son-daughter differences were slight. Both sons and daughters aver-

---

[2]Observations described in this chapter include only those individuals who were sons and daughters in panel families in 1968 and either remained so in 1975 or became a household head or wife. That is, individuals who began the panel period as children and ended it as "others" (niece, nephew, grandchild, etc.) have been excluded from this analysis. These excluded individuals consist of 15 sons and 14 daughters. The reason for this exclusion is the difficulty of clear identification of end-year family income components for the excluded group.

Table 4.1

CHANGE IN INCOME/NEEDS DECILE POSITION, 1967-1974
(Sons Aged 10-29 in 1968)

Change in Decile Position	All	Bottom Decile, 1967*	Top Decile, 1967*
Fell Two or More Deciles	19.1%	-- %	58.7%
Fell One Decile	11.0	--	10.4
No Change	19.9	31.7	30.9
Increased One Decile	17.8	27.4	--
Increased Two or More Deciles	32.2	40.9	--
TOTAL	100.0%	100.0%	100.0%
Number of Observations	1,850	564	60

Table 4.2

CHANGE IN INCOME/NEEDS DECILE POSITION, 1967-1974
(Daughters Aged 10-29 in 1968)

Change in Decile Position	All	Bottom Decile, 1967*	Top Decile, 1967*
Fell Two or More Deciles	20.3%	-- %	54.2%
Fell One Decile	11.8	--	2.0
No Change	17.5	33.2	43.8
Increased One Decile	16.8	20.2	--
Increased Two or More Deciles	33.6	46.6	--
TOTAL	100.0%	100.0%	100.0%
Number of Observations	1,742	577	54

   *The deciles were constructed from the distribution of income/needs for the entire sample of families. For any subgroup, more or less than 10 percent of that subgroup can fall into any one decile. See Tables A4.1a and A4.1b for the complete distribution of 1974 income/needs decile by 1967 income/needs decile.

MTR #8028, 8029

Table 4.3

MEANS AND STANDARD DEVIATIONS
OF COMPONENTS OF CHANGE IN REAL TOTAL FAMILY INCOME/NEEDS, 1967-1974
(Sons Aged 10-29 in 1968)

Income/Needs Change Component	Mean Change	Standard Deviation of Change
Change in Total Family Income	$ 51	$7,918
Change in Needs	-1,248	1,953
Change in Income/Needs	0.57	1.96

Number of Observations: 1,850

Table 4.4

MEANS AND STANDARD DEVIATIONS
OF COMPONENTS OF CHANGE IN REAL TOTAL FAMILY INCOME/NEEDS, 1967-1974
(Daughters Aged 10-29 in 1968)

Income/Needs Change Component	Mean Change	Standard Deviation of Change
Change in Total Family Income	$ -169	$7,903
Change in Needs	-1,430	1,908
Change in Income/Needs	0.62	1.77

Number of Observations: 1,742

NOTE: 1974 income and needs figures have been deflated by the increase in the
Consumer Price Index since 1967.

MTR #8019, 8021, 8030, 8031

aged about the same increase (about 0.6) in family income/needs over the eight-year period, with substantial individual variation. Needs decreased by an average of over $1,000, a much larger average change in absolute terms than the change in income. Most of this decrease in needs undoubtedly resulted from sons and daughters splitting off from their parents' households since parental family members and their needs would not be part of the new household. Mean change in income was small, with sons averaging a slight increase in income ($51) and daughters averaging a small decrease ($-169).

From these tables it appears that, on average, most of the change in income/needs was due to change in needs rather than change in income. However, mean changes mask the extent of individual variation. Change in income was much less uniform among these older children than was change in needs, as indicated by the respective standard deviations of change.

In order to explore further the sources of variability in change in income/needs, and relative contributions of change in income and change in needs in explaining that variability, the *variance* of change in income/needs was divided into its basic components.[3] The resulting decomposition is depicted in Figures 4.1 and 4.2 for sons and daughters, respectively. Note that in both cases the component variances sum to over 100 percent of the total variance. This results from the two components being highly positively correlated. A great deal of this positive correlation is, no doubt, due primarily to the extensive splitting off which occurred over the panel period since splitting off from the parental household entails the loss of both the income and needs of the parental family.

The variance of change in income accounted for, by far, the largest percentage (over 120 percent) of the variance of change in economic well-being, with only a small percentage (about 30 percent) accounted for by the variance of change in needs. However, although change in the needs was a weak source of the variance of change in well-being for older children, it was a slightly more important source of the total variance for them than for the other family members examined.[4] This, again, is no doubt due to the extensive family composition change experienced by the splitoffs.

Changes in Income

As the primary source of the variance of change in economic well-being,

---

[3] To facilitate this decomposition, change in income/needs is measured as the natural logarithm of the ratio of 1974 income/needs to 1968 income/needs. See Chapter 1 for a detailed explanation of this operation.

[4] See Chapter 1, Table 1.1, for comparisons with the other family members examined.

Figure 4.1

COMPONENTS OF THE VARIANCE OF
LOGARITHMIC CHANGE IN FAMILY INCOME/NEEDS, 1967–1974
(Sons Aged 10–29 in 1968)

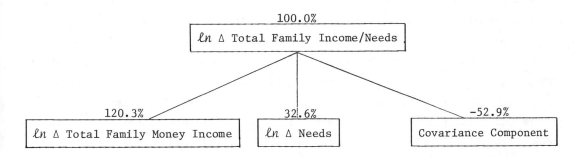

Number of Observations: 1,850

Figure 4.2

COMPONENTS OF THE VARIANCE OF
LOGARITHMIC CHANGE IN FAMILY INCOME/NEEDS, 1967–1974
(Daughters Aged 10–29 in 1968)

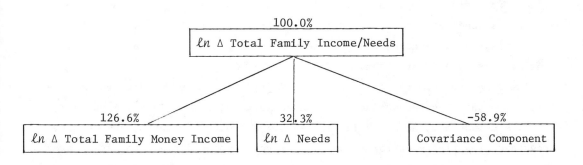

Number of Observations: 1,742

NOTE: The natural logarithm of the change in income/needs is equal to the log
of change in income minus the log of the change in needs. Thus, the *variance* of
the log change in income/needs is equal to the variance of the log of change in
income plus the variance of the log of change in needs minus two times the covariance. Hence, a positive covariance leads to a negative covariance component.
See Chapter 1.

MTR #8012, 8014

changes in family income merit closer scrutiny. Family income is, itself, comprised of several subcomponents, which may help to further identify the sources
of the variance of change in economic well-being. Changes in family income can
result from either changes in family taxable income or changes in family transfer income, or both. Family taxable income can be further decomposed according
to the contributions of the various family members. For older children, further
decomposition is somewhat complicated by a high probability of substantial family composition changes resulting from the splitting-off process. These sons
and daughters may remain in their parents' households or they may split off and,
perhaps, get married. Because of the possibility of such changes in family members, change in the family taxable income of older children was decomposed into
the following categories: change in the child's own taxable income, change in
spouse's taxable income (which is zero when there is no spouse), change in parents' taxable income (which changes from some positive amount to zero when the
child becomes a splitoff), and change in others' taxable income.

This decomposition of change in family income is outlined in Tables 4.5 and
4.6.[5] For both sons and daughters, change in parents' income--which decreased
by an average of over $4,000--was the largest component of mean change in family
income and varied extensively among individuals (its standard deviation was over
$8,000). For sons, the second largest component of mean change in family income
was change in *own* taxable income, which increased by an average of $3,335 and
varied a fair amount (standard deviation, $3,970). For daughters, on the other
hand, the second largest component of mean change in family income was change
in spouse's taxable income, which increased $2,730 on average, and varied sub-
stantially (standard deviation, $4,335).

The relative importance of the variability of these components can be explored by separating the variance of change in total family income into these
same five components, as shown in Figures 4.3 and 4.4. Note that summing the
percentage of variance explained over all five components again totals to over
100 percent. The components' over-explanation of the variance of change in family income is due to strong negative correlations between such components as
changes in own taxable income and changes in parents' taxable income which over-
powered the positive correlations between such other components as change in own
taxable income and change in spouse's taxable income. (See Tables A4.2a and
A4.2b in the appendix for the correlation matrix.)

For both sons and daughters, parents' taxable income was by far the strong-

---

[5]Note that change is now measured in real terms as opposed to logarithmic
terms since the components now sum to the total.

Table 4.5

MEANS AND STANDARD DEVIATIONS
OF COMPONENTS OF CHANGE IN REAL TOTAL FAMILY INCOME, 1967-1974
(Sons Aged 10-29 in 1968)

Income Change Component	Mean Change	Standard Deviation of Change
Change in Own Taxable Income	$ 3,335	$3,970
Change in Spouse's Taxable Income	760	1,757
Change in Parents' Taxable Income	-4,239	8,493
Change in Others' Taxable Income	213	3,277
Change in Family Transfer Income	-15	1,530
TOTAL	$ 51	$7,917

Number of Observations: 1,850

Table 4.6

MEANS AND STANDARD DEVIATIONS
OF COMPONENTS OF CHANGE IN REAL TOTAL FAMILY INCOME, 1967-1974
(Daughters Aged 10-29 in 1968)

Income Change Component	Mean Change	Standard Deviation of Change
Change in Own Taxable Income	$ 1,457	$2,532
Change in Spouse's Taxable Income	2,730	4,335
Change in Parents' Taxable Income	-4,494	8,037
Change in Others' Taxable Income	227	2,569
Change in Family Transfer Income	-85	1,482
TOTAL	$ -168	$7,902

Number of Observations: 1,742

NOTE: 1974 income measures have been deflated by the increase in the Consumer
        Price Index since 1967.

MTR #8012, 8014

126

Figure 4.3

COMPONENTS OF THE VARIANCE OF CHANGE
IN REAL TOTAL FAMILY INCOME, 1967–1974
(Sons Aged 10–29 in 1968)

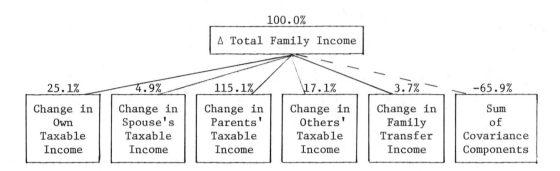

Number of Observations: 1,850

Figure 4.4

COMPONENTS OF THE VARIANCE OF CHANGE
IN REAL TOTAL FAMILY INCOME, 1967–1974
(Daughters Aged 10–29 in 1968)

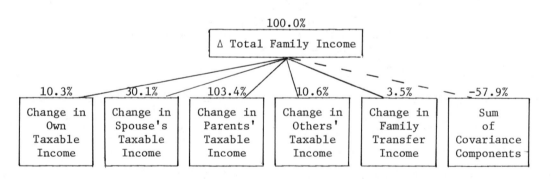

Number of Observations: 1,742

NOTE: The variance of change in total family income equals the sum of (1) var-
        iance of change in own taxable income, (2) variance of change in spouse's
        taxable income, (3) variance of change in parents' taxable income, (4)
        variance of change in others' taxable income, (5) variance of change in
        family transfer income, and (6) the sum of the covariance components (two
        times the covariance between each income source).

MTR #8012, 8014

est source of the variance of change in family income; this component alone accounted for over 100 percent of the total variance. As with mean change in family income, a strong sex differential arises in the relative importance of change in own income versus change in spouse's income. Change in spouse's income was the second most important source of variation in change in family income for daughters (explaining 30.1 percent of the variance), with change in their own taxable income playing a more minor role (explaining 10.3 percent of the variance). For sons, this was reversed--change in spouse's taxable income explained only 4.9 percent of the variance, whereas change in their own taxable income explained 25.1 percent. The third strongest component for both sons and daughters was change in others' taxable income, although its third-place ranking was tenuous for daughters (explaining 10.6 percent of the variance, compared to the 10.3 percent explained by change in their own taxable income). Change in family transfer income played a very minor role in explaining the variation of change in family income, accounting for less than 4 percent of the variance for both sons and daughters.

Changes in Parental Taxable Income

Tables 4.7 and 4.8 provide a breakdown of change in parents' taxable income according to three types of family composition changes experienced by the sons and daughters--becoming a splitoff, remaining within the parental household but with the gain or loss of a parent, and remaining within the parental household with no gain or loss of a parent. As these tables indicate, about half of the variance of change in parents' taxable income was due to the loss of parents as household members through the process of splitting off (47.7 percent for sons and 56.4 for daughters). However, a large part of the variance of change, especially for sons, was also due to changes in the income of the older child's parents (46.1 percent for sons and 37.2 percent for daughters); very little of the variance of change in parents' taxable income was due to the loss or addition of a parent (about 6 percent for both sons and daughters). Since splitting off involved the total loss of parental income, it may be surprising that the explained percentages of the variance of changes in parental income were larger relative to group size for those who remained in their parents' households (especially sons), than for those who became splitoffs. This suggests that substantial changes in parental income occurred in the parental family even with no loss or gain of parents. This did, in fact, seem to be the case. The data indicate that parents' taxable income changed by over $5,000 for as much as one-fifth of older children who remained in their parental families and had no loss or gain of parents.

Table 4.7

CHANGE IN PARENTS' TAXABLE INCOME
BY CHANGE IN FAMILY COMPOSITION, 1968-1974
(Sons Aged 10-29 in 1968)

Change in Family Composition	Number of Observations	Weighted Proportion of Observations	Mean Change in Parents' Taxable Income	Fraction of Variance of Change in Parents' Taxable Income, Explained by Subgroup
Became Splitoff	828	53.2%	$-9,029	47.7%
Remained in Parental Household with Loss or Gain of a Parent	172	7.7	- 842	6.2
Remained in Parental Household with no Loss or Gain of a Parent	850	39.1	1,609	46.1
TOTAL	1,850	100.0%	$-4,239	100.0%

Table 4.8

CHANGE IN PARENTS' TAXABLE INCOME
BY CHANGE IN FAMILY COMPOSITION, 1968-1974
(Daughters Aged 10-29 in 1968)

Change in Family Composition	Number of Observations	Weighted Proportion of Observations	Mean Change in Parents' Taxable Income	Fraction of Variance of Change in Parents' Taxable Income, Explained by Subgroup
Became Splitoff	892	58.4%	$-8,580	56.4%
Remained in Parental Household with Loss or Gain of a Parent	140	6.2	-1,446	6.4
Remained in Parental Household with no Loss or Gain of a Parent	710	35.4	1,699	37.2
TOTAL	1,742	100.0%	$-4,495	100.0%

NOTE: The 1974 income figures have been deflated by the increase in Consumer Price Index since 1967.

MTR #8020

Other Components of Change in Family Income

In addition to change in parents' taxable income, change in the older child's own income and change in spouse's income were also important sources of the variance of change in family income for the sons and daughters. Although change in own taxable income was much more important for sons than daughters (explaining 25.1 percent and 10.3 percent of the variance of change in family income, respectively), son-daughter comparisons may be revealing. Since our data lack wage information for individuals who were neither household heads nor wives, our focus in examining change in own taxable income is on labor force behavior.[6] Tables 4.9 and 4.10 provide breakdowns of change in own taxable income according to labor force participation subgroups for sons and daughters, respectively. Change in labor force status consists of: remaining out of, entering, leaving, or remaining in the labor force between the first and last years of the panel period, plus a category of unknown change in labor force status.

About 50 percent of both sons and daughters entered the labor force during the panel period. Sons entering the labor force averaged considerably larger increases in earnings than daughters who entered ($4,413 as opposed to $2,623). Sons who began and ended the panel period in the labor force, however, averaged even larger increases in their own taxable income, larger relative both to labor force entrants and to daughters who were in the labor force in both years. These sex differentials would be due to larger increases in the hours worked and/or in the wage rates for sons than for daughters. During this transition stage to adulthood, males were likely to increase their labor force commitment more than females. Among those who were in the labor force in both 1967 and 1974, the sons work hours increased an average of 1,018 hours, whereas for daughters the average increase was 443 hours. Among those who entered the labor force during the panel period, sons averaged an increase of 1,594 hours worked, while for daughters the average increase was 1,195 hours. Part of the sex differential with respect to change in own labor income could be due to sex-differentiated wage changes as well; wages for women may be more stable (with fewer increases) during this transition-to-adulthood stage than wages for men. Wage data, however, were not available to test this conjecture.

In terms of explaining variance of change in own taxable income, being in the labor force at the end of the panel period was important for sons (43.7 per-

---

[6]For individuals who were neither household heads nor wives, labor income was not separable from asset income. For these individuals, their own income was decomposable only into taxable (labor plus asset) income and transfer income. Thus, although hours worked is known, wages cannot be computed since labor income cannot be uniquely identified.

Table 4.9

CHANGE IN OWN TAXABLE INCOME,
BY CHANGE IN LABOR FORCE STATUS, 1967–1974
(Sons Aged 10–29 in 1968)

Change in Labor Force Status	Number of Observations	Weighted Proportion of Observations	Mean Change in Own Taxable Income	Fraction of Variance of Change in Own Taxable Income, Explained by Subgroup
Out of Labor Force in Both 1967 and 1974	563	21.9%	$ 88	14.8%
Entered Labor Force by 1974	931	53.3	4,413	43.7
Left Labor Force by 1974	22	1.0	−1,127	1.4
In Labor Force in Both 1967 and 1974	212	15.4	5,096	27.5
Labor Force Status Unknown in 1967	122	8.3	2,244	12.6
TOTAL	1,850	100.0%	$ 3,335	100.0%

Table 4.10

CHANGE IN OWN TAXABLE INCOME,
BY CHANGE IN LABOR FORCE STATUS, 1967–1974
(Daughters Aged 10–29 in 1968)

Change in Labor Force Status	Number of Observations	Weighted Proportion of Observations	Mean Change in Own Taxable Income	Fraction of Variance of Change in Own Taxable Income, Explained by Subgroup
Out of Labor Force in Both 1967 and 1974	735	32.9%	$ 85	10.2%
Entered Labor Force by 1974	763	48.9	2,623	46.2
Left Labor Force by 1974	43	4.0	−1,517	13.1
In Labor Force in Both 1967 and 1974	122	9.1	2,363	11.3
Labor Force Status Unknown in 1967	79	5.0	−130	19.2
TOTAL	1,742	100.0%	$ 1,457	100.0%

NOTE: The 1974 income figures have been deflated by the increase in the Consumer Price Index since 1967. An individual is defined as in the labor force if he worked at least 250 hours during the year.

MTR #8036

cent of the variance was explained by entering the labor force and 27.5 percent
was explained by remaining in the labor force). For daughters, on the other
hand, labor force turnover accounted for most of the variance of change in own
taxable income (46.2 percent was explained by entering the labor force and 13.1
percent was explained by leaving the labor force). Of particular interest are
those sons who were in the labor force at both the beginning and end of the panel period and those duaghters who left the labor force; both groups explained
fractions of the variance of change in own taxable income that were disproportionately large relative to group size. There was extensive individual variability of change in own taxable income within both of these groups.

Change in spouse's income was a much stronger source of variance of change
in family income for daughters than for sons. A breakdown of this change according to whether there was a spouse in the labor force in 1974, a spouse out of
the labor force in 1974, or no spouse (Tables 4.11 and 4.12), revealed that a
larger percentage of sons than daughters had spouses who were not labor force
participants (14 percent versus 1.5 percent). Additionally, the income of wives
in the labor force was, on average, only half that of husbands in the labor
force ($3,316 versus $6,897). The larger difference in means between no spouse
and working spouse for daughters relative to sons was undoubtedly what accounted
for the no-spouse subgroups being more important to the total variance for daughters than for sons.

Another component of change in family income that was an important source
of variance, especially for sons, was taxable income of "others" (siblings,
aunts, uncles, grandparents, etc.). Change in others' income can result from
the gain or loss of individuals classified as others and/or from change in their
incomes. Since over half of the older children became splitoffs and consequently lost those "other" individuals, it seems likely that most of the change in
others' taxable income would result from that family composition change. However, splitting off was *not* the dominant source of change in others' taxable income (Tables 4.13 and 4.14). Although a smaller fraction of older children remained in their parents' households, remaining there explained a larger fraction
of the change in others' income than did becoming a splitoff (67 percent versus
33 percent for sons, and 52.5 percent versus 47.5 percent for daughters). Older
children remaining in their parents' households, especially sons, experienced
greater individual variations in change in others' taxable income than did splitoffs. This could have been, but was not necessarily, the result of the gain or
loss of "others."

Table 4.11

CHANGE IN SPOUSE'S TAXABLE INCOME,
BY SPOUSE'S LABOR FORCE STATUS, 1967–1974
(Sons Aged 10–29 in 1968)

Change in Labor Force Status of Spouse	Number of Observations	Weighted Proportion of Observations	Mean Change in Spouse's Taxable Income	Fraction of Variance of Change in Spouse's Taxable Income, Explained by Subgroup
Spouse In Labor Force in 1974	321	22.0%	$3,316	85.0%
Spouse Out of Labor Force in 1974	208	14.0	207	3.0
No Spouse*	1,321	64.0	0	12.0
TOTAL	1,850	100.0%	$ 760	100.0%

Table 4.12

CHANGE IN SPOUSE'S TAXABLE INCOME,
BY SPOUSE'S LABOR FORCE STATUS, 1967–1974
(Daughters Aged 10–29 in 1968)

Change in Labor Force Status of Spouse	Number of Observations	Weighted Proportion of Observations	Mean Change in Spouse's Taxable Income	Fraction of Variance of Change in Spouse's Taxable Income, Explained by Subgroup
Spouse In Labor Force in 1974	523	39.5%	$6,897	76.1%
Spouse Out of Labor Force in 1974	23	1.5	207	0.5
No Spouse*	1,196	59.0	0	23.4
TOTAL	1,742	100.0%	$2,730	100.0%

*Includes unmarried splitoffs and older children in the parental household in 1975.

NOTE: The 1974 income figures have been deflated by the increase in the Consumer Price Index since 1967.

MTR #8020

Table 4.13

CHANGE IN OTHERS' TAXABLE INCOME,
BY HOUSEHOLD MEMBERSHIP STATUS, 1967-1974[*]
(Sons Aged 10-29 in 1968)

Household Membership Status	Number of Observations	Weighted Proportion of Observations	Mean Change in Others' Taxable Income	Fraction of Variance of Change in Others' Taxable Income, Explained by Subgroup
Household Head in 1975	828	53.2%	$- 353	33.0%
Child in 1975	1,022	46.8	857	67.0
TOTAL	1,850	100.0%	$ 213	100.0%

Table 4.14

CHANGE IN OTHERS' TAXABLE INCOME,
BY HOUSEHOLD MEMBERSHIP STATUS, 1967-1974[*]
(Daughters Aged 10-29 in 1968)

Household Membership Status	Number of Observations	Weighted Proportion of Observations	Mean Change in Others' Taxable Income	Fraction of Variance of Change in Others' Taxable Income, Explained by Subgroup
Household Head or Wife in 1975	892	58.4%	$- 355	47.5%
Child in 1975	850	41.6	1,041	52.5
TOTAL	1,742	100.0%	$ 227	100.0%

[*]"Others" consist of members of the child's household other than his/her parents or spouse. These could include the child's siblings, aunts, uncles, grandparents, etc.

NOTE: 1974 income figures have been deflated by the increase in the Consumer Price Index since 1967.

MTR #8020

Changes in Family Composition

Although change in family income was the overwhelmingly dominant component of the variance of change in economic well-being, change in needs also exerted a substantial influence. Change in needs could result from aging of family members; the largest changes in needs, however, would result from the actual loss or gain of family members. Older children were especially likely to experience changes in family members since a large proportion of them left home to form new households (to become splitoffs). Subdividing older children according to change in family composition allows investigation of the types of changes in family composition that account for the greatest change in family needs. Tables 4.15 and 4.16 show a subdivision according to seven types of family composition change for sons and daughters, respectively. Most of the older children who remained in the parental family experienced declines in family size as their siblings moved out; this was the only group of older children remaining in the parental family who experienced overall mean declines in family needs. The other older children who were still at home in 1975 experienced small mean increases in family needs. Family needs declined substantially for all groups of splitoffs due to the loss of parental family members. For splitoffs who were married as of 1975, some of this needs decline was counteracted by the gain of a spouse and, in many cases, the gain of a child; this group registered lower mean declines in family needs than splitoffs who were not married as of 1975.

As for the variance of change in needs of older children, splitoffs who did not marry during the panel period accounted for the largest proportion (over 26 percent). This group experienced the loss of parental family members with no counteracting gain of other family members. Splitoffs who married and had children accounted for the second highest percentage of the variance of change in needs even though, of all the splitoffs, they had the largest gains in family members. This result appears to be simply due to peculiarities in the economies of scale that have been built into the needs standard.[7]

Changes in family composition can result in changes in family income as well as changes in needs since the family members lost or gained may be income-earners. For this reason, Tables 4.15 and 4.16 provide information concerning change in both income and needs. For older children who remained with their

---

[7]Married splitoffs with children born during the panel period averaged almost the same decrease in needs as married splitoffs with no children born during the panel period, even though they had no significant differences in mean parental family size.

Table 4.15

CHANGE IN INCOME, NEEDS, AND INCOME/NEEDS BY TYPE OF FAMILY COMPOSITION CHANGE, 1967-1974
(Sons Aged 10-29 in 1968)

Family Composition Change	Number of Observations	Weighted Percent	Mean Change in Income/ Needs	Mean Change in Income	Mean Change in Needs	Percent Contribution to Total Variance of Income/Needs Through:	
						Change in Needs	Change in Income
Remained in Parental Household							
No Change in Family Composition	165	9.5%	.50	$ 4,212	$ 670	10.4%	5.1%
Family Size Decreased, with Siblings Moving Out	604	27.7	1.33	3,807	- 944	10.4	16.5
Other Change in Family Composition	253	9.6	.39	2,683	527	11.3	9.7
Became Splitoff							
Married During Panel Period; Widowed, Divorced, or Separated as of 1975	44	3.2	.15	-3,613	-1,921	4.0	3.6
Married as of 1975, with Child Born During Panel Period	333	21.5	.28	-2,099	-1,850	24.3	17.5
Married as of 1975, with No Child Born During Panel Period	196	14.5	.55	-2,044	-1,863	12.9	10.4
Unmarried as of 1975, Did Not Marry During Panel Period	255	14.0	- .20	-5,704	-2,650	26.7	37.2
TOTAL	1,850	100.0%	.57	$ 51	$-1,248	100.0%	100.0%

NOTE: 1974 income and needs figures have been deflated by the increase in the Consumer Price Index since 1967.
MTR #8019, 8031

Table 4.16

CHANGE IN INCOME, NEEDS, AND INCOME/NEEDS BY TYPE OF FAMILY COMPOSITION CHANGE, 1967-1974

(Daughters Aged 10-29 in 1968)

Family Composition Change	Number of Observations	Weighted Percent	Mean Change in Income/ Needs	Mean Change in Income	Mean Change in Needs	Percent Contribution to Total Variance of Change in Income/Needs Through:	
						Change in Needs	Change in Income
Remained in Parental Household							
No Change in Family Composition	150	9.6%	.70	$ 4,423	$ 485	11.5%	5.4%
Family Size Decreased, with Siblings Moving Out	424	21.1	1.26	3,436	- 978	8.3	11.8
Other Change in Family Composition	276	10.9	.45	1,974	400	15.5	6.9
Became Splitoff							
Married During Panel Period; Widowed, Divorced, or Separated as of 1975	71	3.6	.01	-4,050	-2,779	6.5	4.7
Married as of 1975, with Child Born During Panel Period	336	24.0	.65	-1,206	-2,032	19.4	22.7
Married as of 1975, with No Child Born During Panel Period	210	17.0	.80	-1,563	-1,951	12.4	17.7
Unmarried as of 1975, Did Not Marry During Panel Period	275	13.7	- .39	-6,081	-2,874	26.4	30.8
TOTAL	1,742	100.0%	.62	$- 169	$-1,430	100.0%	100.0%

NOTE: The 1974 income and needs figures have been deflated by the increase in the Consumer Price Index since 1967. MTR #8021, 8030

parental families the average family income increased, whereas for those who became splitoffs the average family income declined. The largest average declines
in family income, by far, were those of splitoffs who did not marry during the
panel period ($-5,704 for sons and $-6,081 for daughters). In fact, although
these splitoffs had the largest decrease in needs, their decline in family income was so large that their mean income/needs declined. The mean income/needs
for all other family composition change groups in this population increased over
the panel period.

In terms of the variance of change in income, splitting off and not marry-
ing during the panel period was the dominant type of family composition change.
Due to their large decreases in family income, this group accounted for much
more of the variance of change in income than group size alone would warrant.

Results for Blacks and the Poor

Change in family income was the most important source of change in the variance of economic well-being for the older children as a whole, but what of subgroups of this population? Tables 4.17 and 4.18 offer comparisons of the relative explanatory strengths of change in income and change in needs for the entire
sample of older children and for several of its subgroups, including blacks and
three "nested" subgroups who were poor. The latter three subgroups are (1) the
target population (individuals whose families were in the bottom quintile of
income/needs during at least one year of the panel period), (2) the initially
poor (those who began the panel period in families whose income/needs level was
below the poverty line); and (3) the "climbers-out" (initially poor individuals
whose family income/needs level was above the poverty line by the eighth year of
the panel period). To facilitate comparison across subgroups, percentage contributions to the total variance of change in income/needs of the two basic components have been weighted to sum to 100 percent.

Sons and daughters were virtually identical with respect to the relative
importance of income change versus needs change for all of these groups. In
black families sons and daughters very much paralleled the whole sample in the
relative dominance of change in income over change in needs, with income accounting for almost four times as much of the variance of change in economic
well-being. For the nested poverty subgroups, the relative strength of change
in income in explaining change in economic well-being declined as the subgroups
narrowed. For the final subgroup, the climbers-out, income accounted for only
twice as much of the variance in change in economic well-being as did needs.
The greater relative importance of needs suggests that family composition
changes were important means of climbing out of poverty. Since splitting off

138

Table 4.17

COMPONENTS OF THE VARIANCE OF THE LOGARITHMIC
CHANGE IN REAL TOTAL FAMILY INCOME/NEEDS, 1967-1974
(For Various Subgroups of Sons Aged 10-29 in 1968)

| | | Fraction of Variance of Log Change in Income/Needs, Explained by Component | | |
Group	Number of Observations	Log Change in Real Income	Log Change in Needs	Covariance Component
All	1,850	78.7%	21.3%	- 52.9%
Blacks	829	79.1	20.9	- 54.4
Target Population	1,208	83.5	16.5	- 38.3
Initially Poor	627	74.8	25.2	- 74.2
Climbers Out	408	62.7	37.3	-111.0

Table 4.18

COMPONENTS OF THE VARIANCE OF THE LOGARITHMIC
CHANGE IN REAL TOTAL FAMILY INCOME/NEEDS, 1967-1974
(For Various Subgroups of Daughters Aged 10-29 in 1968)

| | | Fraction of Variance of Log Change in Income/Needs, Explained by Component | | |
Group	Number of Observations	Log Change in Real Income	Log Change in Needs	Covariance Component
All	1,742	79.7%	20.3%	- 58.8%
Blacks	849	78.6	21.4	- 43.8
Target Population	1,201	84.0	16.0	- 40.0
Initially Poor	618	75.7	24.3	- 55.8
Climbers Out	412	66.6	33.4	-100.7

NOTE: The fraction of variance of log change in income/needs explained by log change in real income and log change in needs have been repercentagized to sum to 100 percent in order to facilitate comparison across subgroups. The actual fraction of variance accounted for by these two components can be computed by multiplying the repercentagized figures by one minus the covariance component.

The 1974 income and needs figures have been deflated by the increase in the Consumer Price Index since 1967.

MTR #8014, 8012, 8021, 8023, 8024

was not very much more prevalent among the climbers-out than among all the initially poor,[8] changes in family composition both within the parental family and among splitoffs were probably important for climbing out of poverty.

The figures in the columns labeled "covariance component" in Tables 4.17 and 4.18 have interesting implications. The covariance components for climbers-out (-111.0 percent for sons and -100.7 for daughters) were very large relative to those for other subgroups listed; the figures indicate that there was a highly positive correlation between changes in income and changes in needs for those who climbed out of poverty and that this correlation was much stronger for the climbers-out than for all the initially poor. The covariance component figures also show a somewhat lower positive correlation between changes in income and changes in needs for daughters than for sons in the initially poor and climbers-out subgroups. This could well be tied to the fact that a larger percentage of daughters than sons became splitoffs. Although average family income declined among the entire group of splitoffs, it increased for splitoffs from initially poor families.[9]

The four subgroups differed from the whole sample in the relative importance of components of change in income, as indicated in Tables 4.19 and 4.20. For blacks, as compared to the entire sample, changes in own taxable income, in others' taxable income, and in family transfer income were relatively more important contributors to the variance of change in family income; changes in parents' taxable income (although still the dominant source of variance) were less important for blacks than for the entire sample; and changes in spouse's taxable income accounted for less of the variance of change in family income for black daughters than for all daughters. For black daughters, changes in their own taxable income were equal in importance to changes in spouse's taxable income, while for all daughters the latter kinds of changes were much more important than the former. This may be due to the fact that male domination of the labor market is not as strong among blacks as among nonblacks.

For the initially poor and climbers-out of poverty, change in parents' taxable income was *not* the dominant source of the variance of change in family income. The more minor role of parents' taxable income is undoubtedly due to its low initial level; splitoffs among these groups forfeited relatively little

---

[8] Forty-nine percent of the sons who were initially poor and 55 percent of the sons who climbed out of poverty were splitoffs; corresponding figures for daughters were 62 percent and 70 percent.

[9] Mean family income for initially poor splitoffs was $3,420 in 1967 and $5,771 in 1974; for all splitoffs it was $10,682 in 1967 and $7,801 in 1974.

Table 4.19

COMPONENTS OF THE VARIANCE OF CHANGE IN REAL TOTAL FAMILY INCOME, 1967-1974

(For Various Subgroups of Sons Aged 10-29 in 1968)

Group	Number of Observations	Fraction of Variance of Change in Real Total Family Income, Explained by Component					Sum of Covariance Components
		Change in Own Taxable Income	Change in Spouse's Taxable Income	Change in Parents' Taxable Income	Change in Others' Taxable Income	Change in Family Transfer Income	
All	1,850	15.1%	3.0%	69.4%	10.3%	2.2%	- 65.9
Black	829	28.3	3.5	50.5	12.5	5.2	-106.6
Target Population	1,208	15.9	2.8	67.4	9.9	4.0	- 43.7
Initially Poor	627	37.3	4.0	25.2	24.0	9.5	-118.3
Climbers-Out	408	35.3	4.7	29.3	21.4	9.3	-134.5

NOTE: The fraction of variance of change in real total family income explained by income types have been reper-centagized to sum to 100 percent in order to facilitate comparison across subgroups. The actual fraction of variance accounted for by each income type can be computed by multiplying the repercentagized figures by one minus the sum of the covariance components.

The 1974 income figures have been deflated by the increase in the Consumer Price Index since 1967.

MTR #8014, 8021, 8023, 8024

Table 4.20

COMPONENTS OF THE VARIANCE OF CHANGE IN REAL TOTAL FAMILY INCOME, 1967-1974
(For Various Subgroups of Daughters Aged 10-29 in 1968)

Group	Number of Observations	Fraction of Variance of Change in Real Total Family Income, Explained by Component					Sum of Covariance Components
		Change in Own Taxable Income	Change in Spouse's Taxable Income	Change in Parents' Taxable Income	Change in Others' Taxable Income	Change in Family Transfer Income	
All	1,742	6.5%	19.1%	65.5%	6.7%	2.2%	- 57.9
Black	849	16.3	16.3	43.7	17.6	6.1	- 70.9
Target Population	1,201	8.3	26.6	53.2	7.9	4.0	- 51.6
Initially Poor	618	18.4	32.8	21.5	18.0	9.3	-127.2
Climbers-Out	412	16.1	33.6	24.5	17.4	8.4	-178.2

NOTE: The fraction of variance of change in real total family income explained by income types have been reper-centagized to sum to 100 percent in order to facilitate comparison across subgroups. The actual fraction of variance accounted for by each income type can be computed by multiplying the repercentagized figures by one minus the sum of the covariance components.

The 1974 income figures have been deflated by the increase in the Consumer Price Index since 1967.

MTR #8012, 8021, 8023, 8024

when they chose to leave their parents' households. All other income components were more important for these two subgroups than for the entire sample. Among sons, change in own taxable income was the dominant source of variance in family income change; among daughters, change in spouse's income dominated. For both sons and daughters in these two subgroups, change in others' taxable income was a much stronger component of change in family income than for the whole sample. The importance of change in others' taxable income for the initially poor could be due to intentional attempts at economic improvement through the addition of income earning "others" to the family. In any event, changes in their own income, marriage to an income-earning spouse, and changes in the incomes of other family members were more important sources of change in economic well-being for older children who were initially poor than for the entire sample of older children.

Summary

The population considered in this chapter consisted of those persons who were sons and daughters in the original panel families and who were aged 10-29 in the initial year of the study (1968). These individuals experienced substantial changes over the eight-year period covered by this analysis. By the final year (1975) about 50 percent of these sons and daughters had entered the labor force, over 50 percent had become splitoffs, about 40 percent had married, and over 20 percent had married and become parents themselves. For young adults, changes of this kind were likely to entail drastic changes in economic well-being.

Change in the economic well-being of these sons and daughters over the eight-year period of the panel study was the focal point of this chapter. Economic well-being was measured by the ratio of total family money income relative to a needs standard that was adjusted for family size and the age-sex composition of the family. Since changes in the level of such economic well-being can result from changes in family money income and/or changes in family needs, this analysis of changes in economic well-being decomposed the change into these components. Primary emphasis was placed on the variance of change.

For these sons and daughters in the original panel families, changes in family income accounted for more of the variability in the change in overall economic well-being than did changes in needs. Among the components of change in family income, changes in parents' taxable income were most important. A large part of the change in parents' taxable income came about because many of these

older children split off from their parental households; however, there was a
very large amount of variation in change in parental income within the parental
family as well.

For sons, change in their own taxable income was a very important source of
the overall change in economic status. For daughters, change in spouse's taxable income was very important. Being in the labor force at the end of the panel
period accounted for most of the variance of change in the sons' own taxable income, whereas labor force turnover accounted for most of this variance for daughters. Gaining a working spouse, as would be expected, accounted for most of the
variance of change in spouse's taxable income for both sons and daughters.

In terms of the association between change in economic well-being and family composition change, becoming an unmarried splitoff was the major source of
variance in both changes in family income and changes in needs. Both married
and unmarried splitoffs averaged declines in both family income and needs. However, for splitoffs who did not marry during the panel period, the declines in
income relative to the declines in needs were so large as to result in an average decline in economic well-being. All other types of family composition
change were associated with mean increases in economic well-being.

Although for blacks, the initially poor, and those who climbed out of poverty, change in income also dominated change in needs in explaining the variance
of change in the economic well-being, these subgroups differed from the entire
population with respect to the importance of the components of change in family
income. Change in parents' taxable income was less important, relative to the
other income components, for these subgroups than for the population as a whole.
In fact, for the initially poor and climbers-out of poverty, change in parents'
taxable income was *not* the dominant source of the variance of change in family
income. It was superceded for sons by change in their own taxable income and
for daughters by change in spouse's taxable income. For daughters, one other
subgroup difference stood out. Change in spouse's taxable income was of relatively less importance for black daughters than for the entire sample of daughters. In fact, for black daughters, change in their own taxable income was as
important as change in spouse's taxable income.

APPENDIX 4.1

Table A4.1a

1974 FAMILY INCOME/NEEDS DECILE BY 1967 FAMILY INCOME/NEEDS DECILE
(Sons Aged 10-29 in 1968)

1967 Income/Needs Decile	1974 Income/Needs Decile										
	Lowest Tenth	Second	Third	Fourth	Fifth	Sixth	Seventh	Eighth	Ninth	Highest Tenth	Total
Lowest Tenth	3.4	2.9	1.4	0.9	0.8	0.3	0.6	0.3	0.1	0.0	10.7
Second	1.5	1.2	1.7	1.3	1.1	0.9	0.7	0.2	0.2	0.1	9.0
Third	1.3	0.8	2.7	2.1	1.3	0.9	0.9	0.7	0.6	0.8	12.0
Fourth	0.6	0.6	0.8	2.5	1.9	1.5	2.1	0.9	1.5	0.2	12.5
Fifth	0.2	0.7	1.0	1.4	1.9	1.4	1.2	1.5	0.7	0.6	10.7
Sixth	0.3	0.5	0.5	1.4	1.6	2.2	1.6	1.4	0.9	0.7	11.2
Seventh	0.1	0.5	0.2	0.1	0.9	1.7	1.1	2.2	1.5	1.6	10.0
Eighth	0.6	0.3	0.8	0.4	0.4	0.6	1.2	1.4	2.2	1.7	9.7
Ninth	0.1	0.2	0.6	0.5	0.2	0.8	1.0	1.3	1.4	1.8	7.8
Highest Tenth	0.3	0.4	0.1	0.4	0.3	0.7	1.0	0.4	0.7	2.0	6.3
TOTAL	8.5	8.2	9.8	10.9	10.6	11.2	11.3	10.4	9.8	9.4	100.0

MTR #8028

Table A4.1b

1974 FAMILY INCOME/NEEDS DECILE BY 1967 FAMILY INCOME/NEEDS DECILE
(Daughters Aged 10-29 in 1968)

1967 Income/Needs Decile	1974 Income/Needs Decile										
	Lowest Tenth	Second	Third	Fourth	Fifth	Sixth	Seventh	Eighth	Ninth	Highest Tenth	Total
Lowest Decile	4.3	2.6	1.0	1.6	1.4	0.6	1.1	0.2	0.3	0.0	13.0
Second	2.0	1.2	1.8	1.3	0.7	0.7	0.8	0.8	0.2	0.2	9.7
Third	1.6	1.5	2.1	2.3	1.6	1.3	0.7	0.8	0.5	0.3	12.7
Fourth	0.3	0.8	1.2	1.5	1.6	1.8	1.2	1.3	0.4	0.3	10.4
Fifth	0.1	1.1	0.9	1.1	1.5	1.4	0.9	1.1	1.3	0.5	10.0
Sixth	0.4	0.7	0.7	1.2	1.6	1.1	2.2	1.9	2.4	0.5	12.6
Seventh	0.3	0.5	0.5	0.9	0.8	1.5	1.0	1.9	2.3	0.3	9.9
Eighth	0.0	0.2	0.2	0.6	0.4	1.4	1.3	1.1	1.5	1.3	7.9
Ninth	0.1	0.6	0.0	0.6	0.1	1.1	0.7	1.6	0.9	1.5	7.2
Highest Tenth	0.4	0.1	0.0	0.5	0.4	0.3	0.8	1.0	0.1	2.8	6.4
TOTAL	9.6	9.3	8.3	11.5	10.2	11.2	10.8	11.5	9.8	7.8	100.0

MTR #8029

APPENDIX 4.2

Table A4.2a

CORRELATIONS AMONG COMPONENTS OF CHANGE IN FAMILY INCOME/NEEDS, 1967-1974
(Sons Aged 10-29 in 1968)

Component	1	2	3	4	5	6
1 Change in Income/Needs*	1.00					
2 Change in Family Income*	.86	1.00				
3 Change in Needs*	−.11	.42	1.00			
1 Change in Family Income	1.00					
2 Change in Own Taxable Income	−.02	1.00				
3 Change in Spouse's Taxable Income	−.04	.30	1.00			
4 Change in Parents' Taxable Income	.85	−.34	−.31	1.00		
5 Change in Others' Taxable Income	.26	−.46	−.14	.10	1.00	
6 Change in Family Transfer Income	−.01	−.14	−.11	−.11	.02	1.00

Table A4.2b

CORRELATIONS AMONG COMPONENTS OF CHANGE IN FAMILY INCOME/NEEDS, 1967-1974
(Daughters Aged 10-29 in 1968)

Component	1	2	3	4	5	6
1 Change in Income/Needs*	1.00					
2 Change in Family Income*	.86	1.00				
3 Change in Needs*	−.05	.46	1.00			
1 Change in Family Income	1.00					
2 Change in Own Taxable Income	.10	1.00				
3 Change in Spouse's Taxable Income	.15	.19	1.00			
4 Change in Parents' Taxable Income	.78	−.24	−.36	1.00		
5 Change in Others' Taxable Income	.33	−.23	−.20	.19	1.00	
6 Change in Family Transfer Income	−.07	−.08	−.18	−.13	−.01	1.00

*Variables expressed in logarithms.

NOTE: 1974 income figures have been deflated by the increase in the Consumer
Price Index since 1967.

MTR #8012, 8014

PART II

OTHER ANALYSES

Chapter 5

ECONOMIC GROWTH AND FAMILY WELL-BEING

John W. Holmes

Introduction

Over the life cycle of some households, family income deviates from its normal or expected pattern. That is, such exogenous disruptions as involuntary unemployment or the prolonged disability of a wage earner may create fluctuations in the income of a family over time. One external influence of particular interest is the effect of aggregate economic activity on the well-being of the household. Previous research by Anderson (1964), Aaron (1967), and Madden (1968) has documented that economic growth does have beneficial effects on the economic welfare of some subgroups. However, there has been widespread disagreement on the extent to which various subgroups participate in the overall advance of the economy.

One theory which is consistent with the findings of differential benefits of economic growth is the "backwash thesis." This hypothesis, initiated by Gallaway (1965), contends that the economic status of a substantial proportion of the poor is unaffected by economic growth and that, as a result, sustained economic growth has a decreasing impact on reducing the incidence of poverty. That is, the poverty elimination rate will fall as the poverty population becomes increasingly comprised of individuals who are incapable of improving their economic welfare.

Empirical studies of the backwash thesis have centered on analyzing the relationship between the proportion of families with incomes below a poverty threshold and some indicator of overall economic activity. Unlike these previous empirical studies which used grouped Census data to examine the influence of economic activity on the incidence of subgroup poverty, this chapter explores the impact of macroeconomic fluctuations upon the well-being of the household at the micro level. After partitioning the data according to the race and sex of the family heads, the time-series and cross-section observations from the panel study were pooled to assess the sensitivity of family income to changes in economic activity.

Analysis

I. A POOLED TIME-SERIES CROSS-SECTION MODEL

Research by Anderson on the influence economic growth had on differently situated households indicated a differential sensitivity of subgroup incomes to movements in the overall level of income. While households headed by nonwhite, nonfarm, nonaged males were found to benefit substantially from economic growth, the incomes of families headed by women or by elderly persons were not responsive to changes in the rate of income growth. The importance of disaggregating data while exploring the relationship of the well-being of families to some indicator of economic activity was underscored further in later research by Gallaway and by Aaron. Gallaway initially concluded that the number of families who remained unaffected by economic progress was overstated by the Council of Economic Advisors. However, subsequent research by Aaron demonstrated that Gallaway's approach to testing the backwash thesis suffered from use of aggregate data and the particular functional form of his regressions. Indeed, Aaron refitted Gallaway's basic equation, using a more appropriate functional form, and found the revised estimate of the incidence of poverty in 1980 quite similar to the original projections by the Council.[1] More important, this later research verified that poverty is heterogeneous and that data must be disaggregated to examine the actual relationship of poverty to economic activity.

This chapter extends Anderson's analysis by using the household income, as opposed to median family income, as the dependent variable. The panel data are disaggregated by sex and race of the family head. Finally, since transfer payments tend to be the primary income component for households headed by elderly persons, the analysis is restricted to those panel households where the family head was younger than age 65 in 1973.

While Anderson relied solely on deflated personal income per capita as an

---

[1] In 1964, the Council had forecast that by 1980 the extent of poverty would only be reduced to 10 percent, even if the favorable economic conditions which prevailed in 1947-56 could be maintained. After regressing the logarithm of the percentage in the poverty class on median family income and the national unemployment rate, Gallaway forecasted the incidence of poverty to decline to nearly 6 percent by 1980. He attributed the marked difference between these estimates to an understatement by the Council of the impact of economic growth on the extent of poverty. Consequently, Gallaway maintained that greater consideration should be given to the role which economic growth can play in eliminating poverty. Aaron refitted Gallaway's basic equation using a double logarithmic formulation and found the revised estimate of the projection of families in poverty quite similar to the Council's original projection (9.7 percent versus 10 percent).

overall measure of economic progress, in this analysis we use two indicators of economic activity--GNP and the county unemployment rate--to assess the sensitivity of each group's income to overall movements in the economy. Tight labor markets provide opportunities for other household members to augment the family income by securing employment. Our data have shown that the earnings of these secondary workers were a principal factor, particularly among blacks, in enabling lower income families to improve their economic position. Hence, an inverse association would be expected between family income and the level of unemployment, which is measured at the county level. The county unemployment rate should be a better proxy than the national unemployment rate for differential employment opportunities for the panel households.

The county unemployment rate is solicited annually from the state agencies and was coded into the panel data according to the following scale:

1. Under 2 percent
2. 2 - 3.9 percent
3. 4 - 5.9 percent
4. 6 - 10 percent
5. Over 10 percent
9. Not ascertained.

This measure of the tightness of the local labor market was converted to a continuous variable by using the midpoint of each bracket.[2] Counties designated as areas with unemployment rates in excess of 10 percent were assigned a value of 12 percent. Those few cases where the county unemployment rate was not ascertained were assigned either the average of the prior and succeeding years' levels or the mode.

Variables representing the region of residence and whether the family lived in an urban environment were included to delineate further any subgroup which experienced a differential improvement in economic well-being over the panel. Three dichotomous region variables were constructed for residence in the Northeast, North Central, or Southern region of the country. Since we were interested in whether the incomes of families living in these areas differed from the rest of the sample (and not from the omitted Western region), we applied a simple transformation of variables which enabled us to express the resulting coefficients

---

[2] It should be noted that the estimates of county unemployment rates are, in general, subject to substantial measurement error. An especially acute problem in determining local labor market conditions is estimating the extent of the labor force for a county. Hence, the accuracy implied by point estimates of county unemployment rates provided by the state agencies is quite misleading.

as deviations from the overall mean income level.[3] In general, we would expect
higher than average incomes for households residing in the more urban Northeast
sector and markedly lower than average incomes among households living in the
South. The variable "whether an urban environment" was coded 1 if the family
resided within 15 miles of a city with a population of 50,000 or more and 0
otherwise. Proximity to a large urban area would be expected to provide more
employment opportunities for members of the household and, therefore, higher
family money income.

Analysis based on the first five years of the panel study (1968-1972) showed
that differences in labor incomes of the household heads accounted for nearly
two-thirds of the variance in interfamily income.[4] The importance of the family
head's earnings to the economic well-being of the household persisted when considering change in family money income from 1967 to 1971.[5] Accordingly, the last
set of variables included in this analysis of family economic well-being was
taken from the human capital model of income determination which shows that measures of educational attainment and labor market experience are adequate predictors of individual labor income.[6] Although our primary interest here has been
in the responsiveness of family income to economic activity and not on the differential returns to schooling or experience for various subgroups, these standard human capital variables were included to adjust for differential earnings

---

[3]This was accomplished by constraining the estimated dummy variable coefficients to sum to zero and then rewriting the dummy variables as deviations from
the omitted group. Thus, rather than estimating

$$(1) \quad Y = a_1 + a_2 NE + a_3 NC + a_4 S + \varepsilon$$

where NE, NC and S represent the three dummy variables whether
the household resided in the Northeast, North Central or South,
respectively (West being the omitted group),

we estimated the equation as follows:

$$(2) \quad Y = a_1^* + a_2^*(NE-W) + a_3^*(NC-W) + a_4^*(S-W) + \varepsilon.$$

This implies, of course, that the coefficients for the omitted Western region
would be the negative sum of the other region coefficients.

[4]Morgan (1974), p. 67.

[5]Morgan (1974).

[6]See Mincer (1974).

of the main income provider, the head of the household.[7]

II. ESTIMATION PROCEDURE

The time-series and cross-section observations from the panel are used to relate family income to the two measures of economic activity (GNP and the county unemployment rate) and demographic characteristics of the household. This relationship can be expressed as

$$(3) \quad Y_{it} = \beta_1 + \beta_2 G_t + \beta_3 U_{it} + \beta_4 ED_{it} + \beta_5 EXP_{it} + \beta_6 EXP_{it}^2 + \sum_{k=1}^{4} \gamma_k Z_{it,k} + \varepsilon_{it}$$

with $E(\varepsilon_{it}) = 0$ for i=1,2,...,N and

$\quad\quad E(\varepsilon_{it}^2) = \sigma_i^2$ t=1,2,...,T

where Y_{it} represents family money income for the ith household in time t,

$\quad\quad G_t$ denotes nominal GNP in time t,

$\quad\quad U_{it}$ is the level of the unemployment rate for the county of residence of the ith household at time t,

$\quad\quad ED_{it}$ is the number of years of formal education acquired by the head of the ith household by time t,

$\quad\quad EXP_{it}$ represents the number of years the head of the ith household was employed full time since age 18 by time t,

$\quad\quad Z_{it,k}$ represents dummy variables for region of residence and whether the ith household resided in an urban environment at time t,

and ε_{it} is the disturbance term for the ith household.

As indicated by the above formulation, we are assuming that the parameters are invariant with respect to both households and time. We assumed also that dis-

---

[7]Information on the educational attainment of the household head contained in the panel data reflected only a range for number of years in formal schooling completed (e.g., 0-5 grades, 6-8 grades, 9-11 grades, completed high school, . . .). This scaled education variable was translated to a continuous variable by assignments to midpoints of each bracket and to the mode for missing data cases. Previously, human capital earnings models were limited to using a proxy for the labor market experience of an individual (usually age minus education minus six). The seventh wave of the panel study provided a direct measure of the number of years the household head was employed full time. This measure of accumulated work experience of the family head was limited to employment after age 18 to reflect the expectation that useful labor market experience begins at that age.

turbances are autocorrelated and heteroskedastic.[8]

A three-stage procedure was used (see appendix) to derive efficient estimates of the parameter vectors β and γ. Basically, the first two stages involved correcting for serial correlation and heteroskedasticity in the error term. The derived estimates of β and γ from applying OLS to the final adjusted equation are thus unbiased, consistent, and asymptotically efficient.[9]

III. SAMPLE RESTRICTIONS

Substantial changes occurred in the composition of the original sample households during the panel period. Although some of these changes may have

---

[8]In particular, the disturbance term, ε_{it}, was assumed to follow a first-order Markov process.

$$(4) \quad \varepsilon_{it} = \rho\varepsilon_{i,t-1} + \eta_{it} \qquad \text{with } |\rho| < 1$$

$$E(\eta_{it}) = 0$$

$$E(\eta_{it}\eta_{jt'}) = \begin{cases} 0 & \text{for } i=j \text{ and } t \neq t' \\ \sigma^2_{\eta_i} & \text{for } i=j \text{ and } t=t' \\ 0 & \text{for } i \neq j \end{cases}$$

$$\text{and} \quad E(\varepsilon_{i,t-1}\eta_{jt}) = 0 \qquad \text{for all } i,j.$$

For simplicity, the autocorrelation coefficient, ρ, was assumed to be invariant over households within a particular subgroup (e.g., households headed by white, nonfarm, nonaged males).

[9]The first phase involved obtaining a consistent estimate of the serial correlation parameter for each subgroup. After applying least squares to the entire set of NT observations for equation (3), the resultant least squares residuals (e_{it}) were then regressed on their lagged values to estimate ρ for each subgroup. Equation (3) was then transformed by subtracting from each variable its lagged value times the estimated serial correlation coefficient. Since the least squares residuals from this transformed equation (e^*_{it}) are now consistent, we could proceed to correct for heteroskedasticity. In the general formulation of equation (3), we have allowed the variance of the disturbance to vary over households. Instead of computing a separate estimate of the variance for each household, we assumed that the variance of the disturbance was markedly similar for households with similar economic circumstances. Hence, for each subgroup separate variance estimates were derived for households in the same income range. Four income ranges were established for computing these variance estimates--family incomes less than \$5,000; \$5,000-\$9,999; \$10,000-\$14,999; and \$15,000 and over. After classifying each household into its respective income state, the sum of the squared residuals from the transformed equation (Σe^{*2}_{it}) adjusted for the degrees of freedom was used to derive a consistent estimate of the variance for

represented inevitable life cycle occurrences such as the death of a member of the household, the dominant characteristic of family composition change was a voluntary alteration of the living arrangement of the household (e.g., married couples dissolving their marriage or single heads of households becoming married). For proper comparison of the economic well-being of these subgroups, the analysis was limited to those families with the same head of the household in each wave of the panel. Furthermore, the data were restricted to nonfarm households.

For some households, most notably the self-employed, business losses may partially or even completely offset other income earned in a particular year. These extreme year-to-year fluctuations in entrepreneurial income pose substantial difficulties in assessing the sensitivity of family income to overall economic activity. Hence, to avoid domination by these extreme cases, panel households where the household head was self-employed or with year-to-year variations in income in excess of $25,000 were also excluded from the analysis. Similarly, households whose reported annual incomes were less than or equal to $100 were also filtered from the panel data. These latter restrictions eliminated 69 households from subsequent analysis.

Thus, among the nonaged, nonfarm households with the same family head over the seven-year period from 1967 to 1974, we were left with 559 and 1,386 cases for black and white male-headed families, respectively. The corresponding number of observations for black and white female-headed households were 438 and 254, respectively.

IV. ANALYSIS RESULTS

The adjusted results from the pooled time-series, cross-section regressions are presented in Table 5.1. Since the focus of this analysis was the responsiveness of household income to cyclical fluctuations in economic activity, the coefficient estimates for the education and experience variables were not included in Table 5.1; however, the entire set of coefficient estimates is included in Table A5.1.[10]

A random half-sample was used for some preliminary experimentation in

---

each income range. The final step was to apply the heteroskedasticity correction by dividing each variable of the transformed equation by the estimated standard deviation of the disturbance. The parameter estimates of β and γ from applying ordinary least squares to this adjusted equation are thus unbiased, consistent, and asymptotically efficient.

[10]The unadjusted coefficient estimates in Table A5.1 reflect applying least squares to the entire set of observations. The two adjusted regression results presented in the table for each subgroup are the corresponding coefficient estimates after correcting for autocorrelation and heteroskedasticity.

Table 5.1

REGRESSIONS OF FAMILY MONEY INCOME ON ECONOMIC GROWTH AND UNEMPLOYMENT
RATES, 1967-1974, AND DEMOGRAPHIC CHARACTERISTICS OF THE FAMILY HEAD[c]

Dependent Variable: Log Family Money Income

	Constant	Log GNP	Log Un-employment Rate	Whether North-east[a]	Whether North Central[a]	Whether South[a]	Whether Urban Area[b]
White *nonfarm, nonaged*							
Male Family Head	2.3343	.8414** (.0179)	.0057 (.0057)	.0395** (.0040)	.0345** (.0038)	-.0521** (.0042)	.0687** (.0047)
Female Family Head	3.0725	.6471** (.0588)	.0347 (.0192)	.1319** (.0129)	.0530** (.0132)	-.0760** (.0148)	.1311** (.0159)
Black *nonfarm, nonaged*							
Male Family Head	.8453	1.0119** (.0372)	-.0913** (.0122)	.0436** (.0110)	.1266** (.0100)	-.0614** (.0092)	.0640** (.0124)
Female Family Head	1.1253	.9666** (.0542)	-.2459** (.0188)	.0652** (.0144)	-.0147 (.0125)	-.0915** (.0136)	.1450** (.0179)

** Significant at .01 level.

NOTE: Estimated coefficients are shown with standard errors enclosed in parentheses.

[a] The estimated dummy variable coefficients are constrained to sum to zero and each dichotomous variable is expressed as deviations from the western region.

[b] Coded 1 if family resides within 15 miles of city of 50,000 or more, 0 otherwise.

[c] Corrected for heteroskedasticity and autocorrelation. Human capital variables--the education, labor market experience, and experience squared of the household head--are controlled for. The complete results are shown in Table A5.1.

specifying an appropriate model. This was limited primarily to determining the appropriate functional form for equation (3). After comparing the results from regressions in original units, semi-logarithmic and double-logarithmic form, the last was settled upon as the basis for analyzing the income of panel households in this model. Thus, the dependent variable in this analysis was the logarithm of family money income. The two economic indicators, GNP and the county unemployment rate, were expressed also in logarithmic form.

As shown in Table 5.1, the estimated elasticities of family money income with respect to GNP were significant at the .01 level for all subgroups. The largest subgroup--white, nonfarm, nonaged households headed by males--had an elasticity of family income with respect to GNP of .84. This means that a 1 percent increase in GNP (with no change in unemployment or any of the other variables included in the analysis) was associated with a .84 percent increase in the incomes of families in this subgroup. By contrast, the incomes of their black counterparts were *more* responsive to cyclic changes in GNP. Similar to the earlier findings of Anderson, the 1.01 coefficient for black households headed by males indicates that their income increased by an amount that was slightly more than proportional to the growth in GNP.

As noted above, previous research by Anderson and Aaron suggested that the incomes of female-headed households were not affected significantly by overall economic activity. Table 5.1 shows a mixed pattern regarding the sensitivity of this group's income to overall movements in GNP. The incomes of households headed by white females were less responsive to this measure of economic growth than the income of any other subgroup. In sharp contrast, black female-headed households had an elasticity of family money income with respect to GNP of .97; in other words, their incomes were *more* responsive to advances in the economy than were the incomes of white, male-headed families and were only slightly less responsive than those of black males.[11] This differential sensitivity of family income to economic growth between blacks and whites could reflect a "whiplash" effect. That is, during periods of economic expansion blacks are the last to be

---

[11]At each phase of the three-stage estimation procedure employed to derive efficient estimates of the response of family income to growth in GNP, a systematic lowering of the standard errors of the estimated coefficients was observed for each subgroup. Similarly, the estimated elasticities of subgroup income with respect to GNP uniformly decreased at each stage of the estimation procedure. (See Table A5.1.) This was particularly pronounced for black female-headed households. The responsiveness of this group's income to growth in GNP decreased nearly 12 percent after adjusting for autocorrelation and heteroskedasticity--from 1.084 in the initial OLS stage to a final adjusted estimate of .967.

hired and, conversely, they are the first to be fired during an economic contraction. Thus, blacks not only have lower incomes than similarly situated whites, but also their incomes are more dependent on favorable economic conditions.

We hypothesized that expanded employment opportunities were the main vehicle by which black households improved their economic position. In a tight labor market, the head of the household could expect to benefit by virtue of more steady employment and perhaps even the opportunity to work additional hours. These added earnings of the family head may also be supplemented by increased labor income of the spouse and other family members. Thus, an inverse relationship was hypothesized to exist between family money income and the county unemployment rate, particularly for black households. This relationship was, in general, confirmed in the regression results shown in Table 5.1. The incomes of black households were inversely related to movements in the level of the county unemployment rate and were significant at the .01 level. In the black subpopulation the differential sensitivity of family money income to employment opportunities by sex of the household head was particularly interesting. Incomes of households headed by black females were more than twice as responsive to cyclical fluctuations in the county unemployment rate than for black male-headed households. While the elasticity of family money income with respect to this measure of local labor market conditions for black females was .25, the corresponding estimate for black males was only .09. By contrast, the estimated elasticities for whites were not significant at the .05 level and even had the opposite sign.

In general, the pattern of effects for region and urbanicity conformed to expectations, with southern and rural residents having substantially lower than average family money incomes. For all subgroups, both residence in the Northeast sector and residence in an urban environment had a consistent and significantly positive effect on family income. The latter effect was even more pronounced for female-headed families. Proportionately, the incomes of female-headed households were more than twice as affected by residence within a city of 50,000 population or more as the the incomes of their male counterparts. Finally, households in the South had incomes which were 5 to 9 percent lower than average over the panel period.

Implications and Directions for Future Research

Although expanded employment opportunities and economic growth improve the economic status of black households substantially, this hopeful outlook for the

erosion of poverty as a by-product of sustained economic growth and tight labor
markets must be tempered by an acknowledgment of the reverse effect with any
economic contraction. In any event, the maintenance of favorable economic conditions would only provide for a gradual improvement in economic status for some
households. Rather than rely entirely on economic growth and expanded employment
opportunities to remedy the ills of the poverty-stricken, we could attempt to
accelerate the elimination of poverty by initiating new income maintenance programs and continuing to support any viable existing programs.

Although the results presented above provide some additional insights into
the changing economic status of blacks and whites, they are based on a rather
simplistic model of economic mobility. In particular, much additional work is
needed to disentangle the relationship between labor force participation of
family members and economic activity. To some extent, the decision of the spouse
and other household members to participate in the labor market is conditioned by
the fortunes of the household head. Losses in earnings of the family head due
to unemployment often induce the other potential wage earners to enter the labor
force. The dynamics of these interrelationships should be included in a more
direct fashion. Similarly, the county unemployment rate was used as the indicator of local labor market conditions for members of the household. This proxy
for employment opportunity could be refined to reflect the submarket which each
group faces (e.g., labor market conditions for unskilled workers). In any event,
the above estimates reflect only a modest attempt to explore the underlying
structure between employment, economic growth, and poverty.

Summary

Analysis results indicated that blacks benefited more from favorable economic conditions than similarly situated whites. The estimated elasticity of
family money income with respect to GNP was approximately unity for black households and considerably less for white households. This relative insensitivity
of family income to movements in GNP for whites was particularly pronounced for
white female-headed households, where the estimated elasticity of family income
with respect to GNP was .65.

The differential effects of economic activity on the well-being of black
and white households is extended to local employment opportunities. The incomes
of black households were inversely related to movements in the level of the county
unemployment rate and significant at the .01 level. Thus, sustained economic

158

growth and tight labor markets play an important role in enabling black households to improve their economic position. This is reflected not only in expanded
employment opportunities for the unemployed and low-paid workers during periods
of economic expansion, but perhaps also in a reduction, albeit temporary, in
discrimination against blacks and other minorities in the labor market.

References

Aaron, Henry. "The Foundations of the 'War on Poverty' Reexamined." American
    Economic Review 57 (December, 1967), pp. 1229-40.

Anderson, W. H. Locke. "Trickling Down: The Relationship Between Economic
    Growth and the Extent of Poverty Among American Families." Quarterly
    Journal of Economics 78 (November, 1964), pp. 511-24.

Batchelder, Alan B. "Decline in the Relative Income of Negro Men." Quarterly
    Journal of Economics 78 (November, 1964), pp. 525-48.

Beach, Charles. "Cyclical Impacts on the Personal Distribution of Income."
    Annals of Economic and Social Measurement 5 (Winter, 1976), pp. 29-52.

Council of Economic Advisors. 1974 Economic Report of the President. Washington:
    U.S. Government Printing Office, 1974.

Gallaway, Lowell E. "The Foundations of the 'War on Poverty'." American
    Economic Review 55 (March, 1965), pp. 122-31.

Gallaway, Lowell E. "The Foundations of the War on Poverty: Reply." American
    Economic Review 57 (December, 1967), pp. 1241-43.

Johnson, Harry G. "Unemployment and Poverty." In Poverty Amid Affluence.
    Edited by Leo Fishman. New Haven: Yale University Press, 1966.

Kmenta, Jan. Elements of Economics. New York: The MacMillan Company, 1971.

Madden, John Patrick. "Poverty Projections in Relation to Aggregate Demand,
    Economic Growth, and Unemployment." In Rural Poverty in the United States:
    A Report by the President's National Advisory Commission on Rural Poverty.
    Final Report. Washington: U.S. Government Printing Office, 1968.

Mincer, Jacob. Schooling, Experience and Earnings. New York: National Bureau
    of Economic Research, 1974.

Mooney, Joseph D. "Urban Poverty and Labor Force Participation." American
    Economic Review 57 (March, 1967), pp. 104-19.

Morgan, James N. "Changes in Global Measures." In Five Thousand American
    Families--Patterns of Economic Progress, Vol. I. Edited by James N. Morgan.
    Ann Arbor: Institute for Social Research, 1974.

Orshansky, Mollie. "Counting the Poor: Another Look at the Poverty Profile."
    Social Security Bulletin 28 (January, 1965), pp. 3-29.

Orshansky, Mollie. "Who's Who Among the Poor: A Demographic View of Poverty."
    Social Security Bulletin 28 (July, 1965), pp. 3-32.

Theil, Henri. Principles of Econometrics. New York: John Wiley & Sons, 1971.

APPENDIX 5.1

The normal assumption of a homoskedastic disturbance cannot, in general, be retained when the dependent variable is family income. While families at relatively low levels of income are severely impeded in their ability to alter their economic lot, families at the upper end of the income distribution have considerable flexibility in improving their well-being. Hence, the classical assumption that the variance of the disturbance is invariant over all units is not plausible for this specification. Finally, we assume that the disturbances are autocorrelated.

These specifications regarding the behavior of the disturbances can be summarized as follows:

$$E(\varepsilon_{it}) = 0$$

$$E(\varepsilon_{it}^2) = \sigma_i^2$$

$$E(\varepsilon_{it}\varepsilon_{jt'}) = 0 \qquad \text{for } i \neq j$$

$$\varepsilon_{it} = \rho\varepsilon_{i,t-1} + \eta_{it} \qquad \text{with } |\rho| < 1$$

(5) $$E(\eta_{it}) = 0$$

$$E(\eta_{it}\eta_{jt'}) = \begin{cases} 0 & \text{for } i-j \text{ and } t \neq t' \\ \sigma_{\eta_i}^2 & \text{for } i=j \text{ and } t=t' \\ 0 & \text{for } i \neq j \end{cases}$$

and $E(\varepsilon_{i,t-1}\eta_{jt}) = 0$ for all i, j.

In particular, we are assuming that the disturbance, ε_{it}, follows a first-order Markov process and that the autocorrelation parameter, ρ, is invariant over all families. Also, the error terms for different families are independent—indicating zero contemporaneous covariance.

Thus, the variance-covariance matrix of the disturbance term becomes

$$
(6) \quad E(\varepsilon\varepsilon') = \begin{bmatrix} \sigma^2 P_1 & \Theta & \cdots & \Theta \\ \Theta & \sigma^2 P_2 & \cdots & \Theta \\ \cdot & \cdot & & \cdot \\ \cdot & \cdot & \cdot & \cdot \\ \cdot & \cdot & & \cdot \\ \Theta & \Theta & \cdots & \sigma^2 P_N \end{bmatrix}
$$

where

$$
P = \begin{bmatrix} 1 & \rho & \rho^2 & \cdots & \rho^{T-1} \\ \rho & 1 & \rho & \cdots & \rho^{T-2} \\ \cdot & \cdot & \cdot & \cdot & \cdot \\ \cdot & \cdot & \cdot & \cdot & \cdot \\ \cdot & \cdot & \cdot & \cdot & \cdot \\ \rho^{T-1} & \rho^{T-2} & \rho^{T-3} & \cdots & 1 \end{bmatrix}
$$

A three-stage estimation procedure is used to obtain efficient estimates of the parameter vectors β and γ in this cross-sectionally heteroskedastic time-series autocorrelated model. First, ordinary least squares is applied to the entire set of $N \cdot T$ observations for equation (3). The least squares coefficient estimates,[1] $\hat{\beta}$ and $\hat{\gamma}$, are then used to estimate the autocorrelation coefficient by

$$
(7) \quad \hat{\rho} = \frac{\sum\limits_{i}\sum\limits_{t} e_{it} e_{i,t-1}}{\sum\limits_{i}\sum\limits_{t} e_{i,t-1}^2} \qquad \begin{array}{l} \text{for } i = 1,2,\ldots,N \text{ and} \\[6pt] t = 2,3,\ldots,T \end{array}
$$

where e_{it} is the least squares residual.

Second, equation (3) is transformed using this estimate of the autocorrelation coefficient. That is, we subtract from each variable its lagged value times the estimate of the autocorrelation coefficient.

---

[1] When the disturbances are heteroskedastic (autocorrelated), the least squares estimates of the parameter vectors β and γ are still unbiased and consistent; however, they are not efficient. Furthermore, the estimated variances of the least squares coefficients are biased. For further details see Jan Kmenta, Elements of Econometrics (New York: MacMillan Company, 1971), Chapters 8 and 12.

162

(8)
$$Y^*_{it} = \beta^*_1 + \beta_2 G^*_t + \beta_3 U^*_{it} + \beta_4 ED^*_{it} + \beta_5 EXP^*_{it} + \beta_6 EXP^{2*}_{it} + \sum_k \gamma_k Z^*_{it,k} + \eta^*_{it}$$

where Y^*_{it} $=$ $Y_{it} - \hat{\rho}Y_{i,t-1}$

β^*_1 $=$ $\beta_1(1-\hat{\rho})$

G^*_t $=$ $G_t - \hat{\rho}G_{t-1}$

U^*_{it} $=$ $U_{it} - \hat{\rho}U_{i,t-1}$

ED^*_{it} $=$ $ED_{it} - \hat{\rho}ED_{i,t-1}$

EXP^*_{it} $=$ $EXP_{it} - \hat{\rho}EXP_{i,t-1}$

EXP^2_{it} $=$ $EXP^2_{it} - \hat{\rho}EXP^2_{i,t-1}$

$Z^*_{it,j}$ $=$ $Z_{it,j} - \hat{\rho}Z_{i,t-1,j}$ for $j = 1,2,\ldots,K$

and η^*_{it} $=$ $\varepsilon_{it} - \hat{\rho}\varepsilon_{i,t-1}$.

Ordinary least squares is then applied to this transformed equation to derive consistent residuals for the heteroskedasticity correction.

In the general formulation of the variance-covariance matrix of the disturbance (see equation (6)), each household is allowed to have a different variance.
This implies that N different variances would have to be estimated to derive efficient estimates of β and γ. To avoid computing a separate variance estimate
for each household, we assume that the variance of the disturbance is identical
for households in the same income range. Thus, rather than estimating N difference variances, this simplification reduces the number of parameters to be estimated to M (where M denotes the number of income brackets). The resulting residuals from applying least squares to equation (8), say e^*_{it}, are then used to estimate the variance of η_{it} by

(9)
$$S^2_{\eta j} = \frac{1}{N_j XT-K-7} \sum_{i \varepsilon R_j} \sum_{t=2}^{T} e^{*2}_{it}$$ for $j=1,2,\ldots,M$

where N_j represents the number of households in the jth
income range, and

R_j denotes the jth income range.

The final step is to apply the correction for heteroskedasticity. This is accomplished by dividing both sides of equation (8) by the estimated standard deviation of η_{it}.

$$(10) \quad Y^{**}_{it} = \beta^{**}_1 + \beta_2 G^{**}_t + \beta_3 U^{**}_{it} + \beta_4 ED^{**}_{it} + \beta_5 EXP^{**}_{it} + \beta_6 EXP^2{}^{**}_{it} + \sum_k \gamma_k Z^{**}_{it,k} + \eta^{**}_{it}$$

where
$$Y^{**}_{it} = Y^*_{it}/S_{\eta j}$$

$$\beta^{**}_1 = \beta^*_1/S_{\eta j}$$

$$G^{**}_t = G^*_t/S_{\eta j}$$

$$U^{**}_{it} = U^*_{it}/S_{\eta j}$$

$$ED^{**}_{it} = ED^*_{it}/S_{\eta j}$$

$$EXP^{**}_{it} = EXP^*_{it}/S_{\eta j}$$

$$EXP^2{}^{**}_{it} = EXP^2{}^*_{it}/S_{\eta j}$$

$$Z^{**}_{it,k} = Z^*_{it,k}/S_{\eta j}$$

$$\eta^{**}_{it} = \eta^*_{it}/S_{\eta j}$$

and
$S_{\eta j}$ denotes the estimated standard of deviation of η_{it} for $i \epsilon R_j$.

The disturbance in equation (10) now conforms to the classical assumptions of the linear model.[2] The least squares estimates of the parameter vectors β and γ are now unbiased, consistent and asymptotically efficient.

---

[2] That is, the disturbance term in equation (10), η^{**}_{it}, is asympototically non-autocorrelated and homoskedastic.

Table A5.1 (Sheet 1 of 2)

OLS REGRESSIONS OF FAMILY MONEY INCOME ON
ECONOMIC GROWTH, AND UNEMPLOYMENT RATES, 1967–1974,
AND DEMOGRAPHIC CHARACTERISTICS OF THE FAMILY HEAD

Dependent Variable: Log Family Money Income

White *Nonfarm, Nonaged*

	Male Family Head			Female Family Head		
	Unad-justed	Adjusted for Autocor-relation	Adjusted for Autocor-relation and Heteroske-dasticity	Unad-justed	Adjusted for Autocor-relation	Adjusted for Autocor-relation and Heteroske-dasticity
Constant	1.5445	1.4816	2.3343	2.2041	2.4869	3.0725
Log GNP	.9203** (.0319)	.9327** (.0208)	.8414** (.0179)	.7402** (.0919)	.6947** (.0667)	.6471** (.0588)
Log Unemploy-ment Rate	−.0033 (.0118)	−.0002 (.0067)	.0057 (.0057)	.0363 (.0345)	.0426 (.0218)	.0347 (.0192)
Whether North-east[a]	.0517** (.0084)	.0476** (.0048)	.0395** (.0040)	.1566** (.0231)	.1444** (.0147)	.1319** (.0129)
Whether North Central[a]	.0396** (.0080)	.0368** (.0046)	.0345** (.0038)	.0661** (.0238)	.0710** (.0152)	.0530** (.0132)
Whether South[a]	−.0624** (.0088)	−.0603** (.0051)	−.0521** (.0042)	−.0901** (.0263)	−.0830** (.0169)	−.0760** (.0148)
Whether Urban Area[b]	.1049** (.0098)	.0827** (.0056)	.0687** (.0047)	.2051** (.0283)	.1852** (.0180)	.1311** (.0159)
Family Head Education[c]	.0643** (.0015)	.0647** (.0008)	.0558** (.0008)	.0725** (.0040)	.0758** (.0025)	.0669** (.0025)
Labor Market Experience[c]	.0621** (.0017)	.0614** (.0010)	.0511** (.0008)	.0276** (.0041)	.0274** (.0026)	.0215** (.0023)
Experience Squared[c]	−.0012** (.0001)	−.0012** (.0001)	−.0010** (.0001)	−.0004** (.0001)	−.0004** (.0001)	−.0003** (.0001)
$\bar{R}^2$	.326	*	*	.297	*	*
Number of Observations	9,702	8,316	8,316	1,778	1,524	1,524

Black *Nonfarm, Nonaged*

Constant	.3486	.4894	.8453	.2157	.7293	1.1253
Log GNP	1.0496** (.0577)	1.0310** (.0423)	1.0119** (.0372)	1.0836** (.0699)	1.0248** (.0559)	.9666** (.0542)
Log Unemploy-ment Rate	−.0862** (.0225)	−.1088** (.0141)	−.0913** (.0122)	−.1983** (.0283)	−.2574** (.0195)	−.2459** (.0188)

Table A5.1 (Sheet 2 of 2)

Black *Nonfarm, Nonaged* (continued)

	Male Family Head			Female Family Head		
	Unad-justed	Adjusted for Autocor-relation	Adjusted for Autocor-relation and Heteroske-dasticity	Unad-justed	Adjusted for Autocor-relation	Adjusted for Autocor-relation and Heteroske-dasticity
Whether North-east[a]	.0313 (.0203)	.0529** (.0130)	.0436** (.0110)	.0853** (.0211)	.0628** (.0148)	.0652** (.0144)
Whether North Central[a]	.1448** (.0184)	.1335** (.0118)	.1226** (.0100)	-.0223 (.0184)	-.0229 (.0129)	-.0147 (.0125)
Whether South[a]	-.0667** (.0165)	-.0795** (.0107)	-.0614** (.0092)	-.0776** (.0199)	-.0865** (.0140)	-.0915** (.0136)
Whether Urban Area[b]	.1155** (.0222)	.0661** (.0143)	.0640** (.0124)	.2498** (.0264)	.1625** (.0186)	.1450** (.0179)
Family Head Education[c]	.0862** (.0024)	.0889** (.0016)	.0770** (.0015)	.0471** (.0041)	.0498** (.0028)	.0482** (.0028)
Labor Market Experience[c]	.0600** (.0032)	.0626** (.0021)	.0515** (.0019)	.0389** (.0028)	.0393** (.0019)	.0389** (.0019)
Experience Squared[c]	-.0011** (.0001)	-.0012** (.0001)	-.0010** (.0001)	-.0011** (.0001)	-.0011** (.0001)	-.0011** (.0001)
$\bar{R}^2$	.392	*	*	.283	*	*
Number of Observations	3,913	3,354	3,354	3,066	2,628	2,628

**Significant at .01 level.

NOTE: Estimated coefficients are shown with standard errors enclosed in paren-theses.

[a]The estimated dummy variable coefficients are constrained to sum to zero and each dichotomous variable is expressed as deviations from the western region.

[b]Coded 1 if family resides within 15 miles of city of 50,000 or more, 0 other-wise.

[c]The returns to schooling and experience in the above table are based on family money income, *not* individual earnings. Thus, these estimates also reflect dif-ferences in the extent of multiple earners and transfer income between the various subgroups.

*Since the $\bar{R}^2$ from the adjusted equation is not directly comparable to the original OLS stage, it is not reported in the above table.

Chapter 6

PATHS TO ECONOMIC WELL-BEING

Greg J. Duncan

Introduction

Data from the Panel Study of Income Dynamics are particularly well suited
for analysis of income distribution because its respondents come from a recent,
representative national sample, because questions provide rich detail on the background, attitudes, and skills of the respondents, and because the longitudinal design of the panel study permits a look at not only *level* of earnings but also
changes in earnings over time. In the analysis described in this chapter we used
these data to further our understanding of the *process* by which background, educational, attitudinal, and environmental factors operate to influence earnings.
Among the types of questions we sought to answer were the following: How much do
the attainments of an individual's parents influence his own earnings and to what
extent do the parental attainments operate for the individual through advantageous attitudes and behavior patterns, cognitive skills, institutional factors,
and his own educational attainment? What role do attitudes play in determining
earnings? To what extent do education, attitudes, and job change affect short-
run *change* in earnings?

To help answer these questions, a two-part recursive model of income determination was designed. The first part of the model has as its ultimate dependent
variable the individual's average *level* of earnings in the early years of the
panel. Earnings level is taken to be a function of current economic environment
(e.g., occupation, union status, and urbanicity), personal characteristics, educational attainment, and family background. The second part of the model relates
these factors plus changes in economic environment to the individual's *change* in
earnings between the early and most recent years of the panel.

The two parts of the model were estimated separately by race for the male
household heads who were between the ages of 25 and 55 in 1975 and who worked at
least 500 hours per year during the 1970-1974 period. Females were excluded because complete information was not available for wives and because female household heads who did not marry and who worked continuously during the 1970-1975

period constituted a small and unrepresentative subset of female workers for whom the proposed model may not be properly specified.[1] We hope to replicate this analysis for *all* women when the ninth wave interviews with both husbands and wives have been processed.

We first focus on an explanation of earnings level. The proposed earnings model is explained in Section I. The estimates and results for the model are discussed in the second section. In Section III, the model is extended to account for *changes* in earnings and the analysis results for that part of the model are presented in the fourth section.

Analysis

I. A RECURSIVE MODEL OF EARNINGS LEVEL

Intense interest in income distribution in recent years has resulted in the identification of various factors that seem to (or, for unmeasured variables, ought to) affect the amount of money a person makes. Proponents of the human capital model believe that skills acquired in childhood, in school, and through on-the-job training can be thought of as capital embedded in a worker which pays a return on the time and money expended by the individual or, in the case of early skills, by his parents.[2] Human capital analysis usually explains earnings differentials using the individual's years of education and years of work experience, although religion and certain parental characteristics such as educational attainment levels of the mother and father have been argued to be proxies for the quantity and quality of time "invested" in the child by his parents.[3]

Bowles and Gintis propose a competing explanation of the income distribution process.[4] In it, the bundle of acquired and ascribed traits that a worker brings to the labor market will determine his position in the work hierarchy and, ultimately, his earnings. Many of the traits thought to be most important (such as aspirations, motivation, and modes of speech, dress, and interpersonal behavior)

---

[1] Work experience is an exogenous variable in the model but may well be endogenous for women.

[2] The standard references are Becker (1964) and Mincer (1974).

[3] Leibowitz (1974). Hill and Stafford (1974) show that the increased time spent at home which is associated with the birth of a child is significantly higher for highly educated parents and Catholics.

[4] Bowles and Gintis (1972).

are developed in the home. Schooling plays the minor role of *reinforcing* many traits originated in the home and may also serve as a screening function.

Proponents of both of these views recognize that cognitive skills play a role in the income determination processes. It is necessary to include a measure of cognitive skills both because their direct effects on earnings are of interest and because their effects need to be taken into account in estimating the role of other factors, such as education, which are correlated with them.

Consistent with each view is the idea of a temporal sequence of events leading ultimately to earnings. The sequence begins at birth; some individuals are born into more advantaged homes than others. These background differences plus some factors originating outside of the home determine educational attainment. Education and background plus early work experience determine the set of attitudes, behavior patterns, and skills that characterize an individual. All of these variables, operating through choices of occupation and location, affect earnings. Such sequential models of status determination have been used extensively by sociologists to explain occupational attainment and earnings[5] and by some economists to explain educational attainment and earnings.[6] This analysis builds upon previous work with data that allow more detailed specification of the earnings process.

The proposed earnings model is depicted in Figure 6.1. There are four sets of equations in the model, one for each stage in the earnings cycle.

(1) Education = f_1 (Background, Age)

(2) Personal Characteristics$_i$ = f_{2i} (Background, Education, Age)

(3) Environment$_j$ = f_{3j} (Background, Education, Personal Characteristics, Experience)

(4) ℓn Wage Rate = f_4 (Background, Education, Personal Characteristics, Experience, Environment)

where "Education" is completed years of schooling reported by the respondent in 1975,

"Background" is measured by the following variables:

1. Father's educational attainment (in years).

2. Mother's educational attainment (in years).

---

[5] See, for example, Duncan, Featherman, and Duncan (1972), Duncan and Blau (1968), Jencks (1972), and Sewell and Hauser (1975).

[6] A partial list would include Duncan (1974), Hill (1975), Wachtel (1975), Akin and Garfinkel (1975), Taubman (1975), and Morganstern (1973).

Figure 6.1

PATH MODEL OF EARNINGS LEVEL

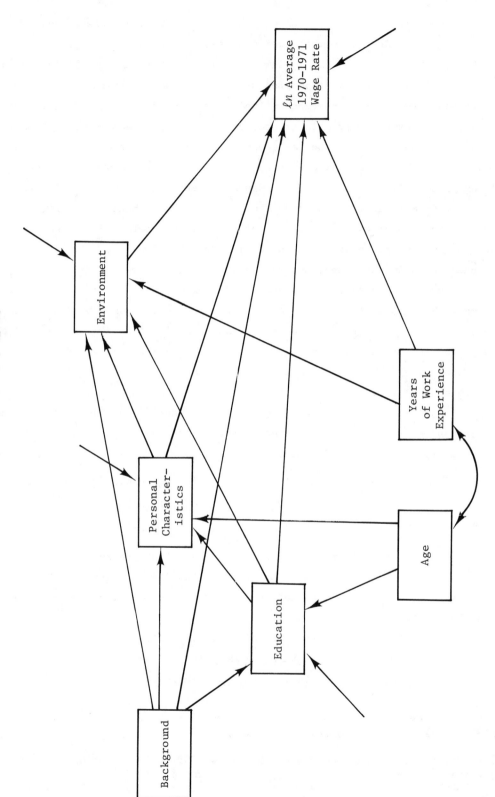

3. Whether Catholic--a dichotomous variable equal to 1 if respondent is Catholic and 0 otherwise.

4. Whether Jewish--a dichotomous variable equal to 1 if respondent is Jewish and 0 otherwise. (This variable was excluded from the analysis of blacks.)

5. Grew up South--a dichotomous variable equal to 1 if respondent reported growing up in the South and 0 otherwise.

6. Grew up Farm--a dichotomous variable equal to 1 if respondent reported growing up on a farm and 0 otherwise.

7. Number of siblings.

"Personal Characteristics" consist of the following variables:

1. Test Score--total score on a 13-question sentence completion test administered to the respondent in 1972. (The test was designed to measure cognitive skills.)[7]

2. Achievement Motivation--total score on a 16-question sequence designed to measure achievement motivation.

3. Efficacy--total score from 1970 and 1971 interviews for six questions concerning the extent to which the respondent carries out plans, is sure life will work out the way intended, and finishes things. (Maximum score is six.)

4. Future Orientation--total score from 1970 and 1971 interviews for four questions about whether the respondent plans his life ahead and saves for the future rather than enjoying life today. (Maximum score is four.)

5. Risk Avoidance--total score from 1970 and 1971 interviews on an index showing extent of avoidance of unnecessary risk. Points are given for using seat belts, having car and medical insurance (or access to free medical care), having savings and smoking less than a pack of cigarettes daily. (Maximum score is 16.)

"Experience" is reported number of years working since age 18.

"Environment" includes the following job and residential characteristics:

1. White Collar--a dichotomous variable which equals 1 if respondent's occupation was white collar in both 1970 and 1971 and 0 otherwise.[8]

2. Self-employed--a dichotomous variable which equals 1 if respondent worked only for self in both 1970 and 1971 and 0 otherwise.

---

[7]Veroff et al. (1971) document the Test Score and Achievement Motivation Indexes.

[8]White collar occupations include professional, technical, and kindred workers; managers, officials, and proprietors; self-employed businessmen; and clerical and sales workers.

3. Whether union--a dichotomous variable which equals 1
   if respondent belonged to a labor union in both 1970
   and 1971 and 0 otherwise.

4. Whether South--a dichotomous variable which equals 1
   if 1970 region of residence was South, 0 otherwise.

5. City size--size of city of residence in 1970, in thousands.[9]

"Wage Rate" is the natural logarithm of the average hourly wage rate for
1970 and 1971, deflated by Consumer Price Index, reported in the spring of
1971 and 1972.[10]

The means and standard deviations of each of these variables are given in
Table A6.1.

To facilitate the estimation of the model, it was assumed that all of the
relationships are linear and additive, that the error term associated with each
equation is independent of the variables in that equation, and that the error
terms are independent of one another. These are rather strong assumptions and
there are several reasons to doubt their validity, particularly for the personal
characteristics equations. These problems are discussed at the conclusion of
this section.

The various background variables are hypothesized to affect earnings in a
number of ways. The *total* effect of a particular background measure is calculated net of the effects of the other background variables and years of work experience. This total effect can be decomposed into the sum of (1) the *direct*
effect of the background variable which is independent of education, personal
characteristics, and environment, (2) an *indirect* effect which comes about because the background factor affects the amount of education and education, in
turn, has a direct effect on earnings, (3) an *indirect* effect operating through
personal characteristics (net of education and environment), and (4) an *indirect*
effect operating through environmental variables.[11] These direct and indirect
effects are expected to account for most, but not all, of the total effect because various second-order indirect effects are possible. A background measure,
for example, may affect educational attainment which, in turn, may affect the
chances of having a white collar occupation which, in turn, affects earnings.

---

[9]Due to the availability of only a one-digit bracket code, this variable
takes on six values--1000, 300, 75, 37.5, 17.5, and 5--which correspond to the
bracket ranges of 500,000 or more, 100,000-499,999, 50,000-99,999, 25,000-49,999,
10,000-24,999, and under 10,000 respectively.

[10]Wage rates are *not* deflated by geographic cost of living differences.

[11]For an algebraic exposition of total, direct, and indirect effects, see the
appendix to this chapter or Duncan (1966).

These second-order indirect effects were found to be generally quite small and are usually ignored in the discussion.

Education's role in the model is somewhat simpler since it cannot operate through any of the background variables which are logically prior to it. The *total* effect of education on earnings is obtained after the effects of the background and work experience measures have been accounted for. As with the background measures, this total effect can be broken down into direct and indirect effects. Specifically, education is allowed to have (1) a direct effect net of the effects of personal characteristics and environment (and, of course, net of background and work experience), (2) indirect effects which operate through personal characteristics, (3) indirect effects which operate through environmental variables, and (4) second-order indirect effects which operate through various pairs of personal characteristics and environmental factors. A close examination of these direct and indirect effects was expected to prove especially interesting since they quantify the extent to which education "pays off" by affecting cognitive skills and attitudes, by affecting one's chances of being in an advantageous occupation, and by operating independently of these factors.

The personal characteristics were hypothesized to be determined by background, education, and age and to affect earnings by operating both through and independently of environment. The *total* effect of each personal characteristic on earnings is calculated by accounting for the effects of all other personal characteristics, educational attainment, background, and work experience. Each total effect is the sum of direct effects which are independent of environmental factors and indirect effects which operate through them.

The environmental variables comprise the final stage of the earnings process. The effect of each on earnings is estimated after controlling for all other variables in the analysis (except age). Since no further variables intervene between environment and earnings, there are no indirect effects possible for the environmental variables.

Many of the hypotheses embodied in this model have received extensive treatment elsewhere. In the following discussion, attention is focused on those parts which will probably be least familiar to the reader.

Background

Educational attainment levels of the parents have been used as measures of the quantity and quality of parental time spent with children,[12] parental status,

---

[12]Leibowitz (1974).

and parental wealth.[13] Measures of both the father's and mother's education
would be expected to have positive total effects on the individual's earnings.
If personal characteristics are developed in early childhood, then we would expect the parental education variables to affect earnings by operating through the
personal characteristics. Since responsibility for child rearing usually resides
with the mother, then the son's personality variables and possibly earnings
should have a stronger association with the educational attainment of the mother
than the father.

Taubman argues that child-rearing practices and values instilled at home may
vary by religious affiliation and that the values imbued by Catholics and Jews
increase their sons' earnings potential more than those instilled by Protestants.[14] An alternative interpretation to an earnings advantage for these groups
is that social networks operate to find good jobs for those in the group. We are
able to differentiate between these competing explanations by calculating the extent to which the effect of religion on wage operates *through* personal characteristics and educational attainment rather than *independently* of them. The larger
the independent effect, the less the support for the child-rearing argument.[15]

Individuals growing up in the South and on a farm might be expected to be at
an earnings disadvantage, partly because they may obtain less and lower quality
education and partly because they are likely to remain in areas with fewer economic opportunities than the urban North.

The final background variable, number of siblings, was expected to have a
negative effect on earnings because the more children in the family, the less
time and money parents can spend on a particular child. The total effect of siblings on earnings, then, should be accounted for by the paths operating through
educational attainment and personal characteristics.

Educational Attainment

Few empirical results show up across different data sets and specifications
as strongly as the positive association between education and earnings. We hope
to add to our understanding of this relationship by accounting for the effects of
the available background measures and, more importantly, by investigating the ex-

---

[13]Bowles and Gintis (1972), Sewell and Hauser (1975), Wachtel (1975).

[14]Taubman (1975), p. 41. See also Featherman (1971).

[15]A third explanation would be that if there are tradeoffs between pecuniary
and nonpecuniary work rewards, then Jews and Catholics might teach their children
to value money more than status, pleasant work, etc. Taubman (1975) provides
some evidence that this might be the case, pp. 190-191.

tent to which education affects earnings by operating through cognitive skills, attitudes, behavior, and locational and occupational choice.

Personal Characteristics

In less guarded moments, even economists sometimes admit to believing what psychologists have been claiming for decades: that certain psychological characteristics have significant, independent effects on economic well-being. Our model includes measures of two key psychological concepts--achievement motivation and sense of personal efficacy. These traits are taken to be functions of background and educational attainment and would be expected to have positive effects on both level and change in earnings.

Achievement motivation is a personality measure representing a propensity to take certain risks in situations where the outcome is ambiguous in order to derive satisfaction from overcoming obstacles by one's own efforts. People with high achievement motivation are believed to take calculated but not extreme risks and to raise their goals after successful experiences.[16]

Measures of personal efficacy gauge the extent to which a person believes personal initiative influences success or failure. Some argue that the more strongly a person believes that outcomes and personal initiative are related, "the more worthwhile initiative becomes and the more likely it is to be demonstrated."[17] Sense of personal efficacy has been shown to be affected by educational attainment and, more importantly, to relate to subsequent economic success.[18]

Both motivation and efficacy would be expected to have positive effects on earnings level and change, but these effects may not be equally strong for blacks and whites. Some psychologists have argued that the association should be strongest for groups--in this case blacks--operating in the least benign environment.[19]

Most scientists agree that cognitive skills affect earnings independently of background, educational attainment, and other skills. Economists have been more interested in the extent to which considering cognitive skills affects estimates of the returns to schooling. Some psychologists have given a much more central role to cognitive skills, coupling findings of heritability of IQ with the im-

---

[16] For a theoretical statement and empirical work on the achievement motivation concept, see Atkinson and Feather (1966).

[17] Andrisani and Nestel (1976), p. 156.

[18] Gurin and Gurin (1976), p. 156.

[19] Duncan, Featherman, and Duncan (1972).

plicit assumption of a strong association between IQ and economic success, and ending up with projections of an "heritability meritocracy."[20] Both links in this causal chain are quite weak. Goldberger has recently shown that estimates of high heritability of IQ are suspect,[21] and no comprehensive study of earnings has found a measure of cognitive skills to account for a substantial fraction of the variance in earnings.[22]

Two final measures round out the list of personal characteristics. The first, future orientation, shows the extent to which future outcomes are valued relative to present ones. We expect that future orientation will have a positive impact on earnings level--although if future orientation determines on-the-job training and if training comes at the worker's expense (in foregone earnings), then the cross-sectional association between earnings and future orientation would have a positive effect on *change* in earnings. Our test of this hypothesis is discussed in the second part of this chapter.

The final personal characteristic measure is an index of avoidance of undue or unnecessary risk. If fastening seat belts, not smoking cigarettes, and having insurance and savings are valid indicators of a propensity to avoid unnecessary risk, then our measure would show whether such a propensity has a favorable effect on success in the labor market.[23] Since some of the indicators may be affected by prior success (e.g., savings and insurance can be more easily afforded by those with higher incomes), the estimated effects of risk avoidance on *change* in earnings (given in Section IV) would be a better test of a causal connection.

Environment

At a given point in time, each labor force participant can be characterized according to his current locational and occupational situation. We included five measures of economic environment: dichotomous measures of whether the individual was employed in a white-collar occupation, worked for himself, was a member of a labor union, or resided in the South, and a continuous measure of the size of the largest city in the immediate area of residence. White-collar occupations, union

---

[20]Hernnstein (1971).

[21]Goldberger (1976), Goldberger and Lewontin (1976). See also Kamin (1974).

[22]See Jencks et al., (1972), Bowles (1973) or Bowles and Gintis (1972). Bowles, for example, estimates that the relative importance (β) of childhood IQ in explaining income differences is less than half the size of the standardized coefficient of years of schooling and socioeconomic background.

[23]It is important to emphasize that the risk measured by this index is undue or unnecessary and does *not* represent potentially beneficial entrepreneurial risk-taking

status, and urban residence were expected to have a positive association with earnings, while self-employment and Southern residence should have a negative effect. In the model, these variables intervene between prior variables and earnings. They are included because they help to show the extent to which background, education, and personal characteristics operate through occupational and locational choice.

Excluded Variables

Some variables not listed above were included in our initial model but were eventually dropped because they consistently failed to show any significant effects for either racial subgroup. The excluded variables were (1) a background measure of whether the father was foreign born, (2) a personal characteristic measure of the extent to which the respondent was connected to sources of information and help (i.e., attendance at social clubs, bars, church, and so on), (3) the education level of the respondent's father-in-law, and (4) an environmental variable measuring whether the respondent was employed in government or construction industries.

Estimation Procedures and Dubious Assumptions

Each equation in the set of recursive equations that comprise the model were estimated by ordinary least squares. The validity of this procedure depends upon whether there are any omitted variables which correlate with included variables in each equation and also upon the independence of the error terms in each equation. These are strong assumptions which deserve some discussion.

Unbiased estimates of the parameters of an equation depend upon the independence of each individual variable from the error term. When a variable which ought to be in an equation is omitted from it, then included variables correlated with the omitted variables will generally be biased, with the size and direction of the bias depending upon the size and direction of the relationships between included, omitted, and dependent variables.[24]

It is likely that important variables have been omitted from the personal characteristics equations. Most of the personal characteristics, especially cognitive skills and achievement motivation, are thought to have early roots (in the case of the genetic component of cognitive skills, at the moment of conception). In this model, each personal characteristic is estimated as a function of background, age, and completed education. But the adult level of each should also be a function of its level during childhood—that is, adult motivation should be a function of childhood motivation, background, age, and completed education.

---

[24]Kmenta (1971), pp. 392-395.

Leaving out the childhood motivation level would *overstate* the effects on adult motivation of such correlated variables as education. While the omission is probably not a serious one for estimating the overall effects of education on the ultimate variable--earnings, it may affect estimates of the extent to which education operates through the personal characteristics. The size of these indirect effects are treated here as upper bound estimates.

As was mentioned above, there may also be problems with the assumption about independent error terms. This assumption may not hold if any omitted variables affect several dependent variables. Consider, for instance, "occupational aspirations," which are formed before the completion of schooling. Such aspirations would affect the amount of schooling attained and so they belong in the education equation. These aspirations may also affect the environmental equation of whether the respondent works in a white-collar or blue-collar occupation.[25] As a result, the education-occupational choice relationship is not completely causal, and estimates of it would overstate the causal relationship.

II. RESULTS FOR EARNINGS LEVEL

In discussing the results, we begin with the factors closest to earnings in the causal chain--environmental variables--and then proceed to personal characteristics, educational attainment, and family background. Moving backwards should facilitate the discussion of indirect effects for early variables since subsequent links will be known and, it is hoped, understood.

Environmental Variables

The estimated effects of environmental variables on earnings were obtained from the regression of earnings on the environmental variables, personal characteristics, education, background, and years of work experience. Raw score (i.e., *not* standardized) coefficients and standard errors for the environmental variables from these regressions are given in Table 6.1. Coefficients which are significantly different from zero at the 1 percent probability level are marked with two asterisks; those significant at the 5 percent level are denoted with a single asterisk; and those significant at the 10 percent level are marked with a cross.

In general, environmental variables showed the expected effects on earnings and these effects were usually similar in magnitude for whites and blacks. The ".199" coefficient in the "white collar" row and "white males" column means that after the effects of all other variables in the analysis (including background,

---

[25]Blinder (1974) recognizes this.

Table 6.1

TOTAL EFFECTS OF ENVIRONMENTAL VARIABLES ON $\ln$ AVERAGE
1970-1971 WAGE RATE FOR MEN
(Controlling for Background, Educational Attainment,
Personal Characteristics, and Experience)

Environmental Variable	White Males	Black Males
White Collar	.199**	.134**
	(.029)	(.045)
Self-Employed	-.494**	-1.005**
	(.044)	(.183)
Whether Union	.215**	.158**
	(.029)	(.036)
Whether South	-.066	-.075†
	(.043)	(.043)
City Size (in thousands)	.00010**	.00030**
	(.00002)	(.00006)
Number of Observations	1,254	423

NOTE: Numbers on the table are raw score regression coefficients, with standard
errors in parentheses.

**Significantly different from zero at .01 level.

† Significantly different from zero at .10 level.

Table 6.2

TOTAL AND DIRECT EFFECTS OF PERSONAL CHARACTERISTICS
ON $\ln$ AVERAGE 1970-1971 WAGE RATE FOR MEN
(Controlling for Background, Educational Attainment, and Experience)

Personal Characteristic	Total Effect		Direct Effect (Net of Environmental Variables)	
	White Males	Black Males	White Males	Black Males
Test Score	.022**	.032**	.023**	.040**
	(.008)	(.010)	(.007)	(.008)
Achievement Motivation	.003	.027**	.005	.018**
	(.005)	(.008)	(.005)	(.007)
Efficacy	.029**	.0003	.030**	.006
	(.009)	(.013)	(.008)	(.010)
Future Orientation	-.027**	.009	-.025**	.016
	(.010)	(.016)	(.010)	(.014)
Risk Avoidance	.029**	.032**	.024**	.034**
	(.005)	(.008)	(.004)	(.007)

NOTE: Numbers on the table are raw score regression coefficients, with standard
errors in parentheses.

**Significantly different from zero at .01 level.

education, personal characteristics, and work experience) were taken into account, white-collar whites earned an average of 19.9 percent more money per hour than blue-collar whites--a highly significant difference. The wage advantage of white-collar work for blacks was also positive and significant but somewhat smaller in magnitude--13.4 percent.

Union membership and urban residence conferred highly significant, positive wage advantages on both blacks and whites; the union/nonunion differential was over 20 percent for whites and just over 15 percent for blacks.[26] Larger cities were associated with a larger wage effect for blacks than whites.

The final two environmental variables--self-employment and living in the South--showed the expected negative association with earnings, although the effects of living in the South were not significant at the 10 percent level for whites and not significant at the 5 percent level for blacks. Self-employed workers often work many more hours than those who work for others and this certainly contributed to the large negative effect of self-employment on hourly earnings.[27] The implausibly high "-1.005" coefficient for blacks was based on an extremely small number of observations.[28]

Including environmental variables in this analysis has enabled us to estimate the extent to which the effects of prior variables operate *through* them and *independently* of them. Let us turn now to an examination of each of these prior variables.

Personal Characteristics

Each of the five measures of personal characteristics--test score, achievement motivation, efficacy, future orientation, and risk avoidance--was hypothesized to have a positive effect on earnings. The results presented in Table 6.2 show that the total effects of only two variables--test score and risk avoidance--were positive and significant for both blacks and whites. The three addi-

---

[26] These differences are similar in magnitude to those obtained from similar data sets. Ashenfelter and Johnson (1972) review this evidence but also propose a simultaneous model that gives considerably *lower* estimates of the union wage effect.

[27] It should be noted that panel study procedures allocated income of the self-employed between capital and labor components. The wage rate used here is based only on the labor part, with no correction for differential tax treatment. Other factors that may contribute to lower earnings for self-employed are the nonpecuniary aspects of their work.

[28] This large coefficient implies that an additive model is not completely appropriate for blacks. Since the self-employment variable plays an extremely minor role as an intervening variable, alternative model specifications were not attempted.

tional measures either worked as expected for only one of the two racial sub-groups or, in the case of future orientation, worked in the negative direction.

Test Score. Regardless of race, the men with high test scores earned sig-nificantly more than those with low test scores. Each correct answer in the 13-question test sequence was associated with an additional 3.2 percent wage advan-tage for blacks and a 2.2 percent wage gain for whites.

These total effects of test score on earnings can be separated into direct effects that are independent of environment and the indirect effect that oper-ates through environment. Results for the direct effects are shown in Table 6.2 and in the second column of Table 6.3, while those for the indirect effects are shown in the final six columns of Table 6.3. The underscored figures for the indirect effects are those for which both coefficients of earnings on environ-ment and environment on personal characteristics were significant at the 5 per-cent level.

In general, environmental variables mediated very little of the test score-earnings relationship. Test scores generally had insignificant effects on the environmental variables. For blacks, the only significant path was a negative one between test score and union status, but the size of that indirect effect was one-tenth the size of the direct effect of test score on earnings.[29] For whites, no path leading from test score to environmental variables was signifi-cant.

Risk Avoidance. The index of avoidance of unnecessary risk had highly sig-nificant and equal total effects on earnings for whites and blacks. Almost none of this total effect operated through environmental measures, with the exception of a small indirect effect through choice of white-collar occupation for both whites and blacks. In other words, those who were more averse to risk-taking earned more, partly because they tended to have white-collar occupations, and those in white-collar occupations earned more, but mostly for reasons not meas-ured by our environmental variables.

Achievement Motivation. As Table 6.2 shows, the achievement motivation var-iable had a significant positive effect on earnings for blacks and had virtually no effect for whites. This differential is consistent with the notion that moti-vation may be superfluous in the benign environment most whites face, but it emerges as an important characteristic for blacks whose labor market environment is more hostile. While most of the total effect for blacks was direct, there was an interesting indirect effect (shown in Table 6.3) operating through city

---

[29]The size of the path between test score and union status can be calculated by directing the indirect effect of test score on earnings listed in Table 6.3 (-.004) by the direct effect of union status on earnings listed in Table 6.1 (.158).

Table 6.3

ACCOUNTING FOR THE EFFECTS OF SELECTED PERSONAL CHARACTERISTICS
ON $\mathcal{L}n$ AVERAGE 1970–1971 WAGE RATE FOR MEN

Population Subgroup and Variable	Total Effects	=	Direct Effects	+	Indirect Effects					
					White Collar	Self-Employed	Whether Union	Whether South	City Size	Other
White Males										
Test Score	.022		.023		.002	.002	-.002	--	-.001	-.002
Efficacy	.029		.030		.003	-.002	.001	-.001	-.002	--
Future Orientation	-.027		-.025		-.001	-.002	--	--	--	.001
Risk Avoidance	.029		.024		.003	--	.001	--	.001	--
Black Males										
Test Score	.032		.040		.001	.002	-.004	--	-.004	-.003
Achievement Motivation	.027		.018		.001	.001	.003	--	.008	-.004
Risk Avoidance	.032		.034		.002	.001	-.001	--	-.003	--

NOTE: "--" denotes indirect effects less than .0005.

Indirect effects where both paths are significantly different from zero at .05 level are underscored.

MTR #7119

size. Blacks with achievement motivation were likely to be living in a large
city (controlling for such background variables as growing up on a farm) and
large cities were associated with higher earnings. Perhaps one mechanism in the
motivation/earnings relationship is rural-urban migration.

Efficacy and Future Orientation. The effects of efficacy and future orientation on earnings were significant for whites but not for blacks. For whites,
efficacy had the expected positive sign, but the relationship between future orientation and earnings was negative. These results are somewhat surprising because, if anything, efficacy should have worked better for blacks than whites
for the same reasons given above for the motivation measure. The future-orienta-
tion result was also contrary to expectation but may stem from the problem that
this index and earnings were measured at roughly the same point in time. It
would be more logical to expect *prior* future orientation to have a positive effect on subsequent economic success; for this reason the results presented in
the last half of this chapter, relating initial future orientation to *change* in
earnings, should be of interest. As explained earlier, one's currently held future orientation may lead to current on-the-job training and, consequently, currently depressed earnings levels. That training opportunities were probably more
readily available to whites than blacks may explain our findings about future
orientation.

Educational Attainment

Most earnings models assign a primary role to education either because education improves productivity-related skills or because it provides a highly visible set of credentials that employers can use to screen job applicants. Results presented in Table 6.4 show that each additional year of education conferred an earnings advantage of about 6 percent on both whites and blacks.[30] The
5.9 and 6.0 percent coefficients represent the total effects of education on
earnings, netting out only the effects of background variables and years of work
experience.

A large part of this earnings advantage was indirect. The ratio of direct
effects (net of all other variables) to total effects was about one-half (.29/.59)
for whites and less than one-quarter (.14/.60) for blacks.

About 25 percent of the total effect of education on earnings for whites

---

[30]This finding of similar coefficients on education for blacks and whites is
contrary to previous work which has found higher coefficients for whites than
blacks. (Blinder [1973], Akin and Garfinkel [1974].) Note that when the effects
of test score, occupation, and other personal characteristics and environmental
measures have been accounted for, the coefficients for whites are twice as high
as those for blacks.

184

Table 6.4

TOTAL, DIRECT, AND INDIRECT EFFECTS OF EDUCATIONAL ATTAINMENT
ON ln AVERAGE 1970–1971 WAGE RATE FOR MEN
(Controlling for Background and Experience)

	White Males	Black Males
Total Effect (of an additional year of education)	.059** (.005)	.060** (.007)
Direct Effect (net of personal characteristics and environment)	.029** (.006)	.014* (.007)
Indirect Effect		
Test Score	.005	.012
Achievement Motivation	--	.005
Efficacy	.004	--
Future Orientation	-.001	--
Risk Avoidance	.009	.010
White Collar	.014	.006
Self-employed	.002	.003
Whether Union	-.008	.002
Whether South	--	.002
City Size (in thousands)	.001	.008
Other	.004	-.002

NOTE: Total and direct effect numbers are raw score regression coefficients with standard errors in parentheses.

"--" denotes indirect effects less than .0005.

Indirect effects where both paths are significantly different from zero at .05 level are underscored.

** Significantly different from zero at .01 level ⎫ Apply to Total and
* Significantly different from zero at .05 level ⎬ Direct Effects Only

MTR #7119

operated through entry into a white-collar occupation. Additional years of education were associated with an increased likelihood of being in a white-collar occupation and, as we saw before, whites in white-collar occupations earned substantially more than whites in blue-collar jobs. This indirect effect was more than twice as large for whites as for blacks. The effect for blacks was small both because the payoff to a white-collar occupation was smaller for blacks and also because the effect of each additional year of education on the probability of being in a white-collar job was considerably lower for blacks than for whites (4.2 percent vs. 7.1 percent).[31] Education, then, seemed to promote entry into white-collar occupations much more for whites than for blacks.

For blacks, education had its most powerful indirect effect by operating through the test score variable. Blacks with more education earned more, and because education increases cognitive skills (or at least ability to take tests), these increased skills paid off in higher earnings.[32] This indirect effect was much stronger for blacks than for whites (.012 vs. .005), both because higher test scores had a greater impact on the earnings of blacks (see Table 6.2) and because education increased test scores by 50 percent more for blacks than whites.

Approximately one-sixth of the relationship between education and earnings for both racial subgroups was explained by risk avoidance. Men with more education tended to be less inclined to take unnecessary risks, which, in turn, seemed to pay off in a similar way for the earnings of both groups. It is important to find such intervening variables because they help to explain the earnings determination process. It is disappointing that we were unable to account for the risk-avoidance/earnings relationship with environmental variables but this may serve to underscore the importance of future work on that topic.

The remaining intervening variables had smaller roles to play in explaining why education affects earnings. For whites, those with more education scored significantly higher on the efficacy scale, were more oriented toward the future,[33] were less likely to be in union jobs, and resided in larger cities. For blacks, educational attainment had a positive, significant association with achievement motivation, living outside the South, and living in large cities.

---

[31] These results are not shown in the table but can be calculated by dividing the indirect effect by the effect of white-collar on earnings.

[32] Since early cognitive skills may effect both education and cognitive skills measured at a later point in life, this interpretation is quite speculative.

[33] The indirect effect for future orientation is negative because it is the product of a positive effect of education on future orientation and a negative effect of future orientation on earnings.

The education/attitude relationships were as expected and, for the most part, were similar to those found by other researchers.[34] That whites with more education should spurn union jobs is reasonable in light of the fact that there is virtually no payoff to additional years of education for union work.[35] The education/location association may relate to migration behavior of the more highly educated.

Background Variables

Results for the various background measures are presented in Table 6.5. In general, the total effects of the variables operated in the expected directions and were usually more significant for whites than for blacks. A comparison of the total and direct effects listed in Table 6.5 showed that virtually all of the total effects could be accounted for by the intervening education, personal characteristic, and environmental variables. The indirect effects, then, warrant closer attention.

Parents' Educational Attainment. Total effects of parents' educational levels on earnings were positive and significant. Each additional year of the father's education was associated with a 1.6 percent increase in average earnings for whites and a 2.9 percent increase for blacks. The wage advantage associated with increased mother's education was small for whites (.8 percent) but was similar to the father's effect for blacks (2.3 percent).

How did these total effects operate? Table 6.6 shows that much of the effects of parents' attainments operated through the individuals own level of education. Both blacks and whites with more highly educated parents received more education themselves and this increased schooling, in turn, has been shown to have a strong direct effect on earnings. For whites, this indirect effect accounts for almost one-third of the total effect of the father's education and one-half of the total effects of the mother's education.

Part of the father's education/earnings relationship was explained by the association between the father's education and the son's test score. It is somewhat surprising that there wasn't also a similar association between the mother's education and test score since the environmental component of cognitive skills is thought to be mainly influenced by the mother and the genetic component should have roughly equal effects from both parents.[36]

---

[34] Gurin (1971).

[35] Dickinson (1974) and Johnson and Youmans (1971).

[36] In Duncan (1974), it is shown that the mother's education level has a significantly more important effect on test score than the father's education. This

Table 6.5

TOTAL AND DIRECT EFFECTS OF BACKGROUND VARIABLES
ON ln AVERAGE 1970–1971 WAGE RATE FOR MEN
(Controlling for Years of Work Experience)

Background Variable	Total Effect		Direct Effect (Net of Education, Personal Characteristics, and Environment)	
	White Males	Black Males	White Males	Black Males
Father's Education	.016** (.005)	.029** (.007)	.004 (.004)	.017** (.006)
Mother's Education	.008† (.005)	.023** (.008)	.005 (.004)	-.003 (.006)
Whether Catholic	.104** (.035)	.073 (.083)	.042 (.030)	.053 (.064)
Whether Jewish	.283** (.063)	--	.184** (.056)	--
Grew up South	-.085* (.033)	-.142* (.061)	.030 (.044)	.023 (.053)
Grew up Farm	-.182** (.033)	-.082† (.049)	-.051† (.029)	.065† (.039)
Number of Siblings	-.018** (.006)	.005 (.003)	.001 (.006)	.006 (.007)

NOTE: Numbers on the table are raw score regression coefficients with standard errors in parentheses.

**Significantly different from zero at .01 level.

* Significantly different from zero at .05 level.

† Significantly different from zero at .10 level.

MTR #7119

Table 6.6

ACCOUNTING FOR THE EFFECTS OF FATHER'S AND MOTHER'S EDUCATION
ON ℓn AVERAGE 1970-1971 WAGE RATE FOR MEN

	Father's Education		Mother's Education	
	White Males	Black Males	White Males	Black Males
Total Effect (of an additional year of parental education)	.016	.029	.008	.023
Direct Effect (net of education, personal characteristics, and environment)	.004	.017	.005	-.003
Indirect Effect				
Education	.005	.003	.004	.003
Test Score	.001	.004	--	-.002
Achievement Motivation	--	-.002	--	.001
Efficacy	--	--	.001	--
Future Orientation	--	.001	-.001	.001
Risk Avoidance	.001	.002	.001	.003
White Collar	.001	.001	--	.001
Self-employed	.001	.001	-.003	.002
Whether Union	-.002	.001	-.002	.004
Whether South	--	--	--	.001
City Size	.001	-.005	--	.002
Other	.004	.006	.003	.010

NOTE: "--" denotes indirect effects less than .0005.

Indirect paths where both paths are significantly different from zero at .05 level are underscored.

MTR #7119

There were, in addition, some small indirect effects which operated through the environmental variables. They do not lend themselves to ready interpretation and will merely be listed. For whites, the father's education operated indirectly by having a negative effect on the likelihood of becoming a union member; the mother's education had a negative association with the likelihoods of both becoming self-employed and becoming a union member. For the blacks, increases in the father's education had a negative effect on size of current city of residence, while the mother's education had a positive relationship with union membership.

A Brief Digression on Background, Education, and Attitudes. One of the ways that the background variables in general, and parental attainments in particular, are thought to affect earnings is by helping to form advantageous attitudes and skills in childhood. Since child care is usually the responsibility of the mother, her attainment was expected to have stronger indirect effects through attitudes than the father's attainment. Table 6.6 showed that there were actually only a few of these indirect effects. This was due in part, however, to the weak links between the attitudes themselves and earnings, a weakness which may stem from the simultaneous measurement of attitudes and earnings that was discussed earlier.

Since the determinants of the attitudes themselves were of interest, we report in Table 6.7 the regression results obtained when each attitude was treated as a dependent variable with background, education, and age as independent variables. Although the fraction of the variance in these attitudinal measures that could be explained by the predictors was generally quite low, two variables showed consistently positive and significant effects: the educational attainment of the mother and the individual's own education level. After accounting for the effects of the father's education level, the respondent's own education, and other background variables, the mother's education level had a significant association with all these attitudes (at the 10 percent level for two of the attitudes) for both racial groups; the relationship with future orientation was especially strong. In contrast, the results for the father's education were never positive and significant and, for two of the attitudes for blacks, were significant and *negative*. It is also important to note that the religion variables were not important in these equations, casting doubt on the hypothesis that differences in child-rearing practices between religious groups instill differentially

---

analysis did not include the individual's own education, however. Sewell and Hauser (1975), on the other hand, find that the father's education level is more important than the mother's, even after controlling for the father's occupation and for parental income.

Table 6.7

EFFECTS OF BACKGROUND, EDUCATIONAL ATTAINMENT, AND AGE ON ATTITUDES

Background Variable	White Males			Black Males		
	Achievement Motivation	Efficacy	Future Orientation	Achievement Motivation	Efficacy	Future Orientation
Father's Education	-.010 (.024)	.006 (.015)	-.016 (.012)	-.128** (.046)	.018 (.027)	-.047* (.021)
Mother's Education	.060* (.024)	.031* (.015)	.034* (.012)	.082† (.048)	.049† (.029)	.077** (.022)
Catholic	.251 (.178)	.184† (.112)	.022 (.090)	-.223 (.518)	.056 (.308)	.114 (.237)
Jewish	-.112 (.324)	-.327† (.204)	-.152 (.165)	---	---	---
Grew up South	-.128 (.174)	-.002 (.110)	.167† (.089)	.412 (.380)	-.189 (.225)	-.014 (.174)
Grew up Farm	-.299† (.170)	.076 (.107)	.120 (.086)	-.689* (.311)	.129 (.185)	-.308* (.143)
Number of Siblings	.036 (.033)	.013 (.021)	.009 (.017)	-.048 (.053)	-.048 (.031)	.003 (.024)
Education	.255** (.028)	.149** (.018)	.034* (.014)	.264** (.050)	.092** (.030)	.018 (.023)
Age	-.003 (.009)	.018** (.006)	-.007† (.004)	.0005 (.012)	.010 (.010)	.014† (.008)
R^2	.114	.086	.023	.129	.077	.066

NOTE: Numbers on the table are raw score regression coefficients, with standard errors in parentheses.

**Significantly different from zero at .01 level.
* Significantly different from zero at .05 level.
† Significantly different from zero at .10 level.

advantageous values and motivation.[37]

The individual's own level of education had an even stronger association with most of the attitudinal measures, especially the achievement motivation and efficacy variables. The causality of the education/attitudes relationship is somewhat ambiguous, however, since early attitudes could influence the amount of education attained.

To summarize, the extent to which one's own education and background operate through attitudes in affecting earnings depends on two links in a causal chain. First, background and education must influence attitudes and, second, the attitudes need to have a significant effect on earnings. Evidence for the first half of the link has been found for two variables--the mother's education level and the individual's own educational attainment. Evidence on the second half is mixed.

Southern and Rural Background. Growing up in the South or growing up on a farm were associated with lower wage rates for both blacks and whites (Table 6.5). White respondents with southern upbringing earned 8.5 percent less than individuals who did not grow up in the South but had otherwise comparable background and work experience. For blacks, the deficit was higher--14.2 percent. Rural background also had a negative effect on earnings, but this effect was considerably higher for whites (-18.2 percent wage difference) than blacks (-8.2 percent).

How do these two background measures operate to effect earnings? When the respondent's own education, personal characteristics, and current location and occupation were taken into account, these background variables showed virtually no significant effect. In fact, three of the four direct effects were *positive* rather than negative.

The indirect effects of these background variables on earnings are shown in Table 6.8. Not surprisingly, men who grew up in the South earned less because they generally still lived in southern states which, in turn, are associated with lower earnings. Similarly, men growing up on farms earned less because they tended to be self-employed or to have blue-collar jobs (many were farmers) and these two occupational groups earned less. The farm background/current occupation link was much stronger for whites than blacks, making the indirect effect larger for whites.

Rural and southern background affected earnings in other ways as well. Men who grew up on a farm and, for whites, in the South, had lower educational at-

---

[37]This negative evidence is consistent with that presented in Featherman (1971). It should also be noted, however, that the results for Jews were based on a relatively small number of observations.

Table 6.8

ACCOUNTING FOR THE EFFECTS OF GROWING UP IN THE SOUTH
OR ON A FARM ON ln AVERAGE 1970-1971 WAGE RATE FOR MEN

| | Grew up South | | Grew up Farm | |
	White Males	Black Males	White Males	Black Males
Total Effect	-.085	-.142	-.182	-.082
Direct Effect (Net of Education, Personal Characteristics and Environment	.038	.023	-.051	.065
Indirect Effect				
Education	-.017	-.009	-.010	-.017
Test Score	-.001	-.065	-.006	-.024
Achievement Motivation	--	.007	-.001	-.012
Efficacy	--	.001	.002	.001
Future Orientation	-.004	--	-.003	-.005
Risk Avoidance	-.009	-.010	.001	-.013
White Collar	.009	.010	-.019	-.012
Self-employed	.004	.003	-.040	-.011
Whether Union	-.019	-.004	-.020	.001
Whether South	-.051	-.046	--	.007
City Size	-.004	-.038	-.019	-.005
Other	-.031	-.014	-.016	.057

NOTE: "--" denotes indirect effects less than .0005.

Indirect effects where both paths are significantly different from zero
at .05 level are underscored.

MTR #7119

tainment which, in turn, led to lower wage rates. For blacks, both background measures operated by lowering test scores. Since the test score/earnings relationship was especially important for blacks, these indirect effects were quite large. It is likely that southern and rural residence for blacks picked up some effects of educational *quality* which would be expected to influence current cognitive skills.

An additional indirect effect operated through a personal characteristic. Blacks who grew up on a farm had significantly less achievement motivation. Since motivation had a positive effect on earnings for blacks, the sign of this indirect effect was negative.

These two background variables had two additional indirect effects which operated through city size and union status. Blacks who had grown up in the South were less likely to be living in large cities, and, as a result, earned less. Interestingly, of the persons who had grown up on farms only the whites earned less because they lived in less urban areas. For blacks, rural background had no relationship with current city size, suggesting much greater residential mobility for blacks than whites. For whites only, southern and rural origins decreased the likelihood of becoming a union member and, since union status was associated with high earnings, there was a negative indirect effect for whites. These two background variables had no significant effect on the union status of blacks.

Religion and Family Size. For whites, measures of religion and number of siblings had highly significant total effects on earnings, as shown in Table 6.5. After controlling for the effects of other background variables, Catholics earned 10.4 percent more and Jews earned 28.3 percent more than the omitted group composed mostly of protestants. The direction and statistical significance of these effects are similar to those found by Taubman on a large sample of air force veterans.[38] Family size had a negative impact on earnings, with each additional sibling associated with a 1.8 percent decrease in hourly earnings. Table 6.5 also shows that the *direct* effects of these variables were considerably smaller than their total effects, suggesting important roles for the intervening variables.

The total, direct, and indirect effects of the religion and family size variables for whites are given in Table 6.9. Not surprisingly, education played an important role in the explanation of the religion and family size effects. When the effects of all background variables and age were taken into account, both Catholics and Jews received more education than Protestants and this addi-

---

[38]Taubman (1975). Since Taubman's equations contain some intervening variables, they are somewhere in between our total and direct effects.

194

Table 6.9

ACCOUNTING FOR THE EFFECTS OF RELIGION AND
NUMBER OF SIBLINGS ON ln AVERAGE 1970–1971 WAGE RATE
FOR WHITE MALES

	Whether Catholic	Whether Jewish	Number of Siblings
Total Effect	.104	.283	−.018
Direct Effect (Net of Education, Personal Characteristics, and Environment)	.042	.184	.001
Indirect Effect			
Education	.011	.039	−.008
Test Score	−.003	.007	.001
Achievement Motivation	.001	--	--
Efficacy	.006	−.011	--
Future Orientation	−.001	.004	--
Risk Avoidance	−.002	.012	−.001
White Collar	.013	.029	.001
Self-employed	−.008	−.053	−.001
Whether Union	.004	−.024	--
Whether South	.002	.001	--
City Size	.022	.038	−.001
Other	.017	.057	.010

NOTE: "--" denotes indirect effects less than .0005.

Indirect effects where both paths are significantly different from zero at .05 level are underscored.

MTR #7119

tional education, in turn, paid off with higher earnings. Those in larger families received *less* education. This is not surprising since parents with large families would generally be less able to afford to educate their children.

For the two religious groups there were additional indirect effects that operated through environment; surprisingly, however, none operated through attitudes, behavior, or test score.[39] Both Catholics and Jews earned more than Protestants because they were more likely to be in white-collar occupations and to live in large cities, both of which were associated with higher earnings. Two additional indirect effects for Jews were negative: Jews were more likely than Protestants to be self-employed (and self-employment had a *negative* earnings effect) and were less likely to be union members (who, other things being equal, earned more than nonunion members). Taken together, these results suggest that the effects of religion do *not* operate through the development of skills and attitudes, as was previously thought, but rather by placing individuals in favorable locations and jobs.

Work Experience

Cross-sectional Census data for white males clearly show that earnings increase steadily with age, peaking around age 50.[40] Mincer and other students of human capital theory argue that this increase results from individual investment in on-the-job training in early years of working life which pays off in later years. Others, such as Rosen, attempt to describe the training process more realistically in terms of the sequence of jobs that individuals hold during their working lives.[41]

In our model, work experience is an exogenous variable that is expected to have indirect effects operating through the environmental variables.[42] The total effect (which is estimated *without* these environmental variables), direct effect,

---

[39]Although the size of some of these indirect effects may appear substantial, none of these personal characteristics was significantly predicted (at the 5 percent level) by the religion dummy variables. These results are quite similar to those of Featherman (1972), who reports that "the adult motivational variables [primary work orientation, materialistic orientation, and subjective achievement evaluation] do not function as intervening variables between religio-ethnic background and socioeconomic career achievements." (p. 120)

[40]Mincer (1974), pp. 65-70.

[41]A discussion of the competing theories which explain age-earnings profile is given in Chapter 7 of this volume.

[42]The effect of work experience is restricted to a linear form. The maximum age of those in the sample in 1970 was 50 years.

and indirect effects of years of work experience on earnings are reported in Table 6.10.

Work experience had a powerful positive total effect on the earnings of whites and an insignificant positive effect for blacks. If returns to work experience are returns to on-the-job training, then either blacks received virtually *no* post-school training or else what training they did get did not pay off in the form of higher wages. Virtually none of these total effects of work experience operated through the intervening environmental variables. For both whites and blacks, work experience had a significant, positive effect on the likelihood of being in a white-collar job. This result is consistent with Rosen's notion of a progression into high paying jobs. But, on the other hand, more years in the labor force increased the likelihood of being self-employed. Since self-employment had a negative effect on wages, this indirect effect was negative.

III. A MODEL OF EARNINGS CHANGE

A correct theory of the income determination process must be consistent not only with cross-sectional data on earnings *level*, such as those presented in the previous section, but also with longitudinal data on changes in earnings over time. Technically, models that explain earnings level of a cross section of individuals are also models of change. Indeed, in the previous section we often spoke of additional units of an independent variable (e.g., an additional year of work experience) as being associated with (influencing, affecting) a certain percentage *change* in wage rates. In the next two sections we use the longitudinal nature of a panel to measure wage changes directly and then relate these changes to a set of independent variables from a model of earnings change.

Expectations

The human capital investment model is not very helpful in understanding change in earnings if investments are not measured directly. According to this model, changes in earnings come about only from some kind of investment in on-the-job training, health, mobility, information or schooling, or possibly from "depreciation" on prior investments. In its most abstract form, the model pictures the investment process as a continuous one, although many kinds of investments (especially mobility) are quite discrete.[43] From this list of investments, only geographic and job mobility are measured in our panel study for a sufficiently large number of individuals to be included in the empirical analysis.

---

[43]Ben-Porath (1967).

Table 6.10

TOTAL, DIRECT, AND INDIRECT EFFECTS OF WORK EXPERIENCE
ON ln AVERAGE 1970-1971 WAGE RATE FOR MEN
(Controlling for Background, Education, and Attitudes)

	White Males	Black Males
Total Effect (of an Additional Year of Experience)	.015** (.002)	.003 (.002)
Direct Effect (Net of Environmental Variables)	.014** (.002)	.002 (.002)
Indirect Effect		
White Collar	.002	.001
Self-employed	-.002	-.001
Whether Union	.001	--
Whether South	--	.001
City Size (in thousands)	--	--
Other	--	--

NOTE: Total and direct effect numbers are raw score regression coefficients
with standard errors in parentheses.

"--" denotes indirect effects less than .0005.

Indirect effects where both paths are significantly different from zero
at .05 level are underscored.

**Significantly different from zero at .01 level.

MTR #7119

198

One of the few unambiguous predictions of the human capital model is that
the volume of individual investments should decline over the life cycle because
the number of years that an investment can pay off obviously declines as retirement age approaches. Declining investment amounts imply declining increments to
earnings and, thus, a *negative* relationship between years of work experience and
change in earnings.[44]

Most competing explanations of the income determination process are essentially noneconomic and give a role to the personal characteristic measures, especially efficacy and achievement motivation. Indeed, change data allow a much
better test of the attitude/earnings relationship because initial attitudes can
be related to subsequent earnings change.[45] At least two studies have found such
a relationship for an efficacy measure.[46]

Environmental factors may also account for some of the variations in earnings change. Labor unions, for example, negotiate multiyear wage contracts with
job security provisions and many have provided members with greater real income
increases during the 1970-1974 period.

The Model

Our model of earnings change is depicted in Figure 6.2. The same measures
of background, education, personal characteristics, work experience, and environment that were included in the model of earning level are treated as exogenous
variables which relate to both ln average 1970-1971 wage rate, changes in environment between 1971 and 1974, and, finally, ln average 1973-1974 wage rate.
Omitting the environmental change variables, the model can be written as

(5) $\quad Wage_{73-74} = \alpha + \beta_1 Wage_{70-71} + \sum_i \beta_{2i} X_i + u_i$

where $Wage_{73-74}$ is the natural logarithm of average deflated
1973 and 1974 wage rate; $Wage_{70-71}$ is the natural logarithm
of average deflated 1970 and 1971 wage rate; and X_i represents
the background, education, personal characteristics, and environmental variables defined in Section I; u_i is an error term.

---

[44]Whether the negative wage change/work experience relationship is *linear* depends upon the functional form of changes in investments. Only the linear relationship is estimated here. The negative relationship will not necessarily hold
if maturity affects the rate of return to human capital investments.

[45]Since change in attitudes might affect changes in earnings, a complete model
would consist of two simultaneous equations with each of the change measures as
dependent variables and a sufficient number of exogenous variables included in
one equation but excluded from the other to identify the system.

[46]Andrisani and Nestel (1976) and Gurin and Gurin (1976).

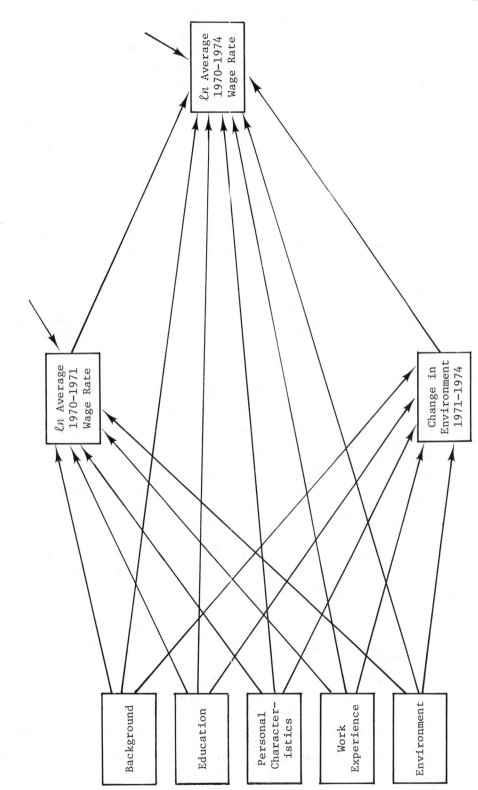

Figure 6.2

PATH MODEL OF EARNINGS CHANGE

Subtracting Wage_{70-71} from both sides, this equation can be rewritten as:

$$(6) \qquad \text{Wage}_{73-74} - \text{Wage}_{70-71} = \alpha_1 + (\beta_1 - 1) \text{Wage}_{70-71} + \sum_i \beta_{2i} X_i + u_i.$$

With this formulation, it can be seen that we are explaining *change* in (the log of) wage rates as a function of initial wage rate and the initial level of the exogenous variables. Equation 6 is used to estimate the *total* effects of the exogenous variables on earnings change. To account for these total effects, we include various measures of environmental change between 1971 and 1974. Specifically, these variables are:

1. <u>Became union member</u>--a dichotomous variable which equals 1 if the "whether union" variable defined earlier equals 0 and the respondent reported membership in a labor union in 1974, and 0 otherwise.

2. <u>Became white collar</u>--a dichotomous variable which equals 1 if the "white collar" variable defined earlier equals 0 and the respondent reported a white collar occupation in 1974, and 0 otherwise.

3. <u>Became self-employed</u>--a dichotomous variable which equals 1 if the "self-employed" variable defined earlier equals 1 and the respondent reported working for himself in 1974, and 0 otherwise.

4. <u>Whether involuntary job change</u>--a dichotomous variable which equals 1 if the respondent reported in 1973, 1974, or 1975 that he lost his job because company went out of business, respondent was laid off, fired, locked out, or on strike, and 0 otherwise.

5. <u>Whether moved to different county</u>--a dichotomous variable which equals 1 if the respondent lived in different counties in 1975 and 1970, and 0 otherwise.

6. <u>Whether moved to a bigger city</u>--a dichotomous variable which equals 1 if the respondent changed residence between 1970 and 1975 and the size of the largest city in the county of residence increased, and 0 otherwise.

These change variables intervene between the exogenous measures and earnings change just as, for example, the environmental variables carried the indirect effects of the personal characteristics on wage *level* as reported in Section II.

IV. RESULTS FOR EARNINGS CHANGE

The total and direct effects of the exogenous variables in explaining changes in wages are shown in Table 6.11.[47] Since the size of the coefficients

---

[47]The table also shows the coefficients on the ℓn average 1971-72 variable (corresponding to β_1 from equations 5 and 6). The R^2 of the equations which did not include the environmental change variables are .601 for whites and .723 for blacks. When the change measures are included, the R^2 increases to .610 for whites and .749 for blacks.

Table 6.11 (Sheet 1 of 2)

TOTAL AND DIRECT EFFECTS OF BACKGROUND, EDUCATION,
PERSONAL CHARACTERISTICS, WORK EXPERIENCE, AND
ENVIRONMENTAL VARIABLES ON CHANGE IN ℓn AVERAGE WAGE RATE

	Total Effects		Direct Effects (Net of Change in Enviornment)	
	White Males	Black Males	White Males	Black Males
Father's Education	.002 (.003)	.004 (.005)	.002 (.003)	.003 (.005)
Mother's Education	-.004 (.003)	.019** (.005)	-.003 (.003)	.026** (.005)
Catholic	.030 (.024)	-.009 (.055)	.033 (.024)	-.027 (.053)
Jewish	.011 (.045)	--	.036 (.045)	--
Grew up South	-.014 (.036)	-.178** (.054)	-.000 (.035)	-.215** (.045)
Grew up Farm	-.035 (.024)	-.023 (.033)	-.029 (.024)	-.038 (.031)
Number of Siblings	-.004 (.004)	-.004 (.006)	-.004 (.004)	.005 (.006)
Education	.011* (.005)	-.009 (.006)	.010* (.005)	-.013* (.006)
Test Score	.001 (.006)	.002 (.007)	-.001 (.006)	-.004 (.007)
Achievement Motivation	.002 (.004)	-.002 (.006)	.003 (.004)	-.001 (.006)
Efficacy	.006 (.006)	-.003 (.009)	.006 (.006)	-.003 (.009)
Future Orientation	-.003 (.008)	.030** (.012)	-.003 (.008)	.027* (.011)
Risk Avoidance	-.001 (.004)	.015* (.006)	-.002 (.004)	.019** (.006)
White Collar	.047* (.024)	.089* (.039)	.065** (.025)	.068† (.038)
Self-employed	.023 (.038)	.236 (.161)	.008 (.038)	.223 (.156)

202

Table 6.11 (Sheet 2 of 2)

	Total Effects		Direct Effects (Net of Change in Environment)	
	White Males	Black Males	White Males	Black Males
Whether Union	.052* (.024)	.130** (.032)	.066** (.024)	.144** (.033)
Whether South	.006 (.035)	.040 (.037)	.000 (.035)	.048 (.036)
City Size	.00012* (.00005)	-.00010* (.00005)	.00010** (.0004)	-.00004 (.00004)
Years of Work Experience	-.001 (.001)	.0044* (.0017)	-.0018 (.001)	.0054** (.0020)
ln Average 1971–1972 Wage Rate	.690** (.023)	.766** (.042)	.686** (.023)	.721** (.043)

NOTE: Numbers on the table are raw score regression coefficients with standard errors in parentheses.

**Significantly different from zero at .01 level.

* Significantly different from zero at .05 level.

† Significantly different from zero at .10 level.

do not lend themselves to ready interpretation,[48] the discussion of these results
focuses on the direction and significance of the coefficients.

As might be expected, the environmental measures were found to be the most
significant predictors of earnings changes. Both blacks and whites who worked
in white-collar jobs or who were members of labor unions did significantly better
than their blue-collar or nonunion counterparts. These regression-adjusted effects were considerably larger for blacks than whites and perhaps reflect relative differences in the amount of job security and stability that these factors
provide to blacks. Additionally, city size had strong effects on earnings change,
although they operated in opposite directions for blacks and whites. Residence in
a large city at the beginning of the panel was beneficial to whites and detrimental for blacks. After netting out the effects of environmental variables, no
other measures were significant for both blacks and whites. A number of other
factors worked for blacks alone, however, including the measures of future orientation and risk avoidance. Avoidance of unnecessary risks, then, was the only
personal characteristic which had positive and significant effects on both earnings level and change for either one of the racial subgroups. For whites, risk
avoidance significantly increased earnings level but had no effect on subsequent
earnings change.

Surprisingly, two background measures showed significant effects for blacks.
Increased levels of the mother's educational attainment had a positive relationship with change, while growing up in the South was detrimental. These results
are puzzling and, unfortunately, the intervening measures of change in environment do little to aid our understanding of those effects.

Years of work experience had a *positive* and significant effect on earnings
change for blacks. This is inconsistent with a theory of declining investments
in on-the-job training over the life cycle and may be caused by the relatively
greater seniority and job security for blacks with longer work experience.

For whites, more education led to greater changes in earnings, perhaps because men with more schooling acquired larger amounts of subsequent training.[49]
This education/earnings change relationship did not hold for blacks, however.

Changes in Environment

To help explain the relationship between the exogenous predictor variables

---

[48]Coefficients show the association between a unit change in the independent
variable and percentage change in average 1973-74 wage rate, after the effects
of $\ln$ average 1970-71 wage rate have been partialed out.

[49]Taubman (1975) also found a positive and significant effect of education on
earnings change for his sample of white Air Force Veterans.

and earnings change, we included six measures of possible changes in job and residence that may have occurred between 1970 and 1974. Four relate directly to job change—joining a union, moving into a white-collar or self-employed occupation, and experiencing an involuntary job change. Two additional measures concern residential mobility—making an intercounty move and moving to a larger city.

Before discussing these variables in the context of earnings change, it is interesting to look first at how well the exogenous variables predict these measures. The results of these regressions are presented in compact form in Table 6.12. Only the direction and significance of coefficients are noted in this table.[50] Some of the environmental variables have definitional associations with some dependent variables—e.g., beginning as a union member and becoming one. They are included as control variables. Most of the significant variables, however, are not definitional and deserve discussion.

Work experience had many significant effects on these environmental change variables, especially for the measures of residential mobility. Older men moved less often. This has been observed by many other researchers, including those who have analyzed the panel data.[51] Additional years in the labor force also reduced the likelihood of an involuntary job change, perhaps through its connection with seniority. Interestingly, additional work experience also increased the likelihood of becoming self-employed—but only for blacks.

Some environmental variables also affected environmental change in interesting ways. Among blacks, union members were less likely to experience involuntary job changes, to move across county lines, or to move into white-collar or self-employed occupations. Only the occupational effects also showed up for whites. Blacks who were working in large cities at the beginning of the panel period had a higher likelihood of joining a union or entering a white-collar occupation; this was not observed for whites.

Some personal characteristics showed significant effects but, taken together, they did not appear to be overwhelmingly important. Achievement motivation "worked" only by increasing the likelihood of an intercounty move for blacks—a result consistent with the findings of Section II. Blacks with high initial

---

[50]The double pluses and minuses indicate significance at the .01 level, single pluses and minuses denote coefficients significant at the .05 level. Note that the dependent variables in those regressions are dichotomous and produce the usual problems associated with limited dependent variables.

[51]Roistacher (1974), Duncan and Newman (1975). The correlation between age and years of work experience is .97 for whites, .92 for blacks.

Table 6.12 (Sheet 1 of 2)

DIRECTION AND STATISTICAL SIGNIFICANCE OF BACKGROUND, EDUCATION,
PERSONAL CHARACTERISTICS, WORK EXPERIENCE, AND INITIAL ENVIRONMENT
AS PREDICTORS OF CHANGE IN ENVIRONMENT, 1970-1974

	Became Union		Became White Collar		Became Self-Employed		Involuntary Job Change		Move to Different County		Move to Bigger City	
	White	Black	White	Black	White	Black	White	Black	White	Black	White	Black
Background												
Father's Education			++									
Mother's Education					+	−						−
Catholic									−		−	
Jewish	−				++							
Grew up South			++		++	+	−	−			−	+
Grew up Farm					+							+
Siblings		+	++	+		−						
Education	−−	−	++			++						+
Personal Characteristics												
Test Score	+								++			
Achievement Motivation										+		+
Efficacy						++				−−		
Future Orientation	++									+	−	
Risk Avoidance						−	−					

Table 6.12 (Sheet 2 of 2)

	Dependent Variable											
	Became Union		Became White Collar		Became Self-Employed		Involuntary Job Change		Move to Different County		Move to Bigger City	
	White	Black	White	Black	White	Black	White	Black	White	Black	White	Black
Environment												
White Collar	--	+	+	--						+		+
Self-Employed	--				--						--	
Union	--	--	--	-	--	--		-		--		
South			-	++	--	--				-		
City Size	++	+							+		--	--
Years of Work Experience			--			++	--	--	--	--	-	--
R²	.007	.158	.164	.051	.043	.337	.046	.104	.067	.184	.093	.217

++Coefficient is positive and significantly different from zero at .01 level.

--Coefficient is negative and significantly different from zero at .01 level.

+ Coefficient is positive and significantly different from zero at .05 level.

- Coefficient is negative and significantly different from zero at .05 level.

levels of future orientation had a greater likelihood of joining a labor union and making an intercounty move. Blacks who avoided unnecessary risks tended not to become self-employed--a sensible result. For whites, the risk avoidance measure decreased the likelihood of suffering an involuntary job change. The test score measure of cognitive skills had only scattered effects--increasing the likelihood of an intercounty move for whites and the chances of moving to a bigger city or joining a labor union for blacks. The final personal character-istic, efficacy, increased the likelihood of becoming self-employed for blacks.

Educational attainment also had a fairly weak set of effects. For whites, additional years of education were associated with an increased likelihood of moving into a white-collar occupation--a result consistent with the strong edu-cation/white-collar link for whites discussed in Section II. For blacks, educa-tion had a significant positive effect on becoming self-employed and a negative effect on joining a labor union.

The background variables also showed some significant effect on the environ-mental change measures. Some were consistent with the findings discussed in the second section--for example, Jews were less likely to join unions and more like-ly to become self-employed, and growing up on a farm increased the likelihood of becoming self-employed. Other effects were intriguing and not inconsistent--for example, for whites only, there was a significant association between the fa-ther's education and moving into a white-collar occupation. Also of interest is the significant, positive association between number of siblings and the likeli-hood of moving into a white-collar occupation for both racial subgroups and join-ing a union for blacks. These findings can be given a "connection" interpreta-tion and suggest that the detrimental effect of family size on education and, hence, on initial earnings may be offset to a certain extent by subsequent bene-ficial job changes obtained informally through the help of siblings. Further evidence that this may be the case for blacks was seen in the highly significant *negative* relationship between number of siblings and the likelihood of becoming self-employed. "Connections" did not lead as readily to self-employment as they did to getting into a union or finding a better job that involved working for others.

The remaining results on these background variables ranged from the sugges-tive--e.g., Catholic whites were less likely to make intercounty moves, to the puzzling--e.g., growing up in the South helped to prevent involuntary job change for both blacks and whites.

Changes in Earnings

Although hardly armed with a complete understanding of the determinants of environmental change, let us proceed to an examination of how these changes fit into the model of earnings change. The first step is to see how the changes in environment relate to changes in earnings when the effects of all exogenous variables have been taken into account. This is shown on Table 6.13. Two of the change measures showed significant effects for both racial subgroups: becoming a union member increased earnings, while experiencing an involuntary job change decreased them. Self-employment was detrimental to the earnings of whites.[52] The two mobility measures were significant only for changes in the earnings of blacks; move to a bigger city was quite advantageous, while an intercounty move (controlling for whether it was to a bigger city) was disadvantageous. It appears that, for blacks, migration paid off only if it was to a more urban environment.

As a final step, we used these changes in environmental variables to help explain the relationship between the exogenous variables and earnings change. A glance back to Table 6.11 shows that they are not likely to be very helpful since direct effects of the exogenous variables were often quite similar to the total effects.

Table 6.14 shows how the significant total effects of Table 6.11 break down into direct and indirect effects. In keeping with the practice of Section II, indirect effects are underscored when *both* the paths leading from the exogenous variables to the environmental changes *and* those leading from changes in environment to change in earnings are significantly different from zero at the .05 level.

The indirect effects do not help us very much in understanding the overall relationships between initial environment and education level and subsequent earnings change for whites. The only result worth noting is that initial union membership was advantageous partly because it had a negative effect on becoming self-employed and those who became self-employed, in turn, did not do as well as the rest of the work force.

Indirect effects for blacks are much more interesting because they involved not only the occupational change variables, but also the migration and involuntary job change measures. Two background measures—growing up in the South and the mother's education—affected earnings change by influencing migration to a bigger city. Southern origin was associated with an *increased* likelihood of moving to a more urban area and such a move was found to increase earnings. It is interesting that *growing up* in the South should have this effect, rather than the environmental measure of whether 1970 region of residence was the South.

---

[52] Both the self-employment and union result for whites is consistent with the findings of Duncan (1974).

Table 6.13

TOTAL EFFECTS OF CHANGE IN ENVIRONMENT
ON CHANGE IN ln AVERAGE WAGE RATE
(Controlling for Background, Education, Experience,
Personal Characteristics, and 1970-1971 Environment)

	White Males	Black Males
Became Union	.133**	.181**
	(.040)	(.055)
Became White Collar	.033	-.105
	(.041)	(.152)
Became Self-Employed	-.141**	.119
	(.042)	(.095)
Whether Involuntary Job Change	-.076*	-.099*
	(.036)	(.049)
Whether Moved to Different County	-.015	-.117*
	(.029)	(.058)
Whether Moved to Bigger City	.022	.410**
	(.042)	(.080)

NOTE: Numbers on the table are raw score regression coefficients with standard errors in parentheses.

**Significantly different from zero at .01 level.

* Significantly different from zero at .05 level.

Table 6.14

ACCOUNTING FOR THE EFFECTS OF VARIOUS EXOGENOUS VARIABLES ON CHANGE IN ℓn AVERAGE WAGE RATE

Population Subgroup and Variable	Total Effect	= Direct + Effect	Became Union	Became White Collar	Indirect Effect — Became Self-Employed	Involuntary Job Change	Moved to Different County	Moved to Bigger City	Other
White Males									
Education	.011	.010	--	.001	-.001	--	--	--	.001
White Collar	.047	.065	-.012	-.007	--	.001	--	--	--
Whether Union	.052	.066	-.016	.002	.006	.001	--	--	.007
City Size	.00012	.00010	--	--	--	--	--	--	--
Black Males									
Mother's Education	.019	.026	--	--	-.001	.001	-.001	-.005	-.001
Grew up South	-.178	-.215	-.014	.001	.011	.010	.002	.029	.002
Future Orientation	.030	.027	.005	.001	--	.001	-.003	--	.001
Risk Avoidance	.015	.019	-.001	--	-.002	-.001	.001	--	-.001
White Collar	.089	.068	.013	-.002	.007	-.002	-.018	.028	.005
Whether Union	.130	.144	-.030	.002	-.008	.007	.013	.009	-.007
Work Experience	.0044	.0054	--	--	.001	.001	.001	-.003	-.0010

NOTE: "--" denotes indirect effects less than .0005.

Indirect effects where both paths are significantly different from zero at .05 level are underscored.

The level of the mother's education also had an indirect effect through this migration variable. Since the mother's education level *decreased* the likelihood of moving to a bigger city, the sign of the indirect effect was negative.[53]

Two of the personal characteristic measures—future orientation and risk avoidance—had significant effects on earnings change for blacks. Part of the future orientation effect operated through joining a labor union. Blacks who were more oriented toward the future were more likely to join a union and those who became union members earned more. A less important indirect effect operated through intercounty mobility; blacks who scored higher on the future orientation index were more likely to make such a move, but since that kind of move had a negative association with earnings change, the sign of the indirect effect was negative. The risk avoidance variable had no significant indirect effects.

The involuntary job changes carried the indirect effects of two environmental variables—union status in 1970 and years of work experience. For blacks, being in a union *decreased* the likelihood of involuntary job change and, thus, increased change in earnings. Work experience had the similar effect of reducing the likelihood of involuntary job change. The remaining indirect effects of the environmental measures operated through the migration variables. Blacks in white-collar occupations initially were more likely to move to a bigger city; those with greater work experience were less likely to make such a move. Both work experience and initial union membership decreased the likelihood of an intercounty move, while white-collar blacks were more likely to make this type of move.

Summary

In this chapter, we have attempted to explain how background, education, cognitive skills, attitudes, and job environment relate to both earnings level and subsequent short-run changes in earnings. To help organize a summary of results, the partial R^2's of each predictor group along the causal chain are shown in Table 6.15.[54] The partial R^2 shows the fraction of the variance of earnings level that a given predictor group can account for over and above the explana-

---

[53]One possible explanation for this, suggested by a reviewer, is that more highly educated mothers are more likely to be in a position to influence the son not to migrate elsewhere.

[54]Table 6.15 also shows the *total* R^2 from the equations which contain the given variable group plus all prior explanatory variables.

Table 6.15

TOTAL AND PARTIAL R^2'S OF BACKGROUND, EDUCATION, PERSONAL
CHARACTERISTICS, WORK EXPERIENCE, AND ENVIRONMENT
ON ℓn AVERAGE 1970–1971 WAGE RATE, BY RACE

	White Males		Black Males	
	Total R^2	Partial R^2	Total R^2	Partial R^2
Background	.107	.107	.145	.145
Education (over and above background)	.161	.060	.256	.130
Personal Characteristics (over and above education and background)	.229	.081	.368	.151
Work Experience (over and above personal characteristics, education and background)	.281	.067	.371	.005
Environment (over and above experience, personal characteristics, education, and background)	.400	.165	.548	.282

tory power of previous groups.

Background variables were important for both racial subgroups. Without accounting for the effects of subsequent variables, the measures of parental education, religion, rural and southern origin, and number of siblings were able to account for about 10 percent of the variance in earnings level for whites and nearly 15 percent for blacks. For whites, the effects of rural origin and religion were especially strong. Growing up on a farm depressed earnings levels principally by placing individuals in an unfavorable job environment (i.e., in nonunion, blue-collar, or self-employed jobs) and also by reducing the quantity and, perhaps, quality of educational attainment. Religious affiliation was also important for whites, with Jews and Catholics earning considerably more than Protestants. These effects seem to operate through increased educational attainment and better job opportunities rather than through advantageous attitudes and other personal characteristics. For blacks, parental education levels and southern origin were particularly important, with the biggest effect of growing up in the South on earnings operating (in a negative direction) through cognitive skills. Both southern origin and the mother's educational level were significant predictors of short-run changes in earnings for blacks.

The level of education attainment added a great deal to the explanation of earnings level, especially for blacks. Each additional year of education was associated with a 6 percent increase in the earnings of both racial groups. Education affects earnings by increasing cognitive skills, by facilitating entry into white-collar jobs, and by instilling advantageous attitudes and behavior patterns. For both groups, increased education was associated with avoiding unnecessary risks. Among blacks, education further affected earnings through achievement motivation; among whites there was an indirect effect through sense of personal efficacy. Since the preschooling measures of these attitudes were not available, the size of these indirect effects may be overstated somewhat. For whites, educational attainment was also important for short-run changes in earnings.

A unique aspect of the panel data is that they contain measures of certain attitudinal variables, cognitive skills, and potentially advantageous behavior patterns. Taken as a group, these variables add as much to our ability to explain the variance of earnings over and above the background and education variables as the latter do over and above the background factors. For both racial subgroups, an index measuring such undue risk avoidance behavior as fastening seat belts, not smoking, and having medical and car insurance had a more significant earnings effect than did any other variable in the group. Residence and occupation measures did not greatly help to explain this risk avoidance/earnings

relationship, although a small indirect effect was found through an increased
likelihood of having a white-collar job. For blacks, the index related to short-
run improvement in earnings.

Scores on a 13-question sequence designed to measure cognitive skills were
especially important for blacks, although they were also highly significant for
the earnings level of whites. Somewhat surprisingly, the cognitive skills measure had no significant effects on short-run changes in earnings for either group.

Levels of all three attitudinal measures--achievement motivation, efficacy,
and future orientation--were successfully predicted by the education level of the
mother and of the individual himself for both blacks and whites. The relationship between the three measures and earnings, on the other hand, was ambiguous--
perhaps because the attitudes and earnings were measured at the same point in
time. Only the future orientation measure related to earnings *change* and showed
up only for the blacks in the sample.

Several measures of job and location were included to help account for the
effects of prior variables. As a group, they reduced the unexplained variance
in earnings substantially, especially for blacks. All of these environmental
variables operated in expected directions and most had similar effects for blacks
and whites. Some were also significant predictors of earnings change. Respondents who belonged to labor unions, especially blacks, did considerably better
over the 1971-1975 period than did their nonunion counterparts. For blacks, this
union effect worked by reducing the likelihood of an involuntary job change.
Both blacks and whites who began the panel period in white-collar jobs fared significantly better than average.

Additional years of work experience had a large, positive effect on earnings
levels for whites but had virtually no effect on earnings levels for blacks.
This could be due to differential amounts of on-the-job training, although such
an explanation would also lead to a prediction of a significant negative relationship between experience and earnings *change*--a result which was not observed
for whites. For blacks, additional years of experience had a positive effect on
earnings *change*, which is more consistent with institutional factors such as
seniority.

Implications for Future Research

Recursive models of income determination are quite useful because, if properly specified, they help us to understand the earnings *process*. The panel data

are well suited for the estimation of such models because they provide detail on such personal characteristics as cognitive skills and motivation and also contain information on the location and occupational characteristics of each respondent.

To a degree, personal and institutional characteristics compete with one another as intervening variables which deserve further investigation. One could argue, for example, that personal skills, values, and motivation ultimately will account for much of the currently unexplained variance in earnings and will account for the effects of background variables on earnings. Institutional detail would be largely irrelevant to this explanation, especially if the number of different ways that personal characteristics could operate through jobs and job changes is quite large. The human capital theory of earnings is obviously of this type, focusing on the acquisition of and the economic return to skills (sometimes defined broadly enough to include values and attitudes). By assuming competitive labor markets and perfectly informed employers and employees, it ignores the process by which skills "pay off" in earnings.

The alternative view would place much more emphasis on the characteristics of *jobs* than the characteristics of *individuals*. Internal labor markets and "connections" explanations of why individuals from different ethnic or socioeconomic backgrounds earn differential labor incomes are examples of this. Personal characteristics might play a role in determining who gets the job and who makes the advantageous job changes, but the focus would be on the process of job acquisition and promotion.

In the empirical results of this chapter, both personal characteristics and institutional details contributed to the explanation of earnings and helped to account for the effect of background factors, but the institutional variables were clearly more important and useful. Earnings differences between individuals with different religious affiliations, for example, had little to do with the psychological measures that were included in our model, largely because differences in religion were not associated with different scores on these psychological variables. Respondents with different religious affiliations *did* differ, however, along a number of occupational and locational dimensions, and these differences account for much of the total effect of religion on earnings.

Belonging to a labor union played a role in explaining both the level of and short-run changes in earnings. The cross-sectional wage advantage associated with union membership was somewhat higher for whites than blacks (20 percent versus 15 percent) but *changes* in earnings for those who belonged to or joined labor unions were larger for blacks than whites (although highly significant for both groups). Additionally, it was seen that one of the ways that union membership paid off for blacks was by reducing the likelihood of an involuntary job change.

In general, the institutional variables were considerably more important than personal characteristics in explaining short-run changes in earnings. For whites, *none* of the psychological variables had a significant effect on earnings *change*; for blacks, future orientation and risk avoidance were significant predictors. On the other hand, several occupational and locational variables were consistently significant predictors of change for both groups.

In sum, longitudinal data sets provide opportunities to study the determinants of wage *change* as well as wage *level*. While various personal characteristics do play an important role in wage determination models, institutional variables do also. In our attempts to understand the complexities of the paths to economic well-being the benefits of additional detail on job acquisition and job change may well exceed the benefits from knowing more about the personal characteristics of the individuals who have the jobs.

References

Akin, John S. and Garfinkel, Irwin. "Economic Returns to Education Quality: An Empirical Analysis for Whites, Blacks, Poor Whites, and Poor Blacks." Mimeographed. Madison: Institute for Research on Poverty, University of Wisconsin, 1974.

Andrisani, Paul J. and Nestel, Gilbert. "Internal-External Control as a Contributor to and Outcome of Work Experience." Journal of Applied Psychology Vol. 61, No. 2:156-165.

Ashenfelter, Orley and Johnson, George E. "Unionism, Relative Wages, and Labor Quality in U. S. Manufacturing Industries." International Economic Review, 13 (October 1972):488-508.

Atkinson, John W. and Feather, David, eds. A Theory of Achievement Motivation. New York: John Wiley, 1966.

Becker, Gary S. Human Capital: A Theoretical and Empirical Analysis. New York: NBER, 1964.

Ben-Porath, Yoram. "The Production of Human Capital and the Life Cycle of Earnings." Journal of Political Economy, 75 (August 1967):352-365.

Blau, Peter and Duncan, Otis D. The American Occupational Structure. New York: John Wiley, 1967.

Blinder, Alan. "Wage Discrimination: Reduced Form and Structural Estimates." Journal of Human Resources, 8 (Fall, 1973).

Bowles, Samuel. "Understanding Unequal Economic Opportunity." American Economic Review, 62 (May 1973):346-356.

Bowles, Samuel and Gintis, Herbert. "IQ in the U. S. Class Structure." Social Policy, Vols. 4, 5 (November/December 1972 and January/February 1973): 65-96.

Dickinson, Katherine. "Wage Rates of Heads and Wives." Five Thousand American Families--Patterns of Economic Progress, Volume I, by James N. Morgan et al. Ann Arbor: Institute for Social Research, 1974.

Duncan, Greg. "Educational Attainment." Five Thousand American Families--Patterns of Economic Progress, Volume I, by James N. Morgan et al. Ann Arbor: Institute for Social Research, 1974.

Duncan, Greg J. "Nonpecuniary Work Rewards." In Five Thousand American Families--Patterns of Economic Progress. Vol. II. Edited by James N. Morgan. Ann Arbor: Institute for Social Research, 1974.

Duncan, Greg J. and Newman, Sandra. "People as Planners: The Fulfillment of Residential Mobility Expectations." In Five Thousand American Families--Patterns of Economic Progress, Volume III. Edited by Greg J. Duncan and James N. Morgan. Ann Arbor: Institute for Social Research, 1975.

Duncan, Otis D. "Path Analysis: Sociological Examples." American Journal of Sociology (July, 1966).

Duncan, Otis D.; Featherman, David L.; and Duncan, Beverly. Socioeconomic Background and Achievement. New York: Seminar Press, 1972.

Featherman, David L. "The Socioeconomic Achievement of White Religio-Ethnic Subgroups: Social and Psychological Explanations." American Sociological Review, 36 (April 1971):207-222.

Goldberger, Arthur S. and Lewontin, Richard C. "Jensen's Twin Fantasy." Mimeographed. Madison: Institute for Research on Poverty, University of Wisconsin, 1976.

Goldberger, Arthur S. "On Jensen's Method for Twins." Educational Psychologist, 12 (1976).

Gurin, Gerald. "The Impact of the College Experience." In A Degree and What Else? Edited by Stephen B. Withey. New York: McGraw-Hill, 1971.

Gurin, Gerald and Gurin, Patricia. "Personal Efficacy and the Ideology of Individual Responsibility." In Economic Means for Human Needs. Edited by Burkhard Strumpel. Ann Arbor: Institute for Social Research, 1976.

Herrnstein, Richard. "IQ." The Atlantic Monthly (September 1971):43-64.

Hill, C. Russell. "Capacities, Opportunities and Educational Investments: The Case of the High School Dropout." Mimeographed. Columbia, South Carolina: Center for Studies in Human Resource Economics, 1975.

Hill, C. Russell and Stafford, Frank. "Time Inputs to Children." In Five Thousand American Families--Patterns of Economic Progress, Vol. II. Edited by James N. Morgan and Greg J. Duncan. Ann Arbor: Institute for Social Research, 1974.

218

Jencks, Christopher et al. *Inequality*. New York: Basic Books, 1972.

Johnson, George J. and Youmans, Kendrick. "Union Relative Wage Effects by Age and Education." *Industrial and Labor Relations Review* (January 1971).

Kamin, Leon J. *The Science and Politics of IQ*. New York: John Wiley, 1974.

Kmenta, Jan. *Elements of Econometrics*. New York: The MacMillan Company, 1971.

Leibowitz, Arleen. "Home Investments in Children." *Journal of Political Economy*, Part II (March/April 1974).

Mincer, Jacob. *Schooling, Experience, and Earnings*. New York: NBER, 1974.

Morganstern, Richard D. "Direct and Indirect Effects on Earnings of Schooling and Socioeconomic Background." *Review of Economics and Statistics*, Vol. LV, No. 2 (May 1973).

Roistacher, Elizabeth. "Residential Mobility." In *Five Thousand American Families--Patterns of Economic Progress*, Volume II. Edited by James N. Morgan. Ann Arbor: Institute for Social Research, 1974.

Sewell, William H. and Hauser, Robert M. *Education, Occupation, and Earnings*. New York: Academic Press, 1975.

Taubman, Paul. *Sources of Inequality in Earnings*. Amsterdam: North-Holland Publishing Company, 1975.

Veroff, Joseph; McClelland, Lou; and Marquis, Kent. *Measuring Intelligence and Achievement Motivation in Surveys*. U. S. Department of Health, Education, and Welfare, Contract No. OEO-4180, October 1971.

Wachtel, Paul. "The Effect of School Quality on Achievement, Attainment Levels and Lifetime Earnings." *Explorations in Economic Research*, Vol. 2, No. 4 (1975).

APPENDIX 6.1

Path Models and Total, Direct, and Indirect Effects

The various effects that an independent variable can have on the dependent variables in a system of recursive equations are best illustrated by the following simple model:

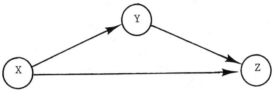

This model is composed of two equations

(1) $Z = a_1 + b_1Y + b_2X$, and

(2) $Y = a_2 + b_3X$

where the b's show the effect of a unit change in an independent variable on the dependent variable.[1] To understand the relationship between X and Z, it is helpful to substitute Equation 2 into 1 to get:

(3) $Z = (a_1 + b_1a_2) + b_1b_3X + b_2X$, or

(4) $Z = (a_1 + b_1a_2) + (b_1b_3 + b_2)X$.

---

[1]The empirical counterpart to the b's are raw score regression coefficients. Although path models are often presented with *standardized* coefficients (β), the empirical results from this chapter are raw score coefficients. Converting one to the other is quite simple:

$$\beta = \frac{b \cdot \sigma_X}{\sigma_Z}$$

where σ_X and σ_Z are the standard deviations of the independent and dependent variables, respectively. The standard deviations of all variables are given in Table A6.1a.

220

Table A6.1a

MEANS AND STANDARD DEVIATIONS FOR ALL VARIABLES, BY RACE

Variable	Mean		Standard Deviation	
	White Males	Black Males	White Males	Black Males
Father's Education	8.78	6.98	3.37	3.34
Mother's Education	9.53	7.81	3.47	3.30
Whether Catholic	.241	.071	.428	.258
Wether Jewish	.055	--	.227	--
Grew up South	.256	.829	.436	.377
Grew up Farm	.281	.373	.449	.484
Number of Siblings	3.34	4.48	2.36	2.70
Age	40.5	40.9	8.60	8.03
Education	12.72	10.61	2.94	3.20
Test Score	10.26	8.54	1.77	2.46
Achievement Motivation	9.46	9.32	2.61	2.83
Efficacy	4.32	3.58	1.62	1.63
Future Orientation	1.63	1.79	1.27	1.25
Risk Avoidance	10.44	8.92	2.96	2.74
Experience	21.71	22.28	8.68	8.50
White Collar	.471	.237	.499	.426
Self-Employed	.079	.007	.270	.086
Whether Union	.267	.441	.442	.497
Whether South	.254	.587	.436	.493
City Size	419.9	544.4	429.4	442.3
$\ln$ 1970–1971 Average Wage Rate	1.693	1.444	0.524	0.462
Became Union	.063	.075	.244	.264
Became White Collar	.068	.007	.252	.086
Became Self-Employed	.055	.028	.229	.166
Whether Involuntary Job Change	.074	.082	.262	.274
Whether Different County	.154	.080	.361	.272
Whether Moved to Bigger City	.066	.040	.248	.196
$\ln$ 1973–1974 Average Wage Rate	1.793	1.500	0.519	0.502
Number of Observations	1,254	423		

MTR #7119

Thus the *total* effect on Z of a unit change in X is composed of two parts:
(1) b_2, which comes from Equation 1 and shows the *direct* effect of X on Z after
partialling out the effects of Y, and (2) $b_1 b_3$, the *indirect* of X on Z which operates through Y. This indirect effect is the product of b_1, the effect of Y on
Z, partialling out the effects of X, and b_3, which is the effect of X on Y. Additional X and Y-type variables merely expand the algebra but not the substance
of total, direct, and indirect effects.

The structure of the earnings *change* model (estimated in Section IV) can be
depicted as follows:

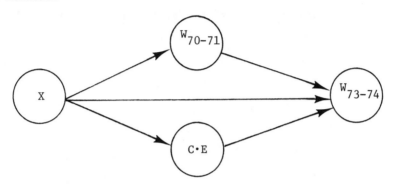

It is composed of three equations:

(5) $\quad W_{73-74} = a_1 + b_1 W_{70-71} + b_2 CE + b_3 X$

(6) $\quad W_{70-71} = a_2 + b_4 X$

(7) $\quad .CE = a_3 + b_5 X$

where W_{73-74} is *ln* average 1973-74 wage rate,

$\qquad W_{70-71}$ is *ln* average 1970-71 wage rate,

$\qquad$ CE is changes in environment between 1970 and 1974, and

$\qquad$ X is the set of exogenous variables.

Equation 5 can be written as a change equation by subtracting W_{70-71} from both
sides:

(8) $\quad W_{73-74} - W_{70-71} = a_1 + (b_1 - 1) W_{70-71} + b_2 CE + b_3 X.$

Substituting Equation 7 into 8,

(9) $\quad W_{73-74} - W_{70-71} = (a_1 + b_2 a_3) + (b_1 - 1) W_{70-71} + (b_2 \cdot b_5 + b_3) X.$

In this case, $(b_2 \cdot b_5 + b_3)$ is the *total* effect of X on change in earnings,
which is composed of the *direct* effect of X on change, from Equation 5, which

partials out the effect of CE, and an *indirect* effect of X on change which operates through CE. This indirect effect is the product of b_2 (the effect of CE on earnings change) and b_5 (the effect of X on CE).

It should be noted that the change model could have been decomposed in a different way, with substitution of both Equations 6 and 7 into Equation 5. This gives:

$$(10) \quad W_{73-74} = (a_1 + b_1 \cdot a_2 + b_2 \cdot a_3) + (b_1 \cdot b_4 + b_2 \cdot b_5 + b_3)X.$$

In this formulation, X is related to the *level* of $\ln$ average wage rates in 1973-74 (and not change in wage rates) with indirect effects operating through both CE *and* 1970-71 wage rate.

Chapter 7

PATTERNS OF CHANGE IN INDIVIDUAL EARNINGS

Saul Hoffman

Introduction

In recent years, the interest of economists in the life-cycle pattern of individual labor market earnings has increased tremendously. This upsurge of interest corresponds roughly to the development and widespread acceptance of the human capital model in the period since the early 1960s. The life-cycle perspective marked the point of departure for the human capital model, and the analysis of life-cycle earnings remains one of its central features. The explanation of life-cycle earnings patterns also figures prominently in the major alternative model of the labor market, the internal labor market/dual labor market analysis. Recent empirical analysis of the poverty population also focused attention on life-cycle earnings. If, as the evidence seems to indicate, a relatively large fraction of the poverty population at a given point in time is only temporarily poor, then an understanding of the nature and determinants of change in individual earnings would be crucial for informed public policy.[1]

Although the human capital model and the internal/dual labor market models suggest very different mechanisms by which earnings are determined, they both predict that individual labor market earnings will increase regularly and gradually throughout most of the working lifetime of most individuals. The human capital model suggests that this pattern will be applicable virtually without exception; in the internal labor market/dual labor market analysis, the monotonic pattern is not thought to be appropriate for workers in the secondary labor market. Although these predictions are fundamental to both models, they have rarely been tested directly since, until recently, a sufficiently long series of longitudinal observations on individual earnings has been unavailable. In the absence of data of this kind, economists have turned to cross-sectional data and have attempted to infer the pattern of earnings of a single individual over his or her life cycle from the pattern of earnings generated by different individuals of different ages. Virtually all of the empirical ideas about the life-cycle

---

[1]Morgan et al. (1974), especially Chapter 1, pp. 27-37.

earnings patterns have been drawn from the age-earnings profiles constructed from cross-sectional data.

In general, cross-sectional analyses have confirmed the prediction of gradual, monotonic increases in earnings. The smooth, concave age-earnings profile of a cross-sectional regression is one of the most familiar and well-replicated empirical findings about individual earnings. In the cross section, earnings are relatively low at the beginning of an individual's career, rise smoothly through middle age, peak at about age 50, and then turn down. This last downturn, it is usually argued, is not a genuine life-cycle phenomenon, but simply an artifact of the cross section itself; it reflects the effects of vintage-related differences in the quality of labor not fully accounted for in the regression equation. But in other respects economists have tended to accept the cross-sectional age-earnings profile as an accurate representation of the life-cycle earnings pattern.

The Panel Study of Income Dynamics provides a longitudinal series suitable for testing the life-cycle earnings prediction in a more direct fashion. Information is available on labor earnings, both annual and hourly, for eight consecutive years for a representative national sample of households. In this chapter, we use the longitudinal earnings data to test the life-cycle predictions of these models directly and to explore the actual pattern of change in individual labor market earnings.

Section I outlines the two basic economic models of life-cycle earnings patterns. In Section II, the panel study data are used to test the life-cycle predictions of the models. Section III extends that analysis to consider the effects of various independent variables on the pattern of earnings. A brief overview, emphasizing both the regularities in and the diversity of individual earnings experiences, is presented in Section IV.

I. ECONOMIC THEORIES OF LIFE-CYCLE EARNINGS

The human capital model and the internal/dual labor market model are the two most prominent contemporary models of the operation of the labor market and the determination of individual labor market earnings. The human capital model is the more widely accepted of the two and its theoretical development has been far more extensive. Before outlining the two models--and their predictions for the life-cycle pattern of earnings--it is important to emphasize that they approach the question of the determination of earnings from essentially different perspectives. The human capital model emphasizes the supply side of the labor market; it can be thought of as a theory which explains the supply of labor quality and the resulting distribution of earnings in a perfectly competitive labor market. In contrast, the internal/dual labor market analysis focuses on the demand side of the labor market and is predicated on the existence of market imperfections.

The Human Capital Model

The emphasis of the human capital model on life-cycle earnings patterns begins with the simple assumption that "many workers increase their productivity by learning new skills and perfecting old ones while on the job."[2] While this statement may sound obvious, it marked a clear departure from what had been, until then, the accepted theory of the labor market. Alan Blinder has summarized the distinction between static marginal productivity theory and the human capital model this way:

> In static theory, an individual's productivity is a datum of the
> problem, given exogenously. However, over a longer period of time,
> this productivity becomes endogenous, that is, a matter of individual
> choice. The entire human capital literature has been built up around
> this notion.[3]

Thus, where static labor market theory ignored the fact that workers did learn on the job and became more productive over time, the human capital model emphasized this learning, treating changes in individual productivity as an endogenous element of the model.

Although many kinds of activities can serve to increase a worker's productivity, in both theoretical and applied work, the human capital model has emphasized the role of investments in on-the-job training as the primary determinant of the life-cycle pattern of labor market earnings. The basic human capital notion about investment in training is that learning does not cease with the completion of formal schooling.[4] Rather, at some point it simply becomes efficient to transfer the site of learning to the labor market and to learn in conjunction with work. It is this learning on the job that the human capital model calls investment in on-the-job training, and it is usually asserted that many, if not most, job skills are learned primarily on the job.[5]

What transforms learning on the job into an investment in human capital is that workers are presumed to pay for the on-the-job training they receive. Training and production are assumed to be mutually exclusive activities, since

---

[2] Becker (1964), p. 9.

[3] Blinder (1974), p. 21.

[4] The basic references here are Mincer (1962), Becker (1964) especially Chapter 2, and Mincer (1974).

[5] See, for example, Rosen (1972) and Mincer (1962).

training requires both the worker's time and perhaps other resources which might otherwise be devoted to production. Consequently, if a worker is learning while working, he or she is producing correspondingly less and, hence, is paid less. But, according to the model, an individual is willing to accept this wage reduction because the acquisition of on-the-job training will lead to increased earnings in the future.

This interpretation is made explicit in the human capital earnings function as developed by Mincer:[6]

$$Y_j = Y_s + \sum_{t=0}^{j-1} r_t C_t - C_j = E_j - C_j$$

where Y_j = earnings in the jth year after completing school,

Y_s = earnings which would be received in the absence of any post-school training,

r_t = the rate of return to on-the-job investments in human capital,

C_j = the dollar cost of investments in human capital in the jth year,

and E_j = earnings capacity in the jth year.

In this formulation, training affects earnings in two ways. First, earnings are depressed (actual earnings, Y_j, are less than earnings capacity, E_j) whenever investment in that period is positive. Second, earnings in any period depend directly on the volume of past investments in training and on the rate of return earned on those investments ($\Sigma r_t C_t$). In fact, the change in earnings over an individual's life cycle depends only on investments in training, since the effect of education (Y_s) is constant over all t. For these reasons, Mincer emphasizes post-school investments (and especially training) as the variable which determines the individual age-earnings profile.[7] Taubman notes that "another way to view Mincer's model is that earnings only change over time because of continued investment in on-the-job training."[8]

The endogenous nature of the pattern of life-cycle earnings is outlined by the theories of optimal investment in human capital. These models, developed in different forms by Becker, Ben-Porath, and Rosen,[9] focus attention on the maxi-

---

[6] See Mincer (1974), p. 12.

[7] Mincer (1974), p. 13.

[8] Taubman (1975), p. 14.

[9] See Becker (1967), Ben-Porath (1967), and Rosen (1972).

mizing process inherent in an individual's investment decision. Individuals are assumed to determine the volume and timing of their self-investment in human capital in order to maximize the discounted value of lifetime earnings. It is clearly advantageous for an individual to invest in training early in his or her working career in order to maximize the number of years over which returns can be earned. However, because the marginal costs of investment are assumed to be upward sloping for any single time period, investment costs are reduced if investments are distributed over a number of years. From these conflicting influences, it is possible to demonstrate that there does exist an optimal time path of human capital accumulation.[10] And this optimal investment profile in turn implies, via the human capital earnings function, a characteristic age-earnings profile. During the first few working years, investment will be relatively high and, consequently, earnings will be depressed. Thereafter, labor earnings rise, sharply at first and then more gradually, as the optimal rate of investment declines and the returns to previous investments are received.

The clear prediction of the human capital model, drawn from the analysis of optimal investment behavior, is that earnings over an individual's life cycle will increase monotonically. Mincer's formulation makes this quite clear, since if,

$$Y_j = Y_s + \sum_{t=0}^{j-1} r_t C_t - C_j,$$

then,

$$Y_{j+1} = Y_s + \sum_{t=0}^{j} r_t C_t - C_{j+1}$$

and the change in earnings from j to j+1 is

$$\Delta Y_j = C_j (r_j + 1) - C_{j+1}.$$

By the theory of optimal investment, $C_j > C_{j+1}$, since optimal investments decline monotonically with age. Consequently, $\Delta Y_j > 0$ for all j.

In its broadest theoretical formulation, the human capital model does incorporate a number of factors which could serve to qualify the prediction of a monotonic pattern of increases in individual labor market earnings. One set of these factors includes things which are usually held constant--in particular, the rate of return to human capital and the rate of interest. Large, sudden

---

[10]Ben-Porath (1967) and Rosen (1972).

changes in the rate of return and perhaps also in the rate of interest could
lead to a decrease in earnings. The model would not, for example, have predicted
regular increases in earnings during the depression of the 1930s. A second possible factor is depreciation of an individual's stock of human capital. Some
versions of the model do allow for depreciation of human capital similar to the
depreciation of physical capital and, if the depreciation rate increased sufficiently so that a worker's net investment was negative, then earnings would
also be expected to fall. The depreciation rate, like the rate of return and
the rate of interest, is considered a purely exogenous effect; it is difficult
to imagine that it could be severe enough and sudden enough to account for many
downturns, except perhaps for the oldest workers in the labor market. Finally,
although the maximand of the investment decision is usually taken in empirical
work to be discounted lifetime income, it is acknowledged that psychic income
and nonpecuniary benefits also influence the human capital investment decision.
It is possible, then, that a decrease in observed earnings may simply reflect a
changed distribution of "full income" between its monetary and nonmonetary components.

In general, relatively little emphasis has been given to most of these factors and, consequently, they were not emphasized in the presentation of the model
above. They are, as yet, not well-integrated into the main body of theory and
are almost never included in empirical work. The mainstream of human capital
theory, from Becker to Mincer, has tended to treat these factors as asides or to
refer to them in footnotes. To assign them a primary role in the determination
of individual life-cycle earnings patterns would necessitate a major change in
the theoretical and especially the empirical emphases of the model.

Internal Labor Market/Dual Labor Market Analysis

As the compound title[11] above indicates, this strand of labor market analysis
represents a synthesis of two distinct approaches. Both parts of the analysis
are crucial to the model's predictions about the life-cycle pattern of earnings:
The analysis of internal labor markets describes a general pattern of life-cycle
earnings, while the dual labor market analysis suggests that for one sector of
the labor market this pattern will not, in fact, be applicable.

The dual labor market model differs from the human capital model primarily

---

[11]Although this model is popularly known as the dual labor market model, it
is important, particularly in a life-cycle context, to emphasize its focus on
internal labor markets. Consequently, we use the compound title rather than the
popular one throughout this paper.

in its focus on the characteristics of jobs and job markets, rather than the characteristics of individuals, and on the role of institutional forces. The most important of these institutional forces is the internal labor market, a concept first introduced by Clark Kerr in the early 1950s.[12] Kerr argued that competitive labor markets were increasingly being replaced by what he called "institutional markets." A primary characteristic of these markets was that customary work rules and practices, frequently formalized by collective bargaining agreements, tended to establish separate markets for those already hired and those seeking employment—an internal labor market for the former group and an external market for the latter. Doeringer and Piore described the internal labor market in similar terms as an administrative unit "within which the pricing and allocation of labor is governed by a set of administrative rules and procedures."[13] They further argued that most promotion takes place within internal markets according to well-structured job ladders. Like Kerr, they contend that only workers who have gained access to the internal labor market via a limited number of "ports of entry" at the bottom of promotion ladders are considered for higher slots on the job ladder.

The dual labor market theorists also adapted Kerr's concept of "balkanized" labor markets. The labor market is not so much balkanized, they argued, as dichotomized into a primary labor market and a secondary labor market, with extremely limited mobility between the sectors. In the secondary labor market, jobs "tend to have low wages and fringe benefits, poor working conditions, higher turnover, little chance of advancement, and often arbitrary and capricious supervision."[14] Jobs in the primary sector are alleged to possess many of the opposite characteristics: employment is steady, wages are higher, and there are significant opportunities for promotion. The dual labor market model emphasizes that the primary sector is characterized by highly structured internal labor markets, while the secondary market is closely tied to conditions in the external labor market.

The dual labor market theorists do acknowledge the importance of on-the-job training, but they interpret it differently than do the human capital theorists. To the former, training is largely technologically determined by the design of jobs, so that a specified amount of training is intrinsic in any given job. The individual acquires training by gaining access to a job which offers a fixed,

---

[12] See Kerr (1953).

[13] Doeringer and Piore (1971), pp. 1-2.

[14] Doeringer and Piore (1971), pp. 165-66.

automatic training component.

This technological determinism would be of little importance if individuals could choose freely among jobs. But restrictions on mobility, particularly between the primary and secondary sectors, are central to the model. "Workers," Wachter writes in his summary of the model, "are barred from the primary sector not so much by their own lack of human capital as by institutional restraints (including discrimination)."[15]

In practice, analysis along these lines has tended to focus on the labor market problems of low-wage urban workers, especially blacks. It is usually argued that one of the effects of labor market discrimination is to confine blacks to secondary market jobs in disproportionate numbers, and, once there, they find it difficult to escape to the better jobs in the primary sector.

One implication of this approach is that the life-cycle pattern of labor earnings is largely dependent on an individual's ability to gain access to training ladders in the primary sector. The key determinant of an individual's earnings, then, is not the stock of human capital he or she possesses; instead, earnings are determined by the job he or she holds and the job market he or she participates in. Because of institutional imperfections in the labor market-- including discrimination--workers with identical stocks of human capital may well receive different current and future wages. Contrary to what the human capital model would suggest, workers do not invest freely in on-the-job training according to some optimizing formula. Workers in the primary sector do receive training, along with regular promotions and increases in earnings, as they progress through well-structured job ladders. For this group of workers, earnings over the life cycle should increase monotonically and gradually, exactly as the human capital model would predict. In contrast, for workers in the secondary sector, training opportunities are rarely available, seniority confers few benefits, and the nature of employment is itself unsteady. Earnings over the life cycle will show not a pattern of regular, gradual increases, but rather a series of fluctuations with no discernible pattern.

II. PATTERNS OF LIFE-CYCLE EARNINGS: SOME EMPIRICAL EVIDENCE

With the eight consecutive years of data available from the panel study, it is possible to make seven comparisons of year-to-year earnings. A simple counting of the number of years in which earnings increase provides a strikingly direct test of the two models. The human capital model, as we have seen, would

---

[15]Wachter (1974), p. 638.

predict that almost all individuals would show monotonic increases in earnings, while the internal/dual labor market analysis predicts a similar pattern for workers in the primary sector and a much more erratic one for secondary market workers.

The analysis is restricted to males who were between ages 18 and 55[16] in 1968 and who were actively in the labor force (either employed or only temporarily unemployed and looking for work) in each of the eight years. Students or those who were disabled were excluded from the sample. This left 1,617 individuals, about one-quarter of them black.

Before turning to the analysis results, a few caveats are in order. Our aim in this paper is a modest one: to test whether the actual longitudinal pattern of change in earnings is consistent with the predictions of the two labor market models. To do this, we examine the pattern of earnings increases for various groups within the population. We do not, however, go on to present a full-scale regression analysis of the determinants of year-to-year change in individual earnings. That is a far more extensive task for which the material here represents only a preliminary stage.

Table 7.1 presents the distribution of individuals by the number of years in which real annual earnings increased. No one, of course, would expect any theory to hold all the time or for all individuals; nevertheless, the results are astonishing--by whatever standards one chooses to apply. The black and

Table 7.1

PATTERN OF INCREASES IN REAL ANNUAL EARNINGS, 1967-1974, BY RACE
(Males, Age 18-55, Continuously in Labor Force, 1967-1974)

Number of Years with Increases	White	Black
1	1.2%	1.8%
2	9.3	6.5
3	27.5	30.6
4	33.8	35.4
5	21.4	22.0
6	6.3	3.7
7	0.4	0.1
TOTAL	100.0%	100.0%
Number of Observations	1,177	440

MTR #7516

---

[16]The age restriction should reduce the importance of depreciation as a determinant of the pattern of earnings.

white distributions are similar, but neither conforms even roughly to the predicted pattern. Less than one-half of 1 percent of the individuals--all of whom
were regular labor force participants in each year during the period--exhibited
a monotonic pattern of increases. The mode is four years (about 34 percent of
the observations), with about a quarter each at three and five years, and far
smaller proportions at either tail.

Proponents of the models might make two objections to the use of real annual
earnings as the earnings measure. First, labor supply considerations--the negative elasticity of supply which has been found in most studies--would operate to
weaken the monotonic pattern. As earnings increase, hours of labor offered would
decrease, and, as a result, annual labor earnings might not actually show an increase. In that case, hourly earnings, uncontaminated by labor supply considerations, would be a more appropriate measure. Second, although the theory clearly
pertains to real earnings over the life cycle, the period 1967 to 1974 was such
a chaotic one in terms of inflation that the normal life-cycle pattern of increases was distorted.[17] Nominal earnings, however, would, in this view, show
the expected pattern.

We consider these objections in Table 7.2, which presents comparable distributions for real and nominal hourly earnings. Neither of these modifications
was sufficient to alter the earlier finding. The distribution of real hourly
earnings shows even less of a regular pattern of increases than did the distribution using real annual earnings. No blacks and only 0.2 percent of the whites
enjoyed monotonic increases. The peak at four years is somewhat higher (38 percent) than previously and the tails are much sharper. The use of undeflated
hourly earnings does lead to an upward shift in the distribution, but even so,
only 3 percent of the whites and 1.7 percent of the blacks had increases each
year. An additional 17.7 percent of the whites and 14.2 percent of the blacks
had increases in all but one year.

It is possible, of course, that the apparent lack of a monotonic pattern of
increases does not reflect actual labor market outcomes, but rather is due to
measurement error in the earnings measures themselves. One can never safely
ignore measurement error in microdata, but it is worth noting some of the reasons
why it should be minimized by the panel study interviewing procedures. Panel
members are interviewed each spring, and a large number report their annual
earnings directly from tax records. Hourly wage rates are also carefully computed: Actual labor income in the preceding year is divided by actual work hours

---

[17]Actually, the rate of inflation was unusually high in only three of the
eight years--1970, 1973, and 1974.

Table 7.2

PATTERN OF INCREASES IN REAL AND NOMINAL
HOURLY EARNINGS, 1967–1974, BY RACE
(Males, Aged 18–55, Continuously in Labor Force, 1967–1974)

Number of Years with Increases	Using Real Hourly Earnings		Using Nominal Hourly Earnings	
	White	Black	White	Black
1	0.5%	0.0%	0.0%	0.0%
2	7.2	6.8	2.2	2.5
3	27.3	26.0	11.9	14.4
4	38.1	38.4	32.3	33.1
5	21.0	25.8	32.8	34.2
6	5.7	3.0	17.7	14.2
7	0.2	0.0	3.0	1.7
TOTAL	100.0%	100.0%	100.0%	100.0%
Number of Observations	1,177	440	1,177	440

Table 7.3

PATTERN OF INCREASES IN REAL AND NOMINAL
"ERROR-ADJUSTED" HOURLY EARNINGS, 1967–1974, BY RACE*
(Males, Aged 18–55, Continuously in Labor Force, 1967–1974)

Number of Years with Increases	Using Real "Error-Adjusted" Hourly Earnings		Using Nominal "Error-Adjusted" Hourly Earnings	
	White	Black	White	Black
1	0.0%	0.0%	0.0%	0.0%
2	0.5	0.4	0.4	0.1
3	7.4	7.7	2.8	3.1
4	16.9	19.0	11.6	11.9
5	33.1	41.6	25.5	36.6
6	30.4	26.2	33.3	33.0
7	11.6	5.1	26.4	15.2
TOTAL	100.0%	100.0%	100.0%	100.0%
Number of Observations	1,177	440	1,177	440

*Earnings are adjusted for possible 10 percent measurement error, i.e., a year-to-year decrease of less than 10 percent is counted as an increase in earnings.

in that year calculated from specific questions about paid vacation, illness, unemployment, strikes, overtime, and second jobs. Finally, the presence of measurement error might just as plausibly overstate the number of increases as understate them.

In any event, we can consider the effects of possible measurement error by allowing for a 10 percent margin of error in the annual earnings comparisons; that is, if earnings (however measured) in year N+1 are at least 90 percent of those in year N, then we will count that as an increase in earnings. It is difficult to imagine that errors of measurement would be larger than 10 percent. In addition, of course, the 10 percent margin would misclassify as increases some changes which actually represent declines in earnings, as much as 15 to 20 percent in real terms. Allowing for measurement error in this way should provide an absolute upper bound estimate of the monotonic pattern of increases.

Rather than present distributions for all three of the earnings measures considered earlier, we concentrate now on two of them--real hourly earnings (which is the most conceptually appropriate measure) and nominal hourly earnings (which previously showed the most monotonic pattern). This last measure with the measurement error allowance should be considered as the upper bound of the upper bound estimate; it surely overstates the actual monotonic pattern.

Table 7.3 shows that the allowance for measurement error does shift the entire distribution upward but that, in either case, we are still left far short of the prediction of universal monotonic increases for most workers. Less than a tenth of the individuals (11.6 percent for whites and 5.1 percent for blacks) enjoyed steady increases in real, "error-adjusted" wages, while about a quarter (26.4 percent for whites and 15.2 percent for blacks) experienced similar increases in undeflated, "error-adjusted" hourly earnings. For both measures, an additional 30 percent of both whites and blacks had increases in all but one year. About a quarter of the individuals had increases in real, "error-adjusted" earnings in four years or less, and about 15 percent had four increases or less in the nominal hourly earnings measure.

In summary, the simple distributions are hardly supportive of either model. The frequency of monotonic increases ranged from a low of 0.2 percent for real hourly earnings to an upper-bound figure of 25 percent for undeflated hourly earnings, when allowance was made for a 10 percent measurement error. Furthermore, there is no evidence at all of any significant differences between whites and blacks in the pattern of increases.

III. FURTHER EVIDENCE ON PATTERNS OF LIFE-CYCLE EARNINGS

Although the predicted monotonic pattern of increases does not appear to hold in general, one might expect that the pattern of observed increases would vary in some systematic fashion for different subgroups of the population. In this section, we extend the analysis to examine a number of variables which might be expected, on theoretical or empirical grounds, to influence the pattern of increases in earnings. The variables considered in this way are age, education, occupation, industry, job tenure, union status, and initial earnings level. In order to make the presentation manageable, we limit the analysis to two earnings measures--real and nominal hourly earnings. The question addressed here is not how monotonic the pattern of increases is--that question was considered for five earnings measures in Section I--but only whether any of the independent variables makes a difference in the observed pattern. The restriction to two earnings variables should not affect the results, since any variable which makes an important difference for one measure will almost certainly affect the other measures similarly.[18]

The human capital model makes its most unambiguous prediction of a monotonically increasing pattern of earnings for younger workers. They are beginning to receive the returns to their large volume of initial investment, their currently optimal investments are declining rapidly, and depreciation can hardly be expected to be important. Additionally, in cross-sectional analyses, the age-earnings profile is usually steepest in this age range. In general, it is difficult, within the human capital framework, to explain why the earnings of young workers should ever fail to increase. The internal/dual labor market analysis would probably predict the opposite result, namely, that the number of individuals with regular increases in earnings would increase with age as more workers gained a secure spot in the primary sector.

As Table 7.4 shows, age does have a mild effect along the lines suggested by the human capital model, but it is hardly overwhelming. The distribution shifts downward (that is, becomes less monotonic) as age increases, but none of the younger workers had a monotonic pattern of increases in real wages, and just under 15 percent of them had increases in every year but one. The general pattern is similar for nominal wages; younger workers tended to have more years with increases, but less than 5 percent had increases in every year, while about 27 percent missed a single year only. There appears to be almost no support at

---

[18]Separate results are not presented by race in this section. In what follows, there are almost no important differences between blacks and whites for any of the variables considered.

Table 7.4

PATTERN OF INCREASES IN REAL AND NOMINAL HOURLY EARNINGS, 1967-1974, BY AGE IN 1967
(Males, Aged 18-55, Continuously in Labor Force, 1967-1974)

Number of Years With Increases	Using Real Hourly Earnings					Using Nominal Hourly Earnings				
	< 25	25-34	35-44	45-54	All	< 25	25-34	35-44	45-54	All
1	0.0%	0.7%	0.4%	0.4%	0.5%	0.0%	0.0%	0.0%	0.0%	0.0%
2	3.7	6.0	9.3	6.5	7.1	1.9	2.1	2.9	1.6	2.2
3	16.8	24.4	29.9	30.1	27.2	10.2	11.8	12.1	15.0	12.1
4	36.8	36.6	37.9	40.6	38.1	27.3	31.9	33.0	34.2	32.3
5	28.0	24.6	19.1	18.7	21.3	28.7	35.7	31.9	31.9	32.8
6	14.7	7.1	3.2	3.7	5.5	27.4	15.5	16.4	16.8	17.4
7	0.0	0.4	0.2	0.0	0.2	4.5	2.9	3.5	1.5	2.9
TOTAL	100.0%	100.0%	100.0%	100.0%	100.0%	100.0%	100.0%	100.0%	100.0%	100.0%
Number of Observations	159	462	565	431	1,617	159	462	565	431	1,617
Mean Number of Increases	4.33	4.01	3.76	3.82	3.89	4.83	4.59	4.56	4.46	4.60

MTR #7516

all for the internal/dual labor market model: There was only a slight mean increase for the oldest group using real earnings and almost no trend at all for the three oldest groups using nominal hourly earnings.

Predictions about the pattern of increases according to occupation are much less specific. The human capital model, for example, makes virtually no references to occupation at all. The internal/dual labor market analysis would probably assign many unskilled laborers to the secondary labor market and many skilled or semiskilled workers to the primary sector, although this classification is imprecise at best.[19] We would, therefore, expect unskilled workers to have a somewhat more erratic earnings pattern and skilled and semiskilled workers to show a more monotonic pattern of increases. Finally, one would probably expect managers and professionals to have a more regular pattern of increases and farmers and self-employed workers to have the least monotonic pattern, since their earnings are known to be highly unstable.

As Table 7.5 shows, these expectations are, in general, confirmed; but, just as with age, the differences by occupational group are relatively small. No occupation shows a strong monotonic pattern of increases in either real or nominal earnings. Indeed, the mean number of increases for six of the nine occupation categories lies within a range of only .15 years for real earnings and .16 years for nominal earnings,[20] with a peak of just over four years using real earnings (managers, officials, and proprietors, and a miscellaneous category made up of primarily policemen and firemen) and of 4.73 years for nominal earnings (professional and technical workers). Professional and technical workers exhibited the most monotonic pattern of increases; 4.5 percent had increases in nominal earnings every year and about another fifth had increases in every year but one. The three remaining occupations which differed from the rest were those expected to have the least monotonic pattern--unskilled laborers, self-employed workers, and farmers. Even here, however, the differences were moderate. The maximum mean difference between the most monotonic and the least monotonic occupation was just over half a year for real earnings and under a year for nominal earnings. The difference in the mean number of increases between the skilled and semiskilled blue-collar workers (craftsmen, foremen, and operatives) and the

---

[19]One of the more frustrating and frequently criticized features of the internal/dual labor market model is its reluctance (or inability) to make specific, testable statements about which jobs fall into which market.

[20]In a one-way analysis of variance, a nine-category occupation variable explained only 1.7 percent of the variance in number of increases in real hourly earnings and 4.0 percent of the variance in increases in nominal earnings.

Table 7.5

PATTERN OF INCREASES IN REAL AND NOMINAL HOURLY EARNINGS, 1967-1974, BY OCCUPATION IN 1967
(Males, Aged 18-55, Continuously in Labor Force, 1967-1974)

Using Real Hourly Earnings

Number of Years with Increases	Profes-sional/ Technical	Managers, Officials, Proprietors	Self-Employed	Clerical and Sales	Foremen	Operatives	Laborers	Farmers	Miscel-laneous	All
1	0.9%	1.1%	0.0%	0.8%	0.4%	0.0%	0.0%	0.0%	0.0%	0.5%
2	7.7	7.2	11.6	5.7	7.5	5.4	9.9	7.8	1.6	7.1
3	29.9	20.4	38.7	26.3	24.6	24.6	31.8	38.6	34.5	27.2
4	30.6	43.6	39.0	38.7	39.7	41.0	37.6	40.9	27.7	38.1
5	24.6	17.5	9.1	19.9	24.6	24.4	16.4	9.8	28.6	21.3
6	5.9	9.6	1.7	8.6	3.3	4.7	4.3	2.9	7.6	5.5
7	0.6	0.7	0.0	0.0	0.0	0.0	0.0	0.0	0.0	0.2
Mean Number of Increases	3.90	4.01	3.51	3.97	3.90	3.98	3.74	3.61	4.06	3.89

Using Nominal Hourly Earnings

Number of Years with Increases	Profes-sional/ Technical	Managers, Officials, Proprietors	Self-Employed	Clerical and Sales	Foremen	Operatives	Laborers	Farmers	Miscel-laneous	All
1	0.0%	0.0%	0.0%	0.0%	0.0%	0.0%	0.0%	0.0%	0.0%	0.0%
2	1.4	1.2	6.6	2.8	2.8	1.1	1.7	7.1	0.0	2.2
3	13.0	9.6	13.0	7.7	9.0	12.5	20.9	34.0	20.1	12.1
4	27.4	36.3	47.5	35.8	31.3	25.9	38.5	36.3	29.1	32.3
5	32.1	29.6	23.6	33.7	36.0	39.1	27.2	19.2	28.0	32.8
6	21.3	21.1	8.6	15.7	18.0	18.2	10.3	3.3	19.5	17.4
7	4.5	2.2	0.6	4.4	2.8	2.7	1.2	0.0	3.3	2.9
Mean Number of Increases	4.73	4.66	4.14	4.64	4.67	4.69	4.31	3.81	4.57	4.60
Number of Observations	229	143	65	160	339	353	222	60	46	1,617

MTR #7516

unskilled laborers was only about 5 percent for real earnings and 8 percent for nominal earnings. It would be difficult to argue that this difference reflected the differential reward pattern predicted for workers in the primary and secondary labor markets. Only farmers and self-employed workers lagged far behind the rest. None of the farmers and only 0.6 percent of the self-employed had increases every year, even using nominal earnings, while over half of the self-employed and just under half of the farmers had increases in real earnings in three years or less. In general, then, although one does observe some interesting differences in earnings patterns among occupations, no occupational group-- not the most highly trained white-collar workers nor the skilled blue-collar workers--shows anything close to a monotonic pattern of increases in either of the earnings measures.

Rather than present the entire distribution for the rest of the explanatory variables, we present the mean number of increases for each subgroup, the percentages of individuals with a monotonic pattern of increases, and the explanatory power (and significance level) for each of the variables. This information is presented in Table 7.6 for education, industry, union status, job tenure, and 1967 labor income.

The simplest summary statement one can make for all of these variables is that none make very much difference in the pattern of increases in earnings. Only one of the variables--industry--explains as much as 5 percent of the variance in number of increases, and almost all of the rest of the variables explain less than 2 percent.[21] The most significant predictor is industry, where government workers had by far the highest mean number of increases of any subgroup considered. In an analysis where even the smallest differences stand out, government workers averaged almost .4 of a year above the mean in both earnings measures and had the greatest percentage of individuals with monotonic increases. Using nominal earnings, workers in manufacturing, both durable and nondurable, also showed a more monotonic trend. The relative importance of a worker's industry is difficult to explain within the human capital model, since industry does not, in general, reflect any component of a worker's skill. Its significance is more compatible with the internal/dual labor market analysis, since it does focus on the behavior of specific job markets. However, the differences among industries that do exist are a good deal less than would be consistent

---

[21] The explanatory power shown for each variable in Table 7.6 is that from a one-way analysis of variance. In spite of their low explanatory power, in all but two cases the independent variables are statistically significant at the 5 percent level. With a sample size as large as 1,600, a variable which explains as little as 1 percent of the variance is usually statistically significant.

Table 7.6 (Sheet 1 of 2)

BIVARIATE PATTERN OF INCREASES IN HOURLY EARNINGS, 1967-1974, FOR SELECTED INDEPENDENT VARIABLES
(Males, Aged 18-55, Continuously in the Labor Force, 1967-1974)

Variable	Number of Cases	Weighted Percentage	Using Real Hourly Earnings		Using Nominal Hourly Earnings	
			Mean Number of Increases	Percent with Increases All Seven Years	Mean Number of Increases	Percent with Increases All Seven Years
Education			$\eta^2=.003$		$\eta^2=.011^*$	
0-5 Grades	122	3.2%	3.92	0.0%	4.64	4.0%
6-8	268	12.6	3.78	0.0	4.32	2.2
9-11	314	16.0	3.96	0.0	4.58	3.8
12	315	21.7	3.94	0.4	4.69	3.3
12 + Nonacademic Training	162	11.5	3.88	0.0	4.67	3.0
College, No Degree	219	16.6	3.92	0.7	4.65	4.1
B.A. Degree	138	11.6	3.88	0.0	4.61	1.8
Advanced or Professional Degree	79	6.8	3.89	0.0	4.56	1.4
Industry (1971)			$\eta^2=.017^*$		$\eta^2=.050^*$	
Agriculture; Mining	138	7.1	3.75	0.0	4.16	0.0
Manufacturing (Durables)	327	21.3	3.88	0.0	4.79	5.2
Manufacturing (Nondurables)	142	8.1	3.99	0.0	4.85	4.8
Construction, Transportation, Communication	357	19.7	3.92	0.1	4.58	4.0
Trade (Retail and Wholesale)	207	13.5	3.87	0.0	4.49	0.8
Finance; Business and Personal Services	143	9.8	3.78	0.0	4.27	0.0
Professional Services	181	12.7	3.82	0.8	4.52	2.4
Government	122	7.8	4.29	1.1	4.95	9.2

Table 7.6 (Sheet 2 of 2)

Variable	Number of Cases	Weighted Percentage	Using Real Hourly Earnings		Using Nominal Hourly Earnings	
			Mean Number of Increases	Percent with Increases All Seven Years	Mean Number of Increases	Percent with Increases All Seven Years
Number of Years in Union			$\eta^2=.008$		$\eta^2=.014$*	
Zero	871	55.5%	3.90	0.2%	4.55	2.6
One	119	6.0	3.78	0.0	4.36	1.1
Two	83	4.4	3.60	0.0	4.42	6.6
Three	52	2.5	4.16	0.0	4.61	0.0
Four	53	3.3	3.87	3.0	4.67	10.1
Five	74	4.6	4.07	0.0	4.84	6.4
Six	77	4.0	3.89	0.3	4.50	4.1
Seven	288	19.7	3.95	0.0	4.78	4.3
Job Tenure (1974)			$\eta^2=.027$*		$\eta^2=.012$*	
Self-employed	87	4.7	3.86	0.0	4.24	0.0
< 1 Year	169	9.6	4.03	0.0	4.44	2.5
1 - 1½ Years	81	5.4	3.91	0.0	4.55	4.2
1½ - 3½ Years	193	12.0	3.89	0.7	4.48	3.0
3½ - 9½ Years	440	26.6	4.08	0.0	4.71	3.1
9½ - 19½ Years	362	22.9	3.90	0.4	4.70	3.8
> 19½ Years	285	18.7	3.59	0.0	4.43	4.0
Labor Income (1967)			$\eta^2=.018$*		$\eta^2=.007$*	
< $5,000	490	18.2	4.00	0.0	4.47	3.4
$5,000 - $7,499	471	28.0	3.96	0.0	4.65	3.6
$7,500 - $9,999	292	22.2	4.00	0.4	4.71	3.8
$10,000-$12,499	212	17.4	3.81	0.5	4.66	3.8
> $12,500	152	14.2	3.60	0.0	4.52	1.3
Mean Value			3.89	0.2%	4.60	3.0%

*Significant at 0.5 level.

MTR #7516

with a division of industries into the primary and secondary labor markets.[22]

A particularly striking example of a variable with almost no effect at all
is education. On the basis of both theory and previous empirical work, one
would expect there to be a positive correlation between years of schooling and
the number of increases in earnings. The human capital model suggests that more
highly educated workers will be more efficient learners on the job and will, as
a result, invest more in on-the-job training. Consequently, their age-earnings
profile will rise more sharply, a finding confirmed by most cross-sectional
analyses. Additionally, the internal/dual labor market analysis frequently argues that education is used as a screening device to assign workers to different
labor markets. Yet, except for one group--those with six to eight years of edu-
cation--the maximum difference in mean number of increases in real earnings is
less than one-tenth of a year. Even the deviant group is only .11 years below
the mean. When nominal earnings are used instead, the differences between the
subgroups are only slightly greater. The explanatory power is only 0.3 percent
for real earnings and 1.1 percent for nominal; and, as low as these figures are,
they actually overstate the explanatory power by allowing education to affect
the pattern of earnings in a nonlinear fashion. There simply appears to be no
correlation at all between years of schooling and the number of years in which
earnings increased.

Neither union status, job tenure, nor initial level of labor earnings made
a systematic difference in the pattern of increases. Although union membership
had a slight positive effect on increases in nominal earnings, it had no effect
on increases in real earnings. The effects of job tenure were nearly random,
and, if anything, the number of increases appears to be negatively related to
initial earnings level.

We have considered in this section whether a set of independent variables,
regularly used in earning regressions and important to either or both of the two
models, made a significant difference in the pattern of increases in real or
nominal hourly earnings. Simply put, they did not. We have, of course, found
some differences, many of them interesting and predicted by the models themselves.
But none of these differences were large. In no case did any single subgroup,
whether defined by age, occupation, industry, job tenure, union status, race, or
initial earnings level, differ from the mean by as much as half a year. No subgroup averaged less than three increases, using real hourly earnings, or more

---

[22]It is possible that some other grouping of industries would produce results
more consistent with the internal/dual labor market analysis. The model does
not, as noted earlier, offer specific guidance on what would be an appropriate
classification scheme.

than five, for nominal earnings. The cumulative weight of the evidence seems clear: A monotonic pattern of increases in earnings is not the norm.

IV. REGULARITIES AND DIVERSITY IN THE PATTERN
     OF LIFE-CYCLE EARNINGS: A BRIEF OVERVIEW

One might reasonably conclude from the evidence of the last two sections that the life-cycle pattern of individual labor market earnings is essentially a random one, with no basic trend and few important empirical regularities. This section takes a brief look at that issue. We contend that both positions are at least partially correct: There are some important regularities and trends, but there is also a great deal more diversity in earnings behavior than was suggested in the previous two sections.

First, even though the mean number of increases was only 3.89 for real hourly earnings and 4.60 for nominal earnings, the general earnings trend over the eight-year period was generally upward. As shown in Table 7.7, over 70 percent of the individuals had higher real hourly earnings in 1974 than in 1967, and over 90 percent had an eight-year net increase in nominal earnings. Almost 60 percent of those with only three increases in real earnings nevertheless had a net increase in earnings, and of those with four increases, nearly three-fourths experienced real income growth. For nominal earnings, the percentages were, naturally, higher: 75 percent of the men with three increases and over 90 percent of the men with four increases had a net increase in earnings over the analysis period. Thus, the lack of a significant monotonic pattern of earnings increases is not inconsistent with a general upward trend in individual earnings over the life cycle.

The proportion with increases in any single year was extremely stable. Table 7.8 reports these figures for each pair of years. Over each two-year interval, with the sole exception of 1973-1974, between 55 percent and 60 percent of the individuals experienced real growth in hourly earnings. The 1973-1974 dip in the percentage with real increases in earnings was due, presumably, to the double-digit inflation rate which prevailed in 1974. For nominal earnings, the annual percentage with increases ranged from 62.1 percent to 68.6 percent. One might be tempted to infer from figures such as those in Table 7.8 that there was, indeed, a large group of individuals--at least half and perhaps as much as two-thirds of the population--who experienced increases in earnings every year. But, as Sections II and III clearly demonstrated, that conclusion is certainly incorrect. While the aggregate figures may be stable, the individuals who compose those aggregates are not.

On the other hand, the diversity of earnings experiences can be seen by

Table 7.7

TREND IN REAL AND NOMINAL HOURLY EARNINGS
BY NUMBER OF INCREASES IN EARNINGS, 1967–1974
(Males, Aged 18–55, Continuously in Labor Force, 1967–1974)

Number of Years with Increases	Using Real Hourly Earnings		Using Nominal Hourly Earnings	
	Weighted Percentage of Cases	Percentage with Increase in Earnings, 1967–1974	Weighted Percentage of Cases	Percentage with Increase in Earnings, 1967–1974
1	0.4%	17.2%	0.0%	0.0%
2	7.2	21.2	2.1	29.5
3	27.2	59.3	10.3	75.4
4	38.1	74.3	29.8	93.1
5	21.4	92.4	33.7	96.6
6	5.5	95.8	20.3	99.9
7	0.2	100.0	3.8	100.0
TOTAL	100.0%	71.2%	100.0%	92.7%

Table 7.8

PERCENTAGE WITH INCREASES IN
REAL AND NOMINAL HOURLY EARNINGS BY YEAR, 1967–1974

Comparison Years	Using Real Hourly Earnings	Using Nominal Hourly Earnings
1967–1968	58.3%	64.8%
1968–1969	59.5	68.6
1969–1970	55.0	66.1
1970–1971	56.0	62.1
1971–1972	59.9	64.7
1972–1973	55.6	67.5
1973–1974	45.7	66.0

considering the actual individual earnings paths. Over the eight-year period, there were 128 (2^7) possible paths of year-to-year increases and decreases in earnings. A single path, for example, represents a monotonic pattern of increases, while 35 distinct paths represent increases in three or four years. The diversity of earnings experience revealed by the paths is striking. Using real hourly earnings as the earnings measure, 123 of these paths were actually realized, with the most common of the paths (two consecutive increases, followed by an alternating sequence of decreases and increases) accounting for only 2.2 percent of the sample. Two others (one with a regular alternation of increases and decreases, the other alternating but with three consecutive increases in the middle years) were each followed by 2.1 percent of the sample. When nominal hourly earnings were used, there were still 115 different paths, and the largest (six increases with a decrease in the middle) included 4 percent of all cases.

There were, of course, far too many paths to present them in full detail, but we can describe some of their major features. In general, the paths confirmed the finding of the earlier analysis. For example, monotonic increases, even over intervals shorter than eight years, were far from universal. Only 36 percent of the sample had, at any time during the eight years, three consecutive increases in real earnings, and less than 15 percent had four such increases. The percentages were higher for increases in nominal earnings, but still less than three-fourths ever had three successive increases and just over half had increases four years in a row. Finally, there was a great deal of regular alternation of increases and decreases. Eighty-five percent of the individuals had two or more nonconsecutive decreases in real earnings, and 72 percent had a similar record with respect to nominal earnings.

Summary

The overall picture of the pattern of individual earnings over the life cycle is, in many ways, a perplexing one. The pattern of monotonically increasing earnings, predicted by theory and noted in the cross section, appears to be the exception rather than the rule. Even with a generous allowance for possible measurement error, the results suggest an upper-bound estimate of just over a quarter of the sample with monotonic increases in nominal earnings and just over 10 percent with increases in real earnings. Moreover, none of the characteristics of an individual (age, education, race, or level of income) or of his job (occupation, industry, union status, or job tenure) had a strong effect on the observed pattern of increases. There is, however, a general, although by no means universal, upward trend in the earnings over the life cycle and, in this respect at least, the models are consistent with the movements of individual earnings over time. The models may capture the trend, but they are simply not rich enough to explain the detail. And it is the detail--the nonmonotonic pattern-- which appears to dominate.

It is, perhaps, tempting to interpret the results of this paper in terms of transitory and permanent components of earnings. A division of that kind is consistent with both the trend and the frequent deviations that are observed. The question that remains, however, is what does in fact account for the deviations. To dismiss the deviations as transitory is frequently to relegate them to a secondary role in the analysis of earnings patterns. In the light of the findings presented here, that would seem to be unwarranted.

References

Becker, Gary S. _Human Capital_. New York: National Bureau of Economic Research, 1972.

Becker, Gary S. _Human Capital and the Personal Distribution of Income_. Ann Arbor: The University of Michigan, 1967.

Ben-Porath, Yoram. "The Production of Human Capital and the Life Cycle of Earnings." _Journal of Political Economy_ 75 (August, 1967), pp. 352-365.

Blinder, Alan. _Towards an Economic Theory of Income Distribution_. Cambridge: MIT Press, 1975.

Doeringer, Peter B. and Piore, Michael J. _Internal Labor Markets and Manpower Analysis_. Lexington, Mass.: Heath Lexington Books, 1971.

Kerr, Clark. "The Balkanization of Labor Markets." In _Labor Mobility and Economic Opportunity_. Edited by E. Wight Bakke. Cambridge: MIT Press, 1954.

Mincer, Jacob. "On-the-Job Training: Costs, Returns, and Some Implications." _Journal of Political Economy_ 70 (October, 1962), pp. S50-S79.

Mincer, Jacob. _Schooling, Experience, and Earnings_. New York: National Bureau of Economic Research, 1974.

Morgan, James N. "Change in Global Measures." In _Five Thousand American Families--Patterns of Economic Progress_, Volume I. James N. Morgan et al. Ann Arbor: Institute for Social Research, 1974.

Rosen, Sherwin. "Learning and Experience in the Labor Market." Journal of Human Resources 7 (Summer, 1972), pp. 326-342.

Taubman, Paul. Sources of Inequality in Earnings. Amsterdam: North-Holland Publishing Co., 1975.

Wachter, Michael. "Primary and Secondary Labor Markets: A Critique of the Dual Approach." Brookings Papers on Economic Activity, 3. Washington, D.C.: Brookings Institution, 1974.

Chapter 8

PARTICIPATION IN THE FOOD STAMP PROGRAM AMONG THE POVERTY POPULATION

Richard D. Coe

Introduction

In July 1975 almost 19 million people in the United States were receiving food stamps, an increase of nearly 5 million from July 1974.[1] Although it has been estimated that approximately one-third of the increased number of participants was a result of the opening of new areas to the food stamp program (e.g., Puerto Rico),[2] it is clear that many families in areas which previously had been served by the program have recently decided to avail themselves of its benefits. Despite the fact that this rapid increase in the number of persons receiving food stamps has drawn widespread attention (and often sharp criticism) from the press and the politicians, the most remarkable aspect of this issue is the low participation rate by families eligible to receive food stamps. Most estimates place the nationwide participation rate in the program at less than 50 percent.[3]

Despite this recognition of the low participation rate in the program, there seems to be no clearly understood reason why the rate is as low as it is. Various explanations have been put forth: eligible families don't know about the potential benefits of the program; people are not willing to face the stigma attached to receiving welfare; benefit levels are too low to make it worthwhile for a family to expend the time and energy necessary to obtain the food stamps; eligible families do not have the necessary transportation to enable them to acquire their food stamps; and other possible reasons.

This chapter attempts to test the relative importance of some of these diverse influences in determining whether an eligible family decides to participate in the food stamp program. The results, though not conclusive, are suggestive. It would appear that one major reason why eligible families do not participate in the program is because they simply are not well-informed either about their eli-

---

[1] Food and Nutrition Service (1975), p. 1.

[2] Seagrave (1975), p. 53.

[3] See, for example, Bickel and MacDonald (1975).

gibility or about the benefit to which they are entitled. A family's attitude
toward receiving welfare income also appears to be influential. The more surprising results of this study, however, are those concerning the factors which
are *not* influential. The amount of the bonus value of the food stamps to which
a family is entitled, the availability of transportation to the recipient family,
and the race of the eligible family are all insignificant in predicting participation in the food stamp program, after controlling for other factors. What
emerges from this study is the suggestion that participation in the food stamp
program is determined primarily by noneconomic factors such as information and
attitudes, rather than economic incentives such as the amount of the bonus value
to which eligible families are entitled.[4]

This chapter is organized as follows: Section I details the data source
and the selection of the sample used in the analysis; Section II discusses the
general framework of the analysis; Section III describes the variables used in
the estimating equation; Section IV presents the empirical results; and Section
V contains a summary of the findings.

I. THE DATA SOURCE

The data source for this study is the eighth wave of the Panel Study of Income Dynamics. As such, it is a one-year, cross-sectional sample. The eighth
wave of data was collected from interviews with 5,725 families conducted in the
spring of 1975. Information was gathered at that time concerning participation
in the food stamp program in 1974, income levels in 1974, and a host of other
variables. Although most of the crucial information collected covered calendar
year 1974, certain variables (as noted below) related to a family's status at
the time of the interview rather than 1974. Thus, there is not a perfect matching of data for all the key variables, but it is not thought that this creates
any substantial problem with the results of the analysis.

In this study the sample was limited to those panel families residing in
the continental United States whose annual money income was below the official
federal poverty guidelines for 1974. This limitation resulted in a subsample of
809 families. Annual family money income for 1974 was defined as the sum of
labor money income, asset money income, and transfer money income, both public
and private, received by all members of the family in 1974. The official federal
poverty guidelines are based on the "Economy Food Plan," as estimated by the De-

---

[4]For a detailed elaboration of a similar theme concerning all welfare programs, see Piven and Cloward (1971).

partment of Agriculture.[5] It is assumed in this study that all families whose money income was below the federal poverty level were eligible for food stamps at some time during 1974.[6] Table 8.1 shows the relationship for different family sizes between the official poverty line[7] and the maximum (net) income a family may receive and remain eligible for food stamps.[8]

----

[5]These guidelines were estimated from a needs standard compiled by the Survey Research Center of the Institute for Social Research at The University of Michigan. The SRC needs standard is slightly more complex than that employed by the Bureau of Census (which conducts the official federal count of the poor), but is virtually equivalent, with one major exception--the poverty threshold for single females aged 65 or more. The SRC needs standard for these people has been adjusted in this chapter to correspond to the Bureau of Census standard.

[6]An exception would be families who had sufficient assets so as to disqualify them from the program. It is doubtful that many families below the official poverty line have sufficient assets to disqualify them, especially when one considers that assets held in the form of a home or a car are generally not included in determining eligibility for the food stamp program. However, financial assets do count, and this may disqualify some poverty families, especially some elderly families. Of the 809 panel families in poverty, 768 (88.2 percent on a weighted basis) reported no income from dividends, rent, or interest. Of the remaining 41 families who reported such income, 31 had a total of less than $500 from such sources. These figures would seem to indicate that few of the poverty families would be ineligible for the food stamp program due to their asset holdings, although it is possible that some families would hold nonincome earning assets.

[7]The single poverty threshold for each family size shown in Table 8.1 does not correspond exactly to the poverty thresholds used by the Bureau of Census. The Bureau employs a total of 124 different poverty thresholds based on the age-sex composition of the family and whether it is a farm or nonfarm family. The figures presented in Table 8.1, however, should be a close average of these various thresholds for nonfarm families of a particular size.

[8]The income measure relevant for determining eligibility for food stamps is *not* gross money income, the income measure used in this study. The food stamp program allows deductions from gross money income for taxes, excess medical and shelter costs, and other items. Since most families have some deductions which they can claim for food stamp purposes, the income measure used in this study represents a conservative estimate of the maximum income a family can receive and still be eligible for food stamps.

Another point should be noted in determining the accuracy of the assumption that all families below the official poverty line are eligible for food stamps. Eligibility for the food stamp program is determined on a *monthly* basis, while the figures used in this study are on an annual basis. The effect of these different time horizons is to underestimate the maximum income eligibility requirements of families. A family could receive more than the monthly maximum income for a few months of the year and still be eligible for food stamps at some time during the year if its income fell below the monthly maximum for any one month.

Also, it might be noted that the income maximums established by the food stamp program apply to nonpublic assistance recipients. Recipients of ADC pay-

Table 8.1

COMPARISON OF FOOD STAMP INCOME MAXIMUMS AND FEDERAL
POVERTY LEVELS, FOR DIFFERENT FAMILY SIZES, 1974

Family Size	Maximum Food Stamp Net Income*	Official Federal Nonfarm Poverty Line**
1	$2,532	$2,330
2	3,288	3,070
3	4,728	3,810
4	6,012	4,550
5	7,128	5,290
6	8,172	6,030

* The figures are the maximum monthly net income allowances, multiplied by 12, as published in the Department of Social Services, State of Michigan, Publication 74, for June, 1974. Net income is gross money income minus certain deductions allowable for food stamp purposes. These figures are equivalent to those published in Characteristics of Households Purchasing Food Stamps (1976) p. 43 (Table B-3), *except* for one-person households. There appears to be a discrepancy in Tables B-3 and B-4 concerning the maximum monthly nonpublic assistance income which a one-person household can receive and still be eligible for food stamps. The figure in the above table corresponds to the one in Table B-4 of the publication. These maximums apply to the 48 contiguous states and the District of Columbia.

**Figures taken from "CSA Income Poverty Guidelines," Community Services Administration, CSA Instruction #6004-If, Community Services Administration, Washington, D. C., for April 1974.

As the figures in Table 8.1 indicate, it would appear that the 809 panel families who did not have sufficient income to exceed the federal poverty line would have been eligible to participate in the food stamp program.[9]

II. THE FRAMEWORK OF ANALYSIS

This analysis attempts to determine the relative importance of various factors which might influence whether or not an eligible family participates in the food stamp program. Specifically, participation is hypothesized to be dependent upon (1) the information received by the family about the program, (2) the attitude of the family toward receiving welfare income, (3) the attitude of local administrators of the program toward the family's participation in the program, (4) the monetary benefit to the family from participating in the program, and (5) the ease of access which a family has in receiving their food stamps. Unfortunately, due to data limitations (discussed more fully below), it was not possible to ascertain the unique influence of each of these various factors. However, reasonable conjectures about the relative importance of some of these factors can be made from the pattern of effects discovered in the analysis. In particular, the contrasting importance of two policy-relevant variables--the information about the program received by the family and the amount of the bonus value for which the family is eligible--is tentatively indicated by the analysis.

The general rationale underlying the hypothesis that food stamp participation is dependent on each of these factors is quite straightforward. In order for the members of a family to receive food stamps, they must have some knowledge of the program. However, even if the members know of the potential benefits which the program has to offer, they may not care to participate in the program because of unfavorable attitudes toward welfare income. The most prominently mentioned source of such attitudes is the stigma attached to accepting welfare income. Even if the members have no personal dislike toward receiving welfare income, they may be sufficiently discouraged from participating in the program because of hostile attitudes on the part of the administrators of the program. If

---

ments are categorically eligible for food stamps and are therefore not subject to the income maximums.

[9]There is another possible exception. Recipients of Supplemental Security Income payments are categorically *ineligible* for food stamps in five states-- California, New York, Massachusetts, Wisconsin, and Nevada. These five states "cash out" food stamp bonus value in determining SSI payments. Three of the 809 families of the subsample would not have been eligible because of this restriction. Eliminating them from the analysis resulted in virtually no change in the results reported here.

these obstacles to participation are overcome, the benefit from the program for which the family is eligible must be large enough to make participation worthwhile in terms of the time and energy which participation involves. Finally, even if all these conditions are met, the family still must be physically able to get the stamps. If physical access to the food stamp distribution center is difficult, a family may choose not to participate in the food stamp program.[10]

III. THE VARIABLES

The following is a description of the dependent and independent variables employed in the empirical analysis of food stamp participation.

Participation in the Food Stamp Program

The dependent variable is whether a family participated in the food stamp program at any time in 1974. A dichotomous dependent variable was formed which assigned a value of 1 to a family if they reported saving any money with food stamps in 1974, and a value of 0 if they did not.

Age-Sex-Marital Status

"Age-Sex-Marital Status" is a nine-category variable combining three age groups (under 25 ["young"], 25-64 ["middled-aged"],[11] 65 or more ["elderly"], the

---

[10] It should be noted that one factor often thought to influence participation has not been included in the above list--the purchase price required to buy the food stamp allotment. It has been argued that an eligible family, although wishing to participate, may not be able to come up with the purchase money because of other demands on a limited budget. While this may have once been a critical problem in the program, administrative reforms in effect in 1974 would seem to have mitigated to a large degree the adverse effects of high purchase prices. Eligible families have the option of purchasing as little as one-fourth of their stamps for a given month at one-quarter of the full-allotment purchase price. In fact, families can receive their monthly allotment in semi-monthly installments, each with the one-fourth option, thereby reducing the cash requirement for participation to one-eighth of the monthly full-allotment purchase price. According to the food stamp regulations the full-allotment purchase price should not exceed 30 percent of the monthly income net of basic living expenses (as defined by the food stamp program). As a result, the variable purchase options, if administered properly, should reduce the cash requirement to less than 10 percent of a family's net income. It would seem that this would not be such a great burden as to prevent many families from participating in the program, athough the bonus value for which the families would be entitled would be proportionately reduced. Thus, while it is not thought that the cash flow problem itself would cause eligible families not to participate, such problems could result in an overestimate of the level of bonus value for which the families are eligible, a problem which should be kept in mind during the discussion of the results concerning bonus value. Furthermore, the argument assumes that eligible families are aware of these options, an assumption whose validity may be questioned.

[11] To those persons in their late twenties or early thirties who object to being labelled as "middle-aged," the author offers as his only defense the fact

two sexes, and whether the household head resided with a spouse. Families were assigned to categories based on these characteristics of the head in the spring of 1975.

Welfare Status

"Welfare Status" is divided into three categories: families which received AFDC or other welfare[12] in 1974; families which received no AFDC or other welfare but reported payments from Social Security or Supplemental Security Income; and families which reported no income from any of these sources in 1974.

Employment Status

"Employment Status" is divided into five categories: employed now or only temporarily laid off; unemployed; retired or permanently disabled; housewife; and student or other. This variable refers to the employment status of the head at the time of interview.

Number of Children Aged 0-13 Years

This variable counts the number of children in the household in the spring of 1975 who were younger than 14 years.

Size of the Largest City in the County

A family was assigned to one of four categories of this variable on the basis of the population of the largest city within the county in which the family resided at the time of the interview. The categories are: (1) a population of 500,000 or more; (2) 100,000-499,999; (3) 50,000-99,999; and (4) fewer than 50,000 people.

Food Stamp Bonus Value

A variable was constructed which estimated the annual bonus value for which each family was eligible in 1974. The bonus levels were bracketed into eight categories: under $200, $200-299, $300-399, $400-599, $600-799, $800-999, $1,000-1,499, and $1,500 or more. Because it was impossible to calculate from the data the deductions from gross income allowable by the food stamp program,[13] gross income rather than net income for food stamp purposes had to be used as the basis for estimating bonus values. Since net income is never larger than

that he, 28 years old, is labelling himself as middle-aged.

[12]"Other Welfare" is essentially general assistance cash payments.

[13]Probably the most important of these deductions is for excess shelter costs, for which 57.6 percent of food stamp participants were estimated to be eligible, for an average deduction of $55 per month. See Peskin (1975), p. 18.

and is generally less than gross income, the use of gross income results in an underestimate of the actual bonus value for which families were eligible.

Another possible source of error resulted from the implicit assumption that annual family money income was received equally in the 12 months of 1974. In estimating the bonus value, the *monthly* income levels appropriate for each bonus value (for different family sizes) were multiplied by 12 to arrive at annual income figures. The corresponding bonus values were also multiplied by 12 to arrive at annual benefit levels. If monthly income fluctuated greatly (and if food stamp administrators responded immediately), this procedure could result in misestimation. Although it is not clear from the food stamp benefit schedule what the direction or the magnitude of this error would be, a few examples appear to indicate that the likely error is small.[14]

Data for the calculation of benefit levels were obtained from the "Food Coupon Issuance Tables," Department of Social Services, State of Michigan, for June 1974.[15] A set of equations was derived from these tables to assign the annual benefit level for families of different sizes. Using a single equation for each family size resulted in an additional small error. These equations and resulting errors at selected income levels are presented in Appendix 8.1.

Distance to Nearest City of 50,000 or More

A family was assigned to one of the five categories of this variable depending on the distance of their place of residence in the spring of 1975 from the nearest city of at least 50,000 people. The five categories were: (1) less than 5 miles, (2) 5-14 miles, (3) 15-29 miles, (4) 30-49 miles, and (5) 50 miles or more.

Transportation

A family was assigned to one of four categories depending on the type of

---

[14] For example, take a family of four with an annual net income of $1,200. If this income were received equally in the 12 months, thus resulting in a monthly income of $100, the monthly bonus value of food stamps would be $125. The annual benefit would be $1,500. If the family received $200 a month for six months and nothing in the other six months, annual benefit would equal (6 × $97) + (6 × $150), or $1,482--$18 less than the steady income situation. If the family received the entire $1,200 in one month and nothing in the remaining eleven months, the annual benefit would equal (1 × $0) + (11 × $150), or $1,650--$150 more than the steady income state. If the family received $600 for two months and nothing in the remaining ten months of the year, the annual benefit would equal (2 × $0) + (10 × $150), or $1,500--exactly the same as the constant monthly income case.

[15] These same benefit levels apply for the 48 contiguous states and the District of Columbia. See Characteristics of Households Purchasing Food Stamps (1976), p. 43.

transportation which was available to them in the spring of 1975. The four categories were: (1) public transportation only, (2) private transportation only,
(3) both public and private transportation, and (4) no transportation available.

Race

A family was assigned to one of the three categories of this variable
(white, black, other) based on the race of the head of the family.

Region

The "Region" variable was divided into four categories (Northeast, North
Central, South, and West). A family was placed in one of these categories based
on their residence in the spring of 1975.

Whether County Started Food Stamp Program in 1974

Before 1974, an individual county had the option of entering the food stamp
program. However, in 1974 a federal court ordered the Department of Agriculture
to administer the program in all counties.[16] As a result, some counties did not
begin administering the food stamp program until 1974. Families were assigned
to one of the two categories of this variable depending on whether or not their
county of residence began the program in 1974.[17]

IV. THE RESULTS

The influence of each of these variables on a family's decision to participate in the food stamp program was estimated by the dummy variable regression
program Multiple Classification Analysis (MCA). By listing the independent variables in rank order according to the value of Beta^2, one can see the relative
importance of each predictor in explaining variation in the dependent variable
after adjusting for the effects of other predictors.[18] In addition, an F-test
can be performed on the value of Beta^2 to see if the differences in the subclass
means of the independent variable are statistically significant.

As shown in Table 8.2, the noneconomic variables dominated in importance,
with the age-sex-marital status and the welfare status of the family being the

---

[16]*Bennet v. Butz*, 386 F. Supp. 1059 (D. Minn. 1974).

[17]Due to difficulties with the data, families residing in Virginia could not
be categorized in such a manner. Thus, all families living in Virginia in the
spring of 1975 were assigned to the category "County Started Program Before
1974." Of Virginia's 132 counties, 43 did not begin administering the food
stamp program until some time during 1974.

[18]For a full explanation of the MCA program, see Andrews et al. (1973), or
Appendix D of Volume IV of this series.

Table 8.2

UNADJUSTED (ETA^2) AND ADJUSTED ($BETA^2$) EXPLANATORY POWER OF
PREDICTORS OF PARTICIPATION IN THE FOOD STAMP
PROGRAM BY THE POVERTY POPULATION, 1974

Predictor	Eta^2	$Beta^2$
Age-Sex-Marital Status	.144	.102**
Welfare Status	.245	.081**
Employment Status	.052	.077**
Number of Children Age 0-13	.126	.059**
Size of Largest City in County	.044	.023**
Food Stamp Bonus Value	.097	.014
Distance to Center of Nearest City of 50,000 or More	.020	.012*
Transportation	.014	.006
Race	.031	.004
Region	.003	.003
Whether County Started Food Stamp Program in 1974	.003	.001

Number of Observations = 809

Adjusted R^2 = .379

* Significant at .05 level, as calculated by an approximation to the F-test.

**Significant at .01 level, as calculated by an approximation to the F-test.

MTR #7028

two most important explanatory variables. The amount of the bonus value, the
availability of transportation, race, region, and whether the county started administering the program in 1974 were all statistically insignificant. Overall,
the independent variables did an impressively strong job of explaining the decision to participate in the food stamp program, with an R^2 of .379--quite high
for a dichotomous dependent variable using microdata.

The unadjusted and regression adjusted participation rates of the different
categories of the independent variables provide a more detailed picture of the
influence of the independent variables on the decision to participate. (See
Table 8.3.) Overall, 37.1 percent of the poverty population participated in the
food stamp program at some time during 1974. This estimate is very close to the
Census Bureau's estimate of the participation rate of poverty families; the Bureau estimated that 40 percent of all poverty families and 20 percent of unrelated individuals in poverty purchased food stamps in 1974.[19]

The age-sex-marital status of the household head was the single most powerful explanatory variable, with a Beta^2 of .102. The unadjusted mean participation rates of the different subgroups indicate that elderly single people have
substantially lower-than-average participation rates, a sharp contrast to the
participation rate of elderly married couples. (Caution is required in interpreting the results for elderly single males, due to the low number of observations (N=13).) The unadjusted rates also show that single males of all ages
have low participation rates, while households headed by middle-aged single females have the highest participation rate. When other factors are held constant
to arrive at an adjusted mean participation rate for the individual subgroup,
these results hold, with the exception of households headed by young single
males. The exceptionally low unadjusted participation rate of this subgroup was
adjusted markedly higher, a result which will be discussed below.

These results suggest an interesting interpretation of the influence of informational and attitudinal factors on the decision to participate in the food
stamp program. Concerning informational factors, elderly persons are often
thought to be one group that is particularly cut off from the mainstream of society, and this could lead to poor information concerning the food stamp program.
This problem would be most acute for single elderly people, considered by many

---

[19] "Characteristics of Households Purchasing Food Stamps," Current Population
Reports, Series P-23, No. 61, p. 4. The Census Bureau defines an unrelated individual as a person 14 years old or older who is not living with any relatives.
A family is a group of two or more persons related by blood, marriage, or adoption and residing together. No such distinctions are made in this paper.

Table 8.3 (Sheet 1 of 3)

UNADJUSTED AND ADJUSTED MEAN PARTICIPATION RATES
IN FOOD STAMP PROGRAM BY POVERTY POPULATION, 1974

Family Characteristic	Percent of Poverty Population	Unadjusted Mean Participation Rate	Adjusted Mean Participation Rate
TOTAL	100.0%	37.1%	--
Age-Sex-Marital Status of Head			
Young Married Couple	3.9%	28.5%	53.6%
Middle-Aged Married Couple	17.0	39.6	42.5
Elderly Married Couple	9.1	51.7	42.1
Young Single Female	10.3	28.8	36.5
Middle-Aged Single Female	23.2	64.4	52.3
Elderly Single Female	20.8	17.8	12.9
Young Single Male	8.0	17.2	48.8
Middle-Aged Single Male	4.5	25.4	26.8
Elderly Single Male	3.3*	12.9	7.3
Welfare Status			
AFDC or Other Welfare	23.6	78.7	59.8
Social Security or SSI Only	37.5	31.3	36.4
No Welfare	38.9	17.5	24.0
Employment Status			
Working Now, or Only Temporarily Laid Off	29.6	22.9	21.2
Unemployed	9.1	44.6	29.6
Retired, Permanently Disabled	37.0	44.4	52.5
Housewife	19.2	46.7	39.5
Student, Other	5.2	17.3	22.0
Number of Children Age 0-13			
None	69.5	26.6	30.1
One	8.4	62.9	51.9
Two	7.9	48.9	45.7
Three	6.0	52.9	44.7
Four	4.5	83.2	66.0
Five or More	3.6	69.4	69.0

Table 8.3 (Sheet 2 of 3)

Family Characteristic	Percent of Poverty Population	Unadjusted Mean Participation Rate	Adjusted Mean Participation Rate
Size of Largest City in County			
500,000 or More	28.9	46.2	40.0
100,000-499,999	20.6	24.9	30.9
50,000 - 99,999	10.8	55.4	55.5
49,999 or Less	39.7	31.8	33.2
Food Stamp Bonus Value			
Under $200	16.8	25.4	44.1
$ 200 - 299	24.5	32.7	34.6
$ 300 - 399	13.8	21.4	33.6
$ 400 - 599	14.4	28.]	33.8
$ 600 - 799	8.6	57.7	45.7
$ 800 - 999	7.8	64.2	43.5
$1,000 - 1,499	7.3	46.7	25.6
$1,500 or More	6.7	65.3	37.0
Distance to Nearest City of 50,000 or More			
Less Than 5 Miles	19.3	44.2	40.6
5 -14 Miles	18.6	38.2	37.1
15-29 Miles	10.8	41.5	40.2
30-49 Miles	7.3	15.3	18.9
50 Miles or More	44.0	36.0	37.8
Transportation			
Public Transportation Only	32.2	44.6	39.5
Private Transportation Only	25.3	29.7	33.6
Both Public and Private Transportation	18.7	37.4	31.9
No Transportation	23.8	34.6	41.6
Race			
White	63.4	30.6	39.3
Black	33.1	48.6	33.4
Other	3.5*	45.5	32.5

Table 8.3 (Sheet 3 of 3)

Family Characteristic	Percent of Poverty Population	Unadjusted Mean Participation Rate	Adjusted Mean Participation Rate
Region			
Northeast	14.5	41.8	30.2
North Central	26.4	38.7	38.5
South	45.2	35.8	38.0
West	13.9	33.5	38.7
Whether County Started Food Stamp Program in 1974			
County Started Program Before 1974	91.1	37.9	37.6
County Started Program in 1974	8.9	28.5	31.8

Number of Observations = 809

Adjusted R^2 = .379

*Less than 25 observations.

MTR #7028

to be the most isolated segment of our society. Furthermore, it has been alleged that elderly people have a greater distaste for welfare income than the younger generation. If so, we would expect lower participation rates for elderly persons, thus compounding the effect of presumably lower information. The results reported above provide support for some of these conjectures, but not others, and the differences are crucial. The above-average participation rate of elderly married couples argues against the idea that elderly persons are less inclined to participate in the food stamp program because they have strong adverse attitudes toward welfare income, as it is difficult to see how these attitudes would be affected by marital status. However, the sharply contrasting result for single elderly persons--presumably the most isolated group of the sample--indicates that informational factors may have a substantial impact on the decision to participate in the food stamp program.

As mentioned above, nonelderly single males had lower than average participation rates, at least on an unadjusted basis. A probable explanation of this result is that the stigma effect of receiving welfare income would likely be higher for males, the traditional breadwinners in our society, thus leading to a lower inclination to participate in the food stamp program. However, as noted above, after adjusting for other factors, single men below the age of 25 had an above-average participation rate of 48.8 percent. This upward adjustment is a result of the fact that the young single males for the most part received no welfare income, were either working or were students, and had no children in their households, circumstances which lead to lower than average participation. If, as might be argued, households with these characteristics have lower-than-average participation rates because of adverse attitudes toward receiving welfare income, then the upward adjustment for young single males would reflect the assignment of "normal" attitudes to young single males. Thus, even though the adjusted participation rate of young single males was above average, the results still could support the hypothesis that nonelderly single men have less favorable attitudes toward participating in the food stamp program.

The second most powerful explanatory variable was the welfare status of the family. Recipients of AFDC or other welfare income had a participation rate which was markedly above average, both on an unadjusted and adjusted basis, while families which received no transfer income had a substantially lower-than-average participation rate--24 percent when other factors were held constant. Recipients of Social Security or Supplemental Security Income payments had an adjusted participation rate comparable to the overall mean. Although it is not possible to pinpoint precisely the reason for these widely divergent participation rates, this author believes that the major reason for these differences is the varying levels of information concerning the food stamp program which these groups possess. Recipients of AFDC payments are categorically eligible for the food stamp program[20] and routinely receive information about the program when applying for AFDC, as well as assistance in completing the necessary paperwork. This is in sharp contrast to recipients of Social Security payments,[21] who may not be routinely informed about the program.[22] Families receiving no public transfer payments also would not be routinely informed. Thus, it is likely that the higher participation rate of AFDC and other welfare recipients can be attributed primarily to the fact that these families were more informed about their eligibility and benefits under the program. However, it is also obviously true that a family which is receiving AFDC or general assistance payments does not have such a negative attitude toward welfare income that it chooses not to receive any, and this factor may account for part of the difference in food stamp use between welfare recipients and those who received no welfare income--who simply may not have wanted to have any income of this nature. In addition, families receiving AFDC or other welfare had convinced local administrators that they were entitled to welfare support. Families receiving no welfare may have tried to obtain it, but were unable to persuade (rightly or wrongly) local officials that they were entitled to such aid. This may further explain the difference in participation rates between these two groups. Hence, although the results concerning the welfare status of the family are consistent with the hypothesis that the information available to the family concerning the food stamp program exerts a powerful influence in determining the family's decision to participate, this conclusion should be tempered with the realization that other factors may be operating to influence the results.

---

[20]This is not quite correct. Households in which *all* members are eligible for AFDC payments are categorically eligible for food stamps. This may have eliminated some of the AFDC recipients in the sample from categorical eligibility because they may have been living with a person who was not eligible for AFDC payments--an elderly parent, for example. However, these households would still be eligible for food stamps on an income basis, and the arguments advanced in this chapter would still stand.

[21]Although there is an element of redistribution in the Social Security program, this section is not meant to imply that Social Security is a purely redistributive program.

[22]Some recipients of Social Security and Supplemental Security Income payments, upon inquiry about their benefit payments, may be told about the food stamp program by administrators at the local Social Security office. However, this still generally involves a trip and subsequent dealings with another government agency, a difficulty which AFDC recipients usually do not face.

A third highly significant variable in explaining the decision to participate was the employment status of the head. On both an unadjusted and adjusted
basis, those heads of poor households who were either working (or only temporarily laid off) or in school had substantially lower-than-average participation
rates--around 20 percent. On the other hand, the retired or permanently disabled
and those heads of households who listed themselves as housewives had higher-than-
average participation rates, on both an unadjusted and adjusted basis. Households
headed by an unemployed person had higher-than-average unadjusted participation
rates, but when other factors were held constant, the rate fell to 29.6 percent--
below the overall mean. A primary reason for this large downward adjustment is
that 52 percent of the households which had unemployed heads received either AFDC
or some other form of welfare payment--a situation which leads to high participation. Controlling for this factor resulted in the downward adjustment.

Why these differences in participation among the subgroups? It would seem
quite probable that the low participation rate of students can be attributed to
the negative public attitude toward students receiving food stamps, an attitude
which would likely be reflected in a student's own feelings toward participation
and in the attitude of local administrators of the program toward dispensing food
stamps to students. The differentially higher participation rates for the retired or the permanently disabled and of housewives can perhaps best be explained
by the fact that external constraints on labor market participation are much
greater for these people, due to age, disability, or household responsibilities.
These severe external constraints on finding adequate employment may lead to more
favorable attitudes toward receiving welfare income, and thus to greater participation in the food stamp program. A similar argument could be advanced concerning households whose heads are unemployed, that is, they would prefer to find employment rather than receive welfare income, but external constraints prevent
this. Consequently, they are more favorably inclined to receive welfare income
and to participate in the food stamp program. The higher-than-average unadjusted
participation rate of this group is consistent with this interpretation. The
lower-than-average adjusted participation rate of this group would appear to
speak against this line of argument, until one recalls that the reason for the
large downward adjustment in the participation rate is that 52 percent of these
households received either AFDC or other welfare payments, a fact which is compatible with the above interpretation.

Speculating further along this line of reasoning, an examination of the results for the age-sex-marital status variable, the welfare status variable, and
the employment status variable suggests an interpretation of the effect of infor-

mation and attitude factors on the participation rate of elderly people. Virtually all elderly people are either retired, disabled, or housewives (40 percent of the single elderly females listed themselves as housewives), and few elderly people receive AFDC or other welfare income. In the context of the arguments developed in this chapter, the picture which emerges is that elderly people actually may have favorable attitudes toward receiving welfare income due to the fact that they are prevented from earning labor income by factors beyond their individual control, such as age or disability. Support for this conclusion is found in the higher-than-average participation rates of the retired and/or permanently disabled and of households headed by elderly married couples, and to a degree by the higher-than-average participation rate of housewives. However, this favorable attitude is stifled for elderly single people because their isolated existence prevents them from learning about the program.

The number of children in the household under fourteen years old exerted a significant and distinct influence on the decision to participate. Having any younger children in the household leads to higher-than-average participation, and the greater the number of children, the more likely is participation in the food stamp program. The adjusted participation rate of households with no children was 30.1 percent, households with one to three children had participation rates in the 45-50 percent range, and households with four or more children had adjusted participation rates of approximately 70 percent. This author would attribute this pattern of participation to the fact that younger children are totally dependent on older members of the household for their food, while older children (and other older members of the household) may find alternative means of feeding themselves. This total dependence leads to greater pressure on the household head to provide food for younger children than for older children, and this pressure would increase with the number of younger children, and would lead to a greater willingness to receive food stamps. In addition, local officials may be more sympathetic toward families with younger children to feed. This combination of influences would lead to greater participation as the number of younger children increased. However, certain reviewers have questioned this interpretation, and at present it should be considered as an interesting conjecture rather than a firm conclusion.

Perhaps the most surprising result of this analysis was the insignificance of of the amount of the bonus value to which the family was entitled in predicting the decision to participate.[23] It was thought that the greater the bonus value,

_____

[23]Although the bonus value variable had a higher Beta^2 than the distance to nearest city of 50,000 or more, the latter was significant while the former was

the more likely a family would be to participate. There was a strong bivariate association between amount of bonus value and participation in the program, as evidenced by the relatively large Eta^2 of .097. A look at the unadjusted participation rates shows that families entitled to a bonus value in excess of $600 had substantially higher participation rates than families eligible for lower bonus values. However, when other factors were held constant in the multivariate analysis, this strong association between bonus value and participation no longer held. (See Figure 8.1.) In effect, these results indicate that if a poverty family is informed about the food stamp program, has favorable attitudes toward receiving welfare income, and is certified as eligible to participate by local welfare officials, the family 's participation will be *independent* of the amount of bonus value to which it is entitled. Conversely, if a poverty household is ill informed about the program, has unfavorable attitudes toward receiving welfare income, or is not considered entitled to the benefits of the program by local officials, the household will probably not participate in the program, no matter how large a bonus value they are eligible to receive. However, it should be kept in mind when considering these results that the amount of the bonus value to which a family was entitled was estimated and subject to error. It is also possible that the amount of the bonus value, even if correctly estimated, would not measure the value of the in-kind transfer to the recipient.[24] The bonus value actually represents the monetary cost to the government of providing the in-kind transfer. Furthermore, if cash flow problems are critical and a household must consider the variable purchase options, the actual bonus value which they would be able to receive would be less than the one assigned by this variable, thus weakening the results presented here. (See footnote 10 for more elaboration on this point.)

It was also somewhat surprising that the availability of transportation was not a significant predictor of the decision to participate. It was thought that eligible families which had private transportation available would be more likely to participate because of the greater convenience (generally) of private transportation. Families which had only public transportation available were expected to be somewhat less likely to participate, while families which had no means of transportation (except possibly walking) were hypothesized to be least likely to participate. The results did not support these expectations, and cast some doubt

---

not. This is because the bonus value variable had eight categories while distance to center of nearest city had only five, and the statistical significance tests depend upon the number of degrees of freedom that a variable uses up.

[24]For a full development of this argument, with special attention given to food stamps, see Peskin (undated).

Figure 8.1

FOOD STAMP PARTICIPATION RATE OF POVERTY FAMILIES
BY AMOUNT OF BONUS VALUE

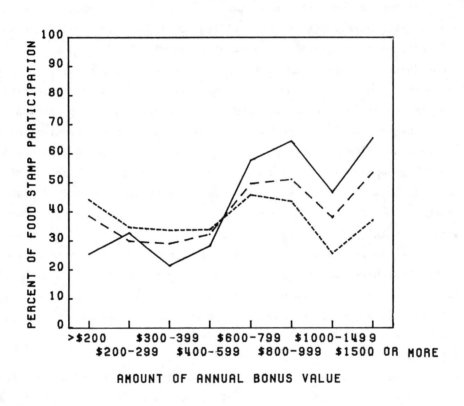

——— Unadjusted

— — — Adjusted for *all* other variables *except* "Number of Children Aged 0-13"

- - - - Adjusted for *all* other variables

on the importance of access costs on the decision to participate in the food
stamp program.

Because it has been alleged that a favorable attitude toward welfare is
passed down intergenerationally among poor families, it may be that persistent
poverty is more strongly associated with participation in the food stamp program
than is "temporary" poverty. Since black families are much more likely to be
persistently poor than white families,[25] race was entered as a measure of persistent poverty. The insignificance of this variable argues against the above
hypothesis. However, the race variable is a weak measure with which to test this
argument, so one should be cautious in rejecting the argument on the basis of
the results presented here.

A set of geographical variables was entered to control for any locational
factors which might influence the decision to participate in the food stamp program. These variables included the size of the largest city in the county where
the family resided, the distance to the nearest city of 50,000 or more, the region of residence, and whether the family resided in a county which began administering the food stamp program in 1974. The latter two variables were statistically insignificant. The other two geographical variables were statistically
significant, but the pattern of participation exhibited by the subgroups of
these variables do not lend themselves to any consistent interpretation. These
results imply that locational factors have little influence on the decision to
participate.

V. IMPLICATIONS OF THE ANALYSIS

The reader will have realized that because of limitations of the data this
analysis does not lend itself to many concrete conclusions. However, the results are suggestive of the importance of certain factors in influencing the decision to participate in the food stamp program. The fact that AFDC recipients
are much more likely than non-AFDC recipients to participate in the food stamp
program argues strongly for the importance of informational factors on influencing the decision to participate. The fact that single elderly people are
much less likely to receive food stamps than elderly married couples provides
some additional support for the importance of informational factors. The results
also suggest that a person's attitude toward receiving welfare income may exert
a strong impact on the participation decision. Support for this conjecture is
found in the low participation rates of nonelderly single males and of students,

---

[25]See Coe (1975).

and in the higher participation rates of the retired or permanently disabled, housewives, and households with younger children. On the other hand, the results of the analysis indicate that other factors thought to be influential are relatively unimportant in determining participation. The amount of bonus value for which the family is eligible was found to be insignificant, contrary to expectations. The transportation available to the family was also insignificant, a finding which hints at relative unimportance of access costs in determining participation.

In short, the results of this analysis point out that we must be careful in assessing the relative impact of various factors in determining whether a family participates in the food stamp program. For example, although it would seem straightforward that higher bonus values would lead to greater participation, little empirical support was found for this proposition. However, due to data limitations, one cannot be certain what the truly dominant variables are, although we can form reasonable conjectures. Further research may enable us to firm these conjectures into documented conclusions.

References

Andrews, Frank; Morgan, James; Sonquist, John; and Klem, Laura. Multiple Classification Analysis. Ann Arbor: Institute for Social Research, 1973.

Bickel, Gary and MacDonald, Maurice. "Participation Rates in the Food Stamp Program: Estimated Levels, by State." Discussion Paper 253-75. Madison: Institute for Research on Poverty, 1975.

Bureau of the Census. Characteristics of Households Purchasing Food Stamps. Current Population Reports, Series P-23, No. 61. Washington, D. C.: U. S. Department of Commerce, 1976.

Coe, Richard. "Sensitivity of the Incidence of Poverty to Different Measures of Income." In Five Thousand American Families--Patterns of Economic Progress, Vol. 4. Edited by Greg J. Duncan and James N. Morgan. Ann Arbor: Institute for Social Research, 1976.

Community Services Administration. CSA Income Poverty Guidelines. CSA Instruction #6004-If. Washington, D. C.: Community Services Administration, 1974.

"Food Coupon Issuance Tables." Lansing, Michigan: Department of Social Services, 1974.

MacDonald, Maurice. "Why Don't More Eligibles Use Food Stamps?" Discussion Paper 292-75. Madison: Institute for Research on Poverty, 1975.

Peskin, Janice. "The Shelter Deduction in the Food Stamp Program." Technical Analysis Paper No. 6, Office of Income Security Policy. Washington, D. C.: U. S. Department of Health, Education and Welfare, 1975.

Peskin, Janice. "In-Kind Income and Measurement of Poverty." Washington, D. C.: U. S. Department of Health, Education and Welfare, undated.

Piven, Frances Fox and Cloward, Richard A. Regulating the Poor: the Functions of Public Welfare. New York: Pantheon Books, 1971.

Seagrave, Charles. "Food Stamps." In The Cyclical Behavior of Transfer Income Programs: A Case Study of the Current Recession. Washington, D. C.: U. S. Department of Health, Education and Welfare, 1975.

APPENDIX 8.1

The following equations were used to assign annual food stamp net benefit levels to families of different sizes.

Family Size	Assignment Equation
1	$B = 528 - .2(Y-360)$
2	$B = 996 - .3(Y-360)$
3	$B = 1428 - .3(Y-360)$
4	$B = 1812 - .3(Y-360)$
5	$B = 2138 - .3(Y-360)$
6	$B = 2448 - .3(Y-360)$
7	$B = 2748 - .3(Y-360)$
8	$B = 3048 - .3(Y-360)$
9	$B = 3316 - .3(Y-360)$
10	$B = 3580 - .3(Y-360)$
11	$B = 3840 - .3(Y-360)$
12	$B = 4104 - .3(Y-360)$
13	$B = 4368 - .3(Y-360)$
14	$B = 4632 - .3(Y-360)$
15	$B = 4896 - .3(Y-360)$

B = annual food stamp net benefit level
Y = annual family gross money income

The following table shows the difference, for selected levels of income, between the annual level of net benefit as assigned by the above equations and the actual annual benefit.

Average Income (Poverty Threshold Income)	Family Size								
	1	2	3	4	5	6	7	8	9
	($2330)	($3070)	($3810)	($4550)	($5290)	($6030)	---	---	---
$ 660	+12	+42	+42	+42	+44	+42	+42	+30	+34
$1260	+12	0	+30	+42	+44	+54	+54	+54	+58
$1920	+60	0	+24	+36	+38	+48	+48	+48	+52
$3120	X	X	+24	+36	+38	+48	+48	+48	+52
$4500	X	X	X	+18	+20	+20	+30	+30	+34
$6660	X	X	X	X	X	X	-24	+30	+34

Chapter 9

THE FIRST GENERATION FAMILY
AND SECOND GENERATION FERTILITY

Arland Thornton

Introduction

The influence of the parental home in shaping the behavior of children is a well-established fact in social science. In fertility research, two aspects of the parental home have been identified as important forces affecting second generation childbearing: the parental standard of living and the size of the first generation family. The influence of these two factors on second generation fertility is examined in this chapter.

Parental economic status holds a crucial position in the socioeconomic explanation of the post-World War II fertility swing. Easterlin argued that following World War II the American economy was growing rapidly, creating particularly favorable circumstances for young couples, the most important childbearing group.[1] The hypothesis suggested that the baby boom was, in part, a response of these young people to the good economic conditions; young couples translated their high incomes into increased fertility.

In the late 1950s, however, fertility began to decline, while economic growth and prosperity continued. Easterlin found that while economic conditions in general were still favorable, circumstances for young people were not keeping pace and by the 1960s were actually deteriorating.[2] The specific economic conditions existing for young people were seen as accounting for some, but not all, of the reduction in fertility. To account for the rest of the decline, Easterlin introduced a new factor: "desired consumption level" or "tastes for consumer goods." He argued that young people in the 1960s had greater tastes for consumer goods than those of the 1940s and 1950s and that these consumption aspirations were competing with children for economic resources. As a result, increased tastes for goods were hypothesized to be contributing to the fertility decline. By including consumption tastes in the economic model, the framework could explain both the rise and subsequent decline in childbearing which occurred in the

---

[1] See Easterlin (1962).

[2] Easterlin (1966 and 1973).

post-World War II period. During the 1940s and early 1950s, consumption aspirations were hypothesized to remain at a fairly constant low level while income increased, resulting in relatively high fertility. During the 1960s, the incomes of young people began leveling off while their aspirations increased greatly; the outcome was a decline in childbearing.

In testing the hypothesis, Easterlin was able to measure the income of cohorts of couples in a straightforward manner; however, it was not possible to measure consumption desires. But, by making some assumptions about the way tastes are formed, he devised an indirect strategy to measure this factor. He hypothesized that children obtain their consumption desires from their parents while they are growing up. The consumption desires of children were thought to be greatly influenced by the standard of living enjoyed by their parents; children raised in poor homes were hypothesized to have fewer aspirations for material goods than those raised in wealthy homes. With these assumptions, Easterlin was able to argue that an index of the parental standard of living would provide an adequate proxy for their children's consumption desires.

The actual variable used in Easterlin's research was the ratio of the children's income to their consumption desires. The numerator, the income of the young adults, was expected to be positively related to fertility; the denominator was the parents' income, Easterlin's proxy for consumption desires, and it was hypothesized to be negatively related to fertility. The expectation, therefore, was that this ratio would be positively related to childbearing. When Easterlin compared time trends and movements in this measure with fertility levels, he found a correspondence. The hypothesis that income and consumption desires work together to influence fertility, or even more specifically, the idea that the income of a couple relative to the income of their parents affects childbearing, has come to be known as the "Easterlin hypothesis." In its more specific formulation the hypothesis predicts that the higher the son's income relative to his father's, the more children he will have.

Several studies have shown that the family sizes of successive generations are positively correlated. Children from large families were more likely to have many children themselves. Berent reported this association for a sample of British couples,[3] while Duncan reported similar results from the 1955 Growth of American Families Study as well as from a 1962 Current Population Survey.[4] The

[3]See Berent (1953).

[4]Duncan et al. (1965).

positive correlation was also found in the Princeton Study.[5] Weaker, but still positive, findings were reported from the Indianapolis Fertility Study.[6] A recent study of Pennsylvania women reconfirmed the positive association.[7]

When these results are placed within a broad theoretical framework, it is clear that there are several mechanisms which could produce a positive correlation between the family sizes of successive generations. First, it is possible that natural fertility or fecundity itself is transmitted through genetic mechanisms: couples with physical attributes conducive to high fertility may pass them on to their children. Second, it may be that parents are a prime source of knowledge concerning birth control and its effective use. If so, children from homes where contraception is effectively used would be better able to limit their own childbearing; similarly, it is plausible to expect that the attitudes of parents toward birth control would be passed on to their children through the socialization process. Third, it is possible that the orientation, desires, and norms of parents toward family size may be learned by their children. As a result, children from large families may desire or plan to have more children than others. Finally, as Duncan suggested, children may try to recreate role relationships existing in the family of orientation,[8] and these relationships depend to some extent upon the number of children in that family. The tendency to recapitulate those relationships would produce successive generations of families of similar sizes and could, therefore, operate independently of direct tastes and norms concerning family size. Johnson and Stokes investigated the relationship between family size in successive generations and concluded from their data that both ". . . norms and role relationships encountered in the family of orientation exert an influence on fertility behavior."[9]

The Panel Study of Income Dynamics provided an opportunity to study the influence of parental attributes and behavior on children since those older children who left their parental homes, married, and established their own households were added to the original panel, and annual interviews were conducted with these new household heads. As a result, the data set included information about a substantial group of recently married couples and about the parental home of

[5]Bumpass and Westoff (1970).

[6]See Kantner and Potter (1954).

[7]Johnson and Stokes (1976).

[8]Duncan et al. (1965).

[9]Johnson and Stokes (1976).

one of the spouses.

Analysis

I. PARENTAL STANDARD OF LIVING AND SECOND GENERATION INCOME

The behavior and expectations of the couples were examined at several points in their lives. Cumulative childbearing through 1972 and 1974 was studied, limiting the analysis to those couples married by the 1971 and 1973 interviews, respectively. In addition, all couples married by 1972 were asked whether or not they expected to have any more children, and if so, how many they expected altogether. These questions measured the total expected family size of these couples as well as the number of children expected in addition to those already born.

Extensive information concerning the parental homes of either the husband or wife in each family studied was obtained from the parents themselves. As a result, several measures of the economic status of those parental homes were available. Those used in this paper are outlined below:

1. Parental family head's income—the income of the father if present in the home; otherwise, the income of the mother.

2. Father's and mother's income—the income of both parents together.

3. Parental family income—the income of all earners in the parental family.

4. Parental welfare ratio—the ratio of family income to family needs.

5. Parental house value—the reported value of the house if owned; if rented, the value was estimated at ten times the annual rent.

6. Parental house value per person—parental house value divided by the number of persons in the family unit.

The indicators of parental economic status were obtained during each year of the study. To estimate an overall measure for each household, the average for the various years was obtained. These averages, however, were estimated using only data for the years the son or daughter was still in the parental home. In addition, the averages took into account inflation during the years following the initial interview.

Two other measures of parental status were used in the analysis. First, the husband was asked to report on his father's educational attainment. Second, the husband was asked to report the financial status of his parents when he was growing up.[10]

The measure of second generation well-being was the husband's income during the year prior to the interview (i.e., 1971 income and 1973 income). Several ratio variables, similar to the one created by Easterlin, were used to indicate the ratio of the husband's income to the various indicators of parental living levels.

Not all couples were included in the analysis. Excluded were those for whom the present marriage was not the first, those who had experienced a marital disruption during the study period, and those with more than one child at the first interview following marriage. Also excluded were couples in which the husbands were not in the labor force.

Undoubtedly, the composition of the parental home influenced its economic organization and standard of living. Families headed by single persons, especially females, would be expected to have substantially lower income than others. Since a substantial number of the parental homes contained only one parent, it seemed possible that the analysis could be influenced by this factor, and thus, preliminary analysis was conducted using data only for children from two-parent homes. The results obtained for this group, however, did not differ significantly from those for the whole sample, and, therefore, the analysis reported here included children from both one and two-parent families.

Basic data for the variables of interest are shown in Table 9.1, including estimates of means and standard deviations for the four dependent variables. Also shown in Table 9.1 are the zero order correlations between these four variables and the measures of economic status. Included in the bottom panel of the table are zero order correlations between the fertility measures and variables which were used in the multivariate analysis. The correlations between the indicators of parental financial status and the number of children already born were almost all negative. The correlations tended to be larger in 1974 than in 1972 and, with almost 600 cases, most were statistically significant. The correlations of the dependent variables with total expected and additional expected fertility were quite inconsistent in direction, and none were large enough to discount the possibility that they were produced by sampling variability.

The correlation between fertility and the husband's income depended on the year and measure examined. Parity and income in 1972 were positively and signif-

---

[10] The question was: "Were your parents poor when you were growing up, pretty well-off, or what?" Answers to this question were scored one for "poor," three for "average" or "it varied," and five for "pretty well-off."

278

Table 9.1

MEANS, STANDARD DEVIATIONS, AND ZERO ORDER
CORRELATIONS OF CHILDREN IN THE FAMILY IN 1972 AND 1974,
AND TOTAL EXPECTED AND ADDITIONAL EXPECTED CHILDREN IN 1972

	Children Born 1972[a]	Children Born (1974)[b]	Total Expected (1972)[c]	Additional Expected (1972)[c]
Number of Couples	293	566	454	454
Mean	.73	.82	2.38	1.79
Standard Deviation	.70	.76	.98	1.23
Correlation with:				
Parental Head's Income	−.052	−.144*	−.026	.012
Father's and Mother's Income	−.117*	−.155*	−.022	.024
Parental Family Income	−.061	−.114*	.005	.015
Parental Welfare Ratio	−.135*	−.123*	−.041	−.005
Parental House Value	.024	−.054	.032	−.005
Parental House Value Per Person	−.066	−.063	−.022	−.009
Father's Education	−.091	−.115*	.030	.031
Parental Financial Status (Reported by Son)	−.055	−.108*	−.005	.001
Husband's Income[d]	.123*	−.004	.002	−.082
Husband's Income ÷ Parental Head's Income[d]	.092	.102*	.097	.011
Husband's Income ÷ Father's and Mother's Income[d]	.119*	.123*	.087	−.008
Husband's Income ÷ Parental Family Income[d]	.111	.082	−.018	−.103*
Husband's Income ÷ Parental Welfare Ratio[d]	.169*	.113*	.081	−.031
Husband's Education	−.215*	−.226*	.098	.190*
Wife's Education	−.239*	−.159*	.056	.163*
Year Married	−.291*	−.432*	.108*	.301*
Race (White=0, Other=1)	.142*	.109*	.038	−.026
Religion (Catholic=1, Other=0)	.156*	−.062	.165*	.106*

*Correlations which are larger than two times their standard error.

[a]Includes couples married by 1971 interview.

[b]Includes couples married by 1973 interview.

[c]Includes couples married by 1972 interview.

[d]For the 1972 analysis husband's income refers to 1971 income; for the 1974 analysis, 1973 income is used.

icantly related. There was, however, virtually no correlation between the husband's income and parity in 1974, nor between income and total children expected. The correlation between income and additional children expected was negative. Note that the ratio of the husband's income to the various measures of parental status was positively related to 1972 and 1974 parity and to total expected fertility, but it was not positively related to additional children.

In analyzing the influence of the economic variables on fertility, a multivariate approach permits the influence of other important variables to be controlled. In this research two different sets of multivariate controls were used. The first, referred to as Model 1, controlled the year the couple married (scored one for the first year of the panel, through five for the fifth year), race, and religion. The last two variables were operationalized as dichotomies: for race, the values were zero for whites and one for nonwhites; for religion, Catholics were coded one, while all others were coded zero.

Model 2 controls were designed to ascertain the extent to which the inclusion of parental economic status into a fertility model increases understanding of the mechanisms involved. Research has shown a negative relationship, albeit decreasing with time, between a couple's level of education and childbearing.[11] In addition, stratification research has shown a positive correlation between the socioeconomic statuses of successive generations.[12] These two relationships alone would produce a negative correlation between first generation status and second generation fertility.

This raises an important question concerning the place of parental status in a fertility model. If the relationship between parental status and second generation childbearing were entirely the result of the parents transmitting their status to their children and high status children bearing few children themselves, then the inclusion of parental status in a model of childbearing would add very little to our understanding. If, however, there is an influence of parental status that is not translated indirectly through the socioeconomic status of the second generation family, then the inclusion of parental status would increase predictive power. The latter result would indicate that parental status implied something more than just second generation social status.

The Model 2 controls permitted the examination of whether or not parental status had a direct effect upon second generation childbearing, net of the influence of second generation status. This was accomplished by including the

[11]Kiser et al. (1968), Ryder and Westoff (1971), and Blau and Duncan (1967).

[12]Blau and Duncan (1967).

education of both husband and wife of the second generation in an equation along with the measures of parental status and the income of the second generation husband. In addition, to take into account the effect of the other background factors, all controls from Model 1 were also included in Model 2. With Model 2 controls, a substantial relationship between parental status and children's fertility would indicate that parental status did add to the model.

For the multivariate part of the analysis it was decided to limit the indicators of parental status and use only parental head's income and parental welfare ratio. The first, a measure of one person's earnings, eliminates the effect of multiple earners. The second measure provides a more adequate definition of the actual living standards in the family. The regression coefficients reported are standardized; that is, all variables have been divided by their own standard deviations.

The results of the analysis of children born through 1972 are shown in Table 9.2. Equation 1 of each model contains only the control variables of that particular model. Equations 2 and 3 add husband's income and one measure of parental economic status to the variables contained in Equation 1, while Equations 4 and 5 each add one ratio variable to the basic equation.

In Equations 2 and 3 of both models, the husband's income was found to be positively related to the number of children born. However, the relationship was not large enough to be statistically significant in the modest-sized sample of couples married by 1971. Also note that in Model 1 both measures of parental status were negatively related to fertility, with the welfare ratio variable having enough impact to be statistically significant. However, when Model 2 was used, the negative coefficients were reduced substantially, with the effect of the parental head's income reversing its sign. Similarly, when the ratio variables were entered into the models, they had a positive sign as expected in Model 1, but in the second model their direct influence was very minor (and even negative in one case).

The results for 1974 parity, presented in Table 9.3, were quite different from those obtained for 1972 parity. The husband's 1973 income did not have the expected positive influence on the number of children born. Rather, in Model 1 its impact was negative and large enough to be statistically significant. With the addition of education into Model 2, the magnitude of the coefficient was reduced, but it remained negative. It should be observed that the reverse in sign from 1972 to 1974 was not the result of changing the sample; when the 1972 sample was analyzed in 1974, the same negative coefficients were observed (the results are not shown here).

Table 9.2

MULTIPLE REGRESSION ANALYSIS OF 1972 PARITY

Standardized Regression Coefficients

	Model 1					Model 2				
	(1)	(2)	(3)	(4)	(5)	(1)	(2)	(3)	(4)	(5)
Year Married	-.286*	-.274*	-.272*	-.282*	-.271*	-.253*	-.241*	-.240*	-.255*	-.249*
Race (White=0, Other=1)	.121*	.117*	.106	.117*	.101	.090	.099	.092	.093	.084
Religion (Catholic=1, Other=0)	.156*	.144*	.146*	.156*	.151*	.174*	.139*	.145*	.174*	.172*
Wife's Education						-.154*	-.172*	-.155*	-.155	-.149*
Husband's Education						-.097	-.106	-.091	-.098	-.090
Husband's 1971 Income		.064	.079				.097	.104		
Parental Head's Income		-.045					.025			
Parental Welfare Ratio			-.139*					-.046		
Husband's Income/Parental Head's Income				.018					-.015	
Husband's Income/Parental Welfare Ratio					.094					.038
R^2	.124	.129	.145	.125	.133	.171	.180	.181	.171	.172
R^2 (Adjusted)	.115	.114	.131	.113	.121	.157	.160	.161	.154	.155

*Coefficient is at least two times its standard error.

Table 9.3

MULTIPLE REGRESSION ANALYSIS OF 1974 PARITY

Standardized Regression Coefficients

	Model 1					Model 2				
	(1)	(2)	(3)	(4)	(5)	(1)	(2)	(3)	(4)	(5)
Year Married	-.434*	-.454*	-.468*	-.431*	-.430*	-.451*	-.460*	-.466*	-.452*	-.453*
Race (White=0, Other=1)	.122*	.090*	.082*	.118*	.108*	.085*	.076*	.074	.087*	.089*
Religion (Catholic=1, Other=0)	-.035	-.017	-.020	-.034	-.035	-.022	-.015	-.016	-.022	-.021
Wife's Education						-.150*	-.140*	-.134*	-.150*	-.152*
Husband's Education						-.128*	-.113*	-.105*	-.128*	-.129*
Husband's 1973 Income		-.089*	-.084*				-.040	-.041		
Parental Head's Income		-.096*					-.035			
Parental Welfare Ratio			-.135*					-.054		
Husband's Income/Parental Head's Income				.018					-.008	
Husband's Income/Parental Welfare Ratio					.044					-.014
R^2	.203	.221	.229	.203	.205	.258	.261	.262	.258	.258
R^2 (Adjusted)	.199	.214	.223	.197	.199	.252	.252	.253	.250	.250

*Coefficient is at least two times its standard error.

While the husband's income did not show a positive effect, the hypothesized negative influence of parental status did exist. In Model 1 both indicators of parental finances had large negative coefficients. The coefficients persisted but with reduced magnitude in Model 2. These results imply that parental status had a large overall impact on childbearing but that much of the influence was transmitted through the education of the offspring. In fact, the effect remaining in Model 2 was not large enough to be statistically significant.

The analysis shown in Equations 4 and 5 of the two models indicates that the ratio variables were only modestly related to parity, and the direction of the relationship depended upon the model. Furthermore, neither variable contributed anything to the explanatory power of the models. These results are undoubtedly due to both the numerator and denominator of the variables being negatively correlated to number of children. By using the ratio form, the two effects cancelled each other.

The analysis of total expected family size is reported in Table 9.4. These data are not consistent with the hypothesis that greater income increases childbearing. In both models, the husband's income failed to show a positive influence. However, parental status did show the hypothesized effect in both models. Indeed, the parental coefficients were larger (but still not twice their standard errors) in Model 2 than in Model 1. This result indicates that the direct or net influence of parental status on expected childbearing was larger than the gross or zero order influence. Also, as hypothesized, the ratio variables were positively associated with expected fertility. In fact, these variables added more to our predictive power (increase in R^2) than did their components when entered individually.

The analysis documented by Table 9.4 concerned all children expected by the family, both those already born and those expected in the future. It is often useful to study expectations for additional children separately. This strategy was employed with the dependent variable being the number of children expected in the future (Table 9.5). The number of children currently in the family was controlled in both models since this factor would greatly influence future plans.

A review of the data in Table 9.5 indicates that the results were very similar to those reported in Table 9.4. Education was positively related to fertility in both cases. The husband's income was not related to the dependent variable, and the impact of parental status was negative. As before, the estimated direct influence of parental income was larger in Model 2 than in Model 1. The ratio of the husband's income to the parental standard of living was also positive as hypothesized. The similarity of the results in Tables 9.4 and 9.5

Table 9.4

MULTIPLE REGRESSION ANALYSES OF 1972 TOTAL EXPECTED FERTILITY

	Standardized Regression Coefficients									
	Model 1					Model 2				
	(1)	(2)	(3)	(4)	(5)	(1)	(2)	(3)	(4)	(5)
Year Married	.100*	.100*	.097*	.114*	.112*	.099*	.094	.085	.114*	.114*
Race (White=0, Other=1)	.033	.022	.026	.002	.007	.045	.027	.030	.013	.014
Religion (Catholic=1, Other=0)	.160*	.167*	.162*	.163*	.160*	.156*	.171*	.163*	.158*	.154*
Wife's Education						.011	.030	.040	.019	.028
Husband's Education						.086	.102	.105	.092	.099
Husband's 1971 Income		.000	-.001				-.017	-.018		
Parental Head's Income		-.045					-.082			
Parental Welfare Ratio			-.032					-.087		
Husband's Income/Parental Head's Income				.113*					.123*	
Husband's Income/Parental Welfare Ratio					.090					.117*
R^2	.039	.040	.040	.050	.046	.047	.053	.053	.061	.059
R^2 (Adjusted)	.032	.030	.029	.042	.037	.036	.038	.038	.048	.046

*Coefficient is at least two times its standard error.

Table 9.5

MULTIPLE REGRESSION ANALYSIS OF ADDITIONAL CHILDREN EXPECTED, 1972

Standardized Regression Coefficients

	Model 1					Model 2				
	(1)	(2)	(3)	(4)	(5)	(1)	(2)	(3)	(4)	(5)
Current Parity	-.556*	-.559*	-.561*	-.561*	-.566*	-.538*	-.536*	-.537*	-.541*	-.546*
Year Married	.078	.080	.076	.086*	.084*	.083*	.083	.074	.094*	.093*
Race (White=0, Other=1)	.025	.017	.018	.001	.003	.034	.019	.020	.009	.008
Religion (Catholic=1, Other=0)	.129*	.131*	.127*	.131*	.128*	.123*	.133*	.126*	.125*	.121*
Wife's Education						.001	.016	.028	.006	.014
Husband's Education						.089	.101*	.106*	.093	.099*
Husband's 1971 Income		.015	.016				-.003	-.002		
Parental Head's Income		-.039					-.071			
Parental Welfare Ratio			-.039					-.086		
Husband's Income/Parental Head's Income				.089*					.097*	
Husband's Income/Parental Welfare Ratio					.080					.101
R^2	.357	.359	.359	.365	.363	.365	.369	.371	.374	.374
R^2 (Adjusted)	.352	.350	.350	.358	.356	.356	.358	.359	.364	.364

*Coefficient is at least two times its standard error.

is probably due to the fact that the couples studied were still very much newly-
weds. For them, additional expected childbearing was a much larger component of
the total number of children expected than was the number already born.

II. PARENTAL FAMILY SIZE AND IDEAL FAMILY SIZE

The analysis described in this section was focused on the influence of
parental family size on second generation fertility. The data also provided the
opportunity to investigate the importance of parental family size preferences on
the childbearing, expectations, and behavior of the children. Unfortunately,
the survey did not contain measures of fecundity, birth control attitudes, or
family role relationships, so their influence could not be explored.

Measures of the actual fertility behavior and the expressed fertility preferences of the parental generation were available in the data and are shown in
Figure 9.1. First, the number of siblings of the husband (obtained from either
a son in the original panel or the husband of an original panel daughter), indicated the actual family size of the parental generation. Second, ideal family
size was indicated by the response of the head of the original panel family to a
standard question about the ideal size of the average American family; this variable was used to indicate the first generation respondent's perception of social
norms concerning family size, flavored by his or her actual feelings and values.
This measure was available from the parents of one member of a second generation
couple, either a son in the original panel (and not his wife) or a daughter in
the original panel (and not her husband). Thus, it was possible to examine both
the inheritance of tastes and norms concerning children and the correlations between actual fertility behavior of the two generations.

The above two measures concerning the parental family were related to several additional measures taken from the newly married couples. First, the ideal
family size of the second generation husband was obtained in 1971, so the analysis concerning this variable was limited to couples married by 1971. The other
two measures were the total expected family size of the husband, measured in
1972, and parity achieved by 1972 and by 1974.

The analysis was conducted by first determining the zero order relationships
between first and second generation fertility and then, as described in the previous section, controls were added in a stepwise fashion. First, we controlled
the average income of the parental head and successively controlled religion,
race, and year married. Finally, the educational attainment of the second generation husband and wife were taken into account. This procedure permitted us to
test the influence of the first generation variables by controlling factors which

Figure 9.1

MEASUREMENT OF THE FAMILY SIZE VARIABLES
FOR THE FIRST GENERATION

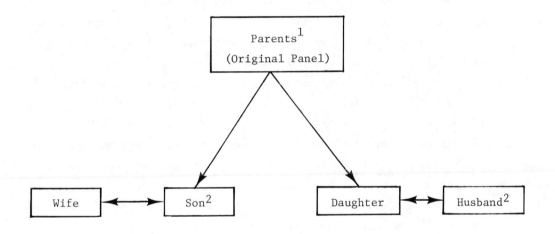

[1]Ideal family size of the first generation family was obtained from interviews with the head of this family.

[2]The actual family size of the first generation family was ascertained by asking the second generation husband how many siblings he had.

might bias the observed relationship and allowed us to examine the extent to
which fertility behavior or attitudes of parents operate through the education
of the spouses themselves. The statistical approach again was to use product-
moment correlation coefficients and ordinary least squares multiple regression.

The results of the statistical analysis of the ideal number of children reported by the second generation husband (see Table 9.6) show a positive zero
order correlation between both measures of parental fertility and the dependent
variable. Only the coefficient for parental ideal family size was statistically
significant, and it was almost three times as large as that for actual parental
fertility.

Columns 2 through 7 of Table 9.6 demonstrate that the introduction of controls reduced the magnitude of the observed relationship. For actual parental
fertility, the standardized regression coefficient was reduced to .05 with all
controls employed. However, for the parent's ideal number of children, the coefficient with all controls was almost .24. The unstandardized coefficients for
the parental fertility variables are also shown in Table 9.6. Using all controls, a difference of one child in actual fertility increased the preferred
number of children for the second generation by about .02, while a difference of
one child in the parent's ideal number netted an increase of .16.

The analysis of the total number of children expected by the husband of the
second generation family is reported in Table 9.7. As expected, there was a
positive correlation between total expected children and the measures of parental fertility. However, the coefficients were not as large as the ones observed
in Table 9.6. Again, the ideal family size of parents was a better predictor of
the fertility of the second generation than was the actual family size of the
parents. Both the zero order correlation coefficient and standardized regression coefficients for the ideal measure were substantially larger than those for
the number of siblings. The unstandardized coefficients were about .08 for
ideal size and in the .01-.03 range for actual fertility.

It should be noted from Table 9.7 that the introduction of the first two
groups of controls reduced the observed relationships somewhat. With the introduction of education, however, the observed coefficients increased. This result
is due to the unexpected positive relationship between education and expectations
of fertility. Thus, for total fertility expectations the overall influence is
not mediated through the children's own social status.

The results concerning parity achieved by 1972 and 1974 are shown in Tables
9.8 and 9.9. It should be kept in mind that the maximum marital durations possible by these points in time were only three and five years, respectively.

Table 9.6

MULTIPLE REGRESSION ANALYSIS OF HUSBAND'S 1971 IDEAL FAMILY SIZE

	Zero Order Correlation	Standardized Regression Coefficients					
	(1)	(2)	(3)	(4)	(5)	(6)	(7)
Siblings of Husband	.113				.106	.097	.053
Ideal Family Size of Head of Parental Family	.282*	.278*	.264*	.237*			
Income of Head of Parental Family	-.071	-.018	-.031	.026	-.059	-.069	-.006
Year Married	-.002		.010	.034		.000	.031
Race (White=0, Other=1)	.085		.041	.026		.066	.048
Religion (Catholic=1, Other=0)	.099		.085	.092		.106	.114
Wife's Education	-.195*			-.106			-.127
Husband's Education	-.208*			-.122			-.126
R^2		.080	.088	.122	.016	.032	.073
R^2 (Adjusted)		.073	.072	.100	.009	.015	.050
Unstandardized Coefficients for Either "Siblings of Husband" or "Ideal Family Size of Head of Parental Family"		.184*	.174*	.156*	.038	.035	.019

Number of Cases: 293

*Coefficient is at least two times its standard error.

290

Table 9.7

MULTIPLE REGRESSION OF TOTAL CHILDREN EXPECTED IN 1972

	Zero Order Correlation	Standardized Regression Coefficients					
	(1)	(2)	(3)	(4)	(5)	(6)	(7)
Siblings of Husband	.070				.068	.029	.058
Ideal Family Size of Head of Parental Family	.102*	.100*	.096*	.103*			
Income of Head of Parental Family	-.026	-.015	-.035	-.076	-.012	-.039	-.076
Year Married	.108*		.101*	.099*		.097*	.091
Race (White=0, Other=1)	.038		.014	.019		.018	.020
Religion (Catholic=1, Other=0)	.165*		.166*	.166*		.164*	.159
Wife's Education	.056			.034			.026
Husband's Education	.098			.102			.115
R^2		.011	.049	.063	.005	.041	.056
R^2 (Adjusted)		.006	.039	.049	.001	.030	.041
Unstandardized Coefficients for Either "Siblings of Husband" or "Ideal Family Size of Head of Parental Family"		.080*	.077*	.082*	.029	.012	.024

Number of Cases: 454

*Coefficient is at least two times its standard error.

Table 9.8

MULTIPLE REGRESSION ANALYSIS OF 1972 PARITY

	Zero Order Correlation	Standardized Regression Coefficients					
	(1)	(2)	(3)	(4)	(5)	(6)	(7)
Siblings of Husband	-.044				-.051	-.040	-.089
Ideal Family Size of Head of Parental Family	.205*	.202*	.173*	.145*			
Income of Head of Parental Family	-.052	-.014	-.002	.058	-.058	-.040	.031
Year Married	-.291*		-.282*	-.257*		-.279*	-.244*
Race (White=0, Other=1)	.142*		.096	.082		.116*	.095
Religion (Catholic=1, Other=0)	.156*		.144*	.152*		.166*	.174*
Wife's Education	-.239*			-.150*			-.150*
Husband's Education	-.215*			-.088			-.136
R^2		.042	.154	.192	.005	.127	.179
R^2 (Adjusted)		.036	.139	.172	.000	.112	.159
Unstandardized Coefficients for Either "Siblings of Husband" or "Ideal Family Size of Head of Parental Family"		.115*	.098*	.082*	-.016	-.013	-.028

Number of Cases: 293

*Coefficient is at least two times its standard error.

Table 9.9

MULTIPLE REGRESSION ANALYSIS OF 1974 PARITY

	Zero Order Correlation	Standardized Regression Coefficients					
	(1)	(2)	(3)	(4)	(5)	(6)	(7)
Siblings of Husband	.032				-.004	.030	.001
Ideal Size of Head of Parental Family	.054	.035	.052	.047			
Income of Head of Parental Family	-.144*	-.140*	-.106*	-.034	-.145*	-.106*	-.038
Year Married	-.432*		-.434*	-.452*		-.434*	-.450*
Race (White=0, Other=1)	.109*		.088*	.073		.088*	.076*
Religion (Catholic=1, Other=0)	-.062		-.032	-.024		-.034	-.020
Wife's Education	-.159*			-.142*			-.143*
Husband's Education	-.226*			-.121*			-.121*
R^2		.022	.217	.262	.021	.215	.259
R^2 (Adjusted)		.019	.210	.252	.017	.208	.250
Unstandardized Coefficients for Either "Siblings of Husband" or "Ideal Family Size of Head of Parental Family"		.022	.032	.029	-.001	.010	.000

Number of Cases: 566

*Coefficient is at least two times its standard error.

Therefore, in this instance, current parity actually reflected timing decisions as much as completed family size. It is possible that the relationships may be quite different when actual childbearing is completed.

These tables also suggest that there was no relationship between parental family size and actual parity achieved by 1972 and 1974. In the 1972 data the correlations were all negative but not statistically significant. The 1974 coefficients, though mostly positive, again were not significant.

The ideal family size of the first generation was related to parity in both years. In 1972 the relationship was substantial and large enough to exclude sampling error as the force producing it. Even with full controls, the standardized coefficient was .145 while the metric coefficient was .082. In the 1974 data the coefficients were substantially smaller and, even with a larger sample, not statistically significant. Note that the difference between the two years was only partially the result of adding couples between the two time periods. When the 1974 analysis was limited to couples examined in 1972, the coefficients were still much smaller than in 1972 (results not shown).

Discussion

Several points should be made about the observed results. First, as a whole, the findings concerning parental family size are consistent with the conclusions of earlier research. Family size in the first generation was positively related to fertility in the second. While the relationships between the size of the parental family and fertility preferences and expectations were not large enough to be statistically significant, they were in the predicted direction. However, there did not appear to be a positive relationship between actual parental family size and parity achieved during the first three or first five years of second generation marriages. This result may have been due to the fact that the measures of current parity reflected spacing decisions more than family size decisions. In addition, it should be noted that the effect of parental family size on ideals and expectations was smaller than the effects reported by Duncan concerning the influence of parental fertility on second generation family size.[13]

Second, the ideal family size of parents related positively to the second generation fertility variables examined. In addition, in three of the four analyses the effect was large enough to be statistically significant. Also, the influence of the variable was fairly substantial, perhaps not large in terms of explained variance, but quite large in terms of practical and demographic significance. Using the regression coefficients with full controls, a one-child in-

---

[13]Duncan et al. (1965).

crease in parental preferences enlarged second generation ideal family size by
over .15, total expected fertility by .08, achieved parity in 1972 by .08, and
1974 parity by .03.

It is important to observe that parental family size preferences were more
closely related to second generation fertility than was actual first generation
family size. For some variables this effect was much larger than the effect of
family size itself. This result is especially important in light of the way the
variables were measured. As second generation information was obtained from the
husband, second generation ideals and expectations were those of the husband
rather than those of the wife. The measure of first generation family size was
also obtained by asking the husband about the number of siblings he had. On the
other hand, the ideal family size of the first generation could have been reported
by either the wife's parents or the husband's parents, depending on who had been
in the original panel (see Figure 9.1). The analyses related the husband's ideal
family size and expectations to his parents' family size and also to the ideal
family size of either his or his wife's parents. While the procedure should provide an unbiased estimate of the correlation between parental family size and
second generation measures, the relationship between the ideal family size of the
parents and the variables measured for the children are probably biased negatively.
The results of Duncan suggest that the fairly low correlation we observed between
the actual fertility in the parental family and that in the second generation was
not the result of using measures for the husband's, rather than the wife's, family.[14] That research showed second generation fertility to be as closely related
to that in the husband's family as to the wife's family.

These results are consistent with the hypothesis that conditions existing
in the family of orientation influence childbearing in the family of procreation.
On the average, children raised with many siblings apparently plan and have
larger families than others. Furthermore, these data indicate that values and
attitudes concerning family size play an even more important role in the process.
It appears that while the transmittal process is certainly less than perfect,
parental tastes concerning children are passed on to their children.

Third, if only the number of children born by 1972 had been analyzed, we
would have found evidence consistent with the hypothesized positive effect of
second generation income. Current parity in 1972 was positively and significantly
correlated to 1971 income (Table 9.1). With controls, the relationship remained
positive but was not large enough to be statistically significant. Income, how-

---

[14]Duncan et al. (1965).

ever, failed to have a substantial positive influence on any of the other three fertility variables examined. Depending on the model and measure employed, the husband's income had either a very small positive effect or a negative influence. Thus, the results, taken as a whole, do not support the hypothesis that income increases childbearing. They also fail to verify on the microlevel the mechanism Easterlin used to explain the increase in fertility following World War II.

Fourth, concerning parental economic status, we found that virtually all indicators were negatively correlated with children born by 1972 and 1974 (Table 9.1). When controls for other variables were employed and the influence of the variable was examined within the context of Model 1, the negative association persisted and remained large. However, when the two intervening variables of the husband's and the wife's education were entered in the equation (Model 2), coefficients were reduced substantially. These results suggest that the overall impact of parental status on children born was negative and fairly substantial, but most of the influence was transmitted through education. The direct influence was small and not statistically significant.

The correlation of parental status with fertility plans was less consistent and striking. The overall influence seemed small and was statistically insignificant, but when Model 2 controls were used, the magnitude of the direct effect was larger. The increase of the coefficients with Model 2 was due to the positive correlation of education to childbearing plans. However, in none of the Model 2 analyses were the coefficients for parental status twice as large as their standard errors.

The ratio of the husband's income to parental financial status was positively correlated with parity in 1972 and 1974. The relationships persisted at a reduced level using Model 1 controls, but they either disappeared or were negative in Model 2. When fertility plans were studied, however, the influence of the ratio variables was positive and fairly substantial in both Model 1 and Model 2.

While the results of this analysis are not completely consistent, they generally support the hypothesis that high parental status decreases childbearing. This microlevel result gives credence to the Easterlin hypothesis that during the 1960s young couples were coming from affluent homes and, as a result, had lower fertility. However, we cannot specifically say why these couples were having fewer children. The results of the research reported here indicate that much of the overall impact of parental status on actual second generation childbearing was transmitted through the education of the second generation. That is, children from high status homes had few children largely because they themselves were high status. There was very little effect of parental status that could not be accounted for by the children's own status.

This brings us back to the basic question: How is parental economic status transmitted into second generation fertility? Easterlin indicated that the mechanism was consumption standards. He argued that children internalize the parental living levels as their own standard of consumption. Therefore, children raised in wealthy homes would have greater aspirations for material goods. Since Easterlin's model hypothesizes that high aspiration levels decrease childbearing, it follows that high parental living levels would decrease second generation fertility.

Unfortunately, neither Easterlin's data nor the data used in this research permitted the influence of consumption aspiration to be tested directly. We have shown, however, that *if* education is *not* a proxy for aspiration or at least fairly closely related to it, the influence of aspiration cannot be very large. The supporting evidence is that when we controlled the effect of education, the net or direct effect of parental status was very small and not statistically significant; there was little effect operating independently of education. However, it is quite possible that education is, indeed, a reasonable proxy for aspiration. If so, our results are consistent with the notion that the influence of parents operates through consumption standards.

All of this, of course, leaves us with the problem described by Schultz:[15] We do not know exactly what education specifies. As he indicates, education affects many different things, and a review of the literature would indicate that it has been used in empirical research as a proxy for several concepts. This ambiguity suggests the need to move from using the global concept of education as a proxy for some particular theoretical concept and to try to measure the theoretical notion itself. This is necessary because, as Ryder points out, " . . . the data are blind to the concepts of the theorist, and wife's education means whatever it means."[16]

Fortunately, there are models of fertility which outline the specific concepts which should be measured. One useful model was provided by Easterlin.[17] Expanded to include parental economic status and family size, it clearly demonstrates that the relationship between first generation variables and children's fertility is neither simple nor straightforward. Easterlin's hypothesis that parental income influences tastes for consumer goods is represented by the posi-

[15]See Schultz (1973).

[16]See Ryder (1973).

[17]Easterlin (1969 and 1973).

tive arrow between parental status and consumption aspiration (tastes for non-
parenting). However, if parental income affects consumption tastes, it should
also influence standards about inputs necessary to rear children (child quality)
as well as increasing knowledge of, and access to, means of regulating childbearing. Both of these factors should operate to decrease second generation
childbearing. We also know that parental status enhances the occupation and
education of children.[18] Economic models suggest that increased human capital
should raise the price of child care inasmuch as most of it is done by parents,
and this would decrease family size. At the same time, education and occupation
increase income, which is hypothesized to raise fertility. Note that while child
survival, natural fertility, and desires for children are shown to influence
childbearing in Figure 9.2, the influence of the parents' standard of living on
these variables is assumed to be zero. However, even these assumptions may be
overly simplistic.

The mechanisms hypothesized to produce the overall positive relationship
between family sizes in two generations are also shown in Figure 9.2. Parental
family size is hypothesized to be related to the desires for children and to
natural fertility or fecundity, which in turn decrease childbearing. First
generation fertility is also hypothesized to be related to the use of birth control in the second generation. All of these mechanisms could be producing the
observed positive association between family sizes. Note that the figure does
not include direct links between parental family size and tastes for nonchildren,
tastes for child quality, income, prices of children, and child survival. Again,
these exclusions are only hypotheses; additional research might establish direct
links. Figure 9.2 does not include one possible link between first and second
generation family sizes: the hypothesized desire of children to imitate role
relations existing in the parental home. This exclusion is motivated not by a
hypothesis that the mechanism is not important, but rather by the fact that the
mechanism is complex and difficult to diagram in a simple figure.

If measures of all the variables in the theoretical system were available,
it would be possible to estimate the influence of parental attributes on the
second generation variables. In addition, one could estimate the mechanisms
through which parental variables operate to influence childbearing. That is,
with measures of all variables it would be possible to determine which intervening variable was transmitting the influence of parental status. It is crucial
to note that without measuring all intervening variables it is possible to es-

---

[18]Blau and Duncan (1967).

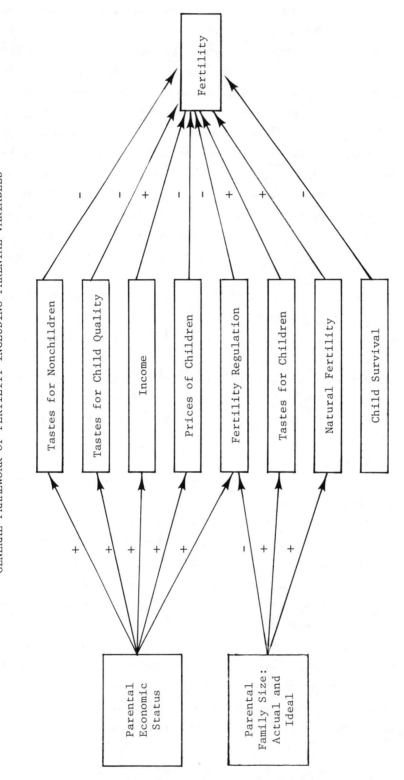

Figure 9.2

GENERAL FRAMEWORK OF FERTILITY INCLUDING PARENTAL VARIABLES*

*Hypothesized signs of effects are shown.

timate only the overall influence of parental background, but it is not possible to estimate the mechanisms. Thus, for example, in the absence of measures of the intervening variables, any relationship observed between parental income and second generation family size would have to be considered as the sum of the influences operating through all of the intervening variables. Without making assumptions that many of the influences shown are zero (which seems rather unlikely), it would not be possible to state that the relationship was the result of only one mechanism. Although a relationship may exist between parental economic status and fertility, it would seem hasty to conclude the effect was only (or even in part) transmitted through tastes for consumption goods. While it is certainly possible that some or even much of the influence is so transmitted, the model is too complex to discover this fact without measures of the intervening variables themselves. By measuring the variables specified and then estimating their effects, it would be possible to better understand the mechanisms involved.

Summary

The data were not consistent with the hypothesis that for second generation husbands high incomes increase childbearing. In all of the multivariate analyses, the coefficient for husband's income was not statistically significant or was negative.

The data were generally consistent with the hypothesis that high parental economic status is related to low second generation fertility. Couples coming from wealthy families tended to have fewer children and to expect fewer in the future.

The relationship between first generation economic status and actual second generation fertility was examined, controlling the educational attainment of the second generation husband and wife. It was found that the relationship was greatly decreased by these controls, suggesting that much of the impact operated through second generation social status. This result, in turn, raised the issue of the meaning of education in fertility research, and a model specifying the actual mechanisms which could be operating was outlined in the discussion section.

It was found that the family sizes of two successive generations were correlated. Even more important, the results indicated that the parents' concept of the *ideal* family size had a larger impact than *actual* parental family size. This finding implies that at least some of the influence of parents on second generation family size does *not* operate through intergenerational inheritance of physiological capability, but rather through one or more of the other mechanisms suggested.

References

Berent, Jerzy. "Relationship Between Family Sizes of Two Successive Generations." Milbank Memorial Fund Quarterly 31 (1953).

Blau, Peter M., and Duncan, Otis Dudley. The American Occupational Structure. New York: John Wiley & Sons, Inc., 1967.

Bumpass, Larry L., and Westoff, Charles F. The Later Years of Childbearing. Princeton: Princeton University Press, 1970.

Duncan, Otis Dudley et al. "Marital Fertility and Size of Family of Orientation." Demography 2 (1965).

Easterlin, Richard A. "The American Baby Boom in Historical Perspective." National Bureau of Economic Research Occasional Paper 79, 1962.

Easterlin, Richard A. "On the Relation of Economic Factors to Recent and Projected Fertility Changes." Demography 3, no. 1 (1966).

Easterlin, Richard A. "Toward a Socioeconomic Theory of Fertility: A Survey of Recent Research on Economic Factors in American Fertility." In Fertility and Family Planning. Edited by S. J. Behrman, Leslie Corsa, Jr., and Ronald Freedman. Ann Arbor: The University of Michigan Press, 1969.

Easterlin, Richard A. "Relative Economic Status and the American Fertility Swing." In Family Economic Behavior. Edited by Eleanor Bernert Sheldon. Philadelphia: J.B. Lippincott Co., 1973.

Easterlin, Richard A. "The Economics and Sociology of Fertility: A Synthesis." Revised version of a paper prepared for the Seminar on Early Industrialization, Shifts in Fertility, and Changes in Family Structure, Institute for Advanced Study, Princeton, New Jersey, June 18-July 9, 1972. Revised version dated July 1973.

Johnson, Nan E., and Stokes, C. Shannon. "Family Size in Successive Generations: The Effects of Birth Order, Intergenerational Change in Lifestyle, and Familial Satisfaction." Demography 13, no. 2 (1976).

Kantner, John F., and Potter, Robert G. Jr. "The Relationship of Family Size in Two Successive Generations." Milbank Memorial Fund Quarterly 32 (1954).

Kiser, Clyde V. et al. Trends and Variations in Fertility in the United States. Cambridge: Harvard University Press, 1968.

Ryder, Norman B. Comment on "A New Approach to the Economic Theory of Fertility Behavior" by Robert J. Willis. Journal of Political Economy 81, no. 2, Part II (1973).

Ryder, Norman B., and Westoff, Charles F. Reproduction in the United States: 1965. Princeton: Princeton University Press, 1971.

Schultz, Theodore W. "The Value of Children: An Economic Perspective." Journal of Political Economy 81, no. 2, Part II (1973).

Chapter 10

LABOR FORCE PARTICIPATION DECISIONS OF WIVES

Daniel Hill

Introduction

The labor force behavior of married women has become a policy issue of major importance since the declaration of war on poverty in 1964. The general failure of the various programs which comprised the war on poverty has stimulated renewed interest in various income maintenance programs. The major political objection to these programs is the fear that they will result in drastic reductions of work effort by the poorer, able-bodied male heads of households. As yet, there is no political consensus on whether married women should work in the marketplace, and a large body of empirical literature on the *family* labor supply response has developed. Naturally, to understand the family response, one must understand the labor response of married women.

Mincer, in his path-breaking study of 1962, concluded that an understanding of life-cycle patterns is crucial to the understanding of the labor supply of married women because:

> . . . the timing of market activities during the working life
> may differ from one individual to another. The life cycle in-
> troduces changes in demands for and marginal costs of home work
> and leisure. Such changes are reflected in the relation between
> labor force rates and age of women, presence, number and ages of
> children. There are life-cycle variations in family income which
> may affect the timing of labor force participation.

Although there has until recently been no successful, unified, life-cycle model of the labor supply of married women to guide empirical research, quite a bit has been learned about income and substitution effects on their labor supply. Examples of studies which address these issues are the works of Ashenfelter and Heckman (1974), Boskins (1973), and Heckman (1974). Their findings are typical of those found in most labor supply studies. Income effects are negative, substitution effects are positive, and the labor supply of wives is more responsive to both income and wages than that of husbands. The policy implications are clear. Income maintenance programs are likely to have little effect on the labor supply of husbands but may cause significant decreases in

302

wives' labor supply. This result is consistent not only with the findings of
most other major supply studies using area and cross-sectional data, but also
with the results from studies using experimental data.[1]

Since 1962, much has also been learned about the relation of children and
education to the labor force participation of married women. The first major
works to document these relationships were those by Cain (1966) and Bowen and
Finegan (1969). More sophisticated theoretical structures have been employed
by the "new home economists" to examine the interrelation of fertility, education,
and the value of the wife's time. Foremost in this field are the findings of
Willis (1973), Gronau (1973), Gramm (1975), and Leibowitz (1975). In general,
their empirical results are consistent with the hypothesis that children (especially young children) have the effect of raising the value of the wife's time
in home production to the extent that it is not worth her while to work in the
marketplace while she has small children at home. Indeed, Leibowitz, who is
struck by the fact that better educated women spend more time in the labor market than less educated women in all phases of their life cycle except during the
25-40 year age span, hypothesizes that more highly educated women are induced by
high wage rates to substitute market goods for their own time in home production.
The elasticity of technical substitution, however, will vary from one home activity to another. Using a variety of types of data, Leibowitz finds that market
goods are quite substitutable for time in activities such as laundry and meal
preparation, but not for time in child care. She concludes by saying, "In child
care, women with more schooling show even lower elasticities of substitution
than average, since available substitutes cannot provide as high-quality care as
they themselves can." This, then, explains why education does not increase the
labor force participation rates of women in the child-rearing ages.

None of the above theories presents a life-cycle model of the labor supply
of married women, although all touch upon some aspect of it. Such a model has
recently been attempted and is drawn upon here to investigate the labor supply
of married women over the eight years of the Panel Study of Income Dynamics.[2]

The most important implication of the model with respect to the pattern of
labor supply over the life cycle derives from the relation of the reservation
wage to the optimal pattern of asset accumulation and expenditures.[3] The rule

---

[1] See, for instance, Journal of Human Resources (1974).

[2] For a detailed explanation of this model, see Hill (1977), Chapter 3.

[3] The reservation wage is defined as the value of the wife's time when she is
doing no market work.

for optimal timing of expenditure and asset accumulation calls for continuously declining marginal benefits of expenditures. In the absence of strong life-cycle time preference, this rule, via the principle of diminishing marginal benefits of market goods, implies that expenditures will start out low early in the life cycle when households try to accumulate assets and end up high later on when assets are liquidated. Because of the close association of the value of the wife's time and the marginal benefits of expenditures, such a pattern of expenditures would result in the wife's reservation wage increasing throughout the life cycle.[4]

For the purposes of this paper, the conclusion that the optimal saving plan involves steadily declining saving activity over the life cycle is inappropriate. This conclusion is based on the assumption of zero life-cycle time preference. When talking about households that buy homes and have children during their lifetime, this assumption is unreasonable. A plan which calls for relative deprivation in a period immediately before the purchase of a house or the birth of a child, succeeded by a period of relatively great expenditures after the purchase or birth, might well be superior to a plan with constantly decreasing levels of saving throughout time. This argument is best illustrated diagrammatically. Assuming positive interest rates and no life-cycle time preference, the intertemporal optimization condition represented in Figure 10.1(a) implies an optimal dissaving plan such as that depicted in Figure 10.1(b). With life-cycle time preference regarding the birth of a child at time 1, however, the saving plan in Figure 10.1(b) would correspond to a pattern of marginal welfare of dissavings as represented in Figure 10.1(c). Here the presence of the infant with its concomitant financial demands increases the marginal welfare of dissaving dramatically. The effect of the child on the marginal welfare of spending disappears after the child reaches some age (e.g., 30).

The pattern depicted in Figure 10.1(c) violates the rule for optimal declining marginal welfare of spending, and, as a result, the dissaving pattern represented by Figure 10.1(b) is no longer optimal and should be rearranged as depicted in Figure 10.1(d). Such a plan would restore an optimal marginal welfare profile such as depicted in Figure 10.1(a). The saving profile in Figure 10.1(d) can be interpreted as saying that it is optimal for the household to save more than it otherwise would prior to the birth of the child and dissave more than

---

[4] This association results from the fact that the value of the wife's time is equal to the ratio of the marginal-utility product of her time in home production to the marginal-utility product of market goods in home production, and this latter is directly proportional to the marginal welfare of expenditures.

Figure 10.1

MARGINAL WELFARE OF EXPENDITURES
AND EXPENDITURES OVER TIME

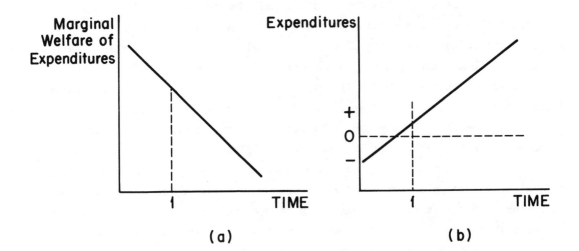

(a)

(b)

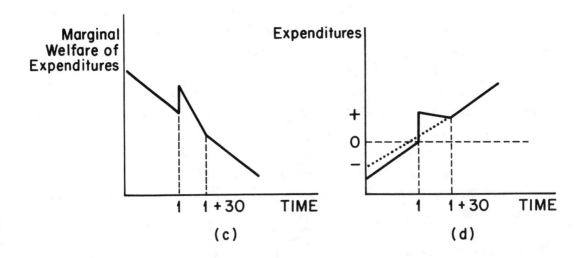

(c)

(d)

it would after the birth.

As a result of these arguments and the fact that children can be expected to affect the productivity of the wife's time in the home, the life-cycle reservation wage profile for a typical woman might appear as in Figure 10.2. The profile is generally upwardly inclined, with sharp peaks at the time of birth of each of the children (times a, b, and c).

Figure 10.2

TYPICAL RESERVATION WAGE PROFILE

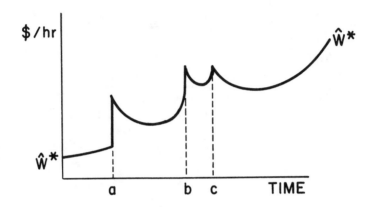

Whether or not it is optimal for a woman to work in any given period depends on the relation of her reservation wage to the market wage. If the market wage which she can obtain is greater than her reservation wage, she would increase the family's total utility by getting a job.

Although not explicitly mentioned, it is assumed that the household takes into account the effects of the investment component of work and education when deciding on the optimal stream of expenditures and work effort over the life cycle. These effects can be treated explicitly by incorporating the human capital model of wage determination. These models have been popularized in the literature by Mincer and Polachek (1973) and others during the last decade and a half. Earnings (net of investment) in any period can be represented as the sum of earnings power (less depreciation) in the preceding period and the returns (net of depreciation) to any investments made in that preceding period.

This model can be shown to imply a life-cycle market wage pattern, as depicted in Figure 10.3, for a hypothetical individual with three periods of market employment.

Combining this model with the life-cycle model of consumption yields the life-cycle model of labor force participation which we have used to analyze the

Figure 10.3

MARKET WAGE PROFILE FOR A WOMAN WITH THREE
SPELLS OF MARKET EMPLOYMENT

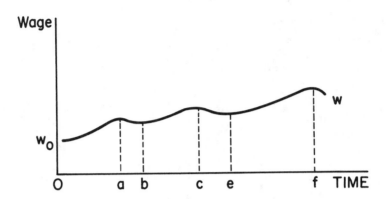

Figure 10.4

HYPOTHETICAL MARKET AND RESERVATION WAGE PROFILES FOR A
WOMAN WITH THREE SPELLS OF EMPLOYMENT AND THREE CHILDREN

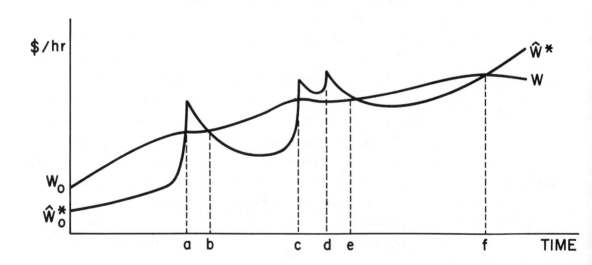

participation patterns of married women. An example of the type of behavior suggested by this model is depicted in Figure 10.4. The woman worked from time o to time a, and, as a result of investments she made on the job, she became more proficient. Her increased proficiency was rewarded with increased wages over the period. At time a the woman quit her job and devoted herself full time to home production until time b. During this period her job-related skills became rusty through disuse and, as a result, her marketable human capital declined. From time b to c and c to f, the woman worked in the market and accumulated skills, and during the period c to e she worked in the home and her market skills depreciated. To reiterate, the woman entered marriage with an initial level of human capital which implied a market wage of w_o. The plan that she and her husband adopted and the value of the variables in the system implied that her reservation wage was $\hat{w}_o^*$. Since $w_o > \hat{w}_o^*$, the wife got a job and remained employed until her first child was born at time a. The presence of the infant in the household drove the reservation wage well above the market wage. The woman quit her job and devoted herself full time to home production. As her first child grew older, it became less of a burden, and the reservation wage declined. At the same time, the woman's marketable human capital depreciated, which caused her market wage to decline. The former declined faster than the latter, and at time b it became optimal for the wife to re-enter the labor force. She remained employed until her second child was born at time c and, because the third child came close on the heels of the second, she did not re-enter the work force until time e when her third child was e-d years of age. She remained employed until time f, at which point the desire to use her time to produce satisfaction (along with goods purchased with assets and the husband's income) again drove the reservation wage over the market wage.

Analysis

I. THE DEPENDENT VARIABLES

Two distinct measures of labor force participation over the eight years of the panel study are discussed in this chapter. The first, employment incidence, is simply a dichotomous variable which takes on the value of unity when a woman has done some market work in any of the eight panel years. For the entire sample this variable averaged 69.1 percent, which can be interpreted as the probability of randomly selecting from the sample of married women a woman who has worked at some time during an eight-year period.

The second measure of labor supply over the panel period will be referred to as the "overall labor force participation rate." This variable is equal to the fraction of weeks the woman worked in the labor market over the panel period. The overall labor force participation rate varied from zero, for women who did no work for money, to one, for those (few) women who reported working 52 weeks in each of the eight years. The average value of the overall labor force participation rate was 32.8 percent, which implies that women in the sample averaged slightly more than 136 weeks of paid employment out of the 416 weeks of the panel period.[5]

II. THE SAMPLE

The sample employed in this analysis consisted of women who were stably married to heads of panel families throughout the panel period and for whom there are complete eight-year work histories. There were 1,694 such cases.

III. EXPECTATIONS

The model outlined above has a number of implications about the amount and timing of the labor supply of married women which can be tested with data from the panel study. The first of these implications concerns life-cycle events such as children being born, children leaving home, purchasing a house, and retiring. Both the probability of a woman working at all and the amount of time she worked during a period should be negatively affected by the presence of children. Hence, the number of children in 1968 and the number of children born since 1968 should negatively affect measures of employment incidence and labor supply over the period, while the age of the youngest child and the number of children who left home should affect these measures positively. Because the model suggests that women should work less as they approach retirement, age should affect the measures of labor supply negatively. Since purchasing a home is largely an asset accumulating activity, we would expect those people who purchased homes over the panel period and even those people who owned their homes in 1968 to be more likely to work and to work more than renters.

The second set of implications about the probability of working over the panel period and the amount of labor supplied concerns human capital variables. Since education and previous work experience should have a positive effect on the wage a woman can receive in paid employment, measures of each of these variables should be positively associated with measures of employment incidence and labor

---

[5] See Table A10.1b for distribution of the labor force participation rate.

supply.

The model's third set of implications for the labor supply of married women over the panel period concerns the effects of household characteristics such as race and income. Eight-year average family money income—other than the wife's labor income—should have the effect of shifting the reservation wage profile up (because of diminishing marginal benefits of expenditures) and, hence, should reduce both the probability of working at all and the amount of labor supplied. Although there are no *a priori* reasons to expect transfer income to affect work decisions differently from other types of income, the policy relevance of any such difference justifies examining the effects of transfer income separately. Through its effects on tastes for work, race should have an impact on labor supply. In particular, because of the historical tendency for black and other non-white women to work in the marketplace, women of these races should have acquired a taste for market work which should positively affect their labor supply. Alternatively, employers may prefer black women because of their historically more stable work patterns. In any event, race is included in the analysis to provide statistical control.

The nature of the local job market should also affect the labor supply of married women. Since women characteristically have less seniority than men, they are generally first to be affected by cyclical downturns in the job market and the last to benefit from recovery. Thus, the labor supply of married women should be negatively related to the local unemployment rate.

A final set of variables which should influence the amount and timing of labor supply over the life cycle are measures of disruptive events. These include measures of the number of years the husband had substantial unemployment, number of times the family relocated, whether the husband changed jobs, and whether the household changed counties over the eight years of the panel study. In general, we would expect each of these variables, because they destabilize the reservation and market wage profiles, to positively affect the probability that the wife would work over the panel period.

IV. RESULTS

Overall Labor Force Participation Rate

Table 10.1 presents the raw-score regression coefficients obtained when overall labor force participation and employment incidence are regressed on the independent variables suggested above. The standard error for each coefficient is presented in parentheses below the coefficient.

Table 10.1 (Sheet 1 of 2)

REGRESSION COEFFICIENTS (AND STANDARD ERRORS) FOR OVERALL LABOR
FORCE PARTICIPATION RATE AND EMPLOYMENT INCIDENCE
(All Stably Married Women, 1967-1975)

Variable		Overall Participation Rate	Employment Incidence
Age		-.0106** (.0009)	-.0179** (.0013)
Number of Children		-.0151* (.0060)	-.0110 (.0081)
Whether Child < 6 in 1968		-.1093** (.0210)	-.0727* (.0287)
Whether No Children Born over Panel Period[a]		.0984 (.0131)	.0950** (.0179)
	Adjusted[b]	.0438	.0442
Whether Two or More Children Born over Panel Period		-.0996** (.0176)	-.0823** (.0240)
	Adjusted[b]	-.1541	-.1331
Number of Children Moved Out over Panel Period		.0708** (.0092)	.0873** (.0126)
Whether Owned Home in 1968		.0565* (.0242)	.0297 (.0330)
Whether Became Homeowner over Panel Period		.0724* (.0286)	.0578 (.0390)
Years of Work Experience		.0139** (.0009)	.0145** (.0013)
Less than High School Education[a]		-.0757** (.0131)	-.0996** (.0179)
	Adjusted[b]	-.0696	-.0700
College Education or More[a]		.0664** (.0162)	.1263** (.0221)
	Adjusted[b]	.0725	.1529
Transfer Income ($1,000)		-.0313** (.0053)	-.0131 (.0072)
Income Other than Transfer or Wife's Labor Income ($1,000)		-.0091** (.0010)	-.0105** (.0013)
Whether Black		.0753* (.0449)	.0758 (.0612)
Whether Other Nonwhite		.1434** (.0299)	.1069 (.0409)
Number of Years Husband Unemployed Two or More Weeks		-.0051 (.0065)	-.0046 (.0088)

Table 10.1 (Sheet 2 of 2)

Variable	Overall Participation Rate	Employment Incidence
Number of Times Family Moved	−.0072 (.0075)	.0211* (.0103)
Unemployment Rate (1974 County)	−.0079 (.0043)	−.0006 (.0059)
Number of Observations	1,694	1,694
$\bar{R}^2$	.279	.245

*Significant at the 95 percent level of confidence.

**Significant at the 99 percent level of confidence.

[a]These variables are expressed as deviations from the omitted categories, and their coefficients represent deviations from an unweighted mean. (See Appendix 10.2 for details.)

[b]These coefficients are adjusted for uneven distributions of cases over the categories of the independent variable and can be interpreted as deviations from the overall sample mean. (See Appendix 10.2 for details.)

Life-Cycle Variables

The life-cycle variables included in the analysis are of two types. The first type measures initial conditions. These 1968 variables include age, number of children, whether any of the children were less than six years old, and whether the family owned their home. The second type measures change over the panel period; these include number of children born over the panel period, number of children who left home over the period, number of other relatives who moved in or out over the period, and whether the family bought a house during the panel period.

Age of wife had a very strong negative impact on both measures of labor supply over the eight-year panel period. Even after the effects of other age-related variables such as household income and number of children were partialed out, each year of age reduced the participation rate by 1.06 percentage points and reduced the probability of being employed at all during the panel period (employment incidence) by 1.79 percentage points.[6] While these coefficients are consistent with the hypothesis that women are less likely to work and less likely to work long hours as they age and approach retirement, they may also reflect cohort differences in tastes for work.

The number of children in the household in 1968 had a significant negative impact on the overall labor force participation rate for these stably married women. Each additional child reduced the overall rate by an average of 1.51 percentage points. This is consistent with the notion that children increase the value of the wife's time in home production. Number of children also had a negative effect on employment incidence, although it was not sufficiently strong to achieve statistical significance at conventional levels of confidence. Far more important as a determinant of work incidence over the eight-year period was the age of the youngest child. Women who had at least one preschool child (i.e., a child younger than six years of age in 1968) were 7.27 percent less likely to be workers than were other women. Similarly, age of children also had a strong significant impact on women's overall labor force participation rate. Women who had children under six years of age in 1968 had average participation rates which were almost 11 percentage points below those of otherwise similar women.

In order to facilitate the discussion of interactive effects presented below, the number of children born to women over the panel period was included in

---

[6]Both age of wife in 1968 and its square were included in another specification model in order to capture age's linear and quadratic effects on the participation rate. The two were so colinear, however, that neither's coefficient was sufficiently large relative to its (inflated) standard error to achieve statistical significance.

the analysis as two dummy variables. Each of these variables was expressed as a deviation from the excluded group and, thus, the coefficients presented are the effects of membership in the group from the overall mean. That is, the .0438 coefficient on "no births" means that the labor force participation rates of women who did not bear children during the panel period were 4.38 percentage points higher than that of similar women who had an average number of births. Similarly, the -.1541 coefficient on "two or more births" means that women who had two or more children during the panel period had participation rates averaging more than 15 percentage points lower than those of average women.

Birth of children was also a very strong determinant of employment incidence. Women who had no children over the panel period were 4.4 percent more likely to go to work than average, while women who bore two or more children over the panel period were 13.3 percent less likely to work. Again, this indicates that young children had a particularly strong impact on the value of the wife's time in home production and, hence, on her reservation wage.

Children leaving home had a strong positive impact on the mother's labor force participation over the panel period. On average, each child who left home was associated with a seven-point increase in the fraction of the woman's time spent in the labor force. Each child who left the household was also associated with an 8.73 percent increase in the probability that the mother would work during the eight-year period. These findings indicate that even older children had a significant impact on the reservation wage of their mothers.[7] This finding is particularly interesting from a policy perspective since women who wait until children leave home before returning to work are likely to face particularly adverse market conditions. In general, those women will have been out of the labor market for a considerable period and their market skills will have depreciated significantly. While further research is clearly indicated on this point, it nonetheless would seem that "manpower" programs for these women might be particularly effective.

The existence of money markets diffuses the effect of purchasing a home on the value of the wife's time, and hence, on her labor supply. Nevertheless, the

---

[7]The effects of the exit and entry of relatives other than the woman's own children into and out of the family are less clear. In another specification the measures of these events were included, and neither "number of other relatives moved out" nor "number of relatives moved in" had sufficiently strong effects to achieve statistical significance. This is more likely due to the fact that these other relatives were more heterogeneous in terms of age and the amount of care they required than were children, than to the fact that relatively few families experienced changes in number of other relatives in the household.

coefficients in Table 10.1 indicate that a woman whose family purchased a house over the panel period (and presumably was saving for a down payment at some time during the period) averaged 7.27 percent higher participation rates than did otherwise similar women. Wives in families who owned their homes in 1968 had higher participation rates than did renters. Home ownership also had a positive but insignificant effect on work incidence, as did "whether became owner" during the panel period.

Human Capital Variables

Both of the human capital variables had the expected strong effects on employment incidence and on the overall labor force participation rate. In terms of explanatory power, years of previous work experience was the most powerful predictor in the entire analysis, even after the effects of experience-related variables such as age were controlled for. Each year of work experience prior to 1968 increased the probability that the wife would work at some time during the panel period by 1.45 percent and increased the overall participation rate by 1.39 percent. In terms of the theory, then, work experience shifted the market wage profile upward relative to the reservation wage and thereby increased the probability that the former would exceed the latter at some point during the eight-year interval. Of course, this variable measures both experience and commitment to the labor market, and it would be wrong to interpret these effects as purely human capital outcomes.

Education was entered into the analysis in the same manner as number of births over the panel period. That is, it was entered as two dummy variables expressed as deviations from the excluded group. The -.0696 coefficient on "less than high school" means that the participation rate of women who did not complete high school was 6.96 percent lower than average. The participation rate of women who had a bachelor degree or more, on the other hand, averaged 7.3 percentage points higher than average. Education also had a positive significant effect on employment incidence. Women with less than a high school education were 7.0 percentage points less likely to work in the marketplace, while those who had a college education (or more) were 15.29 percent *more* likely to work than were other women. This is exactly what Ashenfelter (1974) found with his static maximum likelihood estimation. That is, the market wage is far more sensitive to education than is the reservation wage.

Family Characteristics

The eight-year average transfer income of the family had a negative impact on overall labor force participation of the wife. Each thousand dollars of such income was associated with a 3.1 percent reduction in the fraction of weeks spent in the labor force. Similarly, family income (again, the eight-year average) other than the wife's labor income or transfer income decreased the fraction of time spent in the labor force by an average of 0.9 percent per thousand dollars. Because this income was much more variable than transfer income, its $-.009$ coefficient represents a more powerful overall relationship than does the $-.0313$ coefficient on transfer income. Furthermore, eight-year average income (other than transfer or wife's labor income) had a significant impact on employment incidence. Each thousand dollars of income was associated with a 3.64 percent decrease in the probability that a wife would work for money during the period. In theoretical terms, these findings are evidence that, because of the diminishing marginal-utility product of market goods in producing of desirable household characteristics, family money income increases the reservation wage of the wife.

Race of the family head (and hence most often of the woman herself) had a significant effect on the overall labor force participation rate but not on employment incidence. Blacks spent an average of 7.53 percent more time in the labor force, and other nonwhites spent an average of 14.34 percent more time than did whites.

Disruptive Variables

Although all four of the measures of events which could cause radical changes in the value of the wife's time had negative effects on the overall participation rate, none of them were sufficiently powerful to achieve statistical significance.

The number of years the husband was unemployed for two or more weeks had only a slight (and insignificant) negative effect on employment incidence for wives. The number of moves, however, had a strong positive effect on the probability that the wife would work at some time during the eight years. Each relocation was associated with a 2.11 percent increase in employment incidence. Since each locality has its own set of jobs, the more localities a woman lives in, the more likely she is to find a job of the sort she wants.

Environmental Variables

Because preliminary analysis indicated that the county unemployment rate was the only measure of the local environment likely to have any impact on the labor supply of married women, it was the only measure included in the analysis. The local unemployment rate had a significant negative effect on the overall labor force participation rate. Each percentage point of unemployment was associated with a 0.79 percentage point reduction in the fraction of weeks the wife worked for money. The unemployment rate for the 1974 county of residence, however, had no significant impact on employment incidence.

The moderately high $\bar{R}^2$ indicates that the model fits the data fairly well. Indeed, previous specifications which included "number of relatives moved in," "number of relatives moved out," "whether family changed county," "whether head changed jobs," and four regional dummies, in addition to the variables discussed above, provided significantly poorer fits to the data.

The Combined Effects of Education and Births on the Timing of Labor Supply

Perhaps the most rigorous way to test the model mentioned above is to examine the combined impact of education and births on the amount and timing of labor supplied. The model implied that education, through its effect on the market wage a woman can receive, would tend to increase the amount of labor supplied. The number of children the woman gave birth to over the period, however, should modify the manner in which education affects labor supply. In particular, if the theory is correct, for women who did not bear children over the panel period education should have increased overall participation by increasing the probability that the woman would do some work during the period *and* by increasing the total amount of work done by increasing the stability of the woman's labor supply (i.e., by decreasing the number of spells and increasing their average duration). For women with multiple births, on the other hand, the theory suggests that education would still increase the incidence of employment but would increase the total amount of work by decreasing its stability (i.e., having more but somewhat shorter spells of work). That is, the more educated mothers would be expected to work more than less educated mothers during the childbearing years because they would find it optimal to work in between the births of children, while the relatively low wages available to their less educated counterparts would be simply too low to make it worthwhile for them to work between births. This argument is depicted graphically in Figure 10.5. Suppose that the reservation wage profile for two women, who differ only by the amount of education they have acquired, is shaped as the curve $\hat{w}^*$ in the figure. The profile has a general upward slope with sharp peaks at time a and at time c, at which points the women have their first and second children. Suppose further that the market wage rate available to woman #1 (with the lower level of education) is depicted by curve w_1 and that for woman #2 is depicted by curve w_2, which is above w_1. The result of this higher wage rate is that woman #2 would find it optimal to work in three distinct spells over the time period o to g (from point o to point a where the first child is born; from points b to c when the second

Figure 10.5

MODEL OF LIFE-CYCLE LABOR SUPPLY FOR WOMEN
WITH DIFFERING AMOUNTS OF EDUCATION

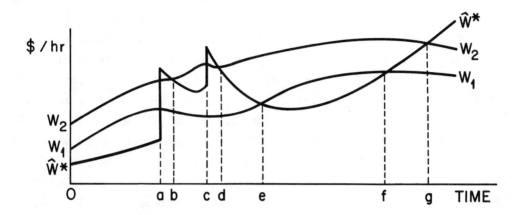

Figure 10.6

MODEL OF LIFE-CYCLE LABOR SUPPLY OF WOMEN WITH DIFFERING
AMOUNTS OF EDUCATION: LIEBOWITZ'S HYPOTHESIS INCORPORATED

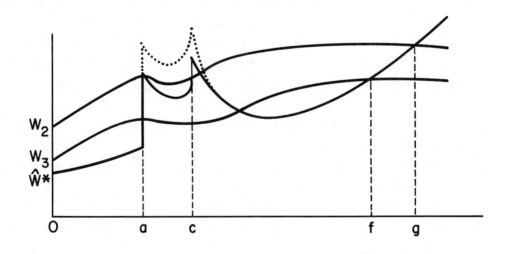

child is born; and from points d to g). Her less educated counterpart, woman #1, as a result of her less attractive market opportunities, would only work two spells (o to a and e to f). Because of the fairly short spell of employment between the births of the children, woman #2's average duration of spells of employment would perhaps be somewhat shorter than woman #1's, but because there are more of them, the total labor supply over the period would be greater.

At this point it is worth recalling that Leibowitz also argued that the relation of education to the labor force participation of a married woman would depend upon whether the woman had small children to care for. In terms of the model described earlier, education (particularly college education) would have the effect of raising the *reservation* wage for women with small children. The reasoning behind this conclusion is that college-educated women would be less likely to find market substitutes of a quality comparable to their own time in child-rearing. Hence, according to Leibowitz, the reservation profiles for woman #1 and woman #2 (equal in all respects except education) would appear as in Figure 10.6. In this case the more educated woman #2 would experience a larger increase in her reservation wage upon the birth of her children than the less educated woman, and, hence, her reservation wage profile would appear as depicted by curve $\hat{w}_2^*$. As a result of this shift, woman #2 would no longer find it worthwhile to re-enter the work force between births and would behave in the same way as her less educated counterpart.

What Leibowitz suggests is in conflict with what this model predicts because her hypothesis implies that the education effect on the labor supply of married women would disappear during the childbearing years. The most appropriate way to test the Leibowitz hypothesis in the context of the present model is to include interaction terms for the combined effects of education and number of births in the empirical models and test for their significance. If the Leibowitz argument adds significantly to our understanding of the labor supply of married women, these interaction terms should be significant. Such tests were conducted for both the overall labor force participation rate and employment incidence, but in neither case did interaction terms add significantly to the proportion of variance explained.

Tables 10.2 and 10.3 show the adjusted mean labor force participation rate and employment incidence rate, respectively, of women with each of the nine possible combinations of education and number of births. These coefficients are simply the sum of the appropriate adjusted education and birth effects from the equation discussed earlier in this chapter.

The education effect for each dependent variable can be seen by reading

Table 10.2

EFFECTS OF EDUCATION AND BIRTHS
ON THE OVERALL LABOR FORCE PARTICIPATION RATE
(Stably Married Women, 1967-1975)

	< HS	HS+	Col +
0 Births	.30	.39	.44
1 Birth	.21	.29	.35
2+ Births	.10	.19	.25

Table 10.3

EFFECTS OF EDUCATION AND BIRTHS
ON EMPLOYMENT INCIDENCE
(Stably Married Women, 1967-1975)

	< HS	HS+	Col +
0 Births	.66	.73	.89
1 Birth	.56	.62	.78
2+ Births	.49	.55	.71

across the rows of each of the tables. The top row gives the education effects for women who did not bear children during the panel period; the second row gives these effects for women who bore one child; the bottom row gives the effects for women who bore two or more children during the eight years. Because the additive model was found to be most appropriate for these variables, the education effects shown in these tables were, of course, constant for each category of the births variable.

If Leibowitz was correct, we would expect the education effect to disappear for women who bore children. For neither of the dependent variables did this happen. Hence, the above model which predicts that women with more education would be more likely to work between the births of children provides a better fit with the data than does the Leibowitz hypothesis.[8]

The conflict between the implications of Leibowitz's hypothesis and the data examined here could result from either of two things. First, it may be that the structure of the world has changed since the period of time to which Leibowitz's data pertained. Indeed, there have been substantial improvements in the quality and availability of child care since the 1950s. Furthermore, attitudes toward using these market substitutes for the wife's time in child-rearing may have become more permissive. Second, the differences in substitutability of the wife's time for market goods which Leibowitz observed may never have been sufficiently important to affect women's labor supply appreciably. Unfortunately, there are not 1950s data which are comparable to the panel study data, and, hence, we cannot isolate which of these factors explains the conflict.

Summary

In this chapter, a theoretical model of labor force participation behavior has been subjected to empirical test. By and large, the model was found to be

---

[8]Further evidence that the theory mentioned above is more appropriate to the data than is the Leibowitz hypothesis is given by the very strong education effect observed for (logarithm of) number of spells of employment for women having had two or more children during the eight-year period. The adjusted mean (logarithm of) number of spells for college-educated women with two or more births was 75 percent higher than even the number suggested by the additive model, while that for comparable women with less than a high school education was approximately equal to the number suggested by the additive model. This latter effect strongly suggests that more educated women do indeed find it advantageous to enter the work force between the births of their children.

consistent with data on the work patterns of 1,694 stably married women which
were derived from the first eight years of the Panel Study of Income Dynamics.
In particular, it was found that the life-cycle, human capital, and family
characteristics variables had the expected effect on the overall labor force
participation rate and employment incidence. As women aged and approached retirement, it became less likely that they would work at all, and the amount of
actual labor supply declined. The existence of children, especially younger
ones, was seen to reduce work effort. Purchasing a house or owning one had the
effect of increasing labor supply by increasing work incidence.

The human capital variables also had the expected positive effects on employment incidence and on the overall labor force participation rate.

Family income seems to raise the reservation wage, as is consistent with
the notion of diminishing the marginal-utility product of market inputs in home
production. Women from more prosperous homes were likely to work fewer hours
than their less affluent counterparts and were more likely not to work at all.
Race, which presumably affects tastes for goods and market work, was a significant determinant of overall labor force participation.

The measures of household disruptions had no significant effect on the
overall amount of labor supplied by women.

The nature of the local labor market as measured by the unemployment rate
of the 1974 county of residence also had little effect on the overall labor
force participation rate.

The most rigorous test of the notion that the pattern of labor supply is
determined by the relationship of the reservation wage profile (upward sloping
with peaks at the birth dates of children) to the market wage (positively shifted
by education) involves the examination of the interactive effects of education
and number of births over the given period. It was found that, contrary to
Leibowitz's suggestion, the education effect does not disappear during the childbearing years.

References

Ashenfelter, O., and Heckman, J. "The Estimation of Income and Substitution
    Effects in a Model of Family Labor Supply." Econometrica 42 (1974),
    pp. 73-85.

Boskins, Michael J. "The Economics of Labor Supply." In Income Maintenance
    and Labor Supply. Edited by Glen G. Cain and Harold W. Watts. Institute
    for Research on Poverty Monograph Series. Chicago: Rand-McNally, 1973.

322

Bowen, W., and Finegan, T. The Economics of Labor Force Participation.
    Princeton, N.J.: Princeton University Press, 1969.

Cain, Glen G. Married Women in the Labor Force. Chicago: University of
    Chicago Press, 1966.

Gramm, Wendy L. "Household Utility Maximization and the Working Wife." American
    Economic Review 65, no. 1 (March, 1975), pp. 90-100.

Gronau, Reuben. "The Effect of Children on the Housewife's Value of Time."
    Journal of Political Economy 81, no. 2, part II (March/April 1973), pp. 51,
    68-199.

Heckman, James. "Shadow Prices, Market Wages, and Labor Supply." Econometrica
    42, no. 4 (July, 1974), pp. 679-694.

Hill, Daniel. "Labor Force Participation of Married Women: A Dynamic Analysis."
    Ph.D. Dissertation, University of Michigan, 1977.

Leibowitz, Arleen. "Education and the Allocation of Women's Time." In Educa-
    tion, Income and Human Behavior. Edited by F. T. Juster. New York:
    McGraw-Hill, 1975.

Mincer, Jacob. "Labor Force Participation of Married Women." In Aspects
    of Labor Economics. Edited by H. Gregg Lewis. Universities-National
    Bureau Conference Series, 14. Princeton, N.J.: Princeton University
    Press, 1962.

Mincer, J., and Polachek, S. "Family Investments in Human Capital: Earnings
    of Women." Journal of Political Economy 82, no. 2, part II (March/April
    1974), pp. 576-608.

Willis, Robert J. "A New Approach to the Economic Theory of Fertility Behavior."
    Journal of Political Economy 81, part 2, supplement (March/April 1973),
    pp. 14-64.

APPENDIX 10.1

Table A10.1a

MEANS OF THE VARIABLES USED IN THE ANALYSIS

Variable	Mean
Age	40.39
Number of Children	1.64
Whether Child Less than 6 Years Old in 1968	.346
Whether No Children Born over Panel Period	.655
Whether One Child Born over Panel Period	.241
Whether Two or More Children Born over Panel Period	.103
Number of Children Moved Out over Panel Period	.597
Whether Owned Home in 1968	.727
Whether Became Homeowner over Panel Period	.160
Years of Work Experience Prior to 1968	7.82
Less than High School Education	.273
High School Education	.590
College Education or More	.137
Transfer Income ($1,000)	.875
Income Other than Transfer or Wife's Labor Income ($1,000)	12.537
Whether Black	.068
Whether Other Nonwhite	.027
Number of Years Husband Unemployed Two or More Weeks	.537
Number of Times Family Moved	.743
Unemployment Rate (1974 County)	4.32
Less than High School Education and No Births over Panel Period	.193
High School Education and No Births over Panel Period	.375
College or More Education and No Births over Panel Period	.087
Less than High School Education and One Birth over Panel Period	.059
High School Education and One Birth over Panel Period	.153
College Education or More and One Birth over Panel Period	.029
Less than High School Education and Two or More Births over Panel Period	.021
High School Education and Two or More Births over Panel Period	.062
College Education or More and Two or More Births over Panel Period	.020
Overall Labor Force Participation Rate	.328
Employment Incidence	.691

324

Table A10.1b

DISTRIBUTION OF THE OVERALL LABOR FORCE PARTICIPATION RATE, BY AGE
(Stably Married Women, 1967-1975)

Overall Labor Force Participation Rate	Weighted Percent of Cases	
	Whites	Nonwhites
0%	32.2%	16.8%
1 - 9	12.5	11.9
10 - 19	7.5	9.8
20 - 29	5.6	3.4
30 - 39	5.2	7.4
40 - 49	6.6	7.4
50 - 59	4.8	4.9
60 - 69	4.9	3.0
70 - 79	5.2	13.7
80 - 89	5.5	6.7
90 - 100%	10.0	15.0
TOTAL	100.0%	100.0%

Appendix 10.2

Suppose we are interested in determining the effects of membership in each category of a three-category independent variable on some dependent variable. One of several methods of doing this is multiple regression. We can define three new independent dummy variables (X_1, X_2, and X_3) on the basis of whether a given case belongs in the first, second, or third category of the original independent variables. The model we would like to estimate can be written as:

(1) $Y = a + b_1 X_1 + b_2 X_2 + b_3 X_3$

Unfortunately, we cannot directly estimate this model because "...there are more coefficients than there are independent normal equations based on the least-square criterion."[1] In order to estimate the model we must have one more independent equation involving the coefficients b_1, b_2, and/or b_3. The equation employed is some sort of arbitrary constraint placed upon the coefficients.

The most commonly employed constraint is that one of the coefficients must equal zero. Suppose we set

(2) $b_3' \equiv 0$

Then, substituting (2) into (1) yields

$$Y = a' + b_1' X_1 + b_2' X_2 + 0 X_3 = a' + b_1' X_1 + b_2' X_2$$

This modified model can be estimated and the resulting coefficient can be interpreted as the deviation associated with membership in the appropriate category *when measured from membership in the omitted category.*

. . . .

---

[1]Another way of putting this is that the full set of dummy variables are perfectly colinear.

See Melchiar, Emanuel. "Least Squares Analysis of Economic Survey Data," in 1965 Proceedings of the Business and Economic Statistics Section of the American Statistical Association, Washington: ASA (1965).

326

Proof:

Since in least squares the sum of the vertical deviations must be zero, it follows that

$$\Sigma Y = \Sigma \hat{Y}$$

In the case of a three-category independent variable this may be rearranged according to membership in the categories.

$$\Sigma Y = \sum_{i=1}^{n_1} \hat{Y}_1 + \sum_{i=n_1+1}^{n_1+n_2} \hat{Y}_2 + \sum_{i=n_1+n_2+1}^{n_1+n_2+n_3} \hat{Y}_3$$

under the constraint that $b_3' = 0$, then this can be written as:

$$\Sigma Y = n_1(a'+b_1') = n_2(a'+b_2) + n_3 a'$$

Since:

$$\Sigma Y = n\bar{Y} = n(\frac{n_1}{n}\bar{Y}_1 + \frac{n_2}{n}\bar{Y}_2 + \frac{n_2}{n}\bar{Y}_3)$$

it follows that:

$$0 = n_1(a'+b_1' - \bar{Y}_1) + n_2(a'+b_2'\ \bar{Y}_2) + n_2(a'+b_2'\ \bar{Y}_2) + n_3(a'-\bar{Y}_3)$$

Since this relationship must hold for all possible distributions of cases across the categories of the independent variable (including the case $n_1 = 0$, $n_2 = 0$, $n_3 = n$) it must be true that $a' = \bar{Y}_3$.

. . . .

The major shortcoming of this technique, according to Melichar, is that they may have difficulty in interpreting these coefficients, especially "...if they have limited knowledge of the general character of the base (omitted) classes...)"[2]

A technique which yields more easily interpreted coefficients and standard deviations involves implementing the constraint that the weighted sum of the coefficients equals zero. Algebraically this is represented as:

(3) $\quad p_1 b_1^* + p^2 b_2^* + p_3 b_3^* = 0$

_____

[2] Ibid., p. 374.

where p_i: the proportion of cases falling in the ith category of the dependent variable.

Solving (3) for b_3^* yields:

(3a) $$b_3^* = -\frac{P_1}{P_3} b_1^* - \frac{P_2}{P_3} b_2^*$$

Substituting this into (1) yields:

(4) $$Y = a^* + b_1^* X_1 + b_2^* X_2 + (-\frac{P_1}{P_3} b_1^* - \frac{P_2}{P_3} b_2^*) X_3$$

$$= a^* + b_1^* (X_1 - \frac{P_1}{P_3} X_3) + b_2^* (X_2 - \frac{P_2}{P_3} X_3)$$

$$a^* = \bar{Y} - b_1^* \overline{(X_1 - \frac{P_1}{P_3} X_3)} - b_2^* \overline{(X_2 - \frac{P_2}{P_3} X_3)} = \bar{Y}.$$

The coefficients b_1^* can be interpreted as deviations *from the overall mean of the dependent variable* associated with membership in the appropriate category.

The major shortcoming of this technique is that its implementation requires prior knowledge of the distribution of cases across the categories of the independent variable. A compromise technique involves constraining the *unweighted* sum of the coefficients to equal zero.[3] That is

(6) $$b_1^{**} + b_2^{**} + b_3^{**} = 0$$

Solve (6) for b_3^{**}, substituting into (1) and collecting terms yields:

(7) $$Y = a^{**} + b_1^{**} (X_1 - X_3) + b_2^{**} (X_2 - X_3)$$

These coefficients can be interpreted as deviations from the *unweighted* mean associated with membership in the appropriate category of the independent variable.

. . . .

---

[3] For certain purposes, such as forecasting, these coefficients are superior to those obtained under constraint (3) since they are less sensitive to the distribution of cases across the independent variable.

328

Proof:

Since it is true for each case that:

$$a^{**} = Y_i - b_1^{**}(X_1 - X_3) - b_2^{**}(X_2 - X_3) + \varepsilon$$

where ε is the error term.

It is also true for the sum of cases in each category of the independent variable. Thus, it holds that:

(a) $\quad \displaystyle\sum_{i=1}^{n_1} a^{**} = \sum_{i=1}^{n_1} Y_i - b_i^{**} \sum_{i=1}^{n_1} \varepsilon_i \quad$ for all i in X_1

(b) $\quad \displaystyle\sum_{i=n_1+1}^{n_1+n_2} a^{**} = \sum_{i=n_1+1}^{n_1+n_2} Y_i - b_2^{**} \sum_{i=n_1+1}^{n_1+n_2} X_{2i} + \sum_{i=n_1+1}^{n_1+n_2} \varepsilon_i \quad$ for all i in X_2

and

(c) $\quad \displaystyle\sum_{i=n_1-n_2+1}^{n} a^{**} = \sum_{i=n_1+n_2+1}^{n} Y_i - (-b_1^{**} - b_2^{**}) \sum_{i=n_1+n_2+1}^{n} X_3$

$$+ \sum_{i=n_1+n_2+1}^{n} \varepsilon_i \quad \text{for all i in } X_3.$$

Since under least squares the regression line runs through the mean of each category:

$$\sum_{i=1}^{n_j} \varepsilon_{ij} = 0 \quad \text{for all i in } X_j$$

equations (a) through (c) reduce to

(d) $\quad n_1 a^{**} = n_1 \bar{Y}_1 - n_2 b_1^{**} \qquad \rightarrow \quad a^{**} = \bar{Y}_1 - b_1^{**}$

(e) $\quad n_2 a^{**} = n_2 \bar{Y}_2 - n_2 b_2^{**} \qquad \rightarrow \quad a^{**} = \bar{Y}_2 - b_2^{**}$

(f) $\quad n_3 a^{**} = n_3 \bar{Y}_3 + n_3 (b_1^{**} + b_2^{**}) \quad \rightarrow \quad a^{**} = \bar{Y}_3 + b_1^{**} + b_2^{**}$

Summing these last equations (d through f) yields:

$$3a^{**} = \bar{Y}_1 + \bar{Y}_2 + \bar{Y}_3$$

or

$$a^{**} = \frac{\bar{Y}_1 + \bar{Y}_2 + \bar{Y}_3}{3}; \text{ the unweighted mean.}$$

. . . .

   It should be noted that the coefficients yielded when constraint (3) is imposed are identical to those yielded when constraint (6) is imposed if the cases are distributed evenly across categories of the independent variable. Implementation of constraint (6) then yields (whenever cases are roughly evenly distributed across categories of the independent variable) coefficients *and standard deviations* which are more easily interpreted than those obtained from implementation of constraint (2) without necessitating prior knowledge of the exact distributions of cases across the categories of the independent variable.

   Since the coefficients yielded by any two of the above techniques differ only by a constant, it is easy to convert from the coefficients obtained with one constraint to those which would have been obtained under some other constraint. For example, since:

   (9) $b_i^* = b_i^{**} + c$ for all $i <1,n>$

can be substituted into (3) and rearranged to yield

   (10) $c = -\Sigma b_i^{**} p_i$

then

   (11) $b_i^* = b_i^{**} - \Sigma b_i^{**} p_i$

Chapter 11

WORK ROLES AND EARNINGS

James N. Morgan

Analysis

Occupation has many facets—status, prestige, remuneration, risk, mental and physical requirements, and responsibility, to name just a few. Sociologists have generally focused on occupational prestige while most economists have concerned themselves with remuneration. The focus of this chapter is on a third dimension of occupation—work hierarchy.

In the eighth wave of the Panel Study of Income Dynamics, several specific questions about the nature of the work role were added to the usual occupation questions. The relationships among responses to these and other questions about personal and job characteristics and about earnings are discussed in this chapter. Of particular interest is whether aspects of the work role add anything to the explanation of earnings not already accounted for by occupation and education.

I. A WORK HIERARCHY CLASSIFICATION

Self-employed respondents were asked whether they employed other workers, and, if so, how many. Respondents who were not self-employed were asked whether they supervised other persons and, if so, how many, and whether they had any say over the others' pay or promotion. They were also asked whether their own immediate boss, in turn, had a supervisor. Finally, due to the uniqueness of government service, the employed respondents were asked whether they worked for a federal, state, or local government. Those who were both employed and self-employed were asked both sequences.

It is tempting to construct an employment hierarchy from the number of levels of authority above the individuals and a minimal estimate of the number of levels in the organization. At the same time one should keep in mind that hierarchical position has no monotonic relationship with earnings and omits some of the other dimensions of the job. The distribution on an hierarchical scale of the 1975 household heads who worked in 1974 was as follows:

Four percent were self-employed and did not employ others, so were in a one-level hierarchy.

Six percent were self-employed and employed others, so were first in a hierarchy with at least two levels.

Nineteen percent were employed but did not supervise others and their boss had no boss over him, so were second in a two-level hierarchy.

Four percent were employed, supervised others, and had a boss with no boss over him, so were second in a hierarchy of three or more levels.

Thirty-seven percent were employed, did not supervise others, and had a boss with a boss, so were third or lower in a hierarchy of three or more levels.

Thirty percent were employed, supervised others, and had a boss with a boss, so were third or lower in a hierarchy of four or more levels. Of this 30 percent, 17 percent had some say over the pay or promotion of those they supervised; 13 percent did not.

The hierarchical aspects of occupations and their relation to social structure and inequality have been studied by others using some of the panel study data.[1] It is clear from the data on earnings, however, that no monotonic relationship existed between any definable hierarchy and earnings and that some job aspects had far more to do with earnings than others. Therefore, in this analysis we take a more atomistic approach, asking how each aspect of the work role seems to affect earnings, before and after accounting for personal characteristics and other work aspects.

II. ASPECTS OF WORK ROLES AND EARNINGS

In order to be able to incorporate the 1972 Sentence Completion Test scores as part of the explanation of earnings, we have restricted the sample to males who have been heads of households since 1972 and who worked at least 500 hours in each of the years from 1971 through 1974; our earnings measure is four-year average hourly earnings. We introduced separately into the analysis (1) occupation (a ten-category variable), (2) the work hierarchy characteristics:

1. Whether worked for federal, state, or local government
2. Whether worked for others and, if so, whether boss had a boss
3. Number of others employed or supervised with say over pay or promotion
4. Number of others supervised without say over pay or promotion

and (3) the following background characteristics:

1. Years of work experience since age 18
2. Years of tenure on present job
3. Whether born on a farm, small town, or city

---

[1] For some analyses of these data focusing on broader aspects, see Wright (1976).

4. Education and, for three college groups, whether the college had freshmen ACT scores averaging 25 or higher[2]
5. Sentence Completion Test scores (1972)
6. Size of largest city in the area
7. Marital status
8. Race.

The main results, using the four-year hourly earnings (deflated to 1967 prices), in both dollar and natural log form, are given in Table 11.1. These regressions were run on each of the two earnings variables. The first regressions omitted the occupation variable, the second left out the remaining work characteristics (but included occupation), and the third included all of the independent variables. With 2,370 observations, all but one of the variables showed effects that were statistically significant by conventional standards; the lone exception was the measure of supervision *without* having say on pay or promotion. Thus, after taking the effects of other variables into account, those who reported having jobs where they supervised others but did not have a say over pay or promotion did not earn significantly more or less than those in jobs without this feature. Although statistically significant, the wage effect of working for the government or having a boss who had a boss was quite small.

Occupation and work hierarchy each retained some of its explanatory power when the other was included in the analysis. Taken by itself, the ten-category occupational classification was able to account for 22 percent of the variance in the logarithm of average hourly earnings. When adjusted for the various demographic characteristics, this explanatory power fell to 6.9 percent. When the work hierarchy variables were added, the β^2 fell again—to 5.0 percent. Comparable reductions in explanatory power were observed for the work hierarchy variables—especially the measure of number of employees supervised *with* say on pay or promotion. Since it is the pattern of effects (along with their estimated size) that is most crucial and since estimates of explanatory power differ depending on whether one is explaining dollars or logs, we turn to some figures showing the effects on log earnings before and after regression adjust-

---

[2]In the eighth wave, we asked college educated respondents for the names of the colleges they attended. We matched these names with their quality measures—(1) the average ACT test scores of freshmen classes in the last college attended, (2) the expenditure per pupil in that college, and (3) a prestige ranking of that college, prewar for those 45 and older, postwar for those under 45. Initial analysis (see Morgan and Duncan (forthcoming)) showed that the ACT measure had the greatest effect on earnings and so it is used here. For more detail on this quality measure, see the Wave VIII documentation volume.

Table 11.1 (Sheet 1 of 2)

RELATIVE IMPORTANCE OF VARIOUS CHARACTERISTICS OF PERSON OR JOB IN ACCOUNTING
FOR AVERAGE HOURLY EARNINGS 1971-1974, GROSS AND NET OF OTHER EFFECTS[a]
(Male Household Heads Since 1972, Currently Employed, Who
Worked at Least 500 Hours Each Year from 1971 Through 1974)

	Number of Classes	Natural Log of Earnings[b]				Dollar Earnings[b]			
		Gross (Eta^2)	Net ($Beta^2$)			Gross (Eta^2)	Net ($Beta^2$)		
			Omitting Occupation	Omitting Work Hierarchy	All		Omitting Occupation	Omitting Work Hierarchy	All
Education and College Quality	12	.186	.107	.083	.074	.167	.109	.100	.081
Occupation	10	.221	--	.069	.050	.145	--	.028	.025
Years of Work Experience	5	.070	.033	.034	.028	.055	.026	.027	.022
Years on Present Job	7	.034	.023	.027	.027	.032	.021	.025	.024
Number Employed or Supervised With Say over Pay or Promotion	4	.097	.026	--	.020	.109	.037	--	.030
Number Supervised Without Say over Pay or Promotion	4	.004	(.001)	--	(.001)	.005	(.001)	--	(.001)
Self-Employed--Boss Has a Boss	3	.022	.038	--	.014	.006	.004	--	.006
Works for Government	2	(.000)	.003	--	.002	(.001)	.004	--	.003
Size of Largest City in Area	6	.137	.057	.050	.046	.088	.034	.032	.029

Table 11.1 (Sheet 2 of 2)

	Number of Classes	Natural Log of Earnings[b]				Dollar Earnings[b]			
		Gross (Eta²)	Net (Beta²)			Gross (Eta²)	Net (Beta²)		
			Omitting Occupation	Omitting Work Hierarchy	All		Omitting Occupation	Omitting Work Hierarchy	All
Test Score	8	.091	.008	.010	.008	.074	.007	.009	.007
Grew up on a Farm	3	.080	.008	.004	.004	.056	.005	.004	.003
Marital Status	3	.022	.016	.017	.015	.012	.009	.009	.008
Race	3	.021	.005	.004	.004	.015	.005	.005	.005
Mean			1.34 = $3.81					$4.38	
R² Adjusted			.45	.45	.48		.35	.34	.37

Number of Observations: 2,370

( ) = Not Significant at 0.5 level.

[a] Gross Effect (Eta²) is the one-way analysis of variance squared correlation ratio. Net effect is an analogous measure based on adjusted subgroup means. F-tests can be applied to Eta² if one ignores sample design effects and to Beta² if one assumes that predictor is as well-correlated with earnings as with the other predictors. See Andrews et al. (1973), p. 4.

[b] Hourly earnings were deflated to 1967 prices, averaged, increased by 5 percent if the respondent was covered by an employer pension plan, and truncated to $25/hour if above that.

ments.[3]

Figure 11.1 shows the effects of the main occupational classes, before and after adjustments were made for the other characteristics of the job or person. The familiar occupation-earnings pattern remained after the adjustment, but it was severely attenuated.

As Figure 11.2 shows, pay increased with the number of people that the self-employed persons employed or that supervisors supervised with say over pay or promotion. A similar attenuation of the effects resulted from correlations with occupation and education.

On the other hand, supervising others without any say over their pay or promotion had little relation to earnings, as Figure 11.3 shows. As a matter of fact, both before and after adjustments, those who merely supervised others earned less than those who did not, except for a small group who said they supervised 20 or more other people.

As Figure 11.4 shows, the self-employed earned less, and respondents, presumably employed in larger organizations, whose boss had a boss made more. No simple hierarchical power structure seems in evidence here. Indeed, a more flexible search of this data, not reported here, produced little evidence of the systematic interaction effects that hierarchy theories would call for.

A final result, not shown in the figures, is that working for the government apparently involved some financial sacrifice, visible only after the regression adjustments were made. Those who worked for the government made 2 percent more overall, but after adjustments they made 7 percent less (6 percent if one also adjusted for occupation).

III. TEST SCORE, EDUCATION, AND EARNINGS

Education and college quality remained the most powerful correlate of earnings. Since interpretation of the meaning of education and occupation involves questions about the individual differences in ability reflected in our test scores, we present the patterns of effect that each of these had on earnings, before and after adjustment by regression for intercorrelations with other variables. It must be kept in mind that we do not have a proper model for *explaining* earnings, having introduced into a single regression factors operating at different stages in a causal process. In particular, race and rural background may

---

[3]A difference in logs can be thought of as a percentage difference in earnings. One can translate the average log earnings, before or after adjustment, back into dollars, but it is a geometric average and, hence, lower than the arithmetic average--$3.81 instead of $4.38 overall.

Figure 11.1

LOGARITHM OF AVERAGE, DEFLATED HOURLY EARNINGS 1971-1974
BY OCCUPATION
BEFORE AND AFTER REGRESSION ADJUSTMENT

(Male Household Heads Since 1972, Currently Employed, Who
Worked at Least 500 Hours Each Year from 1971 to 1974)

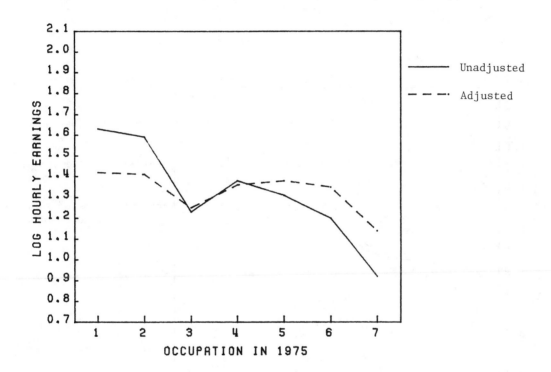

Occupation in 1975:

1 = Professional
2 = Mangerial
3 = Self-employed business
4 = Clerical, Sales
5 = Craftsmen, Foremen
6 = Operatives
7 = Laborers, Service Workers

MTR #1174

338

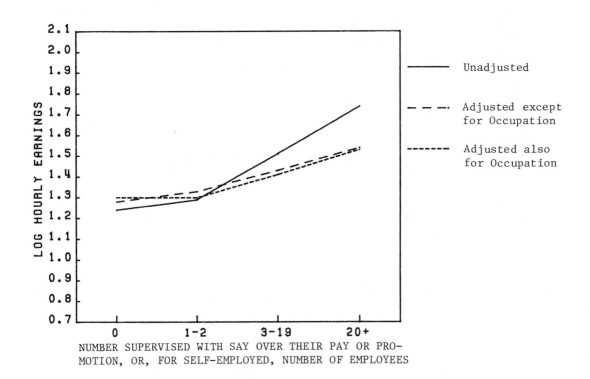

Figure 11.2

LOGARITHM OF AVERAGE, DEFLATED HOURLY EARNINGS, 1971–1974
BY NUMBER SUPERVISED WITH SAY OVER THEIR PAY OR PROMOTION
OR, FOR SELF-EMPLOYED, NUMBER OF EMPLOYEES
BEFORE AND AFTER REGRESSION ADJUSTMENT

(Male Household Heads Since 1972, Currently Employed, Who
Worked at Least 500 Hours Each Year from 1971 to 1974)

Figure 11.3

LOGARITHM OF AVERAGE, DEFLATED HOURLY EARNINGS 1971-1974
BY NUMBER OF OTHERS SUPERVISED WITHOUT SAY OVER PAY OR PROMOTION
BEFORE AND AFTER REGRESSION ADJUSTMENT

(Male Household Heads Since 1972, Currently Employed, Who
Worked at Least 500 Hours Each Year from 1971 to 1974)

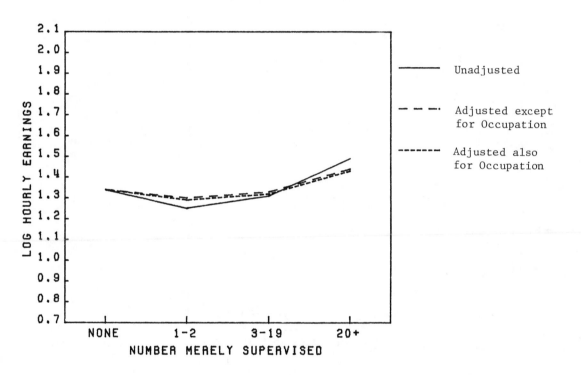

MTR #1174

340

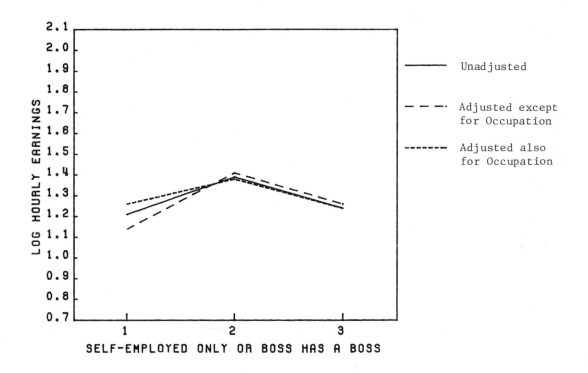

Figure 11.4

LOGARITHM OF AVERAGE, DEFLATED HOURLY EARNINGS 1971-1974
BY WHETHER SELF-EMPLOYED OR HAS A BOSS WHO HAS A BOSS
BEFORE AND AFTER REGRESSION ADJUSTMENT

(Male Household Heads Since 1972, Currently Employed, Who
Worked at Least 500 Hours Each Year from 1971 to 1974)

—————— Unadjusted

— — — Adjusted except
for Occupation

-------- Adjusted also
for Occupation

LOG HOURLY EARNINGS

SELF-EMPLOYED ONLY OR BOSS HAS A BOSS

Self-employed Only or Boss has a Boss:

1 = Self-employed only
2 = Boss has a boss
3 = Boss has no boss

affect the quality of education, and education and test scores may affect earnings *through* the occupation and work role that each person ends up with. Hence, the fact that a substantial relationship between test scores and earnings was almost completely eliminated by the regression adjustments (Figure 11.5) does not mean that test-passing ability does not matter. What it does mean is that its effect operates almost totally through the amount of education completed and the kind of job one has. In fact, most of the adjustment occurred before occupation was introduced into the regression.

On the other hand, the effects of education and college quality remained substantial even after adjustment for occupation and other aspects of the job through which most of the effect of education is assumed to operate. Figure 11.6 shows these patterns.

IV. HIERARCHY, JOB ROLES, OCCUPATION, AND EDUCATION

Since work roles and hierarchy are important, at least in explaining earnings and perhaps in other ways, some summary picture of their relationships with other factors affecting earnings is useful. Table 11.2 shows the proportion of those in each of the main job roles who were black, from farm backgrounds, had high scores on the Sentence Completion Test, or were college graduates. It is clear that people who employed or supervised others and who had a say over others' pay or promotion were much more likely to be college graduates, to have high test scores, and not to have grown up on a farm.

Table 11.3 gives summary measures of association between the main work role categories used to explain earnings and occupation or education. Some of the higher associations were mechanical, since the occupations of the self-employed tended to be in the self-employed businessman category. Perhaps the most interesting is the very low association between education and mere supervision.

Table 11.4, which gives the occupational distribution according to the various characteristics of job roles, reveals some substantial differences and enough spread to indicate that the latter characteristics are not mere reflections of the usual occupation scale. Aspects of the work role, the findings indicate, might add to the explanation not only of earnings, but also of job stability, job satisfaction, and monetary or nonmonetary fringe benefits.

Figure 11.5

LOGARITHM OF AVERAGE, DEFLATED HOURLY EARNINGS 1971–1974
BY SENTENCE COMPLETION TEST SCORE IN 1972,
BEFORE AND AFTER REGRESSION ADJUSTMENT

(Male Household Heads Since 1972, Currently Employed, Who
Worked at Least 500 Hours Each Year from 1971 to 1974)

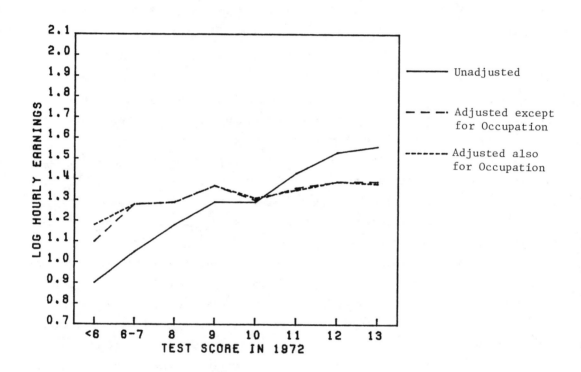

Figure 11.6

LOGARITHM OF AVERAGE, DEFLATED HOURLY EARNINGS 1971-1974
BY EDUCATION AND QUALITY OF COLLEGE
BEFORE AND AFTER REGRESSION ADJUSTMENT

(Male Household Heads Since 1972, Currently Employed, Who
Worked at Least 500 Hours Each year from 1971 to 1974)

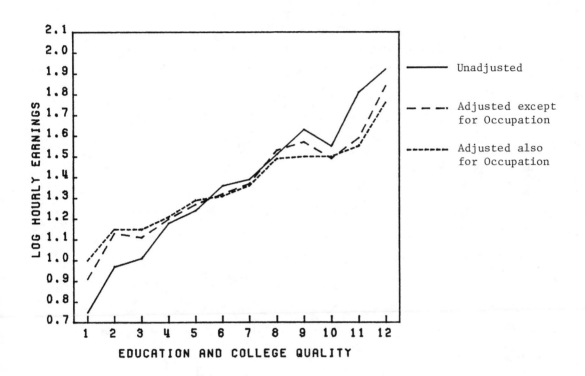

Education and College Quality:

1 = Has trouble reading or writing
2 = No trouble (0-5 grades)
3 = 6-8 grades
4 = 9-11 grades
5 = 12 grades (high school)
6 = 12 grades plus nonacademic training

7 = Some college
8 = College graduate   Colleges with Freshman
9 = Advanced degree   ACT Scores below 25

10 = Some college
11 = College graduate   Colleges with Freshman
12 = Advanced degree   ACT Scores 25 or Higher

Table 11.2

SOME OTHER CHARACTERISTICS OF THOSE IN VARIOUS JOB ROLES
(Male Household Heads Since 1972, Currently Employed,
Who Worked at Least 500 Hours Each Year from 1971 Through 1974)

Job Role	Are Black	Grew up on a Farm	Have a High Test Score (11-13)	Are College Graduates
Employ or Supervise Others With Say over Pay or Promotion				
3-19 Workers	4%	23%	61%	55%
20+ Workers	3	18	64	57
Supervise Without Say over Pay or Promotion				
3-19 Workers	5	31	43	31
20+ Workers	2	23	43	53
Works for Government	12	30	50	46
Self-employed Only	2	33	48	44
Boss Has a Boss	9	29	45	37
ALL	8%	29%	45%	38%

Number of Observations: 2,370

Table 11.3

STRENGTH OF ASSOCIATION AMONG CHARACTERISTICS AFFECTING EARNINGS
(Male Household Heads Since 1972, Currently Employed,
Who Worked at Least 500 Hours Each Year from 1971 Through 1974)

	Number of Classes	Cramer's V[a]	
		With Occupation	With Education (+ Quality of College)
Test Score	8	.16	.22
Grew up on A Farm, City	3	.22	.23
Works for Government	2	.44	.19
Self-employed, or if not, Does Boss Have Boss	3	.51	.13
Number Supervised (With No Say over Pay or Promotion	4	.12	.10
Years on Present Job	7	.12	.26
Years Worked Since 18	5	.12	.19
Number Employed, or Supervised, With Say Over Pay or Promotion	4	.31	.19

[a]Cramer's V is a chi-square-like measure of association that ranges from 0 to 1 and is asymptotically equivalent to the mean square canonical correlation between the two classifications, treated as sets of dummy variables.

Table 11.4

OCCUPATIONAL DISTRIBUTION OF THOSE WITH VARIOUS CHARACTERISTICS OF JOB ROLES

(Male Household Heads Since 1972, Currently Employed,
Who Worked at Least 500 Hours Each Year from 1971 Through 1974)

Occupation	High Test Score (11-13)	Grew up on a Farm	Worked for Government	Self-employed Only	Boss Has a Boss	Supervises Without Say Over Pay or Promotion		Employs or Supervises With Say Over Pay or Promotion		All
						3-19	20+	3-19	20+	
Professional	29%	12%	16%	16%	21%	19%	24%	26%	20%	19%
Managerial	17	9	15	7	12	16	21	25	49	14
Self-employed Business	7	6	8	41	0	0	0	16	6	7
Clerical, Sales	11	7	10	7	11	8	6	5	3	10
Craftsmen, Foremen	15	24	22	6	23	31	30	15	13	21
Operatives	11	19	18	2	19	13	9	4	1	16
Laborers, Service Workers	2	10	7	3	8	7	7	1	1	7
Farmers, Farm Workers	2	10	4	18	0	1	0	4	1	3
Miscellaneous	5	3	1	1	5	5	3	4	6	3
TOTAL	99%	100%	101%	101%	99%	100%	100%	100%	100%	100%
Number of Observations	884	784	421	319	1,646	231	57	351	155	2,370

Summary

We have found that some specific aspects of work are correlated with earnings, even beyond what could be accounted for by their correlation with education, occupation, test scores, or other variables. On the other hand, they do not take the place of occupation. We have a long way to go to develop a set of component elements that account fully for a person's work, particularly if we want to explain not only earnings but also the broader aspects of work--its satisfactions and dissatisfactions, stability, and promise. But just as with college quality, where a single explicit element relating to the quality of fellow students did most of the job, so the single element in work that seems to stand out among the usual occupational distinctions is not self-employment or working for the government, but employing (not just supervising) other people. In addition, however, some of the other aspects of work correlate with education and test scores, indicating that the latter may be important in ways that correlations between aspects of work and hourly earnings do not measure.

References

Andrews, Frank M.; Morgan, James N.; Sonquist, John A.; and Klem, Laura. Multiple Classification Analysis, 2nd edition. Ann Arbor: Institute for Social Research, 1973.

Morgan, James N., and Duncan, Greg J. "College Quality and Earnings." In Research in Human Capital and Development. Edited by I. Sirageldin. Greenwich, Conn.: JAI Press, forthcoming.

A Panel Study of Income Dynamics: Procedures and Tape Codes, 1975 Interviewing Year, Wave VIII Supplement. Ann Arbor: Institute for Social Research, 1976.

Wright, Eric Olin. Class Structure and Income Inequality. Ph.D. Dissertation. Berkeley: University of California, 1976.

Chapter 12

SOME PRELIMINARY INVESTIGATIONS
FOR A MODEL OF MOBILITY

James N. Morgan

An individual makes a set of interlaced discrete decisions, mostly before the age of 50, about job, spouse, and geographic location. Attempts to deal separately with occupational mobility, geographic mobility, and marriage/divorce cannot encompass the jointness of these decisions. It is doubtful that their sequence in time offers a good clue to the best model, since there are long-range plans and expectations and possible lags in execution in each of the acts. A structural equation model that is properly identified currently seems beyond our grasp. However, an approximation that has been proposed by Nerlove and Press (1973, 1976) promises to give results similar to a full maximum likelihood estimate and to give evidence as to how much the proper constraints might affect the other parameters.

Instead of striving for identification so that a system of structural equations can be solved analytically, Nerlove and Press propose to introduce each of the dependent dichotomies into the other equations on the right-hand side but to constrain the coefficients so that the two estimates of jointness--the effect of Y1 on Y2 and the effect of Y2 on Y1--are equal. This requires a "numerical" (iterative) solution. If higher order interactions among the jointly dependent variables are to be allowed, similar constraints can be applied. They find, as we do, that separate solution of the equations without constraints produces reasonably consistent coefficients of jointness and very similar estimates of the other parameters.

I. FOUR RELATED DECISIONS

We need a dynamic model of decision making which allows a reconsideration at any time of any one or more of the following:

1. With whom to live
2. Where to work
3. Where to live
4. Whether spouse should work and in what occupation.

Perhaps for some individuals, these decisions can be thought of as being made sequentially--marriage, job, residential location, and finally where (and whether) the spouse works--but it is more likely that this series of related decisions are made jointly.

Short of a full model which would require far more data than anyone has, we might get at the notion of joint decisions with a model in which disequilibrium in *any* of the four domains leads to decisions to change *one or more* of the decisions. If one can solve a long commuting time problem either by moving or by changing jobs, the model should allow for that. Perhaps the following model would serve:

(1) Change spouse = f (education, age, race, initial hourly earnings + change job, change residence, spouse changes vocation)

(2) Change jobs = f (education, age, race, initial hourly earnings + change residence, spouse changes vocation, change spouse)

(3) Change residence = f (education, age, race, initial hourly earnings + change job, spouse changes vocation, change spouse)

(4) Spouse changes vocation = f (education, age, race, initial hourly earnings + change job, change residence, change spouse)

The effect of any one of these changes on one of the others should be similar to the reverse effect in a second equation. A constrained solution can force this, but it is likely to make little difference in the other coefficients anyway. As a structural equation model, it is clearly underidentified, but we can, a la Nerlove, see whether the bias matters by observing whether the symmetry of the jointness is preserved in the coefficients.

The extent to which these four actions are joint, or at least interrelated rather than independent, can be seen in Table 12.1, which gives the frequency of each of the 16 possible combinations of the four events for seven-year and five-year intervals for families headed by males.[1] A systematic way of looking for interaction effects, differences inside k-way subtables not recapturable from the marginals, has been proposed by Leo Goodman. It involves asking whether a significant reduction in Chi-square results from using more and more detail to predict the full detail, here the 16 frequencies. An application of Goodman's ECTA program reveals that for the seven-year mobility patterns there are indeed nonsymmetrical patterns (interactions) that make it useful to look at various

---

[1] We need a sufficiently long period to reduce the "mover-stayer" problem, the fact that some who do not act have a nonzero probability of acting. We also need enough time for the jointness of the decisions to show up, but a short enough period so that not everyone has done everything.

Table 12.1

PATTERNS OF CHANGE OVER SEVEN AND FIVE YEARS
(For Families with the Same Male Heads for the Entire Period)

Changes 1967-1974, Reported 1968-1975

| | Moved | | Did Not Move | | |
	Changed Jobs	Did Not Change Jobs	Changed Jobs	Did Not Change Jobs	Total
Changed Spouses					
Spouse Changed Vocations*	5.3	2.9	0.3	0.1	8.6
Spouse Did Not Change Vocations	0.2	0.9	0.1	1.0	2.2
Did Not Change Spouses					
Spouse Changed Vocations	16.8	14.9	11.0	25.0	67.7
Spouse Did Not Change Vocations	3.1	4.2	2.2	11.1	20.6
TOTAL	25.4	22.9	13.6	37.2	99.1

Number of Observations: 2,688

Changes 1969-1974, Reported 1970-1975

| | Moved | | Did Not Move | | |
	Changed Jobs	Did Not Change Jobs	Changed Jobs	Did Not Change Jobs	Total
Changed Spouses					
Spouse Changed Vocations	4.8	2.2	0.2	0.9	8.1
Spouse Did Not Change Vocations	0.6	1.0	0.1	0.9	2.6
Did Not Change Spouses					
Spouse Changed Vocations	10.7	7.9	6.6	17.8	43.0
Spouse Did Not Change Vocations	7.6	7.9	6.4	24.6	31.0
TOTAL	23.7	19.0	13.3	44.2	99.8

Number of Observations: 2,350

*Change of vocation means entering or leaving labor market or changing occupation.

MTR 1168

352

combinations:[2]

1. Changing spouses and changing residences.

2. Changing residences and having a spouse change vocation (occupation or labor force status).

3. Changing jobs and having a spouse change vocation and two of the following three: changing spouses, changing residences, and having a spouse change vocation.

The difficulty with this focus only on the four events, however, is that three of them are heavily age-related, the young being the most active. Table 12.2 shows that many of the younger respondents took three or four of the possible types of action, while most of the elderly took none or one. Hence, the interrelation among the four kinds of action may well disappear when we eliminate the "spurious correlation" with age, and/or the age pattern of any one action might alter when we eliminate the effect of the other related actions.

We can examine these questions by treating each of the four actions as the dependent variable in a regression, adjusting the effects of age for other exogenous factors and for the other actions, and adjusting the effects of the other actions for the exogenous factors and the remaining other actions.[3] Starting by ignoring all but the first order interrelations among the four actions, we show the results in Table 12.3.

The effects of initial hourly earnings and of education are substantially attenuated even when we account for the other exogenous variables, particularly age. When the other actions are introduced, the power of age is substantially attenuated, though it remains significant; and as Figures 12.1-12.4 show, the pattern remains, its strength being modified only at the extreme age groups. The Nerlove-Press finding is reinforced: even without constraints to assure it, the symmetry of the estimated effects is remarkably good. The Beta-squares, which are essentially normalized regression coefficients, are almost the same

---

[2]See, for example, Goodman (1970 and 1973) and Bishop et al. (1975).

[3]We have used ordinary least squares, though it can lead to problems of heterogeneous variances and of predictions beyond the 0-1 range. In fact, with probabilities not near either extreme and with substantial sample sizes and not too many omitted interactions in the model, ordinary regression gives very similar coefficients to logit regression (which solves both problems) or to weighted regression (generalized least squares) which solves the heteroskedasticity problem. So we have avoided the cost and complexity of a maximum likelihood solution to the four related equations, and even of the maximum likelihood solution to any one (logit regression). The expected values never threaten to be unreasonable, and the constraints to force symmetry of the jointness among the four actions also appear unnecessary.

Table 12.2

HOW MANY OF THE FOUR POSSIBLE TYPES OF ACTION WERE
TAKEN IN SEVEN OR IN FIVE YEARS, BY AGE GROUPS

Age in 1975	Over Seven Years [*]		Over Five Years [**]	
	Made 3 or 4 of the 4 Changes	Made 0 or 1 of the 4 Changes	Made 3 or 4 of the 4 Changes	Made 0 or 1 of the 4 Changes
25–34	57	11	44	23
35–44	33	28	21	51
45–54	24	41	14	61
55–64	14	62	5	80
65–74	6	68	3	79
75+	4	86	1	92

[*] For 2,350 males who were heads all eight years

[**] For 2,684 males who were heads all six years.

MTR 1168

Table 12.3

FOUR ACTIONS OVER A FIVE-YEAR PERIOD,
REGRESSIONS WITH AND WITHOUT THE OTHER ACTIONS AS PREDICTORS
(For 2,688 Families with the Same Male Heads for Five Years)

	Changed Spouse			Moved			Changed Jobs			Spouse Changed Vocation		
	Eta^2	$Beta^2$	$Beta^2$	Eta^2	$Beta^2$	$Beta^2$	Eta^2	$Beta^2$	$Beta^2$	Eta^2	$Beta^2$	$Beta^2$
Education	.007	.005	.004	.018	.008	.006	.036	.008	.005	.023	.008	.008
Age	.024	.024	.006	.168	.167	.097	.171	.140	.086	.077	.057	.042
Race	.002	.003	.003	.004	.003	.002	.005	.002	.002	.002	.001	.001
Hourly Earnings (1970)	.009	.009	.010	.029	.010	.008	.048	.012	.010	.033	.005	.006
Changed Spouse	--	--	--	.068	--	.037	.015	--	.001	.029	--	.020
Moved	.068	--	.053	--	--	--	.110	--	.036	.025	--	.001
Changed Jobs	.015	--	.002	.110	--	.033	--	--	--	.021	--	.000
Spouse Changed Vocation	.029	--	.020	.025	--	.001	.021	--	.000	--	--	--
R^2 Adjusted	--	.03	.10	--	.18	.25	--	.18	.21	--	.08	.10

MTR 1172

355

Figure 12.1

PERCENTAGE WHO CHANGED SPOUSE 1970-1975,
BY AGE IN 1975, UNADJUSTED AND ADJUSTED BY REGRESSION
(For Men Who Were Heads All Six Years)

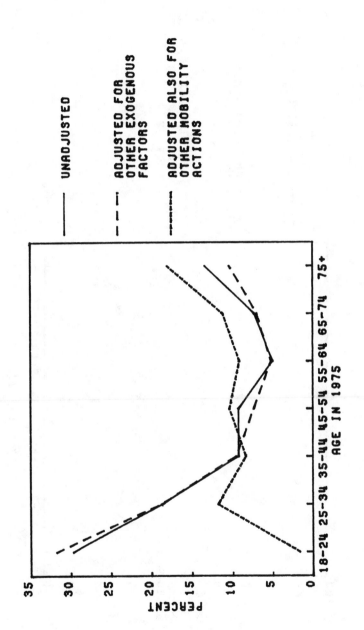

Overall percentage: 10.7

Figure 12.2

PERCENTAGE WHO MOVED 1970-1975,
BY AGE IN 1975, UNADJUSTED AND ADJUSTED BY REGRESSION
(For Men Who Were Heads All Six Years)

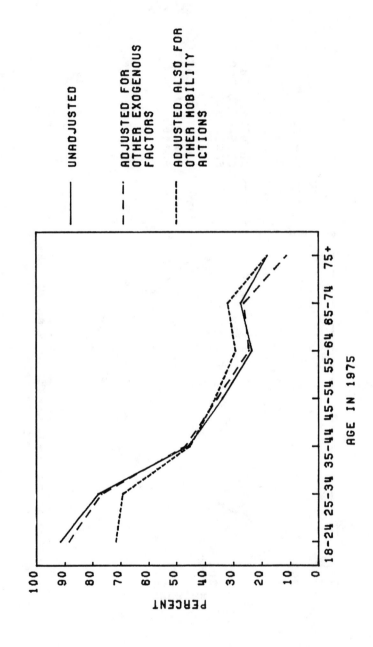

Overall percentage: 42.6

357

Figure 12.3

PERCENTAGE WHO CHANGED JOBS 1970-1975,
BY AGE IN 1975, UNADJUSTED AND ADJUSTED BY REGRESSION
(For Men Who Were Heads All Six Years)

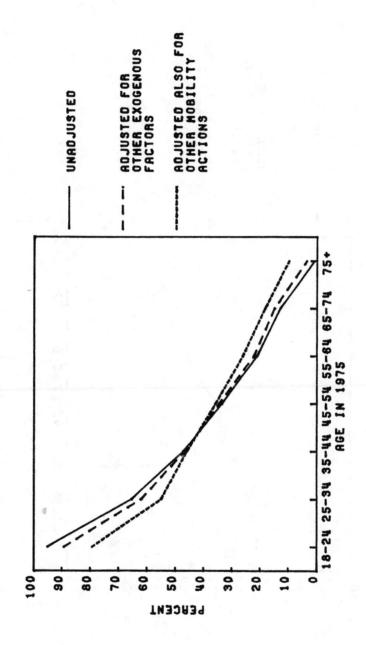

Overall percentage: 51.0

358

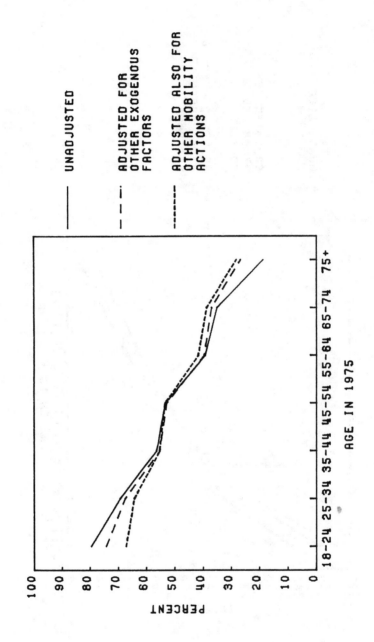

Figure 12.4

PERCENTAGE WHOSE SPOUSE CHANGED VOCATIONS (LABOR FORCE PARTICIPATION
OR OCCUPATION) 1970-1975, BY AGE IN 1975, UNADJUSTED AND ADJUSTED BY REGRESSION
(For Men Who Were Heads All Six Years)

Overall percentage: 51.0

for the effect of action 1 on action 2 as for the effect of action 2 on action 1. For example, the effect of moving on changing spouse (.037) is of the same order of magnitude as the effect of changing spouse on moving (.053), and the other pairs connected by arrows in Table 12.3 are even closer.

The analysis of the seven-year changes for 1967-1974 (not presented here) produced results which were very similar to those for the five-year changes.

If taking account of other actions does not have much effect on the age patterns for the probability of taking any one action, would taking account of other actions and of background alter the estimated effect of one action on another? The answer is clearly yes, particularly where the apparent jointness (effect of one action on another) was small anyway. Table 12.4 gives the unadjusted and adjusted effects of each action on the other three, in terms of difference in expected probability.

On the other hand, there remains a substantial amount of interrelation among these actions. An individual is 31 percent more likely to move if he changes spouses, other things equal, and 19 percent more likely to move if he changes jobs (second row of Table 12.4).

We have the usual double standard problem here of whether to focus on standardized coefficients which are measurement-free estimates of strength of effects or on unstandardized coefficients which ask what a unit change in one probability does to the expected value of the other probability. The former were necessary earlier to check for symmetry, but the latter (Table 12.4) are more useful in talking about behavior patterns.

II. HIGHER ORDER INTERACTION OR JOINTNESS

We noted that the ECTA program indicated some interactions of higher order than the two-way programs whose effects we have just examined. Dealing with these is more complex, and the most obvious way is probably inadvisable. One could simply add to the two dichotomous predictors their product, since these three terms exhaust the information in the four-cell table specifying whether neither, both, or one of the two actions was taken. The cross-product specifies one of the four corners of the table, and the two main effects specify a row and a column. Unless the proper corner of the four is specified, the interpretation is clouded. The more appropriate way is to make a four-class predictor and see whether it explains more than the two dichotomies without any interaction.

In fact, using the seven-year change for this analysis, none of the cross-product terms was very impressive, but in two cases complete interaction terms (four-class predictors) were highly significant: changing spouse was affected

Table 12.4

EFFECTS OF ONE ACTION ON THE PROBABILITY OF ANOTHER, GROSS AND NET OF REGRESSION,
ADJUSTED FOR INTERCORRELATION WITH AGE, EDUCATION, RACE, INITIAL EARNINGS, AND THE OTHER ACTIONS
(2,688 Families with Same Male Heads All Five Years)

Effects on:	Changing Spouses		Moving		Changing Jobs		Spouse Changing Vocation	
	Unadjusted	Adjusted	Unadjusted	Adjusted	Unadjusted	Adjusted	Unadjusted	Adjusted
Changing Spouse	--	--	.16*	.14	.08	.03	.11	.09
Moving	.42	.31	--	--	.34	.19	.16	.03
Changing Jobs	.19	.06	.32	.19	--	--	.14	.01
Spouse Changing Vocation	.27	.23	.16	.03	.15	.02	--	--

*Table reads: (Top row, first entry) movers were 16 percent more likely to change spouses (or acquire or lose one); but after adjustment for other things, including changing jobs or having a spouse change vocation, the difference drops to 14 percent.

MTR 1172

by combinations of moving and having spouse change vocations, and moving was affected by combinations of changing spouse and having spouse change vocations. However, in both cases this may well be the arbitrary result of the fact that gaining or losing a spouse who works automatically causes a "change in spouse's vocation." Hence, we shall not pursue the higher order interaction issue further here. With the exception of those two partly mechanical interaction effects, the regressions did as well or better (adjusted for degrees of freedom) with the three other actions represented as dichotomies in the regression. Table 12.5 gives the multiple R-squares, adjusted for degrees of freedom, for various models. In three of the four actions, adding the other actions increases the power indicating jointness of decisions, but going to higher order jointness—even selectively to save degrees of freedom—does not improve the model.

We are left with the impression, somewhat cavalier perhaps, that investigation of jointly dependent dichotomies can be initiated with ordinary regression introducing the other dichotomies and examining the results for jointness and for symmetry in the estimated jointness. With powerful exogenous variables, examining the jointness of dichotomies without simultaneously considering the exogenous variables (such as age) was not very helpful. Using all the variables in a simultaneous examination for patterns would have led to results difficult to interpret. There is accumulated evidence that better statistical approaches to the individual regressions (logit regression) would make little difference; and there is some reason to believe, given the symmetry of the joint effects, that a constrained, maximum-likelihood, simultaneous solution to the four equations would also lead to very similar results.

Given the rapid decline in activity with age, which comes about almost simultaneously for various kinds of "adjusting" activities, untangling the dynamics of the sequence is bound to be difficult.

III. EFFECTS OF MOVING ON THE PROBABILITY OF MOVING AGAIN

Even if we insist that each type of mobility is joint with the others, can we introduce elements of dynamics into the model by relating the probability of moving to recent moving activity? If moving is adaptive, a recent move could be expected to reduce the disequilibrium and the pressure to move; but if some people—for example, young persons—are more likely to be moving anyway because they are also changing jobs or spouses, there would be a positive autocorrelation rather than a negative one.

This may be true of each type of mobility, but here we focus on changing jobs to provide an example. If changing jobs is to secure a better fit between

Table 12.5

POWER OF VARIOUS MODELS OF MOBILITY,
MULTIPLE REGRESSION R-SQUARED ADJUSTED FOR DEGREES OF FREEDOM
(For 2,350 Men Who Were Family Heads All Seven Years)

Dependent Variable	Four Exogenous Factors Only[d]	Four Exogenous Factors Plus Three Other Joint Actions	Four Exogenous Factors Plus Selected Other Actions and Cross-Problems	Four Exogenous Factors Plus Four Class Combinations of Other Actions
Changed Spouse	.027	.066[a]	.068	.071
Moved	.148	.198[b]	.185	.198
Changed Jobs	.181	.198[c]	.185	.185
Spouse Changed Vocation	.165	.167	.168	.168

[a]Mostly joint with moving.

[b]Mostly joint with changing spouse and/or changing job.

[c]Mostly joint with moving.

[d]Age, race, education, and initial hourly earnings.

MTR 1172

individual capabilities and experience on the one hand and job demands on the other, then the longer a person has been in his present position, other things equal, the greater the likely disequilibrium (assuming he has been learning new skills, or the world has been changing) and the greater the probability of moving. The problem then is how to deal with persistent interpersonal differences that produce positive autocorrelation in order to see the negative autocorrelation that equilibrating moves should produce.

We made one attempt to deal with the dynamics of job-changing decisions by husbands or single family heads. By referring to the interview the year before the last reported change in job, we can ascertain how long the respondent had held his previous job. We also know how long he had held the job he started the year with and whether he changed jobs during the year. This allows us to run a dichotomous regression on whether the respondent changed jobs in 1974 with the following predictors:

1. How long he had been on the same job at the beginning of 1974 (the usual job tenure variable).

2. How long he had held the job previous to the one he had at the beginning of 1974 (a proxy for a persistent propensity not to change jobs).

3. Years of work experience (indicating seniority, invested training, passage of the period of searching and settling, accumulated nonvested pension rights, etc.).

4. Size of largest city in the area (reflecting alternative job opportunities).

5. Sex-marital status (indicating family obligations, sex discrimination).

6. Race (reflecting both job insecurity and restricted alternatives).

The results are striking. Most important, taking account of years of experience and how long the job previous to the early 1974 job was held dramatically changed the estimated effects of job tenure at the beginning of 1974, from a large negative effect on the propensity to change jobs to a positive effect at least after two or three years (Table 12.6 and Figure 12.5). The probability of changing jobs declined with experience, both before and after adjustment for the other predictors, and the adjusted estimates show most of the drop in the first 15 years. A short tenure on the "previous job" also had a persistent association with higher probability of job change in 1974, even in the multivariate context (Figures 12.6 and 12.7).

Table 12.6

IMPORTANCE OF DIFFERENT FACTORS
ACCOUNTING FOR PROBABILITY OF CHANGING JOBS IN 1974
(For Male and Female Household Heads Employed in 1975
Who Worked at Least 250 Hours Each Year, 1967-1974)

	Unadjusted η^2 (Eta^2)	Adjusted β^2 (Beta^2)
How Long Held Job Previous to One in Early 1974	.113	.111
How Long Held Job in Early 1974	.109	.058
Years Worked Altogether	.092	.046
Size of Largest City in Area	.006	.004
Sex and Marital Status	.014	.002
Race	.001	.000

Number of Observations: 3,823

$\overline{Y}$ = .180

R^2 Adjusted = .20

MTR 1157 Reused

Figure 12.5

PROPORTION WHO CHANGED JOBS IN 1974,
BY NUMBER OF YEARS IN SAME JOB IN EARLY 1974
(For Male and Female Household Heads Employed in 1975 Who
Worked at Least 250 Hours Each Year, 1967-1974)

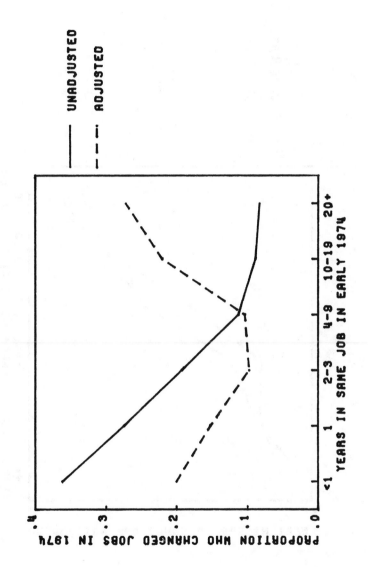

Figure 12.6

PROPORTION WHO CHANGED JOBS IN 1974,
BY NUMBER OF YEARS HELD JOB PREVIOUS TO EARLY 1974 JOB
(For Male and Female Household Heads Employed in 1975 Who
Worked at Least 250 Hours Each Year, 1967-1974)

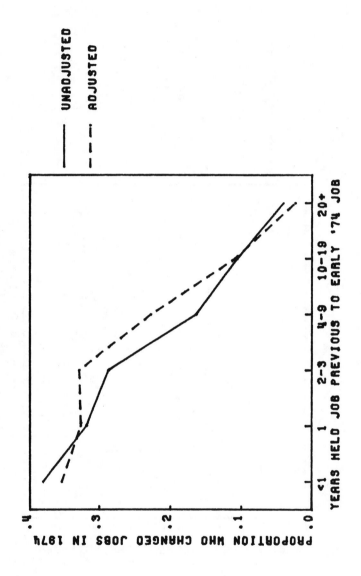

367

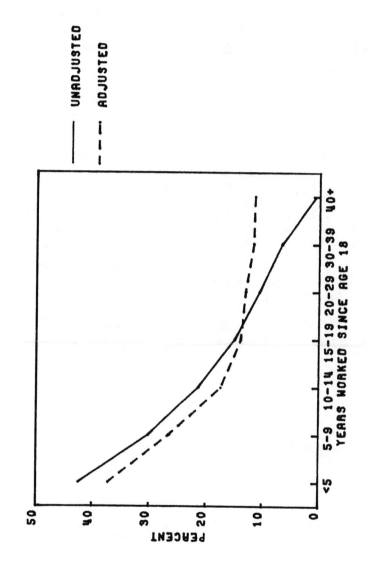

Figure 12.7

PROPORTION WHO CHANGED JOBS IN 1974,
BY NUMBER OF YEARS WORKED SINCE AGE 18
(For Male and Female Household Heads Employyd in 1975 Who
Worked at Least 250 Hours Each Year, 1967-1974)

It seems clear, then, that using recent mobility to "explain" future mobility is unwise unless the model can allow us to sort out its two separate effects: First, there is a stimulation of job change because long tenure allows the fit of person to job to deteriorate, either by change in the person (investment in human capital, perhaps) or by change in the environment. Second, there is a (spurious) decrease in the propensity because prior tenure is a reflection of a persistent interpersonal difference associated with years of experience, individual motivation or personality, or situational or environmental factors.

References

Bishop, Y. M. M.; Fienberg, S. E.; and Holland, P. W. Discrete Multivariate Analysis: Theory and Practice. Cambridge, Mass: The MIT Press, 1975.

Goodman, Leo. "The Multivariate Analysis of Qualitative Data: In Interactions Among Multiple Classifications." Journal of the American Statistical Association 68 (1973), pp. 165-75.

Nerlove, M. and Press, S. J. Univariate and Multivariate Log-Linear and Logistic Models. Rand Corporation Report R-1306. Santa Monica: The Rand Corporation, 1973.

Nerlove, M. and Press, S. J. Multivariate Log-Linear Probability Models for the Analysis of Qualitative Data. Center for Statistics and Probability Discussion Paper No. 1. Evanston, Ill.: Northwestern University, 1976.

Chapter 13

FURTHER RESULTS ON THE DYNAMICS
OF FAMILY LABOR SUPPLY DECISIONS:
Logistic Analysis of Quits and Relocation Decisions

Martin David

Introduction

Extensive analysis of the household head's labor market decisions was undertaken in Chapter 5, Volume II, of the <u>Five Thousand American Families</u> series. The
analysis focused on job changes and related geographical mobility between 1971
and 1972. Voluntary changes were termed quits, and involuntary changes were layoffs. Geographical mobility between counties in combination with a job change
was termed a job-related move; geographic mobility without a job change was termed
a transfer. (Full explanations of these definitions are given in the earlier
article.) Linear probability regressions on these four variables yielded significant relationships to 19 variables chosen to reflect an underlying structural
process of job search in both the internal and external labor markets. These
findings are summarized in Table 13.1 for the reader's convenience.

The findings can be divided into four major groups. First, the level of
wage that the respondent thought would induce him to take another job was thought
to be related to quit behavior. In fact, this variable proved a significant
factor in layoffs, but not in quits where the current wage rate appeared to be
the ruling variable. Second, job history was thought to be an important condition-
ing variable, as people who have experienced job changes and geographical mobility
in the past would be more likely to do so again in the future. In addition,
accommodation to a job and employer would imply that quits and layoffs will decline with job tenure. Third, the explicit plans of respondents were thought to
be an important intervening variable in explaining labor market behavior; planned
moves and planned job changes were seen as positive determinants of job-related
moves, transfers, and quits. Lastly, several factors were seen as forces inhibit-
ing changes. Home ownership would inhibit geographical mobility. Nonwhite or
female status was seen as related to labor market discrimination. High local
rates of unemployment were taken as inhibitors of quits and as pressure for job-
related moves outside the local area.

Table 13.1

SIGNIFICANT EFFECTS IN LINEAR PROBABILITY
REGRESSIONS ON JOB CHANGE AND RELATED GEOGRAPHICAL MOBILITY

		Decision Variable			
Variable[a]		Quit	Layoff	Job-Related Move	Transfer
A1	Age	-*			
A3	Education			-	
A4	Female Head	**		-	
A5	Race: Nonwhite	-	+	+	
B1	Property Income			**	
B2	Homeowner	-		**	-
B3	New Head				-
C1	Took New Job		+	**	
C2	Refused Job	**	+		
C3	1/(Job Tenure)	+	+		+
C4	Number of Employers	+	+		+
D1	Plans to Get New Job (1970)			**	
E2	Wage Rate	-			
E3	Union Member	-			-
F1	R Frequently Late to Work	-	**		-
G1	Plans to Move			+	+
G2	Plans to Get New Job (1971)	+	+		
G3	Wage Rate/Wage Required to Change Jobs		+	**	
H2	R Got Married (1971-1972)				+*
H3	Quit (1971-1972)			+	
H6	Area Unemployment Rate	+			

[a]Numbering refers to the model developed in the earlier analysis.

*Variable omitted from the logistic estimation to avoid convergence problems.

**Variable included in the logistic estimation as the T-ratio was larger than 1.5 in the quit, layoff, or job-related move analysis.

Analysis

The forces described above appeared in significant linear probability relationships when tested with a large number of additional variables. (Compare Table 13.1 here with Table 5.7 of the earlier article.) For methodological reasons, there is some doubt remaining in these findings. The linear probability technique is statistically inefficient; that is, the estimated standard errors of the regression coefficients are too large. Additional variables might be significant if a more appropriate estimating technique were used. However, the estimating technique does not account for clustering in the sample design, and for that reason the regression estimates of the standard errors are too small.

To overcome these technical deficiencies, each regression in the model was reestimated using the logistic function $y_i = (1 + \exp(-b_i x))^{-1}$, where $b_i x$ is a linear form in p independent variables. The logistic has the properties that estimated values of y_i must lie between zero and one, and the relationship of the dependent variable to any one independent variable is roughly S-shaped. The logistics were estimated according to the iterative method of Duncan and Walker which converges to maximum likelihood estimates.[1]

The sampling distribution of the estimated logistic coefficient vectors was computed directly from partitions of the sample. Each observation in the sample was randomly assigned into one of four partitions, in a manner that preserved the sample design within each partition. The variance of the coefficient vectors estimated independently for the four subsamples is an estimate of the variability of the coefficient vector that overcomes the deficiencies of estimates derived from ordinary regression techniques. However, the fact that only four independent subsamples were used implies that the variance is estimated with only three degrees of freedom, so that tests for significant effects are not very powerful.

Computation of the logistic model entailed both mechanical and logical problems. The mechanical problem was that the computing capacity available for solving the iterative estimation procedure would admit either a large number of variables or a large number of observations, but not both. Thus it was necessary to restrict the number of observations under consideration for technical reasons. This could be done easily by using the random quarter-samples required to compute the variance of the coefficients. Estimates of the coefficient vector were obtained as the arithmetic mean of the values from the four subsamples; this procedure is unbiased.

---

[1] See Duncan and Walker (1967) and Amemiya (1973).

The logical problem arises from the relatively low probability of the events studied. If there is a subgroup defined by the independent variables in which there is no variation of the dependent variable, that implies that the best estimated value for y_i must be zero (or unity). However, the logistic function is not defined for $y_i = 0(=1)$, so that the value of the linear form $b_i x$ must increase (or decrease) without limit. In the process of iterative estimation this is revealed by some coefficients growing indefinitely large while others decline; convergence is not achieved. The only way to avoid this problem is to limit the number of explanatory variables to a sufficiently small number so that there is variation in the dependent variable for all possible subgroups.[2]

The logical problem limiting the number of variates included in the logistic is not a reflection on the value of the logistic for modeling dichotomous variables. Rather, it is a clear warning to the investigator that he is attempting to extract more information from the sample than is warranted by the combination of the size of the sample and the number of distinct populations that can be defined on the independent variates.

In order to avoid convergence problems in estimating the logistic functions, the following strategy was followed. For each relationship all effects that were significant in the linear probability relationship were included as independent variates. One exception was made: family units who reported a marriage during the survey year (a significant factor in increasing transfers) were not singled out, as the group included very few cases, and subpopulations with no variance were sure to result. Four additional variables were included to ascertain whether the lack of significant effects was due to the functional form of the linear probability relationship. Female headship was added to the quit function. Property income was added to the job-related move function. Lagged plans to change jobs and the ratio of wages to the level required to induce a job change were included in the job-related move function.[3]

---

[2]Nerlove and Press (1973), p. 41, encounter the same problem and offer a similar explanation.

[3]To eliminate the possibility of subgroups in which no moves, quits, or layoffs were observed, we truncated the models to include only those variables for which T-ratios in the linear regressions exceed 1.5. In addition, age was eliminated from the model because of its high collinearity with job tenure, home ownership, change in marital status, and new family formation. In the case of the transfer regression, this rule was not sufficient to eliminate the problem of nonconvergence. Therefore, variables with T-ratios of less than 2.0 were eliminated for that model.

This manner of truncating the model implies that our results suffer from pretest bias (Bock, Yancey, and Judge, 1973). No practical alternative to the procedure used exists, given that we felt that the entire set of variables was

The estimated logistic functions are displayed in Table 13.2. Only six of the variables that were significant in the linear probability analysis approach significance at a critical probability of 0.2 or more.[4] Job tenure, being late to work, plans to take a new job, and plans to move emerged as the critical behavioral variables affecting the four dependent variables. Education induced a greater probability of job-related moves; female headship inhibited such moves. Thus, the information available in the sample is sufficient to admit only a very simple model of these labor market choices.

The logistic estimation technique implies that significance attached to several variables in the earlier analysis was mistaken. Being nonwhite did not appear to play a role in job change behavior, and home ownership did not seem to inhibit quits or geographical mobility. Neither the wage rate nor the ratio of the wage to that required to induce the head to change jobs appeared to play a significant role in the behaviors studied.

It is possible that pooling of information from several years might reverse these conclusions and such analysis ought to be undertaken. It is worth noting that none of the significant effects in the linear probability analysis emerged in the logistic relationships with opposite signs. The signs of effects in this study are consistent with those observed earlier and are largely in the direction predicted by the theory developed earlier.

One additional investigation of job turnover behavior warrants mention. To the extent that job change is induced by volatile demand on the part of the employer, one would expect some correlation between job changes and the industry for which the respondent works. It is well known that automobile workers are subject to frequent layoffs while postal workers are not. Because of the computation problems involved in adding variables to the logistic relationships of Table 13.2, the effect of industry was estimated by studying the residuals from

---

pertinent at the outset. Also, the realization of our sample in combination with limited computing capability made it impossible to define four quarter-samples in which there was variance on the dependent variable for all subgroups. While it would be numerically possible to redefine the values of y_i so that they lie within the unit interval to avoid this problem, results obtained from that procedure do suggest the true limits of the information used to estimate the functions. We feel that truncation of the model, with collinear effects absorbed in the remaining variates, gives a truer picture of our ability to understand the process underlying job change and relocation. Thus, the logit estimation procedure explicitly warns us when we have reached the limits of our sample data, unlike OLS that allows us to estimate models that are far too complex for the information to support.

[4]Jackknife calculations on the quarter-sample would undoubtedly increase the power of these tests; see Kish and Frankel (1971).

Table 13.2 (Sheet 1 of 2)

MEAN (STANDARD ERROR) OF THE LOGIT
COEFFICIENTS ESTIMATED FROM FOUR QUARTER-SAMPLES

Variable[a]	Quit	Layoff	Job-Related Move	Transfer
Background				
Education	--	--	.305[b] (.167)	--
Sex: Female	-.149 (.324)	--	-3.907[d] (.918)	--
Race: White	-.457 (.342)	.317 (.344)	.244 (.676)	--
Past Allocations of Income				
Property Income	--	--	.267 (.430)	--
Homeowner	-.408 (.631)	--	-.703 (.560)	-.416 (1.143)
New Family Formed	--	--	.--	.452 (.702)
Past Decisions Relating to Search (1970-1971)				
Ever Took New Job	--	.273 (.267)	.790 (.577)	--
Ever Refused Job	.135 (.271)	.113 (.165)	--	--
1/(Job Tenure)	.850[d] (.261)	.898[e] (.152)	--	.524 (.350)
Number of Employers	.011 (.019)	.033 (.038)	--	--
Past Attitudes Towards Search				
Plans to Get New Job (1970)	--	--	-6.031[b] (2.258)	--

Table 13.2 (Sheet 2 of 2)

Variable[a]	Quit	Layoff	Job-Related Move	Transfer
Initial Employment Status (1971)				
Wage Rate	-.052 (.150)	--	--	--
Union Membership	-.173 (.572)	--	--	-2.049 (1.398)
Initial Attitudes to Job (1971)				
Late to Work	-.156 (.183)	.038 (.205)	--	$-.312^b$ (.167)
Initial Attitudes to Search				
Plans to Move (1971)	--	--	1.292^c (.428)	2.61^c (.825)
Plans to Get New Job (1971)	$.725^d$ (.185)	$.572^d$ (.145)	--	--
Wage/Wage Inducing A Move	--	15.579 (27.575)	82.639 (77.173)	--
Changes During Year				
Quit	--	--	1.264 (.776)	--
Unemployment Rate in County	--	.064 (.136)	--	--
Constant	-2.355 (1.422)	-4.250^c (1.350)	-1.066 (1.889)	-3.315^d (.740)

[a]Variables refer to the head.

[b]Significantly different from zero at the .2 level.

[c]Significantly different from zero at the .1 level.

[d]Significantly different from zero at the .05 level.

[e]Significantly different from zero at the .01 level.

those logistic functions. This two-stage procedure tends to understate the full effect of industry when estimated simultaneously with household variables and is, therefore, an extremely rigorous test for industry effects. The 21 categories defined by the industry variable contribute significantly to an explanation of the residuals from the quit, the layoff, and the transfer logistic.

The industries and the associated mean deviation from the predicted value in the logistic are shown in Table 13.3. The industries are ordered according to the size of the residual from the quit logistic. Rankings of the residuals from layoffs and transfers are shown in parentheses for comparison. (The rank order correlation between the residuals from quits and layoffs is not statistically different from zero.) The mean deviations associated with the outlying industry groups (i.e., the smallest and largest) were of the same order of magnitude as the probability of quits for the sample as a whole. Thus, it is clear that these effects were of substantial importance in explaining labor market behavior. The same statement could be made for layoffs. What is not clear is with which underlying forces these effects were associated, and further analysis of the role of industry association is clearly in order to locate the cause of these effects.

Summary

Reestimation of the model developed in the earlier chapter on the dynamics of family labor supply showed that job history and attitudes (plans) were the most important variables in a model of quits, layoffs, and job-related geographical moves. Further investigation of these attitudes may give some clues to the forces that create a predisposition to move and change jobs and may ultimately relate this behavior to other background and situational variables. The results presented here make it clear that behavioral models based solely on nonattitudinal data will miss an important aspect of the problem.

It is equally clear that large differences in the demand for labor and the patterns of work in different industries imply that the industrial affiliation of a worker cannot be omitted from an understanding of the dynamics of his labor market choices. It is to be hoped that in further investigation, pooling data from several years of the panel will provide a synthesis and further explanation of the results presented here.

Table 13.3

MEAN DEVIATION (RANK) FROM PREDICTED
QUIT, LAYOFF, AND TRANSFER FUNCTIONS BY INDUSTRY

Industry	Quit		Layoff		Transfer	
Army	-.053	(1)	-.070	(1)	-.057	(19)
Communications	-.041	(2)	.027	(18)	-.001	(1)
Transport	-.026	(3)	.007	(15)	.023	(9)
Government (Excluding Education Services)	-.021	(4)	-.052	(2)	.025	(12)
Printing	-.015	(5)	.008	(16)	.024	(10)
Business Services	-.012	(6)	-.002	(10)	.055	(18)
Public Utility	-.006	(7)	-.013	(6)	-.000	(2)
Personal Service	-.005	(8)	-.010	(7)	.022	(7)
Manufacturing-- Nondurables	-.004	(9)	-.004	(9)	.008	(3)
Manufacturing--Durables	-.003	(10)	.041	(19)	.030	(14)
Educational Services	.003	(11)	-.041	(3)	.015	(6)
Wholesale Trade	.004	(12)	.065	(21)	.024	(11)
Finance	.012	(13)	.003	(14)	.009	(4)
Agriculture and Mining	.021	(14)	.002	(13)	.025	(13)
Construction	.025	(15)	.017	(17)	.022	(8)
Health Services	.031	(16)	-.007	(8)	.042	(16)
Retail Trade	.032	(17)	-.000	(11)	.014	(5)
Manufacturing--n.e.c.	.038	(18)	.001	(12)	.050	(17)
Repair Services	.059	(19)	.050	(20)	.040	(15)
Professional Services	.079	(20)	-.036	(4)	.096	(21)
Industry Not Ascertained	.30	(21)	-.019	(5)	.079	(20)

The differences shown are significant at the .01 level.

References

Amemiya, T. "The Equivalence of the Nonlinear Weighted Least Squares Method and the Method of Scoring in Binary Regression Models." Technical Report 137, Institute for Mathematical Studies in the Social Sciences. Stanford, Calif.: Stanford University, 1973.

Bock, M.; Yancey, T.; and Judge, G. "Statistical Consequences of Preliminary Test Estimators in Regression." Journal of the American Statistical Association 68 (1973), pp. 109-117.

David, M. "The Dynamics of Family Labor Supply Decisions: Quitting and Relocating as Family Unit Decisions." In Five Thousand American Families-- Patterns of Economic Progress, Vol. II. Edited by James N. Morgan. Ann Arbor: Institute for Social Research, 1974.

Holt, C. and David, M. "The Concept of Job Vacancies in a Dynamic Theory of the Labor Market." In Measurement and Interpretation of Job Vacancies. New York: Columbia University Press, 1966.

Holt, C.; Macrae, J.; and Smith, R. The Unemployment-Inflation Dilemma: A Manpower Solution. Washington: The Urban Institute, 1971.

Kish, L. and Frankel, M. "Balanced Repeated Replications for Standard Errors." Journal of the American Statistical Association 65 (1970), pp. 1071-94.

Lansing, John B. and Morgan, James N. Economic Survey Methods. Ann Arbor: Institute for Social Research, 1971.

Mattilla, J. Peter. "Quit Behavior in the Labor Market." In Proceedings: Business and Economics Section American Statistical Association, 1969. Washington, D.C.: American Statistical Association, 1969.

Morgan, James N. et al. A Longitudinal Study of Family Economics. Ann Arbor: Institute for Social Research, 1969.

Nerlove, M. and Press, S. J. Univariate and Multivariate Log-linear and Logistic Models. Rand Report R-1306. Santa Monica, Calif.: Rand Corporation, 1973.

Parsons, D. O. "Quit Rates Over Time: A Search and Information Approach." American Economic Review 63 (June 1973).

Schroeder, L. "Occupational and Geographical Mobility Within Wisconsin 1946-60: An Economic Analysis." Ph.D. dissertation, University of Wisconsin, 1971.

Toikka, R. "Supply Responses of the Unemployed." Ph.D. dissertation, University of Wisconsin, 1971.

Veroff, J.; McClelland, L.; and Marquis, K. Measuring Intelligence and Achievement Motivation in Surveys. Ann Arbor: Survey Research Center, 1971.

Walker, S. and Duncan, D. "Estimation of the Probability of an Event as a Function of Several Variables." Biometrika 54, pp. 167-79.

Chapter 14

THE CHILD CARE MODE CHOICE OF WORKING MOTHERS

Greg J. Duncan and C. Russell Hill

Introduction

One of the more striking economic and demographic trends of the past half century is the increase in the labor force participation of women with preschool children. In 1970, for example, about one-third of the mothers with children under six were in the labor force, up more than ten percentage points from 1960. This movement of mothers of young children from the home into the labor market has been accompanied by and, in some cases, caused by an increased public and private demand for the provision of formal, institutionalized child care facilities. These facilities and the various subsidy schemes which have been suggested to encourage their use will have an impact on the effective price of (or returns from) working in the market and will probably lead to new choices of child care arrangements used by working mothers.

In Volume III of this series, we investigated the determinants of choice among three different child care modes--formal day care, sitters, and family arrangements. In this chapter we focus on the socioeconomic determinants of the use of formal day care arrangements. The effect of these programs on labor supply is not analyzed here; the interested reader is referred to the paper by Heckman (1974) for an excellent theoretical and empirical analysis of this question.

The great majority of working mothers still use relatively informal modes of child care for their children while they work, most often turning to family members and babysitters.[1] Nevertheless, several recent events have made it increasingly likely that formal day care programs will have a larger role to play in caring for the preschool-aged children of working mothers. In January 1975 the President signed into law Title XX of the Social Security Act. This law provides that state social services will be shaped primarily by decisions made

---

[1]See Duncan and Hill (1975). Daycare centers and nursery schools were chosen by only 12.4 percent of the two-parent households with working wives and young children. Paid babysitters were chosen by more than half of these families, and arrangements *within* the family were made by about one-third of the families.

at the local level, rather than by requirements set by the federal government.
One result of this has been an increase in requests for the provision of formal
child care arrangements by local women's rights organizations, welfare mothers,
and other interested parties during the public review and comment period man-
dated by law in the states' social services plan. The use of formal modes of
child care is also encouraged by the federal tax laws which enable some families
to deduct up to $400 per month for child care expenses if this expense is neces-
sary to enable the parents to find or hold work and if it is paid to individuals
not related to the family head or spouse. Finally, discussions of welfare re-
form have increasingly emphasized the development of child care programs in
addition to income maintenance as a means of developing a comprehensive family
support system. The Gary Income Maintenance Experiment, for example, is now
testing the viability of such a system by offering subsidized child care programs
to those enrolled in the experiment (Shaw, 1974).

The costs of development and subsidization of the institutionalized child
care programs (provided primarily through day care centers and nursery schools)
will depend, in part, upon the likelihood that the eligible population will in
fact use them. Consequently, a question of prime importance for federal and
local policy makers concerns the factors that affect the choice of this mode of
child care.

Analysis

I. A MODEL OF THE CHOICE OF DAY CARE AND NURSERY SCHOOL FACILITIES

In order to determine the factors which affect the likelihood that a family
will use a formal mode of child care, we specified and tested a model using data
from the 1974 wave of the Panel Study of Income Dynamics. Our sample was restricted to 223 two-parent families in which both parents worked and in which
the youngest child was six years of age or younger.[2] The probability that these

---

[2] Our earlier analysis used the 1973 wave of data and did not make this "age
of youngest child" restriction (Duncan and Hill, 1975). We also included families with working female heads and found that a "sex of head" variable was a
totally unimportant determinant of mode choice when included in an additive
linear probability model. We do not know whether the model we are estimating
here would differ for female-headed as opposed to two-parent families. Unfortunately, there were too few observations to allow an estimation of the model
for families with female heads.
    A further restriction limited the sample to the cross-section part of the
original panel study population. This was done because we were unwilling to

families would use a formal day care mode was estimated with a logit regression technique which allowed for the use of categorical independent variables.

The factors which will affect a family's selection of a formal mode of child care can usefully be grouped as follows:

1. Locational factors reflecting both the location of residence and recent mobility.

2. Tastes for different child care modes which primarily reflect attitudes concerning the quality of care provided.

3. Price and income variables which reflect both differences in the price of time of working mothers and the family's ability to pay for the relatively more expensive formal day care arrangements.

Each of these factors and the variables used to capture their effects are briefly reviewed below.

Location

As pointed out in our earlier paper, interest in and support for nursery schools and day care facilities have not been constant across all geographic areas. Whether these differences have reflected different levels of political support for this type of child care, independently of demand or locational differences in preferences for such care, cannot be determined from our data. Nevertheless, an accurate estimate of the probability of use of day care facilities must include locational variables, even though their interpretation will be somewhat difficult. Locational differences have, in part, been captured here by (1) a four-category census region of residence variable and (2) a five-category measure of city size. A dichotomous variable which indicates whether the family reported moving within the past year has also been included. Recent mobility may be associated with either an increase or decrease in the supply of close relatives available for child care purposes and, consequently, may have affected the demand for extrafamily child care modes.

Tastes

The preference which a family has for a formal child care mode is, of course, difficult to measure but certainly reflects the family's perception of the quality of care provided. Whether quality is perceived to be associated with parents' awareness and control of the way their children are cared for or by the developmental outcomes of the mode of care, attitudes concerning quality are

---

include the subsample of poor families without also applying weights to them, and the logit computer program we used did not calculate significant tests using weighted data.

clearly related to the educational attainment of the parents (Nelson and
Krashinsky, 1974). A five-category "average education of parents" variable has
been used to capture the effect of this preference variable. Moreover, religious
affiliation has been shown by Hill and Stafford (1974) to affect the parental
time devoted to preschool child care independently of family income. Consequently,
a categorical measure of religious preference has been included to capture
another dimension of child care preferences. Finally, a dichotomous variable
measuring the race of the family head has been included in order to discover
whether, other things being equal, black and white families differ in their
preference for institutionalized day care.

Price and Income

It takes time to make child care arrangements and to deal with breakdowns
in these arrangements. Consequently, the opportunity cost of taking time away
from the market to make these arrangements should be an important determinant
of the choice of child care mode. The wage rate of the mother was used here as
the measure of the value of time. Since our previous work showed that day care
and nursery schools are somewhat more reliable and regular than other varieties
of child care, we expected a positive relationship between the wife's wage and
the probability of using a formal child care arrangement. A categorical variable measuring other family income (total family income minus wife's earnings)
was also included to control, in part, for a family's ability to pay for different modes of child care. While family arrangements were obviously the least
expensive, there seemed to be little difference between the hourly expense of
formal day care or nursery school and the more informal babysitter care.[3] Consequently, we expected that families with the lowest incomes would be more likely
to make child care arrangements with other family members rather than use day
care or nursery school facilities. Whether the probability of choosing the formal child care mode increases throughout the *entire* income range is unclear,
however, since those with the highest incomes may choose high quality babysitters
rather than day care or nursery schools. Since the income/child care relationship is not necessarily monotonic, the income variable was entered in categorical
rather than continuous form.

*Intra*family child care is not available to all families. Its price, then,
is really a shadow price which is, in part, a function of the structure of the

---

[3]In 1973, only a little over 2 percent of the families who used day care or
nursery school facilities paid nothing for them. The average hourly cost for
those who paid was 63 cents, compared to an average cost of 70 cents for those
using sitters. (Duncan and Hill, 1975, p. 238.)

household (see Heckman, 1974). We attempted to approximate the effect of this price on the probability of choosing a formal child care mode by including a categorical variable for size of family. An increase in family size, *ceteris paribus*, makes it more likely that older children can care for younger ones and, hence, leads to a decrease in the relative nonmarket/market price of child care. An increase in family size also affects a family's ability to pay for institution-alized care for each of its children. For both of these reasons we expected an inverse relation between this variable and the probability of choosing formal child care arrangements.

Formally, the model of child care choice estimated here may be specified as follows:

$$(1) \quad \log_e \left(P/(1-P) \right) = a_o + \sum_i a_i X_i$$

where $P = 1$ if the family chooses a formal mode of child care such as a day care center or nursery school, and $P = 0$ otherwise,[4] and X_i are the variables described above.

All but the wife's wage rate variable were entered in categorical form. This allowed the data to determine the shape of the response function rather than impose an arbitrary functional form upon it. The wife's wage rate was entered in its natural log form. Since the dependent variable is the log of the odds of choosing day care, the estimated coefficient of the wage variable can be interpreted as the wage elasticity of the odds of choosing this mode.

II. RESULTS

The results of the logit estimation of the model are presented in Table 14.1. The first column of the table shows the estimated coefficients and standard errors for all variables. Coefficients for the categorical variables are stand-ardized so that their weighted sum equals zero. In the second column, coef-ficients have been translated into average adjusted probabilities that the day care or nursery school arrangements will be chosen. In the final column, a chi-square statistic is presented for the test of the null hypothesis that the pre-dicted probability of choosing the day care mode is the same for *all* categories of the independent variable.

---

[4]In theory, the logistic model solves many of the estimation problems inherent in the linear probability model. These problems include violation of the con-stant variance assumption of the general linear model, predictions outside the zero-one range, and the nonnormal distribution of the error term. A description of the logit program we used is given in DuMouchel (1974). A more general dis-cussion of logit estimation appears in Theil (1971), pp. 628-36.

Table 14.1 (Sheet 1 of 2)

COEFFICIENTS (AND STANDARD ERRORS) FOR LOGIT
ESTIMATION OF CHILD CARE MODE CHOICE MODEL

Variable	Number of Observations	Coefficient (Standard Error)	Predicted Probability of Choosing the Day Care or Nursery School Mode	χ^2
Region				12.95**
Northeast	20	-1.52 (0.98)	.014	
North Central	66	-0.91* (0.42)	.026	
South	94	1.03** (0.29)	.154	
West	43	-0.16 (0.48)	.053	
City Size				18.63**
500,000 and over	42	1.44** (0.50)	.216	
100,000–499,999	55	0.05 (0.40)	.064	
50,000–99,999	33	1.52** (0.46)	.228	
10,000–49,999	45	-1.00 (0.59)	.023	
9,999 and under	48	-1.42* (0.60)	.016	
Moved in Past Year?				0.08
No	144	-0.05 (0.16)	.059	
Yes	79	0.08 (0.30)	.066	
Average Educational Attainment of Husband and Wife				2.25
6 Grades or Less	22	-0.14 (0.80)	.054	
7–8 Grades	50	0.10 (0.45)	.067	
9–11 Grades	60	-0.45 (0.39)	.040	
12 Grades	42	-0.10 (0.47)	.055	
At Least Some College	49	0.60 (0.48)	.106	

Table 14.1 (Sheet 2 of 2)

Variable	Number of Observations	Coefficient (Standard Error)	Predicted Probability of Choosing the Day Care or Nursery School Mode	χ^2
Religion				7.87*
Baptist	70	0.93* (0.40)	.142	
Protestant	87	-.034 (0.33)	.044	
Catholic	38	0.26 (0.53)	.078	
Other	28	-1.62 (0.85)	.013	
Race				0.21
Nonblack	200	0.04 (0.08)	.063	
Black	23	-0.31 (0.67)	.046	
Natural Logarithm of Wage Rate of Wife	223	0.86* (0.43)	.036[a] .103	
Other Family Income (Total-Wife's Annual Earnings)				3.13
Less than $5,000	21	-0.91 (0.96)	.025	
$5,000-$9,999	102	0.26 (0.26)	.078	
$10,000-$14,999	69	0.23 (0.35)	.076	
$15,000 and over	31	-0.76 (0.60)	.030	
Number of Children				2.99
One	115	0.36 (0.24)	.086	
Two	69	-0.06 (0.34)	.058	
Three or More	39	-0.97 (0.63)	.024	

Constant = 3.53 R^2 = .250

Observed proportion choosing day care/nursery school = .143

NOTE: Sample consists of two-parent families with a child under six years old and wife working. Dependent variable is the log odds that day care or nursery school mode is chosen.

*Significant at .05 level.

**Significant at .01 level.

[a]Predicted values for this variable are evaluated one standard deviation above and below the mean.

In general, these logit results were quite consistent with those we have discussed elsewhere which were based on a linear probability model (Duncan and Hill, 1974). Locational characteristics were the most important determinants of the choice of nursery school and day care facilities, while most socioeconomic measures of the family (most notably income) did not relate to mode choice in any systematic way.

Region and city size were the two most important predictors in the model; the hypothesis that the log odds of choosing the day care or nursery school modes would be equal across regions and city size categories was rejected at the 99 percent confidence level for each. Looking at the individual region categories, it is seen that the choice of the formal child care modes was significantly lower in the North Central region and higher in the South. Probably because they had more of these facilities to choose from, families living in the largest cities were generally more likely to choose day care centers and nursery schools than were families living in smaller cities and towns. The third locational variable, recent mobility, was insignificant.

Of the remaining variables in the model, the natural logarithm of wife's wage rate was the most interesting. Its estimated coefficient, 0.86, is twice its standard error and has the interpretation that a 1 percent increase in the wife's wage rate, *ceteris paribus*, is associated with a .86 increase in the odds that the day care or nursery school mode will be chosen rather than the others. When translated into adjusted proportions, wives with wage rates one standard deviation above the mean were 6.7 percentage points more likely to choose the formal mode than were wives with wage rates one standard deviation below the mean. This result was consistent with our hypothesis that the least time-consuming arrangements were made by those with the highest opportunity cost of time.

Although the patterns of effects for some of the other variables were consistent with our hypotheses (in particular, the number of children), almost all failed to attain statistical significance. We cannot reject the hypothesis that the log odds of choosing day care or nursery school facilities are equal across categories of the variables educational attainment, race, income, and number of children. Only the measure of religious preference was significant, with Baptists more likely to choose the formal child care mode. On the basis of previous work, we had expected that Catholics would be *less* likely to choose day care and nursery school facilities, but this difference did not show up here.[5]

---

[5] See Duncan and Hill (1975), p. 254, and Hill and Stafford (1974), p. 337.

Summary and Conclusion

Few families with working wives and small children chose day care centers or nursery schools for their child care needs. Our analysis has shown that the choice of this mode was largely independent of most socioeconomic characteristics of the family (including income and race). The *locational* characteristics of the family such as city size and region were the most important explanatory variables.

What do these results imply about public policy toward institutionalized child care? First of all, we have reason to doubt that schemes of subsidizing existing day care centers and nursery schools will do much to encourage their use. We found that income played an insignificant role in the choice of these formal child care modes.[6] On the other hand, we did find some evidence that choice was responsive to some of the elements of the price of the child care modes. The wage rate of the mother, for example, had a significant, positive association with the choice of day care and nursery school facilities. If this relationship resulted from the reliability and convenience of the formal modes relative to sitter or family child care arrangements, then perhaps use of the institutional modes could be further encouraged by concentrating on these aspects rather than by simply lowering the nominal price.

Above all, our analysis indicated that the choice of day care centers and nursery schools was heavily dependent upon supply determinants such as region and city size. While some of the effects of these variables might have been related to locational difference in taste for the various child care modes, we found very little evidence that more specific measures of preferences affected mode choice. To the extent that the institutional child care modes were not chosen simply because they were not obtainable, the public role in promoting use should focus on insuring that these services are available to those who want to use them.

References

DuMouchel, William H. "The Regression of a Dichotomous Variable." Ann Arbor: Institute for Social Research, 1974. Mimeographed.

Duncan, Greg J. and Hill, C. Russell. "Modal Choice in Child Care Arrangements." In Five Thousand American Families--Patterns of Economic Progress, Vol. III. Edited by Greg J. Duncan and James N. Morgan. Ann Arbor: Institute for Social Research, 1975.

---

[6]Our income variable was measured net of the wife's earnings.

388

Heckman, James J. "Effects of Childcare Programs on Women's Work Effort."
    Journal of Political Economy (March/April, 1974), Part II.

Hill, C. Russell and Stafford, Frank P. "Time Inputs to Children." In Five
    Thousand American Families--Patterns of Economic Progress, Vol. II. Edited
    by James N. Morgan. Ann Arbor: Institute for Social Research, 1974.

Nelson, Richard R. and Krashinsky, Michael. "Public Control and Economic Organi-
    zation of Day Care for Young Children." Public Policy (Winter, 1974).

Shaw, Lois B. "The Utilization of Subsidized Childcare in the Gary Income
    Maintenance Experiment: A Preliminary Report." Gary, Ind.: Gary Income
    Maintenance Experiment, 1974. Mimeographed.

Theil, Henri. Principles of Econometrics. New York: John Wiley, 1971.

Chapter 15

SUMMARY OF OTHER RESEARCH

In this chapter we summarize some recent analyses of the Panel Study of Income Dynamics data being conducted here at The University of Michigan and elsewhere. A similar summary appeared in Volumes II, III, and IV, and here we attempt to bring up-to-date the list of research completed and in progress.

These analyses are in various stages of completion. Some have already been published in professional journals, some are currently at the "working paper" stage, and the remainder are just getting started.

The list of analyses is certainly not complete. The task of contacting everyone working with the Panel Study data is impossible, but our hope is that the following summaries will help to coordinate future research.

INDEX

Garfinkel, Irwin, and Masters, Stanley. The Effects of Transfer Programs on Labor Supply.

Gordon, Nancy M.; Jones, Carol Adaire; and Sawhill, Isabel V. The Determinants of Child Support/Alimony Payments.

Gordon, Roger H. Horizontal Equity and the Federal Income Tax.

Gregory, Charles Michael. Optimal Income Redistribution.

Hansen, W. Lee, and Cain, Glen G. Labor Supply Behavior as a Function of Market, Household, and Policy Variables: A Simultaneous Equations Approach.

Heckman, James. Labor Supply and Human Capital Investments of Married Women.

Hutchens, Robert M. State Policy Parameters and Recipient Behavior in the Aid to Families with Dependent Children Transfer System.

Knickman, James R. The Effects of Labor-Leisure Preference Variations on Labor Supply Models.

Levy, Frank. How Big is the American Underclass?

Lillard, Lee A., and Willis, Robert. Dynamic Aspects of Earnings Mobility.

Masters, Stanley, and Dickinson, Katherine. The Effect of Income Opportunities on Family Composition.

Nickols, Sharon Y. The Dynamics of Family Time Allocation to Productive Activity.

Parcel, Toby Lee. Individual Investments, Ecological Variables, and Black-White Relative Economic Status.

Rainwater, Lee. A Quantitative Approach to the Study of Life Style.

Schroeder, Larry; Sjoquist, David; and Stephan, Paula. Short and Long-Run Effects of Job Displacement.

Shishko, Robert, and Rostker, Bernard. The Economics of Multiple Job Holding.

Smith, Michael J. The Single-Parent Family: A Comparative Study--Income and Employment Patterns.

Sorenson, Aage B. Relationship Among Individual Characteristics and Social Psychological Rewards of Jobs Held.

Sutton, Gordon F. Color Differentials in Survivorship in Working Years.

Wales, Terence J. Labor Supply and Commuting Time--An Empirical Study.

Wales, Terence J. and Woodland, A. D. Estimation of Household Utility Functions and Labor Supply Response.

Wilson, Franklin D. Effect of Migration on Labor Force Activity of Married Women.

Wright, Eric Olin. Class Structure and Income Inequality.

"SCAR" EFFECTS OF LABOR MARKET PROBLEMS

Michael Barth, Institute for Research on Poverty,
The University of Wisconsin, and
Jonathan Dickinson, Pennsylvania State University

The research plan of this project is to study the persistence of the effects of temporary labor market problems. In a recent study, S. O. Schweitzer and R. E. Smith found that unemployment in one year led to reduced labor supply in subsequent years. Such a scar effect would mean that, of two similar workers facing equivalent current opportunities, the one with more serious prior unemployment would have lower current labor supply. Barth and Dickinson will consider as labor market difficulties short work weeks and work lost due to illness, as well as full unemployment. They will also focus on the conceptual distinction between restricted labor supply choice due to a possible scar effect and restricted current opportunities. The methodological problem in using this distinction is that previous unemployment may be a proxy for limitations on current labor market opportunities, even if the limitations are not manifested in full unemployment. An analysis model is now being constructed. The major data source will be the Panel Study of Income Dynamics.

INVOLUNTARY UNDEREMPLOYMENT AMONG HEADS OF HOUSEHOLDS

Timothy Bates
Institute for Research on Poverty, The University of Wisconsin

This study addresses two interrelated questions: (1) What is the national incidence of involuntary underemployment among nonaged heads of households? (2) What characteristics distinguish household heads who prefer part-time work from those who are involuntarily underemployed?

Utilizing a data file extracted from the Panel Study of Income Dynamics, this study examined the work experiences of a national sample of nonaged heads of households. This data source, which described heads of households and structural characteristics of labor markets, was unique in that underemployed heads of households indicated whether their part-time working status was voluntary or involuntary. Among the heads who were employed during 1971, 15 percent were part-time workers in the sense that they worked, on average, less than 30 hours per week and/or no more than 40 weeks per year. Findings of this study indicated that 54 percent of these part-time workers were involuntarily underemployed, willing but unable to devote more time to gainful employment. Furthermore, household heads who were involuntarily underemployed in 1971 constituted a clear majority of all nonaged heads who were (1) unemployed (58.0 percent) and (2) recent labor force dropouts (55.5 percent) during the spring of 1972. These heads of households were, when working, concentrated in low-wage jobs.

THE DYNAMICS OF HOUSEHOLD BUDGET ALLOCATION TO FOOD EXPENDITURES
J. Benus, Stanford University
J. Kmenta and H. Shapiro, The University of Michigan
Published in *The Review of Economics and Statistics* May 1976

An earlier version of this paper appeared in Volume III of *Five Thousand American Families*.

THE DISTRIBUTION OF PERMANENT INCOME
Dennis W. Carlton and Robert E. Hall
Massachusetts Institute of Technology

Most economists agree that the distribution of well-being is better measured by the distribution of permanent income than by the distribution of annual measured income, but there have been few attempts to put the idea into practice. Further, those attempts have made questionable assumptions about the relation between permanent income and observed variables, either by following Milton Friedman's suggestion that permanent income could be approximated by a moving average of actual income or by defining permanent income as a function of permanent observed characteristics, notably education. In this paper we take a rather different approach in which permanent income is an unobserved variable that cannot be measured at the level of the individual. Stochastic assumptions about transitory income make it possible to identify the distribution of permanent income within a population on the basis of observations on actual income in two years for each member of the population. Even with these assumptions, permanent income at the individual level remains unidentified.

The study calculates that the concentration of the population within various ranges of permanent income will be subject to overestimation more at the high than at the low ranges, when the current income distribution is used as the basis of prediction.

THE EFFECTS OF FAMILY BACKGROUND ON EARNINGS
Mary Corcoran, The University of Michigan
Christopher Jencks, Harvard University
Michael Olneck, The University of Wisconsin

Men with socially and economically privileged parents usually earn more as adults than men with less privileged parents. There is no reason to suppose that men with privileged parents have a stronger preference for cash as against psychic income from their work. If anything, the contrary seems likely. It follows that men with privileged parents are either more valuable to "rational" employers, search more effectively for lucrative jobs, or benefit from positive discrimination by employers based on either background *per se* or its correlates. This paper tries to assess the importance of each of these factors with data from several sources, including the Panel Study of Income Dynamics.

POSTWAR INEQUALITY: TREND AND CYCLE ANALYSIS
Sheldon Danziger and Eugene Smolensky
Institute for Research on Poverty, The University of Wisconsin

This research will undertake a project on trend and cycle in postwar income inequality. The study has three related objectives. First, a consistent time series that captures the trend and cycle in income inequality in the United States over the period since World War II is to be developed and analyzed. Second, the effect of secular trends in the demographic composition of the population and labor force, especially the increase in the number of young people and women in the labor force, on the secular trend in income inequality is to be measured. Finally, the effects of the transfer system on these demographic attributes over both the trend and the cycle will be measured.

Trend analysis from Census and Current Population Survey data will provide the background data required to evaluate a variety of behavioral hypotheses. This research will examine one such hypothesis now being frequently advanced. Specifically, it will relate trend and cycle in postwar inequality to behavioral responses induced by the transfer system. Under this hypothesis the increased inequality in earnings is attributed to the reduction of labor supply by the elderly in response to increased Social Security payments, and to the postponement of labor force entrance and choice of occupation by the young in response to increased educational opportunities. It is further conjectured that the transfer system facilitates investment in education and job search, which affects occupational choice, although the effect on inequality is uncertain.

An important source of information with which to measure these behavioral responses is the Panel Study of Income Dynamics. While others have used this data source, they have usually excluded families in which the head or the spouse of the head changed over the course of the sample. This group, however, may provide an estimate of the effect of the transfer system on family dissolution.

An additional attempt will be made to measure the effect of changes in the labor force participation of women. The panel study data indicate whether a woman worked in the initial year and whether she worked in succeeding periods (this analysis employs data from the first seven years of the panel study). By varying assumptions about future trends in the labor force participation rates of wives, a hypothetical distribution can be created. An upper bound can be computed by assuming that all women with children older than six are employed, whether or not they are married, and whatever their family income. Then for each woman not currently working, an expected income (based on the incomes of similar women who are working) and thus an expected household distribution can be computed. The expected distribution can then be compared to the observed distribution.

INCOME-LEISURE PREFERENCE STRUCTURES OF PRIME-AGED MARRIED MALES
Jonathan Dickinson, Pennsylvania State University

Dickinson will revise for publication the current draft of his monograph on estimating income-leisure preference structures for prime-aged married males. Several sections of his analysis will also be condensed into articles for submission to professional journals.

In this research project, data from the Panel Study of Income Dynamics was used both cross-sectionally--to compare interpersonal differences in labor supply responses, and in the full panel sense--to compare changes in individuals' responses over time. Previous work on the estimation of labor supply parameters from nonexperimental data was extended along three dimensions: (1) The choice of functional form for the labor supply function and the choice of the corresponding preference function were regarded as explicit questions for empirical inference. (2) Careful attention was paid to institutional constraints that may prevent workers from achieving optimal labor supply positions. (3) Diversity of preferences among workers facing the same opportunities was recognized, and estimates of the dispersion of labor supply parameters were obtained.

The main empirical analysis was restricted to employed prime-aged married males who were free to choose their work hours at a defined hourly wage on their primary jobs. The wage and income variables were transformed to account for overtime premiums and increasing marginal tax rates. Cross-sectional estimates based on this select sample of males from the Panel Study indicated that the preference structure is consistent with a parallel utility model or with a linear additive labor supply model. For comparison purposes the simple labor supply model was also estimated for a sample of moonlighters. For each of these samples the estimated income effects were zero or positive and the substitution effects were negative--contratheoretical results tending to confirm the judgment that the simple labor supply model is inappropriate for workers who face demand constraints on work hours.

A second model of labor supply was based on individual responses to time variations in income and wage rates as observed in the panel data. This model included interactions between wage and income changes and the individual's average level of labor supply during the survey period (interpreted as an indicator of the individual's mean preference for labor supply). Individuals with high labor supply preferences were found to be two to three times as responsive to changes in economic incentives as were those who usually work a standard 40-hour week. Although these estimates apply only to the subpopulation of workers who were free to vary their work hours, they do suggest that much of the contraction in work effort by prime-aged males in response to an income maintenance program would take the form of reduced overtime rather than reductions below full-time work.

LABOR SUPPLY BEHAVIOR IN THE PRESENCE OF DEMAND CONSTRAINTS
Jonathan Dickinson, Pennsylvania State University

In this project Dickinson will concentrate on labor supply behavior in the presence of demand constraints--underemployment, moonlighting, and job change. He plans to develop models for simulating the labor supply of workers for whom the simple labor supply model is inappropriate. His previous estimates of the structure and diversity of preferences for the select equilibrium sample will be the starting point for the construction of these models, and the Panel Study of Income Dynamics will be the basic data source.

Three general approaches are planned, involving different levels of technical complexity. First, the responses of constrained workers and moonlighters will be simulated under the assumption that they have the same distribution of preferences as unconstrained workers. Responses to income maintenance programs will be of particular interest. Second, moonlighting behavior will be simulated to test the assumption that the preferences of constrained workers match those of unconstrained workers. A number of simulations will be carried out under plausible alternative assumptions about fixed costs associated with moonlighting. Third, reservation wages and moonlighting behavior of workers with primary job constraints will be estimated directly. It may be possible to adapt and use the generalized Tobit model developed by Heckman. Simpler estimation methods that embody elements of the Heckman approach will also be attempted.

COLLEGE QUALITY AND EARNINGS
Greg J. Duncan and James N. Morgan, The University of Michigan
To be published in *Research in Human Capital and Development*, Volume I.
Edited by Ismail Sirageldin. JAI Press, Greenwich, CT (1977)

In this paper, we related earnings to three measures of college quality and found that for men, the ACT scores of the student body had a much stronger association with earnings than did per-pupil expenditures. In addition, the ACT quality measure was found to be more important than a prestige measure, which presumably takes ACT scores into account. The ACT measure retained its explanatory power even when the effects of the other two quality measures had been taken into account. For women, none of the quality measures affected earnings.

NET EARNINGS CAPACITY MEASURE OF FAMILY ECONOMIC STATUS
Irwin Garfinkel and Robert Haveman
Institute for Research on Poverty, The University of Wisconsin

These two researchers will continue work with David Betson in an attempt to define a comprehensive measure of the economic status of a family (called net earnings capacity) and to estimate this value for a national sample of families. With this measure substituted for current family income, revised estimates of economic inequality can be made, as can an alternative definition of poverty and of the composition of the poverty population. These estimates, to be developed using Current Population Survey data and Panel Study of Income Dynamics data will be used to analyze the "target efficiency" (or poverty effectiveness) of income transfer policies, including H.R. 1, earnings supplements, and wage subsidies.

Aspects of the earnings capacity study to be emphasized include (1) the implications for measuring the composition and incidence of poverty in using the earnings capacity notion in place of the current-income concept as a measure of economic status, (2) the extent to which different groups in the population make use of their earnings capacity, and (3) the use of the earnings capacity concept to decompose observed differences between the incomes of blacks and whites so as to distinguish the role of racial labor market discrimination from the roles of other determinants of income differences.

Virtually all the empirical research and writing have been completed. One paper has been published, and two others have been submitted to journals. A monograph and a paper on earnings capacity and labor market discrimination are in draft. During the coming year these will be reviewed, revised, and submitted for publication.

THE EFFECTS OF TRANSFER PROGRAMS ON LABOR SUPPLY
Irwin Garfinkel and Stanley Masters
Institute for Research on Poverty, The University of Wisconsin

During the coming year, these researchers will complete the revision of their monograph on the effects of transfer programs on labor supply. They will also produce several articles for submission to professional journals and will write a book giving a nontechnical treatment of this whole policy issue.

Employing multiple regression analysis and using data from the Survey of Economic Opportunity and the Panel Study of Income Dynamics, they estimated the labor supply responses of various subgroups of the total adult population. For each subgroup, they analyzed a variety of labor supply measures. This work is part of a long tradition of labor supply studies. (For example, see Income Maintenance and Labor Supply, by Glen Cain and Harold Watts, and the negative income tax experiments.) The topic has attracted much attention because potential labor supply effects are a major consideration in the debate over what kind of income maintenance system this country should have.

The most important independent variables concern wages and unearned income. Several important issues addressed include (1) the determination of the optimal amount of disaggregation by demographic group; (2) the treatment of various kinds of unearned income, many of which are either influenced by a person's labor force status or by his eagerness to accumulate wealth; and (3) the measurement of wage effects when some persons in the sample are not employed or do not receive extra money for working extra hours, when hours-per-week might occur both in the dependent variable and as part of the wage variable, when hourly wages are high because the amount of employment is limited, and when wage rates may be positively related to the nonwage attractiveness of the job. The sensitivity of the income and wage coefficients to alternative methods of resolving these problems is being tested. On the basis of what are considered to be the most appropriate coefficients, the labor supply changes that would result from various income maintenance plans are being estimated.

The findings indicate that the labor supply of prime-aged, married males would not change very much in response to the enactment of such a program. In contrast, married women would reduce their labor supply by a substantial amount. The reduction in the labor supply of prime-aged, single men and women and of married and single older and younger men and women would fall somewhere in between the first two groups.

THE DETERMINANTS OF CHILD SUPPORT/ALIMONY PAYMENTS
Nancy M. Gordon, Carol Adaire Jones, and Isabel V. Sawhill
The Urban Institute

The objective of the research is to examine the determinants of child support/alimony payments within the context of a simultaneous model explaining the amounts of child support/alimony, woman's earnings, and Aid to Families with Dependent Children (AFDC) benefits a family receives. Error components estimation was employed on a six-year household-year file constructed for the analysis. The theoretical determinants tested in the analysis included the father's ability to pay, willingness to pay, the financial need of the mother and children, the mother's desire for support, and the legal enforcement environment. The proxies used for these factors performed well: In general, coefficients were of the expected sign, and the percentage of variation in child support/alimony payments explained by the estimated equations ranged from 0.51 to 0.31. The most important explanatory factors proved to be the father's ability to pay and the financial need of the mother and children.

HORIZONTAL EQUITY AND THE FEDERAL INCOME TAX
Roger H. Gordon, Princeton University

This essay investigates the degree of horizontal inequity resulting from use of the income tax and attempts to measure how successful certain tax reforms would be in lessening this inequity. According to the notion of horizontal equity developed and used in this study, an equitable tax ought to be based on the choice set that an individual has--his opportunities--and ought not to be affected by the nature of the bundle that he actually consumes. In order to compare the incidence of various tax structures, a model was estimated using data from the Panel Study of Income Dynamics which was capable of producing, in simulation, lifetime patterns for a representative group of each of the tax bases. Individual differences were captured in large part through use of individual constant terms in the regressions. The results from the simulation indicated a sizable amount of horizontal inequity from using the current income tax, though this inequity would be moderately relieved by shifting to a tax on lifetime labor income or consumption. These simulation results were also used to compare the distribution of annual income with the distributions of various measures of lifetime income and opportunities. Here, it was found that most observed income differences maintained themselves over a lifetime and that these lifetime differences were due principally to differences in abilities and opportunities, and not to differences in tastes.

OPTIMAL INCOME REDISTRIBUTION
Charles Michael Gregory, University of California, San Diego

Formulas for optimal wage supplement parameters and optimal negative income tax parameters are derived. The models assume a population of utility maximizing individuals who supply labor according to a standard work-leisure choice model. The government then chooses tax parameters which maximize a defined social welfare function subject to a government revenue constraint. The solution equations are highly nonlinear and discontinuous. An iterative search procedure is used to locate the optimum for particular parameter specifications.

In general, both plans will succeed in bringing about an income redistribution which tends towards greater equality. Whereas the wage supplement plan will increase the supply of labor, the negative income tax decreases it. The wage supplement plan with a continuation of current transfer payments increases welfare more than the piece wise linear negative income tax plan; but it should be emphasized that both plans do increase social welfare. More numerical work of this nature is needed to help determine policy recommendations.

Particular value judgments appear in the welfare function. Alternative judgments should be studied. The models did not include education, externalities, lifetime income and inheritance effects, investment, economic growth, family size and stability, occupational choice, criminal activity, or voting behavior. The narrowed data set used probably biased the results toward lower labor supply and higher tax rates under the plans studied. Nevertheless, the framework set down is a beginning in formulating redistribution policies rooted in economic theory. Other redistribution plans can be modeled and compared under similar assumptions.

LABOR SUPPLY BEHAVIOR AS A FUNCTION OF MARKET, HOUSEHOLD,
AND POLICY VARIABLES: A SIMULTANEOUS EQUATIONS APPROACH
W. Lee Hansen and Glen G. Cain
Institute for Research on Poverty, The University of Wisconsin

This study directs and participates in an integrated set of projects on labor supply with empirical estimation of labor supply functions as the principal focus and common theme. Several demographic groups will be studied, with special attention to whites and blacks and to male heads of household, married women, low-income families, and the aged. The principal data sources are the 1960 and 1970 Census and the Panel Study of Income Dynamics. Use will be made of both individual household data and grouped data. The main econometric method involves the estimation of simultaneous equation models, that allow for the interrelations of any individual's labor supply with various market and household behavioral functions. Particular note will be made on the simultaneity or feedback *from* labor supply *to* such variables as earnings capacity (or wage rates) and fertility.

These coordinated research projects are designed to improve predictions about labor force behavior of various demographic groups in response to changes in market, household, and policy variables. A distinction will be drawn between variables impinging on a person's labor supply decision that are generated, on the one hand, by the ordinary workings of the market and household behavior (such as employment opportunities, wage changes, changes in family income, fertility, and schooling decisions) and, on the other hand, by policy interventions (such as taxes, income maintenance programs, retirement benefits, and day care subsidies).

LABOR SUPPLY AND HUMAN CAPITAL
INVESTMENTS OF MARRIED WOMEN
James Heckman, National Bureau of Economic Research,
University of Chicago

The National Bureau of Economic Research has recently been awarded a contract to conduct a study on Labor Supply and Human Capital Investments of Married Women. This research will use the data from the Panel Study of Income Dynamics to analyze the effect of experience versus discrimination interpretations of the earnings differentials between men and women. It is anticipated that this study will be completed by September 1977.

STATE POLICY PARAMETERS AND RECIPIENT BEHAVIOR IN THE AID TO FAMILIES WITH DEPENDENT CHILDREN TRANSFER SYSTEM
Robert M. Hutchens, Cornell University

This thesis investigates the determinants of household transitions to and from the Aid to Families with Dependent Children (AFDC) program. It has two primary objectives. First, it attempts to analyze the relationship between state financial policy parameters and household entry and exit transitions. These "state policy parameters" determine the income level at which families become eligible for AFDC transfers as well as the level of payments received by eligible families. Second, the thesis attempts to analyze changes in household transition probabilities over the 1967-71 period. During this period the number of families receiving payments from the AFDC program doubled.

Economic theories of marriage and and labor supply were used to generate hypotheses about determinants of entry and exit transitions which were tested through application of logistic analysis to a population of female heads drawn from the Panel Study of Income Dynamics. In order to test hypotheses on state policy parameters, new techniques were developed for predicting the parameters confronting each family in the sample.

Analysis indicated that policy parameters did indeed play an important role in determining entry and exit probabilities. Entry probabilities were clearly affected by the AFDC "guarantee" (the payment received when earnings were zero) and the "entry income level" (the income level at which families became eligible for AFDC payments). Exit probabilities were also influenced by the guarantee. No firm evidence was found linking break-even income levels (and thereby tax rates) to either entry or exit. Analysis of remarriage indicated that though the *level* of AFDC policy parameters did not have a statistically significant negative impact on the probability of remarriage, *receipt* of AFDC payments was strongly related to a lower probability. Finally, evidence on changes in household transition probabilities between 1967 and 1971 essentially supported the contention that increases in state policy parameters led to increased entry probabilities during the period.

The analysis also yielded information on the importance of other variables in determining entry and exit transitions. The female household head's wage income, nonwage income, age, and work experience played a particularly significant role.

By expanding our understanding of the factors influencing AFDC entry and exit transitions, the analysis should be useful in AFDC policy debates and future research on transfer program participation.

THE EFFECTS OF LABOR-LEISURE PREFERENCE VARIATIONS ON LABOR SUPPLY MODELS
James R. Knickman, New York University

This research exploits the dynamic nature of the Panel Study of Income Dynamics by estimating a model of labor supply in which all variables are measured as differences between two years. A theory of labor supply which explicitly allows for variations in labor-leisure preference patterns across individuals in different income classes was developed. The demand for leisure equation derived from this model is: $L = f(W,Y,B,T)$ where W is hourly wage rate (the price of leisure), Y is total income, B is a vector of noneconomic determinants of labor supply, and T is not controlled for in the leisure demand function, the wage and income coefficients will be biased and inconsistent since tastes for work are positively correlated with wages and total income.

Since tastes for work are defined as largely time invariant characteristics of individuals, converting all variables to first differences caused the taste variable to vanish from the labor supply equation. The first differences specification, therefore, allowed for unbiased estimates of the wage and income effects, even though labor-leisure preference differences across individuals could not be observed.

The empirical results indicated that the wage and income coefficients estimated with the first differences specification were significantly different from the coefficients estimated with a one-period, cross-section model. The direction of change was that which would be expected if variations in labor-leisure preferences across the sample did in fact bias the cross-section coefficients.

The research also used the first differences model and the multi-period panel data to determine: (1) if transitory wage changes affect labor supply behavior differently than do permanent wage changes, (2) if lagged labor supply adjustments accompany wage changes, and (3) how future wage changes affect current labor supply choices.

HOW BIG IS THE AMERICAN UNDERCLASS?
Frank Levy, University of California at Berkeley

This work analyzed the behavior of a cohort of poor people who might be eli-

402

gible for an income maintenance program--that is, people who are poor before welfare payments are included in their incomes. Levy analyzed the extent to which
their poverty is a permanent versus a temporary condition and discussed the factors associated with a person's movement across the poverty line.

To date, Levy has reached the following conclusions: The principal source
of male-headed poverty was low wages (rather than unemployment); the children of
poor households usually earned incomes much higher than that of their parents;
within an original poverty cohort of 16.35 million (for 1967), there was an "underclass" of 7.7 million who could expect to be poor for most of the near term.

DYNAMIC ASPECTS OF EARNINGS MOBILITY
Lee A. Lillard, National Bureau of Economic Research, and
Robert Willis, National Bureau of Economic Research and
Stanford University

This paper proposes a new econometric methodology for the anlaysis of earnings mobility. It seeks to determine whether poverty is a transitory status or
a permanent condition of individuals. It has the advantage of providing a direct linkage between traditional human capital theory, earnings functions, and
Markov chain type models.

The methodology is fairly simple. First, we estimated an earnings function
with male earnings as the dependent variable, using seven years of data from the
Panel Study of Income Dynamics. We estimated permanent, transitory and serially
correlated components of earnings due to both measured and unmeasured variables.
Measured variables are represented by components of variance. The estimated earnings function and the estimated components were then used to compute the probability that an individual's earnings would fall into a particular, but arbitrary,
time sequence of discrete earnings classes. For simplicity, we focused on the
probability that an individual's earnings would fall below an arbitrary poverty
line defined as one-half of the median of U. S. male earnings each year from 1967
to 1973.

With these techniques, indices of income immobility or the degree of "persistence" in individual income levels were developed for various subgroups of
the population (e.g., by race, experience and education). Such measures included the proportion of earnings variation (gross variation or variation around
a predicted level) among individuals which represents a permanent difference,
the degree to which earnings are correlated from year to year for the same individual, and the rate of decay of correlation around the permanent level.

The variance components analysis of the log of annual earnings of males (in
1970 dollars) indicated that 65.8 percent of total variance in log earnings rep-

resents permanent earnings differences. Of the remaining 34.2 percent stochastic variation, 30.6 percentage points are due to purely stochastic variation, 3.6 to serial correlation.

Blacks and whites had roughly the same size permanent component, but the transitory component of earnings variation was more than twice as large for blacks as for whites. This larger random component was partly offset in total variation by a lower serial correlation component for blacks.

Whites were clearly more insulated from poverty not only because of a higher mean earnings but also because of a much lower transitory and thus total earnings variation. Ninety percent of whites had a less than .158 probability of being in poverty, while only 52 percent of blacks were below that probability. In contrast, 90 percent of blacks had less than a .625 probability. A larger fraction of blacks would be persistently in poverty and would experience more transitory poverty.

Schooling, experience, and race explained 31 percent of total earnings variation, but they explained 47.7 percent of the permanent earnings variation. Within racial groups, schooling and experience alone explained 30 percent of the permanent component for blacks and 37.7 percent for whites.

After completing the analysis of male earnings mobility, a similar analysis will be performed for family income mobility.

THE EFFECT OF INCOME OPPORTUNITIES ON FAMILY COMPOSITION
Stanley Masters and Katherine Dickinson
Institute for Research on Poverty, The University of Wisconsin

During the next year a program will be initiated to study the possible effects of new transfer programs on such aspects of family composition as rates of marital formation and dissolution, the ages at which children leave home, and the extent to which the elderly live with other family members. In addition they will investigate the effects of changes in family composition on poverty, on income distribution, and (to the extent possible) on psychological well-being. They hope to rely fairly heavily on longitudinal data such as the Panel Study of Income Dynamics and to a lesser extent on aggregate cross-section data. The researchers hope to be able to publish a monograph on this topic as well as several papers.

Partly as a result of the pioneering theoretical work of Gary Becker, economists have become interested in the extent to which standard economic analysis can be applied to marital patterns. Although economists have been concerned mainly with marriage (and fertility), other aspects of family composition appear to lend themselves to an economic analysis. In particular, income factors should be important in determining who lives together since it is generally more expensive for family members to live apart than to share the same food and housing. Of course, economics is not the only discipline relevant to a study of family composition. In Time of Transition, Heather Ross and Isabel Sawhill provide a good synthesis of material from economics and various disciplines on the issue of marital dissolutions. Masters and Dickinson hope to take a fairly similar approach, but to cover other components of family composition in addition to marital separations.

This subject is important, not only because family composition has a direct effect on the size of the poverty population, but especially because of its relevance for designing policies to combat poverty. For example, income maintenance programs can be designed with the eligibility unit as the individual (as in a demogrant), but the family programs and most proposals for change have used the family rather than the individual as the eligibility unit. The question then arises as to just how to define the family. Should it be all related people living together or should it be restricted to the nuclear family (husband, wife, and minor children)?

The latter approach is less costly since, *ceteris paribus*, fewer people will be eligible for subsidy. In addition, it corresponds to general notions of equity as reflected, for example, in the poverty line concept. This definition of the family does, however, provide an economic incentive for families to split up so that secondary family members may become eligible for government support. The magnitude of such a splitoff effect needs to be known in order to estimate the budgetary costs of potential new income maintenance programs. Moreover, such splitoffs may be regarded in themselves as good or bad side effects of income maintenance. For example, on the one hand, Social Security and other programs for the aged may be highly regarded for the extra freedom they give to both the aged and their offspring. On the other hand, AFDC has been frequently criticized for leading to marital breakdowns. In addition to budgetary costs, estimates of such potential side effects should also be valuable in considering the case for new income maintenance programs. It is hoped that this research will generate such estimates as a part of the study.

THE DYNAMICS OF FAMILY TIME
ALLOCATION TO PRODUCTIVE ACTIVITY
Sharon Y. Nickols, University of Missouri, Columbia

This study focused on the time allocated to housework and market work by husbands and wives in 1,156 structurally intact families in their "productive years" between 1968 and 1973. In the aggregate, an equitable level of participation in productive activity (time allocated to both labor market and household work) was observed between the husbands and wives.

Factors related to time allocated to housework by husbands and wives were explored through multiple regression analysis for data from 1973. Twenty-six percent of the variance in the wife's housework time was explained by a set of variables including those describing the wife's employment status, family size, and the husband's employment characteristics. The factor which most constrained the wife's housework hours was her employment hours, while family size served as a pressure to increase time allocated to housework. Variables related to intensity of the husband's employment served as a constraint on his time inputs to housework; variables related to extent of the wife's employment induced the husband to spend more time in housework, although the impact was quite modest. Only 7.4 percent of the variance in the husband's housework hours was explained.

Cross-lag analysis of data for each sequence of one-year lags indicated that the impact of the wife's labor force hours upon husband's housework hours was minimal. Change in the wife's labor force hours was ineffectual in causing adjustments in the husband's time allocation to housework.

INDIVIDUAL INVESTMENTS, ECOLOGICAL VARIABLES,
AND BLACK-WHITE RELATIVE ECONOMIC STATUS
Toby Lee Parcel, University of Washington

This research is a contextual analysis of status attainment for blacks and whites. The Panel Study of Income Dynamics provided data concerning the areas of current and former residence of respondents, and this information is being used to associate ecological characteristics with each case. These ecological characteristics included measures of school expenditures and economic conditions in the areas of former residence, and measures of industrial structure, proportions of blacks, unemployment, and residential segregation in the areas of current residence. This analysis estimates the direct and indirect impact of individual and ecological level variables upon dependent variables such as educational attainment, lifetime migration, occupational prestige, and earnings.

A QUANTITATIVE APPROACH TO THE STUDY OF LIFE STYLE
Lee Rainwater, Harvard University

The concept of life style has been a central one in qualitative studies of the patterns of life of particular groups of society. Descriptions of life style strive to capture the texture of life as it is lived on a day-to-day basis by a particular social group. Sometimes the same patterning of the elements of daily lives is called the subculture of the group. In some analyses the life style or subculture of a group is presented as a product of the group's cultural inheritance, as a somewhat autonomous cause of behavior, as a set of human forces independent of the resources the group possesses.

This is not the point of view adopted here. Instead, life style or subculture is conceived as a description of the way of living a group creates out of the resources available to it--material, social, and intellectual--in terms of the tastes and needs of members of the group. Life style is understood to be constrained by the resources of the group and yet to reflect the group's choices in constructing a way of life within those constraints. The Panel Study of Income Dynamics is one of several data sets used in operationalizing the concept of life style.

SHORT AND LONG RUN EFFECTS OF JOB DISPLACEMENT
Larry Schroeder, David Sjoquist and Paula Stephan
Georgia State University

The study examines the short and long run effects of displacement from work. The research is being sponsored by the U. S. Department of Labor, Bureau of International Labor Affairs.

For the purposes of this study, displacement is defined as a job change which results from the company having folded, changed hands, or moved out of town. The displaced population is analyzed relative to four groups: the lay-offs, all unemployed and job quitters who are not displaced, the labor force, and the entire sample. The study examines whether or not the displaced population is representative of the labor force and the effects of displacement on the duration of unemployment. Long run effects considered are: the effect of displacement on future earnings and wages, and the mobility response of the displaced worker. In addition, the study examines the labor market response of secondary workers in the family to the displacement of the head. The study uses the five-year data base and should be completed in early 1977.

THE ECONOMICS OF MULTIPLE JOB HOLDING
Robert Shishko and Bernard Rostker, Rand Corporation
Published in *American Economic Review*, Volume 66, Number 3,
June 1976, pp. 298-308.

This paper uses the traditional model of utility maximization to derive an individual's "moonlighting" labor supply curve when first job hours and wage rates are fixed. The moonlighting supply function was estimated using data from the first three waves of the Panel Study of Income Dynamics and the Tobit technique for estimating relationships with limited dependent variables. We used a two-stage procedure. First we projected moonlighting wages for moonlighters and nonmoonlighters alike based upon a reduced form moonlighting wage equation. Second, we fitted the data set of independent variables, including the reduced form moonlighting wage prediction, to the Tobit model.

To test our basic theory, we considered several hypotheses by comparing the theoretical partial derivatives of the moonlighting supply function with those calculated from the estimated supply curve. The basic theory held up in two of three tests.

The estimated elasticities indicated that an increase in moonlighting wages caused an increase in the labor supplied by moonlighters *and* the entry of previous nonmoonlighters into this secondary labor market. Furthermore, the observed negative effect of a given increase in first-job earnings on moonlighting depended upon whether the increase was affected by a change in the primary wage rate or a change in hours worked on the primary job. The negative elasticity with respect to primary hours was greater than the negative elasticity with respect to primary wage, presumably because a change in the latter affected only earnings, but a change in the former also reduced the time available to moonlight.

THE SINGLE-PARENT FAMILY: A COMPARATIVE STUDY
INCOME AND EMPLOYMENT PATTERNS
Michael J. Smith, Community Service Society, New York

One section of this single parent family research is now completed. Analyses of income and employment patterns for samples of one and two-parent families with children have been carried out on a 1968 cross-sectional sample and a panel sample. The following is a brief summary of these findings.

First, in the cross-sectional sample, heads of two-parent families were employed much more often than heads of one-parent families and received major portions of income from wage-related sources. One-parent families had to rely more often on financial support from welfare and Social Security payments and, to a lesser extent, on alimony/child support, retirement pay and pensions, and help from relatives. Nevertheless, the income that heads of one-parent families received from wages and salaries usually represented over twice the income received from any one of these other sources. One-parent family heads who worked were clearly better off than those who could not work. Two-parent families had over twice the family income of one-parent families. When family need was taken into account, one-parent families were even worse off. Fifty-five percent of the one-parent families were poor in 1968 as compared to only 14 percent of the two-parent sample.

Within the sample of one-parent families, divorced single parents were employed the most often and never married parents were the least often employed.

In assessing the relative position of different types of one-parent families, utilization of the number of income measures included in the data set proved valuable. Widowed parents had slightly higher family incomes than divorced parents and both groups were much better off than separated and never married parents. When family need was taken into account, divorced parents were slightly better off than widows, and separated parents, who usually care for more children, were the most deprived group. When the ratio of income to leisure hours was used as a dependent variable, families headed by widowed parents had more income relative to leisure than families headed by divorced parents, and separated parents had less income relative to leisure time than never married parents.

In the panel sample, families that continued as one or two-parent families until 1974 were followed to assess the effects of remaining in a one or two-parent status for six more years. A high percentage of the two-parent families were employed in both 1968 and 1974, compared to less than one-half of those who headed one-parent families. Twenty-four percent of the one-parent sample changed employment status. Fourteen percent of these single parents were not working in 1968 but were employed by 1974, thus experiencing some economic recovery. This represents 30 percent of those single parents eligible for recovery due to amount of recovery in employment after six more years in the one-parent status. Separated single parents experienced the greatest economic loss; many were employed in 1968 but not in 1974.

Multiple regression analysis was used to establish the effects of family structure variables on income. In the cross-sectional sample, the fact that a family was a one or two-parent family was much more important in terms of family income than the fact that a particular one-parent family was headed by a never married, widowed, divorced, or separated parent. The single-parent status was as important a predictor of income as other status variables such as race, education, or the age of the youngest child in the family. Regression analysis was also used to examine predictors of change in family income from 1967 to 1973. Continuance as a two-parent family was an important predictor of change in income and represented a $5,536 increase in income. Change from a two-parent to a one-parent status over six years was also a significant factor in income change, representing a $2,247 decrease in family income. The implications of these findings for family policy will be presented in the final report which will be available by the end of 1976.

RELATIONSHIP AMONG INDIVIDUAL CHARACTERISTICS AND
SOCIAL PSYCHOLOGICAL REWARDS OF JOBS HELD
Aage B. Sorenson, Institute for Research on Poverty,
The University of Wisconsin

This research focuses on the mechanisms that determine the relationships among individual characteristics such as education, ability and background, and the economic, social, and psychological rewards people obtain from their jobs. These may be conceived of as the mechanisms that match persons to jobs.

One line of research focuses on the consequences of different matching processes for the attainment process over time. If the matching process is a competitive process in a perfect market for skills and jobs, only changes in skills will produce changes in individual attainments. If, on the other hand, job competition and/or bureaucratic promotion prevails, changes in attainment take place as the result of the creation of vacancies that produce mobility, and persons' level of skills need not change for their attainment to change. Formulation of different models of the attainment process based on these considerations is near completion, and the work will be reported on in the coming period in a monograph on the structure of inequality and the attainment of status and income.

A second line of research is addressed to developing indicators for the different mechanisms for the matching of men to jobs. This work ties into recent contributions to labor market research, paricularly dual labor market theory. In collaboration with Arne Kalleberg of the University of Indiana, a monograph is being prepared reporting on this work and on the implications of different matching mechanisms for income and status attainment and for persons' job satisfaction.

Finally, in collaboration with Nancy Tuma of Stanford University, research on developing models for the dependency of the rate of job shifts on the duration of a job will be undertaken. Several competing models for this process have been suggested and the research will try to ascertain the empirical validity of these models using life-history data. This research also has substantive interest, as the various models can be linked to the existence of various types of on-the-job training (general versus specific). Data from a variety of sources will be used: the 1970 Census, the Michigan Panel Study of Income Dynamics, the National Longitudinal History Study, and the Hopkins Life-History Study.

COLOR DIFFERENTIALS IN SURVIVORSHIP IN WORKING YEARS
Gordon F. Sutton, University of Massachusetts

Based upon earlier demographic estimates of widowhood, this analysis proposes to measure the color differences in lifetime economic burden experienced

410

by persons in the working ages who outlive the family "breadwinner" of husband-
wife families. The data analysis tests hypotheses that (1) color differentials
in these survivor measures do not closely reflect simple color differentials in
mortality, and (2) nonwhite population is considerably more disadvantaged than
the white population according to such measures. Important cross-generational
effects were seen to flow from confirmation of these propositions. Economic
burden was measured by computing family lifetime income estimates with and
without widowhood effects using recent Census estimates for income levels and
data from the eight waves of the Panel Study of Income Dynamics to obtain family
income level transitions associated with the widowing of women.

LABOR SUPPLY AND COMMUTING TIME--AN EMPIRICAL STUDY
Terence J. Wales, University of British Columbia

In most of the labor supply literature involving models set in a utility
maximizing framework there is generally no distinction made between commuting
time and other uses of nonwork time; instead, they are combined to form a variable
described as leisure. In a cross-section context such an aggregation procedure
relies on the assumption that the ratio of the price of commuting time to that of
leisure (net of commuting time) is the same for all consumers. This assumption
is likely to be violated by the dependence of housing prices on commuting time
since the cost of commuting another hour will equal the wage rate minus the resulting reduction in housing expenditures. In this paper we estimate a very simple model that attempts to incorporate commuting time in the labor supply analysis.

We assumed that the individual maximizes a utility function with leisure,
commuting time, housing consumption, and nonhousing consumption as arguments.
We then assumed that housing prices depend on commuting time; hence the individual faces a schedule of housing prices with the equilibrium price being determined
as part of the utility maximizing process. Similarly, the implicit price of commuting an additional hour was determined endogenously and equalled the wage rate
less the reduction in housing expenditures from commuting the additional hour.

To implement the model, we assumed a flexible form of the individual's indirect utility function and a constant elasticity form for the relation between
housing prices and commuting time. We linearized the budget constraint about observed values for each individual and, using cross-section data, obtained full
information maximum likelihood estimates of the utility function parameters, as
well as of the gradient of house prices with respect to commuting time.

ESTIMATION OF HOUSEHOLD UTILITY FUNCTIONS
AND LABOR SUPPLY RESPONSE
Terence J. Wales and A. D. Woodland, University of British Columbia
Published in *International Economic Review* 17, June 1976.

A summary of the preliminary version of this article appeared in Volume III of *Five Thousand American Families*.

EFFECT OF MIGRATION ON LABOR FORCE
ACTIVITY OF MARRIED WOMEN
Franklin D. Wilson
Institute for Research on Poverty, The University of Wisconsin

This project involves an analysis of the effects of migration on the labor force activities of married females. The data for this analysis is taken from the 1968-1974 Panel Study of Income Dynamics, and the sample universe includes currently married women. The basic issues to be explored include (1) whether migration affects the labor force participation of married women and whether such effects vary depending on type of geographic move, previous employment history, and the employment status of husbands, and (2) whether migration affects the occupational position of women who worked after the move occurred.

CLASS STRUCTURE AND INCOME INEQUALITY
Eric Olin Wright, The University of Wisconsin

Marxist class categories have been almost totally ignored in systematic quantitative studies of social stratification and income inequality, in spite of the fact that social inequality plays a more central role in Marxist theory than in any other tradition in the social sciences. Nearly all sociological analyses of inequality have focused on position within the occupational structure as the pivotal dimension of stratification in contemporary societies. Class, defined in terms of positions within the social relations of production, is rarely even mentioned, let alone included in empirical investigations.

This study is an attempt to bring the Marxist concept of class into the heart of quantitative research on social stratification. The underlying theme of this analysis is that class, understood as common positions within the social relations of production, plays a central role in mediating income inequality in capitalist society. The immediate purpose of the investigation is to demonstrate the mediating role of class position and then to explore the concrete ways in which this mediation takes place.

The study is divided into two parts. The first consists of a theoretical analysis of the Marxist view of class, with particular attention to the problem of understanding "middle classes" in Marxist terms. The concept of "contradic-

tory positions within class relations" is introduced as a way of rigorously defining the position of middle classes within the class structure. This theoretical analysis of class relations served as the basis for developing a series of
hypotheses about the relationship of class position to income inequality, as
well as an operationalization of class which permitted testing those hypotheses.

The second part of the study consists of an empirical investigation of
these hypotheses. Several general conclusions were firmly established by the
results:

1. Class played an important role in generating income inequality in American society. Not only did position within social relations of production have
a consistent impact on income, but class position influenced the ways in which
other factors affected income. In particular, the income returns to education
varied considerably between class positions: workers got much lower returns to
education than managers, and managers got much lower returns than employers.

2. A simple operationalization of the Marxist concept of class was at
least as powerful a predictor of income as the Duncan occupational status scale.

3. The division between property-owning and nonproperty-owning classes remained substantial even in advanced capitalism, and was much greater than various divisions within classes.

4. Class relations mediated the effects of race and sex on income inequality. While blacks as a whole received much lower returns to education than
whites and women received much lower returns than men. Blacks and women within
the working class received virtually the same returns to education as white men.

While these and other results did not prove the validity of the Marxist perspective as a whole, they did indicate that Marxist categories were crucial to
an understanding of social inequality and must be taken seriously within sociological research.

Appendix A

SOME DESCRIPTIVE TABLES

The rich variety of data collected in the panel study allow many descriptive
findings, and it seems useful to present a selected set of them. The sample is
small, relative to most Census Bureau samples, but it is representative--except
for some panel losses not completely handled by the weighting and for the exclusion of immigrants into the household population of continental United States.
The panel follows members of original panel families and interviews their new
families when they are formed, thus replacing family members who die. The combination of panel complications and small sample size means that the results shown
in this section should be regarded as estimates, inferior to those of the United
States Census Bureau where similar data exist, but largely intended to enrich
our understanding of relationships.

The first 20 tables and the first chart describe families categorized either
by their decile position on 1974 income relative to a needs standard, constructed
in a similar way as the Federal poverty definitions, or by brackets of 1974 money
income.[1] The latter is used to provide a bridge to other data; the former is
used because it is a more meaningful measure of economic status or well-being.
Components of income are given as averages for the entire sample, including
those with none; but in each case a companion table gives the proportion in each
income or income/needs group with nonzero amounts of that component. Dividing
the average income figure by the proportion with nonzero amounts gives the average amount for those who have such an income type only.

Most of the patterns are what one would expect, except for the substantial
amounts of transfer income (income not currently earned or taxable) going to
people with large total incomes. Table A.5 shows the vast differences in the
redistributional impact of different kinds of transfer income--ranging from a
positive correlation with economic status for private pensions and annuities to
a heavy concentration at low incomes of ADC, SSI, and other noncontributory wel-

---

[1]The needs standard used here is based on the "low-cost" food plan which is
approximately 25 percent higher than the "economy" food plan. Federal poverty
definitions are based on the "economy" food plan.

fare incomes. Figure A.1, which follows the first nine tables on income components, depicts the relative importance of the four main components at different levels of economic well-being.

Tables A.10 through A.19 summarize other elements affecting the well-being of families, including nonmoney income components; dollar and time costs of earning income; characteristics of housing, neighborhood; and county environment, family composition, and physical disability of the family head. Selected items are given by family money income as well as by money income/needs, but the latter is heavily used as a better way of ranking families according to their economic well-being and ability to afford the things they need and want.

Tables A.21 through A.27 and Figure A.2 (which follows Table A.27) show for 1975 individuals the transitions between 1974 family income/needs decile position and the decile position in earlier years. These transitions must be thought of as starting with 1974 family income/needs for a 1975 sample of individuals and looking backward to whatever family was the earlier source of the present individual. The reason for this view is that several individuals currently in different families could have sprung from the same 1968 family. The individual is the unit of analysis here, but the family income/needs situation is the measure of economic well-being.

The fraction of individuals in each 1974 income/needs decile is not exactly 10.0 percent because families are of different sizes, and the concentration in the fourth through sixth deciles reflects the fact that middle-income families are larger. The distribution of these same individuals by family income/needs deciles in earlier years is further diverted from 10.0 percent in each decile by the differential splitting up of families.

Each transition table gives the proportion who were in the same decile at both year-points and the percentage in the same or neighboring decile, since a very small shift might put an individual across a boundary. A measure of rank correlation is also given, and these correlations are plotted in Figure A.2. If there were no response or measurement error, the rank correlation would be 1.0 if the measure were repeated with no time interval at all, and the decline in the correlation should reflect only the real world processes that change family incomes and/or needs. If those processes were an evenly spread stochastic process, the correlation would decline toward some asymtote. If the population were made up of "movers" and "stayers," a different model would produce a different asymtote. It seems likely that a reasonable model which assumes no measurement error would not produce a curve that fits Figure A.2 and still curve up to a correlation of 1.0 at zero time interval; readers so inclined might want to infer the level of measurement error, given some particular model of change.

Since the first four chapters in this volume deal with changing economic status of groups of individuals, 1967-1974 transition tables, similar to Table A.21, are given for each of those subgroups in the individual chapters of Part I.

Tables A.28 through A.33 give some three-year and four-year transitions in reported savings and expectations about family economic future and show the relations of changes in these two to age and to changes in income/needs decile. There has been little overall change in reported savings for these same-head families, but the proportion expecting to be worse off increased from 8.8 percent to 16.0 percent, reflecting the increased unemployment and inflation of the historic period.

Tables A.34 through A.37 relate the replies to a new set of questions about the nature of the job, plus some other things, to the occupational class of the respondent (household head). A startling 36 percent of those in "professional" occupations worked for federal, state, or local government. Aside from the self-employed businessmen and artisans, the proportion who said their boss had a boss of his own was relatively uniform.

The common use of education and occupation in human capital studies makes it important to know their intercorrelations, which are given in Tables A.37 and A.38. A separate chapter in this volume goes more deeply into the new detailed questions on the nature of the job and their relations to hourly earnings. (See Chapter 11, "Work Roles and Earnings.")

We have just begun to record the month when crucial changes happen to our panel families; Table A.38 gives the distributions by month. This also allows us to look for response bias, particularly "telescoping" (the tendency to remember things as happening more recently than they did) or memory error (more distant events are often forgotten). In fact, the distribution is relatively even throughout the year, and the smaller fractions immediately after the interviewing period could easily be the result of multiple changes since only the data of the most recent change is coded.

Other simple descriptive data, namely the whole-sample weighted distributions of the answers to each question, appear in the companion documentation volume each year. See A Panel Study of Income Dynamics, Procedures and Tape Codes, 1975 Interviewing Year (Wave VII: A Supplement), Ann Arbor: Institute for Social Research, 1975.

Table A.1

COMPONENTS OF 1974 FAMILY MONEY INCOME BY 1974 INCOME/NEEDS DECILES[a]

(Entries are the averages for all families in each decile including those with no income.)

1974 Income/ Needs Decile	Upper Limit[d]	Head's Labor Income	Wife's Labor Income	Head and Wife Capital Income[c]	Head and Wife Taxable Income	Others in FU Taxable Income	Transfer Income[b] Head and Wife	Others	Total Family Money Income	Annual Needs Standard
Lowest	.89	$ 1,085	$ 125	$ -13	$ 1,197	$ 169	$1,552	$ 79	$ 3,055	$4,807
Second	1.30	2,286	296	114	2,696	529	1,787	164	5,176	4,721
Third	1.70	3,930	426	357	4,713	480	1,669	188	7,049	4,670
Fourth	2.07	5,818	793	372	6,983	618	1,479	140	9,221	4,869
Fifth	2.47	7,643	1,060	570	9,273	858	1,204	140	11,475	5,055
Sixth	2.92	9,481	1,208	664	11,354	705	1,001	156	13,216	4,932
Seventh	3.43	9,833	2,018	689	12,541	1,080	1,209	144	14,974	4,742
Eighth	4.08	11,746	2,676	774	15,195	1,410	1,073	78	17,757	4,761
Ninth	5.27	13,840	3,285	1,363	18,487	1,371	832	87	20,778	4,547
Highest		22,443	4,483	5,255	32,180	1,646	818	62	34,689	4,538
Overall Average		$ 8,813	$ 1,638	$1,015	$11,465	$ 887	$1,262	$ 124	$13,742	$4,764
Below Poverty Line, 1974		$ 931	$ 104	$ -88	$ 948	$ 120	$1,467	$ 83	$ 2,700	$3,316

[a]Based on the 1974 incomes of the 5,725 families interviewed in 1975.

[b]See Tables A.5 and A.6 for composition of Transfer Income of Head and Wife and Others.

[c]Includes Rent, Interest Dividends, Farm, Business.

[d]1967 Needs Standard has been inflated by cost of living increase between 1967 and 1974.

MTR #1162

Table A.2

COMPONENTS OF 1974 FAMILY MONEY INCOME BY 1974 INCOME/NEEDS

(Entries are proportions within the group who have any income of each type.)[a]

1974 Income/ Needs Decile	Upper Limit[d]	Head's Labor Income	Wife's Labor Income	Head and Wife Capital Income[c]	Head and Wife Taxable Income	Others in FU Taxable Income	Transfer Income[b] Head and Wife	Others
Lowest	.89	.46	.10	.15	.56	.12	.77	.05
Second	1.30	.59	.16	.27	.76	.18	.72	.10
Third	1.70	.73	.21	.37	.92	.18	.61	.09
Fourth	2.07	.79	.34	.36	.93	.21	.54	.06
Fifth	2.47	.86	.33	.40	.97	.22	.40	.06
Sixth	2.92	.93	.38	.49	.99	.20	.35	.07
Seventh	3.43	.90	.44	.46	.98	.22	.36	.05
Eighth	4.08	.92	.51	.54	1.00	.27	.30	.05
Ninth	5.27	.94	.52	.67	1.00	.24	.25	.04
Highest		.96	.53	.81	1.00	.27	.20	.04
Overall Average		.81	.35	.45	.91	.21	.45	.06
Below Poverty Line, 1974		.47	.10	.14	.56	.11	.76	.05

[a]Dividing the entry in Table A.1 by the matching entry in Table A.2 will provide an estimate of the mean for those who have such income only.

[b]See Tables A.5 and A.6 for composition of Transfer Income of Head and Wife and Others.

[c]Includes Rent, Interest Dividends, Farm, Business.

[d]1967 Needs Standard has been inflated by cost of living increase between 1967 and 1974.

MTR #1162

Table A.3

INCOME COMPONENTS BY 1974 FAMILY MONEY INCOME

(Entries are the averages for all families in each decile including those with no income.)

1974 Family Money Income	Percent of Families	Head's Labor Income	Wife's Labor Income	Head and Wife Capital Income[a]	Head and Wife Taxable Income	Others in FU Taxable Income	Transfer Income[b] Head and Wife	Others	Total Family Money Income
Less than $1,000	0.7%	$ 367	$ 91	$-1,074	$ -615	$ 13	$ 154	$ 35	$ 426
$1,000-1,999	2.6	388	43	6	437	6	1,126	19	1,588
$2,000-2,999	4.8	600	45	90	735	17	1,761	15	2,527
$3,000-3,999	4.5	795	35	219	1,049	50	2,177	164	3,440
$4,000-4,999	5.1	1,573	183	302	2,059	144	2,120	115	4,439
$5,000-7,499	13.2	3,174	270	372	3,816	345	1,853	184	6,197
$7,500-9,999	12.3	5,430	539	516	6,485	377	1,643	140	8,646
$10,000-14,999	20.7	8,405	1,294	687	10,385	678	1,122	130	12,315
$15,000-19,999	16.2	11,777	2,384	901	15,060	1,103	854	108	17,125
$20,000 or More	19.9	19,699	4,356	2,975	27,030	2,338	623	117	30,100
Overall Average	100.0%	$ 8,812	$1,638	$1,015	$11,465	$ 887	$1,262	$ 124	$13,742

[a] Includes Rent, Interest Dividends, Farm, Business.

[b] See Tables A.5 and A.6 for composition of Transfer Income of Head and Wife and Others.

Table A.4

INCOME COMPONENTS BY 1974 FAMILY MONEY INCOME

(Entries are proportions within the group who have any income of each type.)[a]

1974 Family Money Income	Head's Labor Income	Wife's Labor Income	Head and Wife Capital Income[b]	Head and Wife Taxable Income	Transfer Income[c] Head and Wife	Others
Less than $1,000	.46	.15	.31	.67	.42	.04
$1,000–1,999	.35	.04	.14	.45	.82	.01
$2,000–2,999	.38	.04	.24	.54	.86	.02
$3,000–3,999	.42	.05	.39	.70	.90	.11
$4,000–4,999	.54	.12	.36	.77	.73	.06
$5,000–7,499	.72	.16	.35	.89	.63	.09
$7,500–9,999	.82	.24	.36	.95	.52	.05
$10,000–14,999	.90	.40	.46	.98	.38	.05
$15,000–19,999	.96	.52	.51	1.00	.27	.05
$20,000 or More	.98	.61	.65	1.00	.20	.06
Overall Average	.81	.35	.45	.91	.45	.06

[a]Dividing the entry in Table A.3 by the matching entry in Table A.4 will provide an estimate of the mean for those who have such income only.

[b]Includes Rent, Interest Dividends, Farm, Business.

[c]See Tables A.5 and A.6 for composition of Transfer Income of Head and Wife and Others.

MTR #1162

Table A.5

COMPONENTS OF TRANSFER INCOME BY 1974 INCOME/NEEDS DECILE

(Entries are the averages for all families in each decile including those with no income.)

1974 Income/ Needs Decile	Upper Level	Head and Wife				Others in Family Unit			
		Social Security, Unemployment	Other Retirement Pensions, Annuities	ADC, AFDC Other Welfare, Supplemental Security Income	All Other Transfers	Social Security, Unemployment	Other Retirement Pensions, Annuities	ADC, AFDC Other Welfare, Supplemental Security Income	All Other Transfers
Lowest	.89	$ 658	$105	$635	$154	$ 24	$ 14	$ 42	$0
Second	1.30	1,004	180	405	198	77	16	70	1
Third	1.70	1,021	269	211	168	115	45	21	7
Fourth	2.07	884	352	51	192	90	28	15	7
Fifth	2.47	684	295	24	200	69	29	39	3
Sixth	2.92	425	347	11	217	136	15	4	2
Seventh	3.43	483	548	5	173	88	54	1	1
Eighth	4.08	455	427	0	191	65	5	0	8
Ninth	5.27	310	347	1	174	44	36	0	7
Highest		267	475	0	76	45	13	3	0
Overall Average		$619	$335	$134	$174	$ 75	$ 25	$ 19	$4
Below Poverty Line, 1974		$554	$103	$687	$123	$ 28	$ 12	$ 45	$-2

MTR #1162

Table A.6

COMPONENTS OF TRANSFER INCOME BY 1974 INCOME/NEEDS DECILE[a]

(Entries are proportions within the group who have any income of each type.)

1974 Income/ Needs Decile	Upper Limit	Head and Wife				Others in Family Unit			
		Social Security, Unemployment	Other Retirement Pensions, Annuities	ADC, AFDC, Other Welfare Supplemental Security Income	All Other Transfers	Social Security, Unemployment	Other Retirement Pensions, Annuities	ADC, AFDC, Other Welfare Supplemental Security Income	All Other transfers
Lowest	.89	.40	.08	.33	.21	.02	.01	.03	.01
Second	1.30	.45	.16	.20	.19	.06	.01	.05	.00
Third	1.70	.42	.15	.10	.18	.07	.02	.01	.01
Fourth	2.07	.38	.15	.03	.16	.05	.02	.01	.00
Fifth	2.47	.26	.11	.02	.17	.03	.01	.02	.01
Sixth	2.92	.21	.10	.00	.14	.06	.01	.01	.01
Seventh	3.43	.21	.14	.00	.13	.04	.02	.00	.00
Eighth	4.08	.20	.12	.00	.09	.04	.00	.00	.01
Ninth	5.27	.14	.10	.00	.09	.03	.02	.00	.00
Highest		.12	.08	.00	.05	.04	.01	.00	.00
Overall Average		.28	.12	.07	.14	.04	.01	.01	.01
Below Poverty Line, 1974		.35	.07	.35	.20	.02	.01	.03	.01

[a]Dividing the entry in Table A.5 by the matching entry in Table A.6 will provide an estimate of the mean for those who have such income only.

Table A.7

COMPONENTS OF FAMILY MONEY INCOME BY RACE

(Entries are averages for families below the poverty line in 1974, including those with no income.)

Race	Weighted Percent	Head's 1974 Labor Income	Wife's 1974 Labor Income	Head and Wife Capital Income[a]	Head and Wife Taxable Income	Others in FU Taxable Income	Transfer Income[b]		Total Family Money Income
							Head and Wife	Others	
White n=207	62.2%	$ 845	$118	$-156	$ 807	$ 53	$1,368	$ 36	$2,394
Black n=545	34.7	988	85	24	1,096	234	1,638	172	3,140
Others n=22	3.2	2,012	60	20	2,092	211	1,528	43	3,874
All	100.1%	$ 931	$104	$- 88	$ 948	$120	$1,467	$ 83	$2,700

[a]Includes Rent, Interest, Dividends, Farm, Business.

[b]See Tables A.5 and A.6 for composition of Transfer Income of Head and Wife and Others.

MTR #1162

Table A.8

RACE AND MARITAL STATUS BY 1974 INCOME/NEEDS DECILE
(Entries are proportions of all families within each group.)

1974 Income/Needs Decile	Upper Limit	Race				Marital Status of Head		
		White	Black	Spanish American	Other	Single Male	Single Female	Married
Lowest	.89	.66	.30	.03	.01	.16	.50	.34
Second	1.30	.75	.20	.04	.01	.13	.43	.44
Third	1.70	.83	.15	.02	.00	.13	.34	.53
Fourth	2.07	.86	.11	.03	.00	.09	.24	.67
Fifth	2.47	.85	.12	.03	.00	.12	.18	.70
Sixth	2.92	.91	.06	.02	.01	.09	.19	.72
Seventh	3.43	.91	.07	.02	.00	.09	.19	.72
Eighth	4.08	.93	.05	.02	.00	.12	.14	.74
Ninth	5.27	.94	.05	.01	.00	.11	.13	.76
Highest		.95	.03	.02	.01	.08	.08	.84
Overall Average		.86	.11	.02	.01	.08	.08	.84

MTR #1162

Table A.9

RACE AND MARITAL STATUS BY 1974 FAMILY MONEY INCOME

(Entries are proportions of all families within each group.)

1974 Family Money Income	Race				Marital Status of Head		
	White	Black	Spanish American	Other	Single Male	Single Female	Married
Less than $1,000	.71	.29	.00	.00	.24	.51	.25
$1,000-1,999	.70	.27	.02	.01	.16	.77	.07
$2,000-2,999	.75	.20	.03	.02	.24	.57	.19
$3,000-3,999	.79	.19	.02	.01	.16	.60	.24
$4,000-4,999	.76	.21	.03	.00	.16	.47	.37
$5,000-7,499	.80	.18	.02	.00	.16	.37	.47
$7,500-9,999	.85	.12	.03	.01	.13	.30	.57
$10,000-14,999	.88	.10	.02	.01	.12	.18	.71
$15,000-19,999	.91	.06	.02	.00	.08	.07	.85
$20,000 or More	.93	.04	.02	.01	.04	.03	.93
Overall Average	.86	.11	.02	.01	.11	.24	.65

MTR #1162

Figure A.1

PERCENTAGE OF TOTAL FAMILY MONEY INCOME IN 1974
FROM FOUR MAJOR SOURCES BY INCOME/NEEDS

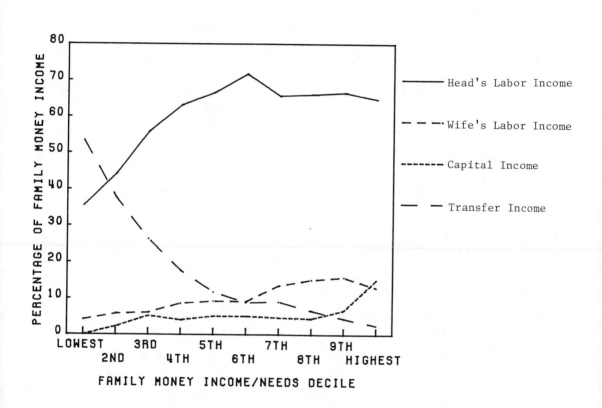

MTR #1162

Table A.10

OTHER COMPONENTS OF WELL-BEING BY 1974 INCOME/NEEDS DECILE
(Entries are the averages for families in each decile)

1974 Income/ Needs Decile	Upper Limit	Value of Free Rent[a]	Food Stamp Subsidy	Support of Outside Dependents	Dollar Costs of Earning Income — Head and Wife Income Taxes	Others Income Taxes	Dollar Costs of Child Care[b]	Work Hours — Head's Annual Work Hours	Wife's Annual Work Hours	Nondollar Costs of Earning Income — Head's Travel to Work Hours	Wife's Travel to Work Hours
Lowest	.89	$110	$229	$ 16	$ 41	$ 3	$ 27	620	74	39	5
Second	1.30	94	117	55	106	26	41	911	145	59	16
Third	1.70	78	43	42	325	26	37	1,259	189	82	17
Fourth	2.07	61	15	28	621	45	86	1,505	334	102	28
Fifth	2.47	38	6	94	995	70	110	1,782	384	130	27
Sixth	2.92	58	4	102	1,340	53	124	1,958	407	145	29
Seventh	3.43	28	1	86	1,625	113	96	1,862	600	128	46
Eighth	4.08	18	0	201	2,113	161	115	1,998	739	145	61
Ninth	5.27	34	0	281	2,868	161	56	2,025	778	173	72
Highest		21	0	801	7,417	221	61	2,235	830	162	74
Overall Average		$ 54	$ 41	$171	$1,746	$ 88	$ 75	1,616	448	116	38
Below Poverty Line, 1974		$110	$262	$ 15	$ 43	$ 2	$ 25	294	73	40	5

[a] For those who neither own nor rent.

[b] From 1974 data.

MTR #1162

Table A.11

OTHER COMPONENTS OF WELL-BEING BY 1974 INCOME/NEEDS DECILE[a]

(Entries are proportions within each group with nonzero amounts)

1974 Income/ Needs Decile	Upper Limit	Value of Free Rent[b]	Food Stamp Subsidy	Support of Outside Dependents	Dollar Costs of Earning Income			Work Hours		Nondollar Costs of Earning Income	
					Head and Wife Income Taxes	Others Income Taxes	Dollar Costs of Child Care[c]	Head's Annual Work Hours	Wife's Annual Work Hours	Head's Travel to Work Hours	Wife's Travel to Work Hours
Lowest	.89	.15	.34	.03	.12	.02	.03	.48	.11	.30	.08
Second	1.30	.09	.22	.04	.41	.09	.05	.59	.16	.44	.14
Third	1.70	.07	.11	.06	.62	.08	.05	.73	.21	.59	.18
Fourth	2.07	.05	.05	.06	.75	.10	.10	.79	.34	.66	.30
Fifth	2.47	.04	.03	.08	.86	.11	.12	.87	.33	.77	.29
Sixth	2.92	.04	.02	.09	.93	.09	.12	.93	.38	.82	.33
Seventh	3.43	.02	.01	.09	.92	.13	.11	.90	.44	.79	.41
Eighth	4.08	.02	.00	.13	.95	.16	.09	.92	.51	.82	.48
Ninth	5.27	.02	.00	.19	.98	.16	.07	.94	.52	.85	.50
Highest		.02	.00	.27	1.00	.15	.05	.96	.53	.81	.50
Overall Average		.05	.08	.10	.75	.11	.08	.81	.35	.69	.32
Below Poverty Line, 1974		.16	.38	.02	.06	.01	.03	.49	.10	.32	.08

[a]Dividing the entry in Table A.10 by the matching entry in Table A.11 will provide an estimate of the mean for those who have such income only.

[b]For those who neither own nor rent.

[c]From 1974 data.

MTR #1162

Table A.12

VARIOUS MEASURES RELATING TO FAMILY AND HOUSING BY 1974 INCOME/NEEDS DECILE

(Entries are the averages for all families in each decile)

1974 Income/ Needs Decile	Upper Limit	Number in Family	House Value (owners only)	Value per Room[a]	Persons per Room	Index of Housing Problems[b]	Index of Neighborhood Problems[c]	Total Housework Hours[d]
Lowest	.89	2.74	$13,769	$3,004	.66	2.04	2.13	1,284
Second	1.30	2.78	18,273	3,398	.64	1.79	2.00	1,476
Third	1.70	2.70	17,994	3,852	.60	1.38	1.70	1,532
Fourth	2.07	2.97	21,385	3,851	.60	1.15	1.44	1,563
Fifth	2.47	3.06	24,688	4,290	.60	1.07	1.43	1,653
Sixth	2.92	2.99	27,896	4,367	.55	.96	1.19	1,771
Seventh	3.43	2.79	33,012	5,076	.53	1.18	1.16	1,627
Eighth	4.08	2.75	31,679	5,117	.51	.73	1.11	1,546
Ninth	5.27	2.57	33,854	5,485	.48	.73	1.06	1,497
Highest		2.62	47,201	6,839	.43	.73	.84	1,336
Overall Average		2.80	$28,829	$4,521	.56	1.17	1.41	1,528
Below Poverty Line, 1974		2.76	$12,292	@2,991	.68	2.08	2.27	1,278

[a]For renters, dwelling unit value is assumed to be ten times annual rent.

[b]The index of housing problems combines answers to questions "Do you have any problems with where you live?" and "Is that a big problem or a small one?" The problems are specified in some detail but can be summarized as focusing on plumbing, structural defects, security from break-ins, insects and vermin, and heat and insulation. With three points for a big problem, one point for other problems, the index can range from zero to 15.

[c]The index of neighborhood problems is similar, focusing on general cleanliness, suitability for kids, noise and traffic, burglaries and robberies, and muggings, rapes, pushers and junkies, or too few police.

[d]From 1974 data.

Table A.13

VARIOUS MEASURES RELATING TO FAMILY AND HOUSING BY 1974 INCOME/NEEDS DECILE[a]

(Entries are proportions within each group.)

1974 Income/Needs Decile	Upper Limit	Fraction Who Own a House	Fraction Who Rent	Fraction Who Neither Own nor Rent	Fraction with at Least One Housing Problem	Fraction with at Least One Neighborhood Problem	Fraction with Housework Hours[b]
Lowest	.89	.38	.47	.15	.55	.50	.94
Second	1.30	.43	.47	.09	.49	.50	.96
Third	1.70	.52	.41	.07	.47	.46	.98
Fourth	2.07	.57	.38	.05	.43	.42	.98
Fifth	2.47	.61	.35	.04	.41	.45	.98
Sixth	2.92	.65	.31	.04	.38	.42	.99
Seventh	3.43	.63	.35	.02	.42	.37	.98
Eighth	4.08	.69	.30	.02	.35	.39	1.00
Ninth	5.27	.72	.26	.02	.34	.40	.99
Highest		.82	.16	.02	.32	.36	.99
Overall Average		.60	.35	.05	.42	.43	.09
Below Poverty Line, 1974		.36	.48	.16	.55	.52	.93

[a]Dividing the entry in Table A.12 by the matching entry in Table A.13 will provide an estimate of the mean for those who have such income only.

[b]From 1974 data.

MTR #1162

Table A.14

VARIOUS MEASURES RELATING TO FAMILY AND HOUSING BY 1974 FAMILY MONEY INCOME
(Entries are averages for all families in each decile)

1974 Family Money Income	Number in Family	House Value (owners only)	Value per Room[a]	Persons per Room	Index of Housing Problems[b]	Index of Neighborhood Problems[c]	Child Care Costs[d]	Total Housework Hours[d]
Less than $1,000	1.64	$13,719	$3,385	.49	2.68	1.92	$ 9	726
$1,000-1,999	1.32	11,239	3,123	.42	2.03	1.98	5	900
$2,000-2,999	1.51	14,567	3,270	.46	1.32	1.51	20	974
$3,000-3,999	1.83	17,304	3,385	.47	1.59	2.22	24	1,128
$4,000-4,999	2.05	17,325	4,115	.54	1.60	1.99	35	1,313
$5,000-7,499	2.37	18,582	3,834	.55	1.52	1.83	43	1,321
$7,500-9,999	2.62	20,439	3,986	.58	1.47	1.64	84	1,468
$10,000-14,999	2.92	24,243	4,222	.58	1.11	1.34	110	1,715
$15,000-19,999	3.28	28,447	4,676	.59	0.81	1.08	112	1,753
$20,000 or More	3.62	44,648	6,422	.58	0.72	0.87	82	1,840
Overall Average	2.80	$28,829	$4,521	.56	1.17	1.41	$ 75	1,528

[a]For renters, dwelling unit value is assumed to be ten times annual rent.

[b]The index of housing problems combines answers to questions "Do you have any problems with where you live?" and "Is that a big problem or a small one?" The problems are specified in some detail but can be summarized as focusing on plumbing, structural defects, security from break-ins, insects and vermin, and heat and insulation. With three points for a big problem, one point for other problems, the index can range from zero to 15.

[c]The index of neighborhood problems is similar, focusing on general cleanliness, suitability for kids, noise and traffic, burglaries and robberies, and muggings, rapes, pushers and junkies, or too few police.

[d]From 1974 data.

MTR #1162

Table A.15

VARIOUS MEASURES RELATING TO FAMILY AND HOUSING BY 1974 FAMILY MONEY INCOME[a]

(Entries are proportions of all families within each group.)

1974 Family Money Income	House Value (owners only)	Fraction Who Own a House	Fraction Who Rent	Fraction Who Neither Own nor Rent	Fraction with at Least One Housing Problem[b]	Fraction with at Least One Neighborhood Problem[c]	Fraction with Child Care Costs[a]	Fraction with Housework Hours[a]
Less than $1,000	$13,719	.40	.24	.36	.62	.48	.02	.91
$1,000-1,999	11,239	.33	.49	.18	.50	.48	.01	.91
$2,000-2,999	14,567	.40	.45	.15	.43	.42	.02	.93
$3,000-3,999	17,304	.46	.46	.08	.48	.51	.02	.95
$4,000-4,999	17,325	.41	.49	.09	.47	.48	.05	.97
$5,000-7,499	17,582	.46	.46	.08	.49	.49	.05	.98
$7,500-9,999	20,439	.46	.48	.06	.47	.45	.09	.98
$10,000-14,999	24,243	.60	.37	.03	.42	.43	.12	.99
$15,000-19,999	28,447	.74	.24	.02	.36	.40	.10	.99
$20,000 or More	44,648	.85	.15	.01	.33	.34	.07	.99
Overall Average	$28,829	.60	.35	.05	.42	.43	.08	.98

[a] Dividing the entry in Table A.14 by the matching entry in Table A.15 will provide an estimate of the mean for those who have such income only.

[b] The index of housing problems combines answers to questions "Do you have any problems with where you live?" and "Is that a big problem or a small one?" The problems are specified in some detail but can be summarized as focusing on plumbing, structural defects, security from break-ins, insects and vermin, and heat and insulation. With three points for a big problem, one point for other problems, the index can range from zero to 15.

[c] The index of neighborhood problems is similar, focusing on general cleanliness, suitability for kids, noise and traffic, burglaries and robberies, and muggings, rapes, pushers and junkies, or too few police.

[d] From 1974 data.

Table A.16

CHARACTERISTICS OF HEAD BY 1974 INCOME/NEEDS DECILE
(Entries are proportions of all families within each group.)

1974 Income/ Needs Decile	Upper Limit	Head is Less Than 35	Head is 65 or Older	Head Has Retirement Plan	Head Has A Child Under 6	Head Has Physical or Nervous Condition That Limits Work
Lowest	.89	.33	.31	.08	.19	.42
Second	1.30	.36	.32	.18	.21	.33
Third	1.70	.39	.26	.24	.21	.25
Fourth	2.07	.39	.22	.36	.26	.20
Fifth	2.47	.42	.15	.46	.27	.16
Sixth	2.92	.45	.11	.50	.25	.12
Seventh	3.43	.47	.12	.56	.22	.11
Eighth	4.08	.40	.11	.59	.20	.09
Ninth	5.27	.31	.10	.66	.12	.08
Highest		.20	.11	.58	.13	.07
Overall Average		.37	.18	.42	.21	.18

Table A.17

CHARACTERISTICS OF HEAD BY 1974 FAMILY MONEY INCOME
(Entries are proportions of all families within each group.)

1974 Family Money Income	Head is Less Than 35	Head is 65 or Older	Head Has Retirement Plan	Head Has A Child Under 6	Head Has Physical or Nervous Condition That Limits Work
Less than $1,000	.56	.14	.07	.12	.31
$1,000-1,999	.26	.44	.03	.07	.51
$2,000-2,999	.27	.52	.08	.08	.46
$3,000-3,999	.26	.52	.06	.11	.43
$4,000-4,999	.30	.38	.11	.13	.39
$5,000-7,499	.42	.27	.23	.19	.24
$7,500-9,999	.50	.16	.35	.25	.17
$10,000-14,999	.48	.12	.51	.28	.11
$15,000-19,999	.36	.07	.64	.24	.07
$20,000 or More	.23	.05	.64	.18	.08
Overall Average	.37	.18	.42	.21	.18

MTR #1162

Table A.18

RESPONDENT'S LOCATION BY 1974 INCOME/NEEDS DECILE

(Entries are proportions of all families within each group.)

1974 Income/ Needs Decile	Upper Limit	Distance to Center of City of 50,000 or More						Region			
		Less Than 5 Miles	5-14.9 Miles	15-29.9 Miles	30-49.9 Miles	50 Miles or More	Not Ascertained	Northeast	North Central	South	West
Lowest	.89	.18	.18	.13	.09	.27	.16	.16	.26	.43	.15
Second	1.30	.20	.17	.08	.11	.26	.19	.20	.24	.38	.18
Third	1.70	.21	.22	.13	.10	.22	.12	.18	.29	.30	.22
Fourth	2.07	.19	.21	.13	.14	.21	.12	.21	.31	.31	.16
Fifth	2.47	.18	.25	.14	.10	.19	.14	.25	.26	.32	.17
Sixth	2.92	.18	.29	.12	.09	.18	.14	.24	.31	.27	.18
Seventh	3.43	.20	.29	.15	.10	.16	.10	.27	.28	.27	.18
Eighth	4.08	.15	.33	.18	.11	.12	.12	.27	.30	.23	.20
Ninth	5.27	.19	.31	.17	.07	.12	.14	.26	.33	.23	.18
Highest		.19	.34	.15	.08	.10	.14	.25	.32	.26	.17
Overall Average		.19	.26	.14	.10	.18	.14	.23	.29	.30	.18

MTR #1162

Table A.19

RESPONDENT'S LOCATION BY 1974 FAMILY MONEY INCOME

(Entries are proportions of all families within each group.)

1974 Family Money Income	Distance to Center of City of 50,000 or More						Region			
	Less Than 5 Miles	5-14.9 Miles	15-29.9 Miles	30-49.9 Miles	50 Miles or More	Npt Ascertained	Northeast	North Central	South	West
Less than $1,000	.17	.17	.16	.13	.18	.20	.12	.23	.41	.24
$1,000-1,999	.17	.12	.12	.06	.36	.17	.11	.34	.44	.11
$2,000-2,999	.19	.24	.07	.10	.25	.16	.17	.26	.39	.18
$3,000-3,999	.21	.16	.09	.10	.25	.16	.17	.26	.39	.18
$4,000-4,999	.22	.18	.11	.10	.22	.17	.22	.26	.35	.16
$5,000-7,499	.21	.21	.12	.12	.18	.17	.19	.30	.34	.17
$7,500-9,999	.20	.25	.10	.11	.22	.12	.21	.25	.33	.20
$10,000-14,999	.19	.28	.13	.09	.19	.12	.24	.29	.31	.18
$15,000-19,999	.17	.29	.17	.10	.14	.13	.25	.31	.27	.17
$20,000 or More	.17	.33	.18	.09	.11	.12	.28	.32	.21	.18
Overall Average	.19	.26	.14	.10	.18	.14	.23	.29	.30	.18

MTR #1162

Table A.20

UNEMPLOYMENT RATE IN AUGUST, 1974 IN RESPONDENT'S COUNTY BY 1974 INCOME/NEEDS DECILE
(Entries are proportions of all families within each group.)

1974 Income/Needs Decile	Upper Limit	Under 2%	2-3.9%	4-5.9%	6-8.9%	9-10%	10.1-12%	More than 12%	Percent in Decile
Lowest	.89	.07	.11	.27	.19	.16	.15	.04	99%
Second	1.30	.07	.16	.28	.14	.16	.15	.04	100
Third	1.70	.06	.11	.30	.17	.18	.15	.04	101
Fourth	2.07	.06	.15	.29	.15	.15	.19	.02	101
Fifth	2.47	.05	.15	.31	.16	.15	.16	.03	101
Sixth	2.92	.05	.11	.38	.15	.14	.14	.04	101
Seventh	3.43	.05	.15	.34	.16	.16	.12	.03	101
Eighth	4.08	.03	.13	.34	.19	.16	.13	.04	101
Ninth	5.27	.05	.13	.31	.14	.15	.17	.05	101
Highest		.04	.17	.31	.19	.14	.13	.02	100
Overall Average		.05	.14	.31	.16	.15	.15	.04	

MTR #1162

Table A.21

1974 FAMILY INCOME/NEEDS DECILE BY 1967 FAMILY INCOME/NEEDS DECILE
(All 1975 Sample Individuals)

1974
Income/
Needs
Decile   1967 Income/Needs Decile

Lowest	4.2	2.2	1.5	0.7	0.4	0.2	0.2	0.2	0.1	0.1	9.9
Second	2.6	1.8	1.7	1.1	1.0	0.6	0.3	0.2	0.2	0.2	9.7
Third	1.1	1.8	2.4	1.3	0.9	0.7	0.7	0.6	0.2	0.1	9.8
Fourth	0.9	0.9	2.0	1.8	1.5	1.6	0.8	0.6	0.4	0.3	10.6
Fifth	0.6	0.6	1.2	1.7	2.2	1.6	1.1	0.8	0.6	0.5	10.9
Sixth	0.3	0.6	0.9	1.2	1.9	1.4	1.4	1.4	0.8	0.6	10.5
Seventh	0.4	0.4	0.5	1.2	1.1	1.7	1.5	1.5	0.6	0.8	9.6
Eighth	0.3	0.4	0.4	0.9	0.9	1.6	1.4	1.4	1.5	0.8	9.8
Ninth	0.1	0.1	0.4	0.6	0.9	0.9	1.5	1.6	2.2	1.0	9.3
Highest	0.1	0.2	0.3	0.2	0.4	0.5	1.1	1.4	2.3	3.5	3.5
Total	10.6	8.9	11.1	10.8	11.1	10.9	10.1	9.6	8.8	8.0	100.0

Rank Correlation (Kendall's Tau-B) = 0.48
Association (Cramer's V) = 0.25
Percentage in same decile = 22.4
Percentage in the same or neighboring decile = 53.0

Table A.22

1974 FAMILY INCOME/NEEDS DECILE BY 1968 FAMILY INCOME/NEEDS DECILE
(All 1975 Sample Individuals)

1974
Income/
Needs
Decile   1968 Income/Needs Decile

Lowest	4.5	2.5	1.2	0.5	0.4	0.3	0.1	0.1	0.1	0.1	9.9
Second	2.5	1.9	2.1	1.2	0.6	0.6	0.5	0.3	0.1	0.1	9.7
Third	1.1	2.0	1.9	1.8	0.8	0.8	0.7	0.3	0.2	0.1	9.8
Fourth	1.0	1.3	1.4	2.2	1.3	1.3	0.6	0.7	0.5	0.2	10.6
Fifth	0.5	0.5	1.3	2.0	2.1	1.4	1.3	0.8	0.7	0.5	10.9
Sixth	0.3	0.4	0.7	1.2	1.8	1.6	1.8	1.3	0.7	0.6	10.5
Seventh	0.2	0.4	0.7	0.8	1.2	1.1	1.9	1.6	1.0	0.8	9.6
Eighth	0.2	0.4	0.5	0.7	0.9	1.4	1.7	1.7	1.5	0.8	9.8
Ninth	0.1	0.2	0.2	0.4	0.8	1.0	1.6	1.5	2.3	1.2	9.3
Highest	0.1	0.2	0.2	0.2	0.3	0.8	0.9	1.0	2.4	3.9	9.9
Total	10.5	9.7	10.1	10.9	10.2	10.2	11.1	9.3	9.4	8.5	100.0

Rank Correlation (Kendall's Tau-B) = 0.50
Association (Cramer's V) = 0.27
Percentage in same decile = 24.0
Percentage in the same or neighboring decile = 55.4

MTR #1162

Table A.23

1974 FAMILY INCOME/NEEDS DECILE BY 1969 FAMILY INCOME/NEEDS DECILE
(All 1975 Sample Individuals)

1974
Income/
Needs
Decile

				1969 Income/Needs Decile						
Lowest	4.7	2.5	1.1	0.7	0.3	0.3	0.1	0.1	0.1	0.1	9.9
Second	2.1	2.7	1.6	1.1	0.9	0.5	0.3	0.2	0.2	0.1	9.7
Third	1.1	1.5	2.3	1.6	1.1	1.0	0.3	0.4	0.3	0.1	9.8
Fourth	0.8	1.1	1.8	2.2	1.7	1.0	0.9	0.5	0.4	0.2	10 6
Fifth	0.4	0.7	1.2	2.0	2.1	1.6	1.0	0.9	0.5	0.5	10.9
Sixth	0.2	0.4	0.6	1.1	1.5	2.2	1.5	1.4	0.8	0.6	10 5
Seventh	0.3	0.3	0.6	0.8	1.4	1.0	1.9	1.5	1.5	0.4	9.6
Eighth	0.1	0.2	0.3	0.6	0.8	2.0	1.5	2.3	1.0	0.9	9.8
Ninth	0.0	0.1	0.2	0.4	0.7	0.7	1.6	1.9	2.4	1.3	9.3
Highest	0.1	0.1	0.1	0.2	0.2	0.7	0.7	0.9	2.1	4.7	9.9
Total	9.9	9.6	10.0	10.6	10.9	11.0	10.0	10.1	9.3	8.7	100.0

Rank Correlation (Kendall's Tau-B) = 0.54
Association (Cramer's V) = 0.25
Percentage in same decile = 22.4
Percentage in the same or neighboring decile = 53.0

Table A.24

1974 FAMILY INCOME/NEEDS DECILE BY 1970 FAMILY INCOME/NEEDS DECILE
(All 1975 Sample Individuals)

1974
Income/
Needs
Decile

				1970 Income/Needs Decile						
Lowest	4.5	2.9	0.9	0.5	0.3	0.3	0.2	0.0	0.1	0.1	9.9
Second	2.5	2.6	1.8	1.0	0.7	0.4	0.2	0.2	0.1	0.1	9.7
Third	1.0	1.7	2.6	1.9	1.0	0.5	0.4	0.4	0.1	0.1	9.8
Fourth	0.7	1.0	2.0	2.3	1.9	1.1	0.9	0.3	0.3	0.2	10.6
Fifth	0.4	0.6	1.4	1.8	1.8	2.0	1.7	0.6	0.5	0.3	10.9
Sixth	0.2	0.4	0.8	0.9	1.7	2.2	1.8	1.2	0.9	0.4	10.5
Seventh	0.2	0.3	0.5	0.8	1.4	1.5	1.7	1.7	0.9	0.7	9.6
Eighth	0.1	0.1	0.5	0.5	0.9	1.4	1.7	2.3	1.6	0.6	9.8
Ninth	0.0	0.1	0.2	0.3	0.5	0.7	1.4	1.9	2.8	1.4	9.3
Highest	0.0	0.1	0.0	0.2	0.3	0.2	0.8	1.1	2.2	4.9	9.9
Total	9.7	9.8	10.6	10.3	10.4	10.4	10.8	9.8	9.4	8.8	100.0

Rank Correlation (Kendall's Tau-B) = 0.57
Association (Cramer's V) = 0.31
Percentage in same decile = 27.7
Percentage in the same or neighboring decile = 61.8

MTR #1162

Table A.25

1974 FAMILY INCOME/NEEDS DECILE BY 1971 FAMILY INCOME/NEEDS DECILE
(All 1975 Sample Individuals)

1974
Income/
Needs
Decile   1971 Income/Needs Decile

Lowest	5.0	2.7	0.9	0.5	0.4	0.1	0.1	0.1	0.1	0.1	9.9
Second	2.3	3.3	1.6	0.7	0.7	0.5	0.2	0.1	0.1	0.1	9.7
Third	1.1	1.5	2.4	2.0	1.1	0.6	0.3	0.4	0.2	0.1	9.8
Fourth	0.7	0.8	1.8	2.7	1.8	1.4	0.6	0.2	0.2	0.3	10.6
Fifth	0.4	0.4	1.3	1.6	2.9	2.0	1.2	0.5	0.4	0.2	10.9
Sixth	0.2	0.3	0.7	1.3	1.9	2.2	1.9	1.1	0.6	0.4	10.5
Seventh	0.4	0.2	0.5	0.5	1.3	1.9	1.8	1.6	1.0	0.4	9.6
Eighth	0.1	0.2	0.3	0.5	0.7	1.1	2.2	2.4	1.8	0.7	9.8
Ninth	0.0	0.1	0.2	0.2	0.5	0.8	0.9	2.2	3.1	1.2	9.3
Highest	0.1	0.1	0.1	0.1	0.3	0.2	0.7	1.2	1.9	5.3	9.9
Total	10.3	9.6	9.8	10.2	11.5	10.9	9.9	9.7	9.4	8.7	100.0

Rank Correlation (Kendall's Tau-B) = 0.61
Association (Cramer's V) = 0.34
Percentage in same decile = 31.1
Percentage in the same or neighboring decile = 64.9

Table A.26

1974 FAMILY INCOME/NEEDS DECILE BY 1972 FAMILY INCOME/NEEDS DECILE
(All 1975 Sample Individuals)

1974
Income/
Needs
Decile   1972 Income/Needs Decile

Lowest	5.6	2.2	0.9	0.6	0.2	0.2	0.1	0.1	0.1	0.0	9.9
Second	2.2	3.5	2.1	0.7	0.5	0.3	0.2	0.2	0.0	0.0	9.7
Third	1.0	1.8	3.1	1.7	0.9	0.6	0.2	0.3	0.1	0.0	9.8
Fourth	0.7	0.9	1.5	3.3	2.0	1.2	0.5	0.2	0.2	0.1	10.6
Fifth	0.3	0.5	0.8	2.2	2.9	2.0	1.2	0.7	0.2	0.1	10.9
Sixth	0.1	0.2	0.4	1.4	2.3	2.3	1.9	1.0	0.6	0.3	10.5
Seventh	0.1	0.3	0.6	0.6	0.8	2.0	2.6	1.5	0.8	0.3	9.6
Eighth	0.1	0.2	0.3	0.1	0.6	1.0	1.9	3.2	1.8	0.6	9.8
Ninth	0.0	0.1	0.1	0.2	0.3	0.7	1.0	2.1	3.5	1.3	9.3
Highest	0.1	0.0	0.1	0.0	0.1	0.3	0.4	0.8	2.2	6.0	9.9
Total	10.1	9.7	9.8	10.8	10.7	10.6	10.0	10.1	9.6	8.8	100.0

Rank Correlation (Kendall's Tau-B) = 0.66
Association (Cramer's V) = 0.39
Percentage in same decile = 36.0
Percentage in the same or neighboring decile = 70.6

MTR #1162

Table A.27

1974 FAMILY INCOME/NEEDS DECILE BY 1973 FAMILY INCOME/NEEDS DECILE
(All 1975 Sample Individuals)

1974
Income/
Needs
Decile   1973 Income/Needs Decile

Lowest	5.6	2.6	0.8	0.5	0.1	0.2	0.0	0.1	0.1	0.0	9.9
Second	2.2	4.1	2.0	0.7	0.3	0.1	0.2	0.1	0.0	0.0	9.7
Third	0.9	1.7	3.4	2.0	0.9	0.4	0.2	0.1	0.0	0.0	9.8
Fourth	0.3	0.6	2.0	3.8	2.0	1.1	0.5	0.2	0.1	0.1	10.6
Fifth	0.1	0.2	1.1	1.8	3.6	2.0	1.2	0.5	0.2	0.1	10.9
Sixth	0.1	0.1	0.3	0.8	2.4	3.1	2.5	0.7	0.2	0.2	10.5
Seventh	0.0	0.0	0.2	0.5	1.0	2.6	2.4	1.9	0.7	0.3	9.6
Eighth	0.0	0.1	0.0	0.3	0.3	0.7	2.1	3.8	1.9	0.4	9.8
Ninth	0.1	0.0	0.0	0.1	0.2	0.3	0.9	2.2	4.2	1.3	9.3
Highest	0.0	0.1	0.0	0.0	0.1	0.1	0.3	0.6	1.9	6.9	9.9
Total	9.3	9.4	9.8	10.4	11.1	10.7	10.3	10.2	9.4	9.4	100.0

Rank Correlation (Kendall's Tau-B) = 0.74
Association (Cramer's V) = 0.45
Percentage in same decile = 40.9
Percentage in the same or neighboring decile = 78.3

MTR #1162

440

Figure A.2

PERSISTENCE OF STATUS (RANK CORRELATION, TAU-B)
BETWEEN 1974 INCOME/NEEDS DECILE AND DECILE OF PREVIOUS YEARS
(All 1975 Sample Individuals)

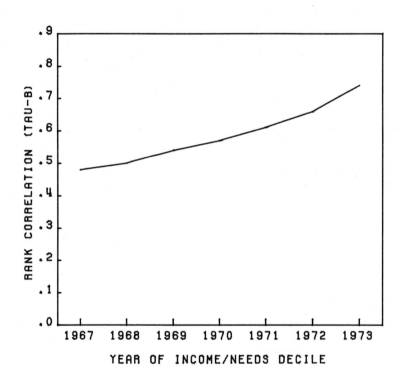

Table A.28

ASSETS OF HEAD IN 1975 AND 1972--A TRANSITION TABLE
(All Families with Same Head, 1972-1975)

Assets in 1972[a]	Assets in 1975[a]			
	None	Some	Equals 2 Months' Income or More	
None	(c) 12.3	(f) 4.8	3.2 (g)	20.3
Some	4.0	(d) 13.3	7.5	24.8
Equals 2 Months' Income or More	(a) 3.3	(b) 10.1	(e) 41.5	54.9
	19.6	28.2	52.2	100.0%
				N = 4,332

[a]The question was: Do you (family) have any savings such as checking or savings accounts, or government bonds? Would they amount to as much as two months' income or more?

Table A.29

EXPECTATIONS OF HEAD IN 1975 AND 1971--A TRANSITION TABLE
(All Families with Same Head, 1972-1975)

Expectations in 1971[a]	In 1975 Expect to Be:			
	Better Off	Same	Worse	
Better	(c) 35.9	13.2	6.2	55.3
Same	11.0	(d) 17.6	(f,g) 7.2	35.8
Worse	(a,b) 3.0	3.2	(e) 2.6	8.8
	49.9	34.0	16.0	100.0%
				N = 3,952

[a]The question was: What about the next few years--do you think you (and your family) will be better off or worse off, or what?

MTR #1171

Table A.30

CHANGE IN REPORTED SAVINGS BY CHANGE IN FAMILY INCOME/NEEDS

(For 4,332 Families with Same Head for All Four Years)

Box in Table A.28	Change in Savings[a] 1972-1975	Change in Income/Needs Decile Position 1971-1974							
		-4-10	-3-4	-1-2	0	+1-2	+3-4	+5+	All
	Less								
(a)	Some Savings in 1972 to None in 1975	10.6	8.7	8.2	5.9	8.1	5.6	3.5	7.3
(b)	Two Months' Savings in 1972 to Less Than Two Months' in 1975	22.9	13.0	10.4	8.6	9.0	11.9	8.8	10.1
	No Change								
(c)	None Both Years	7.1	10.1	12.9	14.3	12.4	8.7	6.0	12.3
(d)	Some Both Years	9.8	13.1	14.3	10.2	13.9	17.1	23.3	13.3
(e)	Two Months' Savings Both Years	40.9	43.1	40.4	45.5	41.2	32.2	32.7	41.5
	More								
(f)	Increased from No Savings in 1972 to Some in 1975	3.1	4.2	3.9	5.5	5.0	7.3	1.2	4.8
(g)	Increased Savings to Two or More Months' Savings in 1975	5.6	7.9	9.9	10.0	10.4	17.2	24.6	10.7
		100.0	100.1	100.0	100.0	100.0	100.0	100.1	100.0
Unweighted Number of Cases		96	263	1,042	1,334	1,111	360	126	4,332

[a]The question was: Do you (family) have any savings such as checking or savings accounts, or government bonds? Would they amount to as much as two months' income or more?

MTR #1171

Table A.31

CHANGE IN REPORTED SAVINGS BY AGE OF HEAD IN 1975

(For 4,332 Families with Same Head for All Four Years)

Box in Table A.28	Change in Savings[a] 1972-1975	Age of Head in 1975							All Ages
		18-21	25-34	35-44	45-54	55-64	65-74	74 or Older	
	Less								
(a)	Some Savings in 1972 to None in 1975	12.8	9.7	8.6	7.0	4.6	4.6	6.1	7.3
(b)	Two Months' Savings in 1972 to Less Than Two Months' in 1975	7.3	13.2	10.3	9.7	8.2	9.3	8.7	10.1
	No Change								
(c)	None Both Years	20.3	10.1	10.2	13.0	12.1	12.3	18.0	12.3
(d)	Some Both Years	27.9	25.3	17.8	10.8	6.2	2.5	1.8	13.3
(e)	Two Months' Savings Both Years	8.6	23.3	35.6	42.7	56.6	59.6	56.6	41.5
	More								
(f)	Increased from No Savings in 1972 to Some in 1975	11.4	5.6	6.7	5.4	2.9	2.7	1.4	4.8
(g)	Increased Savings to Two or More Months' Savings in 1975	11.7	12.8	10.8	11.5	9.5	9.1	7.4	10.7
		100.0	100.0	100.0	100.1	100.1	100.1	100.0	100.0
	Unweighted Number of Cases	241	1,059	825	894	664	433	216	4,332

[a]The question was: Do you (family) have any savings such as checking or savings accounts, or government bonds? Would they amount to as much as two months' income or more?

MTR #1171

Table A.32

CHANGE IN EXPECTATIONS BY CHANGE IN FAMILY INCOME/NEEDS
(For 3,952 Families with Same Head for All Five Years)

Box in Table A.29	Change in Expecta- tions 1971-1975[a]	Change in Income/Needs Decile Position, 1970-1975							All
		-4-10	-3-4	-1-2	0	+1-2	+3-4	+5+	
(a,b)	Improved Expectations	16.9	16.0	16.8	17.4	16.6	20.0	19.2	17.2
	Same								
(c)	*Better* Both Years	33.8	34.9	32.7	32.7	39.0	48.4	42.3	35.9
(d)	*Same* Both Years	17.1	18.7	18.7	19.0	16.9	9.7	17.9	17.6
(e)	*Worse* Both Years	5.0	3.6	3.1	3.0	2.0	0.6	0.0	2.6
(f,g)	Worse Expectations	27.2	27.0	28.7	27.8	25.3	21.2	20.6	26.6
		100.0	100.2	100.0	99.9	99.8	99.9	100.0	99.9
Unweighted Number of Cases		102	264	923	1,203	1,018	307	135	3,952

[a]The question was: What about the next few years--do you think you (and your family) will be better off or worse off, or what?

Table A.33

CHANGE IN EXPECTATIONS BY AGE OF HEAD IN 1975
(For 3,952 Families with Same Head for All Five Years)

Box in Table A.29	Change in Expecta- tions 1971-1975[a]	Age of Head in 1975							All
		18-21	25-34	35-44	45-54	55-64	65-74	75 or Older	
(a,b)	Improved Expectations	11.7	12.5	16.1	18.0	23.9	18.3	15.7	17.2
	Same								
(c)	*Better* Both Years	64.9	61.9	50.6	37.6	20.7	10.1	2.1	35.9
(d)	*Same* Both Years	0.3	4.5	7.2	13.7	19.1	37.9	50.1	17.6
(e)	*Worse* Both Years	0.2	0.3	1.5	2.6	1.6	7.5	5.2	2.6
(f,g)	Worse Expectations	22.9	20.9	24.7	28.1	34.6	26.2	27.0	26.6
		100.0	100.1	100.1	100.0	99.9	100.0	100.1	99.9

[a]The question was: What about the next few years--do you think you (and your family) will be better off or worse off, or what?

Table A.34

ASSOCIATION OF ONE-DIGIT OCCUPATION CLASS
WITH OTHER CHARACTERISTICS OF THE JOB OR PERSON
(For 3,988 Employed Household Heads in Early 1975)

	Measure of Association[a]
Two-Digit Industry	.57
Employed by Government	.46
Self-employed	.40
Boss Has Boss over Him[b]	.40
Has Say in Promotions[c]	.38
Sex	.29
Education	.25
Race	.15
Age	.11

---

[a]Cramer's V is equivalent to the mean square canonical correlation treating each classification as a set of dichotomies.

[b]The question was: Does your boss have a supervisor over him?

[c]The questions were:

For self-employed: Do you employ other people?

Works for others: Do you supervise the work of others, or tell other employees what work to do?

For both: When you work for yourself, do you employ other people?

Table A.35

SOME CHARACTERISTICS OF OCCUPATIONS

(For 3,988 Employed Heads in Early 1975)

Percent within Each Occupation Who . . . .

Occupation[a]	Are Self-employed Only[a]	Work for Government[b]	Have a Say over Pay or Promotion of Others[c]	Have a Boss Who Has a Boss[d]	Are Black	Are Female Heads of Households	Are College Graduates	Are in Durable Manufacturing
Professional	9%	36%	30%	78%	4%	17%	70%	15%
Manager	8	12	69	62	3	8	32	11
Self-employed	88	0	68	0	4	2	16	4
Clerical or Sales	4	17	12	73	11	41	14	9
Craftsman	5	10	21	73	7	2	3	28
Operative	2	7	5	83	15	11	1	41
Laborer and Service Worker	5	18	5	67	26	38	3	7

[a]The question was: What is your main occupation? (What sort of work do you do?) [If not clear] Tell me a little more about what you do. What kind of business is that in?

[b]The question was: Do you work for the federal, state or local government? (If works for self and others): When you work for others, do you work for the federal, state or local government?

[c]The questions were:

For self-employed: Do you employ other people?

Works for Others: Do you supervise the work of others, ot tell other employees what work to do? About how many people are you responsible for? Do you have any say about their pay or promotion?

For both: When you work for yourself, do you employ other people?

[d]Does your boss have a supervisor over him?

MTR #1169

Table A.36

OCCUPATIONAL DISTRIBUTION OF EDUCATION GROUPS

(For 3,988 Employed Household Heads in Early 1975)

Occupation	Cannot Read or Write	0-5 Grades	6-8 Grades	9-11 Grades	12 Grades	12 + Non-academic Training	Some College	B.A. Degree	Professional Degree	All[a]
Professional	1.8	3.0	1.3	3.2	2.5	9.4	16.2	50.1	83.7	18.5
Manager	0.0	2.7	3.2	3.6	9.5	11.6	16.8	20.8	9.2	11.1
Self-employed	4.8	5.3	7.6	4.9	4.7	3.4	6.4	4.5	2.5	4.9
Clerical or Sales	0.0	0.1	7.8	11.1	19.6	16.0	25.2	14.4	1.7	15.2
Craftsman	17.0	24.4	22.9	26.1	22.9	25.1	11.9	2.7	2.3	17.5
Operative	32.8	36.6	26.9	27.0	20.8	14.0	8.7	1.4	0.0	15.2
Laborer	33.7	24.6	21.0	19.9	12.8	11.1	6.8	2.0	0.6	11.2
Farmer	9.4	3.4	8.7	2.4	3.4	1.2	1.3	1.6	0.0	2.5
Miscellaneous (i.e., Armed Forces)	0.6	0.0	0.8	1.8	3.7	8.3	6.8	2.4	0.0	3.9
	100.1	100.1	100.2	100.0	99.9	100.1	100.1	99.9	100.0	100.0
Unweighted Number of Cases	73	113	432	735	785	646	582	410	205	3,988
Weighted Percent	0.9	1.4	8.5	14.6	19.4	17.0	17.0	13.9	7.2	100.0

[a] Includes Don't Know and Not Ascertained

MTR #1169

Table A.37

EDUCATIONAL DISTRIBUTION OF OCCUPATION GROUPS

(For 3,988 Employed Heads in Early 1975)

Education	Professional	Manager	Self-employed	Clerical or Sales	Craftsman	Operative	Laborer	Farmer	Miscel-laneous[a]	All[b]
Cannot Read or Write	0.1	0.0	0.8	0.0	0.8	1.9	2.6	3.2	0.1	0.9
0-5 Grades	0.2	0.3	1.5	0.0	1.9	3.3	3.0	1.8	0.0	1.4
6-8 Grades	0.6	2.4	13.2	4.3	11.1	15.0	15.9	29.1	1.6	8.5
9-11 Grades	2.6	4.7	14.7	10.6	21.8	26.0	26.0	13.9	6.6	14.6
12 Grades	2.6	16.6	18.8	25.0	25.4	26.7	22.4	26.5	18.3	19.4
12 plus Non-Academic Training	8.6	17.7	11.8	17.8	24.3	15.6	16.9	8.2	35.7	17.0
Some College	14.8	25.7	22.5	28.0	11.5	9.8	10.3	8.6	29.1	17.0
B.A. Degree	37.7	26.1	12.9	13.2	2.2	1.3	2.5	8.8	8.6	13.9
Professional Degree	32.6	6.0	3.7	0.8	0.9	0.0	0.4	0.0	0.0	7.2
DK or NA	0.2	0.4	0.0	0.3	0.0	0.5	0.0	0.0	0.0	0.1
	100.0	99.9	99.9	100.0	99.9	100.1	100.0	100.1	100.0	100.0
Unweighted Number of Cases	554	323	142	576	669	749	720	84	170	3,988
Weighted Percent	18.5	11.1	4.9	15.2	17.5	15.2	11.2	2.5	3.9	100.0

[a] i.e., armed forces, police.

[b] Includes Don't Know and Not Ascertained.

Table A.38

TIMING OF JOB CHANGES AND MOVES MID-1974 TO MID-1975[a]

Month	When Changed Jobs	When Changed Residence	When Changed Families	Individuals Moved In or Born[b]
January	1.4	2.0	0.7	0.4
February	1.6	1.9	0.4	0.2
March	1.0	2.3	0.5	0.3
April	0.7	1.2	0.3	0.2
May	0.5	1.5	0.4	0.3
June	0.6	1.9	0.6	0.3
July	1.0	2.1	0.6	0.4
August	1.2	2.5	0.5	0.3
September	1.5	2.3	0.7	0.3
October	1.2	2.5	0.4	0.3
November	0.9	1.6	0.4	0.3
December	0.8	1.9	0.5	0.3
Not Ascertained	0.7	1.0	0.6	0.3
Did Not Change	86.5	75.3	93.2	3.3
	100.0	100.0	100.0	7.2
Unweighted Number of Observations	5,725	5,725	17,329	1,421

[a]This is month when moved to present location or present job, so should be bunched toward recency if there were multiple moves or multiple job changes. Most interviews are in March, April, or May.

[b]This includes splitoff individuals who are all coded as moving in but for whom no month or year is coded.

MTR #1169, 1170

Appendix B

SOME CHECKS ON THE REPRESENTATIVENESS
OF THE PANEL BY EARLY 1975

After the fifth wave, the panel was weighted to adjust both for different sampling fractions and for different rates of nonresponse. At that time we compared distributions of the panel data with the 1970 Current Population Survey, according to race, income, age, sex, family size, number of children under 18, and whether in a Standard Metropolitan Statistical Area.[1] No biases of any significance were detected.

Since then the response rates have been sufficiently high so that there seemed no purpose in reweighting or reassessing; and, logically, by including in the panel those who leave and form new households, we have made this a replacing panel not subject to the usual incremental panel bias. However, in order to provide supplemental evidence about possible biases in the sample, we present here some tables comparing 1975 distributions (1974 income) with data from the 1972-1973 Bureau of Labor Statistics Consumer Expenditure Survey (based on a large, fresh sample interviewed by the Census Bureau) and from the Current Population Survey.[2]

Fortunately the Census-BLS data are sufficiently large for us to recalculate two-way tables of such basic characteristics as family income, age of head, family size, race, and home ownership. Since these factors change little, except for inflation, the fact that we compare our most recent data for Spring 1975 (income for 1974) with their most recent data for Spring 1974 (income for 1973) should not matter. We use our most recent data to allow for the full effect of any panel losses or exposure effects.

We present two-way tables, percentagized into the corner, since this pro-

---

[1] See *A Panel Study of Income Dynamics, Volume 1, Study Design, Procedures, Available Data, 1968-72 Interviewing Years*. Ann Arbor: Institute for Social Research, 1972, pp. 29-32.

[2] The Census data are from United States Department of Labor, Bureau of Labor Statistics Report 455.2 *Consumer Expenditure Survey Series: Interview Survey 1972 and 1973*, U. S. Bureau of Labor Statistics, Washington, D. C., 1976. C.P.S. data are from two publications cited later.

vides a convenient way to check comparability of subgroup sizes in two dimensions as well as the comparability of the one-way distributions. We have used
the 1973 data from BLS, which are given separately from the 1972 data.

Table B.1 gives two-way distributions of income by race for the two samples,
with the comparable subgroup percentages lined up for easy comparison. The BLS-
Census data do tend to place more households in the lowest income categories and
fewer in the highest income categories. However, their income data are a year
earlier and, more important, there is reason to believe that both the reinter-
view nature of the panel and the attention given to work and income in the panel
allow it to elicit fuller reporting of income.[3] In other words, the income differences may reflect response differences rather than nonresponse or sample differences. Aside from that, the two samples produce quite consistent estimates.

Table B.2 looks at income-home ownership combinations. We find the two samples, again aside from income differences that may be differential adequacy of
response, virtually identical.

Table B.3 examines age-race combinations and finds the panel study with
somewhat more young people and somewhat fewer older people. This occurs in
spite of the fact that the (mostly young) splitoffs from the panel families have
a somewhat higher panel loss rate than their parent families. The reason is
partly a technical one: The replacement of families by following splitoffs allows a double chance for replacement when the splitoff marries (the spouse could
also have been a sample member). The weights assigned after the fifth wave took
account of this by halving the weights of married splitoffs.[4] Since then, the
inclusion of married splitoffs without adjusting weights leads to a bias in the
weights, partly offset by the somewhat lower response rate among splitoffs.
(Weights would be adjusted up for the remaining splitoffs so they would represent
the lost ones too.) This problem is easily corrected, and will be corrected in
the future.

We have also included in Table B.3 estimates of the distribution of household heads by age and by race (not jointly) from the March 1974 Current Population Survey, a much larger sample with a focus on demographic information.[5] They

---

[3]Joseph J. Minarik. New Evidence on the Poverty Count, Washington, D. C.:
Brookings Institution, 1975 (unpublished).

[4]See A Panel Study of Income Dynamics, Volume 1, Study Design, Procedures,
Available Data, 1968-72 Interviewing Years. Ann Arbor: Institute for Social Research, 1972, p. 43.

[5]U. S. Department of Commerce, Social and Economic Statistics Administration,
Bureau of the Census, Current Population Reports, Series P-20, No. 276, Popula-

Table B.1

INCOME-RACE DISTRIBUTIONS ESTIMATED FROM
THE BLS CONSUMER EXPENDITURE SURVEY
AND THE PANEL STUDY OF INCOME DYNAMICS

Income	White		Black		Other		Total	
	1974 PSID	1973 BLS	1974 PSID	1973 BLS	1974 PSID	1973 BLS	1974 PSID	1973 BLS
Under $3,000	5.9%	10.4%	1.9%	2.8%	0.3%	0.3%	8.1%	13.6%
$3,000-3,999	3.5	4.5	0.8	0.7	0.1	0.1	4.4	5.2
$4,000-4,999	3.9	4.1	1.1	0.7	0.1	0.1	5.1	5.1
$5,000-5,999	3.9	4.3	1.0	0.5	0.1	0.1	5.0	4.9
$6,000-6,999	4.8	4.3	0.9	0.8	0.1	0.1	5.8	5.1
$7,000-7,999	4.1	4.0	0.6	0.6	0.2	0.1	4.9	4.7
$8,000-9,999	8.1	8.6	1.2	1.1	0.4	0.1	9.7	9.8
$10,000-11,999	7.5	7.8	0.9	0.6	0.2	0.2	8.6	8.6
$12,000-14,999	10.7	11.3	1.1	0.9	0.3	0.1	12.1	12.3
$15,000-19,999	14.7	13.9	1.0	0.9	0.4	0.1	16.1	14.9
$20,000-24,999	8.0	7.3	0.4	0.3	0.2	0.1	8.6	7.6
$25,000 or More	10.5	7.5	0.5	0.2	0.3	0.1	11.3	7.8
	85.6%	88.0%	11.4%	10.1%	2.7%	1.5%	99.7%	99.6%

Table B.2

INCOME-HOME OWNERSHIP DISTRIBUTIONS ESTIMATED FROM
THE BLS CONSUMER EXPENDITURE SURVEY
AND THE PANEL STUDY OF INCOME DYNAMICS

Income	Owns		Rents		Neither		Total	
	1974 PSID	1973 BLS	1974 PSID	1973 BLS	1974 PSID	1973 BLS	1974 PSID	1973 BLS
Under $3,000	3.1%	4.7%	3.6%	8.5%	1.4%	0.3%	8.1%	13.6%
$3,000-3,999	2.1	2.1	2.1	2.9	0.4	0.1	4.5	5.2
$4,000-4,999	2.1	2.3	2.5	2.5	0.5	0.1	5.1	5.1
$5,000-5,999	2.2	2.5	2.4	2.2	0.5	0.2	5.0	4.9
$6,000-6,999	2.7	2.6	2.6	2.4	0.4	0.1	5.8	5.1
$7,000-7,999	2.2	2.2	2.5	2.4	0.3	0.1	4.9	4.7
$8,000-9,999	4.7	4.8	4.6	4.4	0.5	0.6	9.7	9.8
$10,000-11,999	4.8	4.9	3.5	3.2	0.3	0.5	8.6	8.6
$12,000-14,999	7.6	8.6	4.2	3.1	0.3	0.7	12.1	12.3
$15,000-19,999	12.0	11.3	3.9	2.7	0.3	0.9	16.1	14.9
$20,000-24,999	6.8	6.0	1.6	1.1	0.1	0.4	8.6	7.6
$25,000 or More	10.0	6.6	1.3	0.8	0.1	0.2	11.3	7.8
	60.3%	58.6%	34.8%	36.2%	5.1%	4.2%	99.9%	99.6%

Source, Tables B.1 and B.2:

PSID = Panel Study of Income Dynamics

BLS = U. S. Bureau of Labor Statistics, Consumer Expenditure Survey Series: Interview Survey, 1972 and 1973 Report 455-2, Average Annual Expenditures for Selected Commodity and Service Groups Classified by Family Characteristics, 1972 and 1973. U. S. Department of Labor, Washington, D. C., 1976, 1973 data.

MTR #1175

Table B.3

AGE BY RACE DISTRIBUTIONS FROM
THE BLS CONSUMER EXPENDITURE SURVEY,
THE CURRENT POPULATION SURVEY, AND
THE PANEL STUDY OF INCOME DYNAMICS

Age	White			Black			Other			Total		
	PSID	BLS	CPS	PSID	BLS	CPS	PSID	BLS	CPS	PSID	BLS	CPS
Under 25	11.4%	7.5%	7.3%	1.8%	0.9%	1.0%	0.6%	0.0%	0.1%	13.8%	8.6%	8.4%
25-34	20.2	17.9	18.0	2.6	2.3	2.3	0.5	0.4	0.3	23.3	20.6	20.6
35-44	12.2	14.4	14.6	2.1	2.0	1.9	0.7	0.3	0.2	15.0	16.7	16.7
45-54	14.8	15.9	16.5	1.8	1.8	1.8	0.6	0.3	0.2	17.2	18.1	18.5
55-64	11.1	14.7	14.3	1.3	1.5	1.5	0.3	0.2	0.2	12.7	16.3	16.0
65 or older	16.2	17.9	18.1	1.7	1.6	1.6	0.1	0.2	0.1	18.0	19.7	19.8
	85.9%	88.3%	88.8%	11.3%	10.1%	10.1%	2.8%	1.4%	1.1%	100.0%	100.0%	100.0%

Sources:

PSID = Panel Study of Income Dynamics

BLS = U. S. Bureau of Labor Statistics, Consumer Expenditure Survey Series: Interview Survey, 1972 and 1973 Report 455-2, Average Annual Expenditures for Selected Commodity and Service Groups Classified by Family Characteristics, 1972 and 1973. U. S. Department of Labor, Washington, D. C., 1976, 1973 data.

CPS = Current Population Survey data from Household and Family Characteristics, March, 1974, Current Population Reports Series p. 20, No. 276, February, 1975. U. S. Government Printing Office, Washington, D. C.

MTR #1175

reinforce the implication that, with some additional technical reweighting to account for married splitoffs, the panel sample is representative of the population of the United States.

Table B.4 looks at age-home ownership combinations and finds only minor differences in home ownership, some of them potentially reducible when we correct the weighting of splitoffs.

Tables B.5 and B.6 compare samples on combinations of family size and race, and family size and home ownership. Again, the differences appear to be trivial and, where CPS data are available, about as large between BLS and CPS as between CPS and the panel study.

We have not presented all the possible comparisons, but they show the same general pattern. We conclude that there are no major problems with the representativeness of the sample, except for the necessity of adjusting the weights of married splitoffs to reflect their double chances of being included. We propose to introduce a revised set of weights after the tenth wave is in, adjusting for this and for any differential panel losses. It is doubtful that the accumulation of married splitoffs since 1972 has caused any distortion of the analysis, much of which is either of same-headed families (for change analysis) or treats the splitoffs separately.

When we compare, in Table B.7, the family income distribution for 1967 from the first wave of the panel and from the Current Population Survey, it is clear that the differences in income distribution between the panel and the BLS study or the CPS in 1973-74 are not caused by any increasing lack of representativeness in the panel.

As seen in Table B.8, the number of children under 18 appears to agree with the Current Population Survey and the family size distribution (shown in Table B.9) is apparently not affected much by the failure to halve the weights of those who split and marry after 1972. The effects of adjusting the weights first to halve the weights of those who split and married after 1972 and then also to halve the weights of single splitoffs as of 1972 who married since then, are given in Table B.10. It is clear that only the age distribution is much affected.

Another reason for a discrepancy in the number of families at different ages comes from the treatment of splitoffs who return home or move in with other older relatives. We treat them as independent families once they have been independent for a year, whereas a new single-wave survey would incorporate them into the family they live with. This implies that those who want to make aggregate

---

tion Characteristics, Household and Family Characteristics, March 1974, United States Government Printing Office, Washington, D. C., February 1975.

Table B.4

HOME OWNERSHIP-AGE DISTRIBUTIONS ESTIMATED FROM
THE BLS CONSUMER EXPENDITURE SURVEY
AND THE PANEL STUDY OF INCOME DYNAMICS

Age	Owns		Rents		Neither		Total		1972
	PSID	BLS	PSID	BLS	PSID	BLS	PSID	BLS	BLS
Under 25	2.4%	0.8%	9.5%	7.3%	1.9%	0.5%	13.8%	8.6%	9.1%
25-34	11.4	8.2	10.8	10.3	1.0	2.1	23.3	20.6	19.1
35-44	10.4	11.4	4.2	4.5	0.5	0.8	15.0	16.7	17.1
45-54	13.3	13.4	3.5	4.3	0.4	0.5	17.2	18.1	18.4
55-64	9.5	12.2	2.6	3.7	0.5	0.3	12.7	16.3	16.0
65 or Older	13.1	13.2	4.2	6.1	0.8	0.4	18.0	19.7	20.3
	60.1%	59.2%	34.8%	36.2%	5.1%	4.6%	100.0%	100.0%	100.0%

Sources:

PSID = Panel Study of Income Dynamics

BLS = U. S. Bureau of Labor Statistics, Consumer Expenditure Survey Series:
Interview Survey, 1972 and 1973 Report 455-2, Average Annual Expenditures for
Selected Commodity and Service Groups Classified by Family Characteristics, 1972
and 1973. U. S. Department of Labor, Washington, D. C., 1976, 1973 data.

MTR #1175

Table B.5

FAMILY SIZE-RACE DISTRIBUTIONS ESTIMATED FROM
THE BLS CONSUMER EXPENDITURE SURVEY,
THE CURRENT POPULATION SURVEY, AND
THE PANEL STUDY OF INCOME DYNAMICS

Family Size	White PSID	White BLS	Black PSID	Black BLS	Other PSID	Other BLS	Total PSID	Total BLS	Total CPS
1 Person	20.1%	20.5%	3.1%	2.6%	0.5%	0.2%	23.7%	23.3%	21.4%
2 Persons	27.5	25.1	2.0	2.2	0.7	0.3	30.2	27.6	29.4
3 Persons	14.5	13.7	2.4	1.7	0.6	0.2	17.5	15.7	16.7
4 Persons	11.7	14.1	1.6	1.3	0.4	0.3	13.7	15.4	15.4
5 Persons	6.4	8.1	0.9	0.9	0.3	0.1	7.6	9.1	9.1
6 Persons or More	5.5	7.2	1.4	1.5	0.5	0.2	7.4	8.9	8.0
	85.7%	88.7%	11.4%	10.2%	3.0%	1.3%	100.1%	100.0%	100.0%

Table B.6

FAMILY SIZE-HOME OWNERSHIP DISTRIBUTIONS ESTIMATES FROM
THE BLS CONSUMER EXPENDITURE SURVEY AND
THE PANEL STUDY OF INCOME DYNAMICS

Family Size	Owns PSID	Owns BLS	Rents PSID	Rents BLS	Neither PSID	Neither BLS	Total PSID	Total BLS	1973 BLS
1 Person	8.1%	7.9%	12.9%	14.7%	2.7%	0.5%	23.7%	23.3%	23.8%
2 Persons	19.3	17.4	9.8	8.8	1.0	1.4	30.1	27.6	27.0
3 Persons	11.1	9.6	5.7	5.0	0.7	1.1	17.5	15.7	16.5
4 Persons	10.5	11.0	2.9	3.8	0.3	0.9	13.7	15.4	14.5
5 Persons	5.8	6.7	1.6	1.9	0.2	0.5	7.6	9.1	8.9
6 Persons or More	5.4	6.6	1.7	1.9	0.2	0.3	7.3	8.9	9.3
	60.2%	59.2%	34.6%	36.1%	5.1%	4.7%	99.9%	100.0%	100.0%

Sources, Tables B.5 and B.6:

PSID = Panel Study of Income Dynamics

BLS = U. S. Bureau of Labor Statistics, Consumer Expenditure Survey Series:
Interview Survey, 1972 and 1973 Report 455-2, Average Annual Expenditures for
Selected Commodity and Service Groups Classified by Family Characteristics, 1972
and 1973. U. S. Department of Labor, Washington, D. C., 1976, 1973 data.

CPS = Current Population Survey data from Household and Family Characteristics, March, 1974, Current Population Reports Series, p. 20, No. 276, February,
1975. U. S. Government Printing Office, Washington, D. C.

MTR #1175

Table B.7

FAMILY INCOME DISTRIBUTION ESTIMATED FROM
THE 1967 and 1974 CURRENT POPULATION SURVEY,
THE 1973 BLS CONSUMER EXPENDITURE SURVEY, AND
THE PANEL STUDY OF INCOME DYNAMICS

Family Money Income	1967 Current Population Survey	1967 Panel Study	1973 BLS	1974 CPS	1974 PSID
Less than $1,000	5.7	1.1			
$1,000–1,999	8.7	5.8	13.6	12.8	8.1
$2,000–2,999	7.4	8.2			
$3,000–3,999	7.1	7.2	5.2	5.7	4.5
$4,000–4,999	6.8	6.9	5.1	5.1	5.1
$5,000–9,999	36.5	35.0	24.5	23.9	25.5
$10,000–14,999	18.6	22.3	20.9	21.2	20.7
$15,000 or More	9.3	13.6	30.5	31.2	36.1

Sources:

PSID = Panel Study of Income Dynamics. (Distributions of the five-year merged tapes have duplicated records for divided families and have eliminated families lost to the panel and hence are inappropriate for representing the nation in 1967.

CPS = U. S. Bureau of the Census, Current Population Reports, Series P-60, No. 101, "Money Income in 1974 of Families and Persons in the United States," U. S. Government Printing Office, Washington, D. C., 1976, p. 18, Table 9.

BLS = U. S. Bureau of Labor Statistics, Consumer Expenditure Survey Series: Interview Survey, 1972 and 1973 Report 455-2, Average Annual Expenditures for Selected Commodity and Service Groups Classified by Family Characteristics, 1972 and 1973. U. S. Department of Labor, Washington, D. C., 1976, 1973 data.

MTR #1175

Table B.8

NUMBER OF CHILDREN DISTRIBUTION ESTIMATED FROM
THE CURRENT POPULATION SURVEY AND
THE PANEL STUDY OF INCOME DYNAMICS

Number of Children Under 18	1974 CPS	1975 PSID
None	55.8	56.3
One	15.8	17.2
Two	14.5	13.8
Three	7.8	7.2
Four or More	6.1	5.5
	100.1	100.0

Sources:

PSID = Panel Study of Income Dynamics

CPS = Current Population Survey. U. S. Bureau of the Census, Current Population Reports Series P-20, No. 276, "Household and Family Characteristics: March 1974," United States Government Printing Office, Washington, D. C., 1975, Table 17, p. 84.

Table B.9

FAMILY SIZE DISTRIBUTION ESTIMATED FROM
THE BLS CONSUMER EXPENDITURE SURVEY,
THE CURRENT POPULATION SURVEY, AND
THE PANEL STUDY OF INCOME DYNAMICS

	BLS		1975	1975
Family Size	1972	1973	CPS	PSID
One	23.8	23.3	25.3	23.7
Two	27.0	27.6	27.9	30.1
Three	16.5	15.7	16.3	17.5
Four	14.5	15.4	14.8	13.7
Five	8.9	9.1	8.5	7.6
Six or More	9.3	8.9	7.3	7.3
	100.0	100.0	100.1	99.9
Number of Observations	10,000+	10,000+	45,000	5,725

Sources:

PSID = Panel Study of Income Dynamics

CPS = Current Population Survey. Current Population Reports, U. S. Bureau of the Census, Series P-60, No. 101, "Money Income in 1974 of Families and Persons in the United States," U. S. Government Printing Office, Washington, D. C., 1976. (Combines estimates of the number of unrelated males and females from p. 105, Table 52, with the distribution by size of families (of 20 or more) from p. 50, Table 26.)

BLS = U. S. Bureau of Labor Statistics, Consumer Expenditure Survey Series: Interview Survey, 1972 and 1973 Report 455-2, Average Annual Expenditures for Selected Commodity and Service Groups Classified by Family Characteristics, 1972 and 1973. U. S. Department of Labor, Washington, D. C., 1976, 1973 data.

MTR #1175

Table B.10

EFFECTS OF WEIGHT ADJUSTMENT ON SOME BASIC DISTRIBUTIONS
FROM THE PANEL STUDY OF INCOME DYNAMICS

Age	1*	2*	3*
18-24	13.8%	11.5%	11.3%[a]
25-34	23.3	22.8	22.2
35-44	15.1	15.6	15.7
45-54	17.2	18.0	18.2
55-64	12.6	13.2	13.4[b]
65-74	11.3	11.8	12.0
75 or Older	6.7	7.1	7.2
	100.0%	100.0%	100.0%
Race			
White	85.8%	85.8%	85.8%
Black	11.4	11.4	11.5
Other	2.9	2.8	2.8
	100.1%	100.0%	100.1%
Education			
0-5 Grades	1.8%	1.9%	1.9%
6-8 Grades	3.1	3.2	3.3
9-11 Grades	14.1	14.6	14.8
12 Grades	16.1	16.3	16.4
12 Grades plus Nonacademic Training	17.1	16.7	16.6
Some College, No Degree	15.5	15.3	15.3
B.A. Degree	15.3	14.9	14.8
Advanced Degree	11.2	11.2	11.1
Don't Know, Not Ascertained	5.6	5.7	5.6
Cannot Read or Write	0.2	0.2	0.2
	100.0%	100.0%	100.0%
Housing Status			
Own	60.2%	61.8%	62.0%
Rent	34.7	33.1	33.0
Neither Own nor Rent	5.1	5.0	5.1
	100.0%	99.9%	100.1%
1974 Family Money Income			
Under $3,000	8.1%	8.4%	8.5%
$3,000-3,999	4.5	4.7	4.8
$4,000-4,999	5.1	5.1	5.1
$5,000-5,999	5.1	5.1	5.1
$6,000-6,999	5.8	5.7	5.8
$7,000-7,999	4.9	4.8	4.9
$8,000-9,999	9.7	9.5	9.4
$10,000-11,999	8.6	8.4	8.4
$12,000-14,999	12.1	11.8	11.7
$15,000-19,999	16.2	16.2	16.3
$20,000-24,999	8.6	8.7	8.5
$25,000 or More	11.3	11.7	11.7
	100.0%	100.1%	100.2%

*Columns: 1. Present weights.
2. Half weights of splitoffs since 1972 who were married.
3. Half weights of pre-1972 splitoffs who were single in
1972, married in 1975.

[a]1975 CPS estimate is 8.4%.

[b]1975 CPS estimate is 16.0%.

estimates from the panel would be well advised to estimate the criterion of interest separately for each age-of-family-head group and then use Census estimates
of the aggregate number of families headed by people of those ages to "blow up"
to aggregates.

Summary and Conclusions

Comparisons with two other larger sample surveys reveal only one possible
distortion in the panel's representativeness--there are fewer household heads 55
to 64 years old and more under 25 than in data from the Current Population Survey
or the Bureau of Labor Statistics survey. Adjusting the weights to allow for the
double chance married splitoffs since 1972 had to be sampled, reduces the difference but does not eliminate it. However, it is small and apparently does not result in any other appreciable differences in the sample distributions, including
two-way distributions.

One other difference was present from the beginning and has not changed:
there are fewer families with very low incomes and more with substantial incomes.
This may reflect better income reporting in the panel study.

Appendix C

RESPONSE RATES AND DATA QUALITY

In Volume IV of this series we reported that we could discover no adverse effect on the response rate or the quality of the data resulting from our change in 1973 to predominately telephone interviewing, or from the slight drop that seems to accompany it, in the number of interviews taken with the head of the family.

In 1975 the number of telephone interviews increased by 2 percent (Table C.1) and the number of interviews taken with the head decreased by about 2 percent (Table C.2). However, the 1975 response rate remained at 97 percent (Table C.3), and the quality of the data, according to our measure of it in Table C.4, continued its minute year-to-year improvement.

Table C.1

PROPORTION OF INTERVIEWS BY TELEPHONE

Year	Sample Size	Number of Telephone Interviews	Unweighted Percent of Sample
1968	4,802	--	--
1969	4,460	--	--
1970	4,655	67	1.4
1971	4,840	108	2.2
1972	5,060	134	2.6
1973	5,285	4,047	76.6
1974	5,517	4,554	82.5
1975	5,725	4,836	84.5

Table C.2

PROPORTION OF FAMILY HEADS INTERVIEWED

Year	Total Sample	Proportion of Interviews by Head
1968	4,802	92.6%
1969	4,460	93.1
1970	4,655	93.2
1971	4,840	93.3
1972	5,060	93.5
1973	5,285	91.1
1974	5,517	90.0
1975	5,725	88.3

Table C.3^a

ANNUAL AND CUMULATIVE PANEL RESPONSE RATES

	Percent	
Year	Annual	Cumulative
1968	76	76
1969	89	68
1970	97	66
1971	97	64
1972	97	62
1973	97	61
1974	97	59
1975	97	57

^{a}The deceased, those too ill to be interviewed, and recombined families have *not* been removed from the base.

Table C.4$^{\alpha}$

TOTAL ACCURACY CODES ON
HUSBAND AND WIFE INCOME VARIABLES

Year of Data	0	1	2	3	4 or More	Total
1968	94.0	2.5	2.6	0.2	0.8	100.0
1969	95.6	1.6	1.9	0.1	0.8	100.0
1970	96.9	1.3	1.3	0.1	0.5	100.0
1971	97.7	0.9	0.9	0.1	0.4	100.0
1972	97.8	0.8	1.1	0.0	0.3	100.0
1973	97.9	1.1	0.7	0.1	0.2	100.0
1974	98.2	0.9	0.7	0.0	0.2	100.0
1975	98.3	0.8	0.8	0.0	0.2	100.0

$^{\alpha}$Table C.4 is based on three variables:

Accuracy of Head's Labor Income
Accuracy of Wife's Labor Income
Accuracy of Asset Income of Head and Wife.

Accuracy here is determined by the number of assignments made by the editors in order to recreate data missing from an interview. The more assignments, the less reliable the data. The accuracy code values and their meanings are:

0. Adequate response: No assignments made.

1. Minor assignment: Response was inadequate, but estimates could be made within a probable error of under $300 or 10 percent of the assignment by using previous years' data or other data in the interview.

2. Major assignment: Response was inadequate and estimates had a probable error of at least $300 and at least 10 percent of the value of the assignment, using any information available in previous interviews or in the current one. Usually these values were assigned from an assignment table.

This table shows the sum of the accuracy codes for the three different income measures. The maximum number possible here would be six for married couples, four for single heads.

Appendix D

1975 QUESTIONNAIRE

Although the questionnaires, codes, and study procedures are described each year in a separate documentation volume, we reproduce the 1975 questionnaire in this appendix for readers without access to these volumes.

STUDY OF FAMILY ECONOMICS

Project 457680

1975

OMB#85-R0224
Exp. Feb. 1976

```
┌─────────────────────┐
│                     │
│                     │
│ (Interview Number)  │
└─────────────────────┘
```

SURVEY RESEARCH CENTER
INSTITUTE FOR SOCIAL RESEARCH
THE UNIVERSITY OF MICHIGAN

68 Int.	69 Int.	70 Int.
71 Int.	72 Int.	73 Int.
74 Int.		

(Do not write in above space)

1. Interviewer's Label	2. P.S.U. _____
	3. Your Interview No. _____
	4. Date _____
	5. Length of Interview _____

SECTION A: CHILDREN

(MAKE SURE PAGE 2 OF COVER SHEET IS COMPLETED BEFORE ASKING Q. A1)

A1. INTERVIEWER: SEE LISTING BOX, ON PAGE 2 OF COVER SHEET, AND CHECK ONE:

1. CHILDREN UNDER 25 IN	5. NO CHILDREN UNDER 25 IN
FU DURING 1974 or 1975	FU DURING 1974 or 1975
	(TURN TO PAGE 2, B1)

A2. Did any of the children stop going to school in 1974 or 1975?

1. YES   5. NO   (TURN TO PAGE 2, B1)

	Person #1	Person #2
A3. Who was that?	_____	_____
	(RELATION TO HEAD) (AGE)	(RELATION TO HEAD) (AGE)
A4. What was the highest grade (he/she) finished?	_____	_____
	(GRADE FINISHED)	(GRADE FINISHED)

2

SECTION B: TRANSPORTATION

(ASK EVERYONE)

B1. Is there public transportation within walking distance of (here) your house?

    | 1. YES | | 5. NO | (GO TO B3)

    B2. Is it good enough so that a person could use it to get to work?

    _____

    _____

B3. Do you or anyone else in the family here own a car or truck?

    | 1. YES | | 5. NO | (GO TO B6)

    | B4. How many cars and trucks do you (and your family living here) own? _____ |
    | B5. During the last year how many miles did you and your family drive in (your car/all of your cars)? |
    | _____ |
    | _____ |

B6. What is the nearest city of 50,000 or more, including the one you live in?

    _____

B7. How many miles is it from your home to the center of that city? _____

(TURN TO PAGE 3, C1)

3

SECTION C: HOUSING

Now let's talk about where you live.

C1. All things considered would you say you are satisfied or dissatisfied
     with your neighborhood as a place to live?

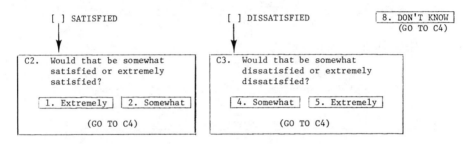

[ ] SATISFIED   [ ] DISSATISFIED | 8. DON'T KNOW |
                                                              (GO TO C4)

C2. Would that be somewhat   C3. Would that be somewhat
     satisfied or extremely   dissatisfied or extremely
     satisfied?   dissatisfied?

     | 1. Extremely | | 2. Somewhat | | 4. Somewhat | | 5. Extremely |

          (GO TO C4)   (GO TO C4)

C4. All things considered would you say you are satisfied or dissatisfied with
     your house or apartment as a place to live?

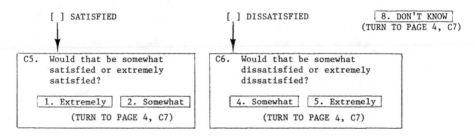

[ ] SATISFIED   [ ] DISSATISFIED | 8. DON'T KNOW |
                                                          (TURN TO PAGE 4, C7)

C5. Would that be somewhat   C6. Would that be somewhat
     satisfied or extremely   dissatisfied or extremely
     satisfied?   dissatisfied?

     | 1. Extremely | | 2. Somewhat | | 4. Somewhat | | 5. Extremely |
        (TURN TO PAGE 4, C7)   (TURN TO PAGE 4, C7)

4

C7. How many rooms do you have for your family (not counting bathrooms)? _____

C8. Do you live in a one-family house, a two-family house, an apartment, or what?

| 1. ONE-FAMILY | | 2. TWO-FAMILY | | 3. APARTMENT | OTHER _____
(SPECIFY)

C9. Do you own the (home/apartment), pay rent, or what?

| 1. OWNS OR IS BUYING | | 5. PAYS RENT | | 8. NEITHER OWNS NOR RENTS |
↓   (GO TO C11)   (GO TO C12)

(IF OWNS OR IS BUYING)

C10. Could you tell me what the present value of your house (farm) is --
I mean about what would it bring if you sold it today?

$_____

(GO TO C14)

(IF PAYS RENT)

C11. About how much rent do you pay a month? $_____
(GO TO C14)

(IF NEITHER OWNS NOR RENTS)

C12. How is that? _____

_____

C13. How much would it rent for if it were rented? $_____ per _____
(MONTH,YEAR)
(GO TO C14)

(ASK EVERYONE)

C14. Have you (HEAD) moved since the spring of 1974?

| 1. YES | | 5. NO | (TURN TO PAGE 5, C17)
↓

C15. What month was that? _____ (MOST RECENT MOVE)

C16. Why did you move? _____

_____

5

C17. Do you think you might move in the next couple of years?

_____ | 5. NO | (GO TO C20)

(IF MIGHT MOVE
OR WILL MOVE)──▶ C18. Would you say you definitely will move, probably will move, or are you more uncertain?

| 1. DEFINITELY | | 2. PROBABLY | | 3. MORE UNCERTAIN |

C19. Why might you move? _____

_____

C20. Do you have any problem with the plumbing where you live -- things like not enough hot water, toilets that don't flush well or old sinks and tubs?

| 1. YES | | 5. NO | (GO TO C22)

C21. Is that a big problem or a small one?

| 1. BIG | | 5. SMALL |

C22. How about the structure of your home -- any problems with sagging floors or ceilings, walls that crack and crumble and things like that?

| 1. YES | | 5. NO | (GO TO C24)

C23. Is that a big problem or a small one?

| 1. BIG | | 5. SMALL |

C24. Is there any problem with lack of security from break-ins?

| 1. YES | | 5. NO | (GO TO C26)

C25. Is that a big problem or a small one?

| 1. BIG | | 5. SMALL |

C26. How about rats, cockroaches and things like that -- any problems there?

| 1. YES | | 5. NO | (TURN TO PAGE 6, C28)

C27. Is that a big problem or a small one?

| 1. BIG | | 5. SMALL |

474

6

C28. Is poor insulation or getting enough heat a problem?

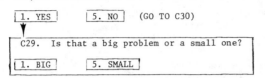

| 1. YES | 5. NO | (GO TO C30) |

C29. Is that a big problem or a small one?

| 1. BIG | 5. SMALL |

C30. How about the general cleanliness of the streets in your immediate neighborhood? Are there unkempt yards or grounds, houses poorly kept up or infrequent and sloppy garbage pickup?

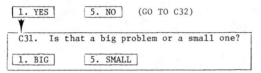

| 1. YES | 5. NO | (GO TO C32) |

C31. Is that a big problem or a small one?

| 1. BIG | 5. SMALL |

C32. Is this a poor neighborhood for kids, with too few places to play, too many ways for kids to get in trouble and things like that?

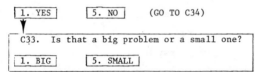

| 1. YES | 5. NO | (GO TO C34) |

C33. Is that a big problem or a small one?

| 1. BIG | 5. SMALL |

C34. Is this a generally crowded area with too many people, too much noise and bad traffic?

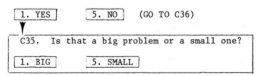

| 1. YES | 5. NO | (GO TO C36) |

C35. Is that a big problem or a small one?

| 1. BIG | 5. SMALL |

C36. How about burglaries and robberies -- is this a problem where you live?

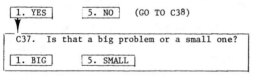

| 1. YES | 5. NO | (GO TO C38) |

C37. Is that a big problem or a small one?

| 1. BIG | 5. SMALL |

C38. How about muggings, rapes, pushers, junkies, or too few police -- any problems there?

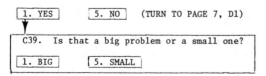

| 1. YES | 5. NO | (TURN TO PAGE 7, D1) |

C39. Is that a big problem or a small one?

| 1. BIG | 5. SMALL |

SECTION D: EMPLOYMENT

D1. We would like to know about your (HEAD'S) present job -- are you (HEAD) working now, looking for work, retired, a housewife, or what?

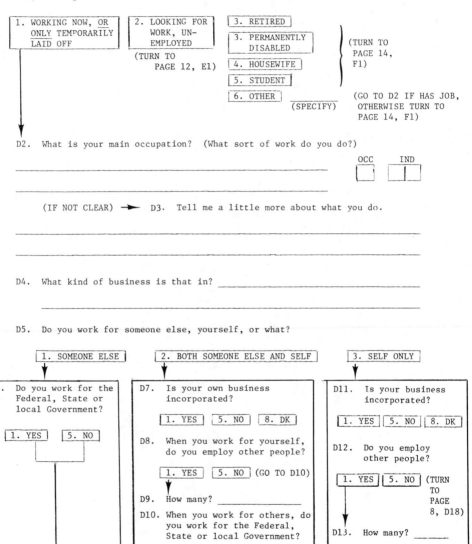

| 1. WORKING NOW, OR ONLY TEMPORARILY LAID OFF | 2. LOOKING FOR WORK, UN-EMPLOYED (TURN TO PAGE 12, E1) | 3. RETIRED
 3. PERMANENTLY DISABLED
 4. HOUSEWIFE
 5. STUDENT
 6. OTHER _____ (SPECIFY) | (TURN TO PAGE 14, F1)

 (GO TO D2 IF HAS JOB, OTHERWISE TURN TO PAGE 14, F1) |

D2. What is your main occupation? (What sort of work do you do?)

_____   OCC   IND

(IF NOT CLEAR) ➤ D3. Tell me a little more about what you do.

_____

_____

D4. What kind of business is that in? _____

_____

D5. Do you work for someone else, yourself, or what?

| 1. SOMEONE ELSE | 2. BOTH SOMEONE ELSE AND SELF | 3. SELF ONLY |

D6. Do you work for the Federal, State or local Government?

  1. YES   5. NO

(TURN TO PAGE 8, D14)

D7. Is your own business incorporated?

  1. YES   5. NO   8. DK

D8. When you work for yourself, do you employ other people?

  1. YES   5. NO (GO TO D10)

D9. How many? _____

D10. When you work for others, do you work for the Federal, State or local Government?

  1. YES   5. NO

(TURN TO PAGE 8, D14)

D11. Is your business incorporated?

  1. YES   5. NO   8. DK

D12. Do you employ other people?

  1. YES   5. NO (TURN TO PAGE 8, D18)

D13. How many? _____

(TURN TO PAGE 8, D18)

8

D14. Do you supervise the work of others, or tell other employees what work to do?

[1. YES]   [5. NO]   (GO TO D17)

> D15. About how many people are you responsible for?_____
>
> D16. Do you have any say about their pay or promotion?
>
> [1. YES]   [5. NO]
>
> (GO TO D17)

D17. Does your boss have a supervisor over him?

[1. YES]   [5. NO]

D18. How long have you had this job? _____

(IF ONE YEAR OR MORE, TURN TO PAGE 9, D24)

(IF LESS THAN ONE YEAR)

> D19. What month did you start this job? _____
>
> D20. What happened to the job you had before -- did the company fold, were you laid off, or what? _____
>
> D21. Does your present job pay more than the one you had before?
>
> [1. YES, MORE]   [5. NO, SAME OR LESS]
>
> D22. On the whole, would you say your present job is better or worse than the one you had before?
>
> [1. BETTER]   [5. WORSE]   [3. SAME] ◄─(TURN TO PAGE 9, D24)
>
> > D23. Why is that? _____
> >
> > _____
> >
> > _____
> >
> > (TURN TO PAGE 9, D24)

D24. How many weeks of paid vacation do you get each year? _____

D25. Did you take any vacation or time off during 1974?

<pre>
| 1. YES | | 5. NO | (GO TO D27)
    |
    ▼
    D26. How much vacation did you take? ____ _____ _____
                                           DAYS WEEKS MONTHS
</pre>

D27. Did you miss any work in 1974 because you were sick or because someone else in the family was sick?

<pre>
| 1. YES | | 5. NO | (GO TO D29)
    |
    ▼
    D28. How much did you miss?   ____ _____ _____
                                           DAYS WEEKS MONTHS
</pre>

D29. Did you miss any work in 1974 because you were unemployed or on strike?

<pre>
| 1. YES | | 5. NO | (GO TO D32)
    |
    ▼
    D30. How much work did you miss?   ____ _____ _____
                                           DAYS WEEKS MONTHS
</pre>

D31. Were those weeks of unemployment all in one stretch, in two periods, or more than two?

| 1. ALL IN ONE STRETCH | | 3. TWO PERIODS | | 5. MORE THAN TWO |

D32. Then, how many <u>weeks</u> did you actually work on your main job in 1974? _____
                                                                        (WEEKS)

D33. And, on the average, how many <u>hours a week</u> did you work on your main job last year? _____

D34. Did you have any overtime which isn't included in that?

<pre>
    [ ] YES   [ ] NO   (TURN TO PAGE 10, D36)
    ▼
    D35. How many hours did that overtime amount to in 1974? _____
                                                              (HOURS)
</pre>

10

D36. If you were to work more hours than usual during some week, would you get paid for those extra hours of work?

| 1. YES | | 5. NO |

| D37. What would be your hourly rate for that overtime?

$ _____ per hour | D38. Do you have an hourly wage rate for your regular work?

\| 1. YES \| \| 5. NO \| (GO TO D40) |

D39. What is your hourly wage rate for your regular work time? $_____per hour

D40. Are you covered by a company retirement plan? | 1. YES | | 5. NO | | 8. DON'T KNOW |

D41. Did you have any extra jobs or other ways of making money in addition to your main job in 1974?

| 1. YES | | 5. NO | (TURN TO PAGE 11, D47)

OCC

D42. What did you do? _____

_____

D43. Anything else? _____

D44. About how much did you make per hour at this? $_____ per hour

D45. And how many <u>weeks</u> did you work on your extra job(s) in 1974? _____

D46. On the average, how many hours a week did you work on your extra job(s)? _____

_____

D47. Was there more work available on (your job) (any of your jobs) so that you
could have worked more if you had wanted to?

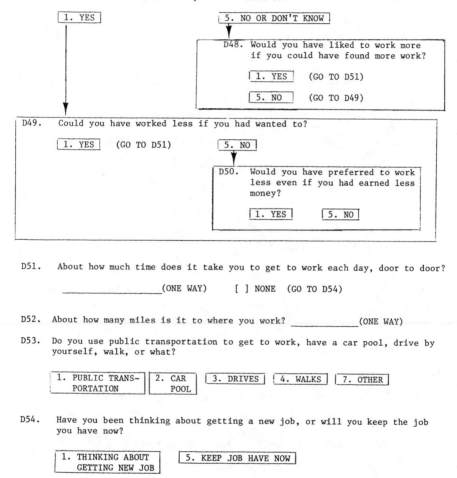

1. YES

5. NO OR DON'T KNOW

D48. Would you have liked to work more
if you could have found more work?

1. YES   (GO TO D51)

5. NO   (GO TO D49)

D49. Could you have worked less if you had wanted to?

1. YES   (GO TO D51)

5. NO

D50. Would you have preferred to work
less even if you had earned less
money?

1. YES   5. NO

D51. About how much time does it take you to get to work each day, door to door?

_____(ONE WAY)   [ ] NONE (GO TO D54)

D52. About how many miles is it to where you work? _____(ONE WAY)

D53. Do you use public transportation to get to work, have a car pool, drive by
yourself, walk, or what?

1. PUBLIC TRANS-   2. CAR   3. DRIVES   4. WALKS   7. OTHER
   PORTATION   POOL

D54. Have you been thinking about getting a new job, or will you keep the job
you have now?

1. THINKING ABOUT   5. KEEP JOB HAVE NOW
   GETTING NEW JOB

(TURN TO PAGE 15, G1)

12

SECTION E: IF LOOKING FOR WORK, UNEMPLOYED IN Q.D1

OCC
☐

E1.   What kind of job are you looking for? _____

_____

E2.   How much might you earn? $_____ per _____

E3.   Will you have to get any training to qualify? _____

_____

E4.   What have you been doing to find a job? _____

_____ | 5. NOTHING | (GO TO E6)

E5.   How many places have you been to in the last few weeks to find out about a job?

| 1. ONE | | 2. TWO | | 3. THREE | | 4. FOUR | | 5. FIVE OR MORE |

E6.   What sort of work did you do on your last job? (What was your occupation?)

OCC   IND
☐   ☐☐

_____

_____

E7.   What kind of business was that in? _____

_____

E8.   Did you supervise the work of others or tell other employees what to do?

| 1. YES | | 5. NO |

E9.   What happened to that job -- did the company fold, were you laid off, or what?

_____

_____

E10. How many <u>weeks</u> did you work in 1974? _____ | 00. NONE | (GO TO E12)

E11. About how many <u>hours a week</u> did you work when you worked? _____

E12. How many weeks were you sick in 1974? _____

E13. Then, how many weeks were you unemployed or laid off in 1974? _____ | 00. NONE |
(TURN TO
PAGE 13, E15)

E14. Were those weeks of unemployment all in one stretch, in two
periods, or more than two?

| 1. ALL IN ONE STRETCH | | 3. TWO PERIODS | | 5. MORE THAN TWO |

E15. INTERVIEWER: REFER TO E10 AND CHECK ONE:

[ ] WORKED IN 1974   [ ] DID NOT WORK IN 1974 (GO TO E19)

E16. On your last job, how much time did it take you to get to work each
day, door to door?

_____   [ ] NONE (GO TO E19)
(ONE WAY)

E17. About how many miles was it to where you worked? _____(ONE WAY)

E18. Did you use public transportation to get to work, have a car pool,
drive by yourself, walk, or what?

| 1. PUBLIC TRANS- PORTATION | 2. CAR POOL | 3. DROVE | 4. WALKED | 7. OTHER |

E19. Are there jobs available around here that just aren't worth taking?

| 1. YES | | 5. NO | (GO TO E21)

E20. How much do they pay? $_____ per _____
(HOUR, WEEK)

E21. Would you be willing to move to another community if you could get
a good job there?

| 1. YES, MAYBE, OR DEPENDS | | 5. NO |

E22. How much would a job
have to pay for you
to be willing to move?

$_____ per _____

E23. Why is that? _____

_____

_____

(TURN TO PAGE 15, G1)

14

SECTION F: RETIRED, HOUSEWIFE, STUDENT, PERMANENTLY DISABLED

F1. During the last year (1974), did you (HEAD) do any work for money?

| 1. YES | | 5. NO |

F2. Are you thinking about going to work?

| 1. YES | (GO TO F8) | 5. NO | (TURN TO PAGE 15, G1)

OCC   IND

F3. What kind of work did you do when you worked? (What was your occupation?)

_____

F4. What kind of business is that in? _____

_____

F5. How many <u>weeks</u> did you work last year? _____

F6. About how many <u>hours a week</u> did you work (when you worked)? _____

F7. Are you thinking of getting a new job in the next year or so?

| 1. YES | (GO TO F8) | 5. NO | (TURN TO PAGE 15, G1)

(IF YES TO F2 OR TO F7)

F8. What kind of job do you have in mind? _____

_____

F9. How much might you earn? $_____ per _____

F10. Would you have to get any training to qualify? _____

F11. What have you been doing to find a job? _____

_____ | 5. NOTHING | (GO TO F13)

F12. How many places have you been to in the last few weeks to find out
about a job?

| 1. ONE | | 2. TWO | | 3. THREE | | 4. FOUR | | 5. FIVE OR MORE |

F13. Are there jobs around here that just aren't worth taking?

| 1. YES | | 5. NO | (TURN TO PAGE 15, G1)

F14. How much do they pay? $_____ per_____

SECTION G: OTHER WORK

(ASK EVERYONE)

G1. Are you married, single, widowed, divorced, or separated?

| 1. MARRIED | 2. SINGLE | 3. WIDOWED | 4. DIVORCED | 5. SEPARATED |

(TURN TO PAGE 16, G14)

(Q's G2-G13 REFER TO WIFE'S OCCUPATION)

G2. Did your wife do any work for money in 1974?

| 1. YES | 5. NO | (TURN TO PAGE 16, G14)

OCC   IND

G3. What kind of work did she do? _____

_____

G4. What kind of business is that in? _____

_____

G5. About how many <u>weeks</u> did she work last year? _____

G6. And about how many <u>hours a week</u> did she work? _____

G7. Did she miss any work in 1974 because she was unemployed or on strike?

| 1. YES | 5. NO | (GO TO G9)

G8. How much work did she miss? _____ _____ _____
                                 DAYS   WEEKS   MONTHS

G9. Was there more work available so that your wife could have worked more in 1974 if she had wanted to?

| 1. YES | 5. NO |

G10. Would she have liked to work more if she could have found more work?

| 1. YES | 5. NO |

G11. About how much time does it take your wife to get to work each day, door to door? _____(ONE WAY) [ ] NONE (TURN TO PAGE 16, G14)

G12. About how many miles is it to where she works? _____(ONE WAY)

G13. Does she use public transportation to get to work, have a car pool, drive by herself, walk, ride with you, or what?

| 1. PUBLIC TRANS-PORTATION | 2. CAR POOL | 3. DRIVES | 4. WALKS | 5. RIDES WITH HUSBAND | 7. OTHER |

16

G14. How much do you (FAMILY) spend on food that you use at home in an average week? $_____(PER WEEK)

G15. Do you have any food delivered to the door which isn't included in that?

[ ] YES   [ ] NO   (GO TO G17)

G16. How much do you spend on that food? $_____per_____
(WEEK, MONTH)

G17. Did you or anyone else now living in your family receive or buy government food stamps last month?

[ ] YES   [ ] NO   (GO TO G22)

G18. For how many members of your family were stamps issued? _____

G19. How much did you pay for the stamps? $_____ per _____
(WEEK, MONTH)

G20. How much food could you buy with the stamps? $_____ per _____
(WEEK,MONTH)

G21. You said you spend _____ on food in the average week.
(MENTION AMOUNT IN G14)

Did you include in that only the amount of money you actually spent or did you also include the extra value of the food you get with stamps?

| 1. INCLUDES ONLY AMOUNT OF MONEY SPENT | 5. ALSO INCLUDES EXTRA VALUE OF FOOD GOT WITH STAMPS (i.e., MONEY SPENT PLUS VALUE OF STAMPS) |

G22. Did you (FAMILY) use government food stamps (commodity stamps) in 1974?

[ ] YES   [ ] NO   (GO TO G27)

G23. How much did you pay for the stamps in 1974? _____ per _____
(WEEK, MONTH)

G24. How much food could you buy with the stamps in 1974?

$_____ per _____
(WEEK, MONTH)

G25. Did you use food stamps regularly during all of 1974?

[ ] YES (GO TO G27)   [ ] NO

G26. For how many months did you use food stamps in 1974?

_____MONTHS   (GO TO G27)

G27. About how much do you (FAMILY) spend eating out, not counting meals at work or at school?

$_____ per _____
(WEEK, MONTH)

17

SECTION H: INCOME

(ASK EVERYONE)

To get an accurate financial picture of people all over the country, we need
to know the income of all the families that we interview.

H1. (INTERVIEWER: CHECK ONE)

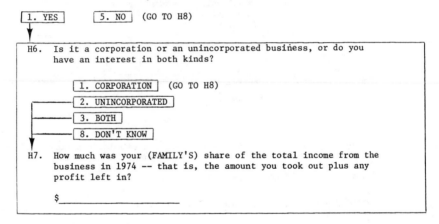

| 1. FARMER, OR RANCHER | | 5. NOT A FARMER OR RANCHER | (GO TO H5) |

H2. What were your total receipts from farming in 1974, in-
     cluding soil bank payments and commodity credit loans? $_____ A

H3. What were your total operating expenses, not counting
     living expenses? $_____ B

H4. That left you a net income from farming of? A-B = $_____ A-B

H5. Did you (R AND FAMILY) own a business at any time in 1974, or have a
     financial interest in any business enterprise?

| 1. YES | | 5. NO | (GO TO H8) |

H6. Is it a corporation or an unincorporated business, or do you
     have an interest in both kinds?

          | 1. CORPORATION | (GO TO H8)
          | 2. UNINCORPORATED |
          | 3. BOTH |
          | 8. DON'T KNOW |

H7. How much was your (FAMILY'S) share of the total income from the
     business in 1974 -- that is, the amount you took out plus any
     profit left in?

     $_____

(ASK EVERYONE)

H8. How much did you (HEAD) receive from wages and salaries in 1974, that is,
     before anything was deducted for taxes or other things?
                                                       $_____

18

H9. In addition to this, did you have any income from bonuses, overtime or commissions?

[ ] YES   [ ] NO   (GO TO H11)

H10. How much was that? $_____

H11. Did you (HEAD) receive any other income in 1974 from:

(IF "YES" TO ANY ITEM, ASK "How much was it?" ENTER AMOUNT AT RIGHT)

(IF "NO" ENTER "0")

a) professional practice or trade? $_____ per _____

b) farming or market gardening, roomers or boarders? $_____ per _____

c) dividends, interest, rent, trust funds, or royalties? $_____ per _____

d) ADC, AFDC? $_____ per _____

e) other welfare? $_____ per _____

f) Social Security? $_____ per _____

g) other retirement pay, pensions, or annuities? $_____ per _____

h) unemployment, or workmen's compensation $_____ per _____

i) alimony? child support? $_____ per _____

j) help from relatives? $_____ per _____

k) the new Supplemental Security Income, the gold (tan, yellow) checks? $_____ per _____

m) anything else? _____ $_____ per _____
                  (SPECIFY)

H12. Did anyone (else) not living here now help you (FAMILY) out financially -- I mean give you money, or help with your expenses during 1974?

[ ] YES   [ ] NO   (TURN TO PAGE 19, H14)

H13. How much did that amount to last year? $_____

```
      (DO NOT WRITE IN THIS SPACE)
           HEAD TYPE INCOME:
   L                A                T

```

H14. INTERVIEWER: REFER TO <u>H11d</u> AND <u>H11e</u> AND CHECK ONE.

| 1. INCOME FROM WELFARE OR ADC, AFDC | 5. NO SUCH INCOME | (GO TO H19)

H15. Was any of your ADC or welfare the new Supplemental Security Income, that is, the gold (tan, yellow) checks?

| 1. YES | | 5. NO | (GO TO H17)

H16. How much did that amount to? $_____ per _____

H17. Did welfare also help you out in any other way, like with your rent or other bills?

[ ] YES   [ ] NO (GO TO H19)

H18. About how much did that amount to in 1974? _____

(GO TO H19)

H19. INTERVIEWER: REFER TO H11f and CHECK ONE.

| 1. INCOME FROM SOCIAL SECURITY | | 5. NO SUCH INCOME | (GO TO H23)

H20. Did your Social Security include any of the new gold (tan, yellow) checks called Supplemental Security Income?

| 1. YES | | 5. NO | (GO TO H22)

H21. How much did that amount to in 1974? $_____ per _____

H22. Did you get any other help? _____

_____

(GO TO H23)

H23. INTERVIEWER: DOES HEAD HAVE WIFE IN FU?

[ ] YES, WIFE IN FU   [ ] NO WIFE IN FU OR FU HAS FEMALE HEAD (TURN TO
PAGE 20, H27)

H24. Did your wife have any income during 1974?

[ ] YES   [ ] NO (TURN TO PAGE 20, H27)

H25. Was it income from wages, salary, a business, or what?

_____   _____
     (SOURCE)   (SOURCE)

H26. How much was it before deductions?

$ _____ $ _____

(DO NOT WRITE IN THIS SPACE)
WIFE TYPE INCOME:

L   A   T

20

H27.   INTERVIEWER: REFER BACK TO COVER SHEET AND LIST
ALL PEOPLE 14 AND OLDER OTHER THAN THE CURRENT
HEAD AND WIFE. LIST THOSE IN THE FU AT ANY TIME
DURING 1974, INCLUDING THOSE WHO MOVED OUT!

[ ] NONE (TURN TO PAGE 22, H40)

_____
RELATION TO HEAD   AGE

H28. Did (MENTION PERSON) have any income   [ ] YES [ ] NO (GO TO H28
in 1974?   FOR NEXT
                                                                   PERSON
                                                                   LISTED)

H29. About how much did that amount to in 1974? $_____ in 1974

H30. Was that from wages, a pension, a
business or what?   _____
                                                        (SOURCE)

TX
TR

IF WAGES OR BUSINESS

H31. What kind of work did (he/she) do?
                                                   _____
                                                          (OCCUPATION)

H32. Can you tell me about how many weeks
(he/she) worked?   _____
                                                           (WEEKS)

H33. About how many hours a week was that?
                                                   _____
                                                           (HOURS)

H34. (IF DON'T KNOW) Was it more than half time? _____

H35. Did (he/she) miss any work in 1974 because
of unemployment or a strike?

[ ] YES   [ ] NO (GO TO H37)

H36. How much work did (he/she) miss?

                                           DAYS   WEEKS   MONTHS

H37. Did (he/she) have any other income?   [ ] YES   [ ] NO (GO TO H28
                                                                 FOR NEXT
                                                                 PERSON
                                                                 LISTED)

H38. What was that from?
                                                   _____
                                                          (SOURCE)

H39. How much was that last year? $_____ in 1974

(DO NOT WRITE IN THIS SPACE)
TYPE: L   A   T

| RELATION TO HEAD | AGE | | RELATION TO HEAD | AGE | | RELATION TO HEAD | AGE |

[ ] YES [ ] NO (GO TO H28 FOR NEXT PERSON LISTED)

$_____ in 1974

_____(SOURCE)

TX TR

(OCCUPATION)

(WEEKS)

(HOURS)

DAYS WEEKS MONTHS

[ ] YES [ ] NO (GO TO H28)

(SOURCE)

$_____ in 1974

[ ] YES [ ] NO (GO TO H28 FOR NEXT PERSON LISTED)

$_____ in 1974

(SOURCE)

TX TR

(OCCUPATION)

(WEEKS)

(HOURS)

DAYS WEEKS MONTHS

[ ] YES [ ] NO (GO TO H28)

(SOURCE)

$_____ in 1974

[ ] YES [ ] NO (GO TO H28 FOR NEXT PERSON LISTED)

$_____ in 1974

(SOURCE)

TX TR

(OCCUPATION)

(WEEKS)

(HOURS)

DAYS WEEKS MONTHS

[ ] YES [ ] NO (GO TO H28)

(SOURCE)

$_____ in 1974

(D O N O T W R I T E I N T H I S S P A C E)

TYPE: L A T   TYPE: L A T   TYPE: L A T

(T U R N T O P A G E 2 2 , H 4 0)

22

(ASK EVERYONE)

H40. Did anyone else living here in 1974 have any income? (INCLUDING CHILDREN UNDER 14)

[ ] YES   [ ] NO (GO TO H42)

H41. Who was that?

_____ ___   _____ ___   _____ ___
RELATION TO HEAD AGE   RELATION TO HEAD AGE   RELATION TO HEAD AGE

(TURN BACK AND ASK H28-H39 FOR THESE ADDITIONAL MEMBERS)

H42. INTERVIEWER CHECKPOINT: REFER TO H28-H40 AND CHECK ONE.

1. OTHER FAMILY MEMBERS WITH INCOME   5. NO SUCH PERSONS   (GO TO H47)

H43. Did anyone else living here in 1974 get any of the new Supplemental
      Security Income, the gold (tan, yellow) checks?

1. YES   5. NO   (GO TO H47)

	PERSON #1	PERSON #2
H44. Who was that?	_____ ___	_____ ___
	RELATION TO HEAD AGE	RELATION TO HEAD AGE
H45. How much did that amount to?	$_____	$_____
H46. Have you already included that?	[ ] YES [ ] NO	[ ] YES [ ] NO

(GO TO H47)

H47. Did you get any other money in 1974 -- like a big settlement from an insurance
      company, or an inheritance?

1. YES   5. NO   (GO TO H49)

H48. How much did that amount to? $_____ in 1974

H49. Do you help support anyone who doesn't live here with you?

1. YES   5. NO   (TURN TO PAGE 23, H54)

H50. How many? _____
H51. How much money did that amount to in the last year? $_____ in 1974
H52. Were any of these people dependent on you for more than half of their
      total support?

1. YES   5. NO   (TURN TO PAGE 23, H54)

H53. How many? _____

H54. Do you (FAMILY) have any savings such as checking or savings accounts, or government bonds?

| 1. YES | | 5. NO |

H55. Would they amount to as much as two months' income or more?

| 1. YES | | 5. NO |⟶

H56. Was there a time in the last five years when you had as much as two months' income saved up?

| 1. YES | | 5. NO |

(GO TO H57)

H57. What about the next few years -- do you think you (and your family) will be better off or worse off or what? _____

_____

_____

| 8. DON'T KNOW |
(GO TO H59)

H58. Why is that? _____

_____

H59. Do you (HEAD) belong to a labor union?

| 1. YES | | 5. NO |

24

SECTION J: FEELINGS

INTERVIEWER: IF RESPONDENT SIMPLY REPEATS ONE OF THE ALTERNATIVES GIVEN IN A
QUESTION, CIRCLE THAT WORD OR PHRASE. "YOU" MEANS <u>RESPONDENT</u> IN
THIS SECTION.

Now I have some questions which ask you to describe yourself or your feelings
about certain things. There are no right or wrong answers; we just want to
know how you would describe yourself.

J1. Have you usually felt pretty sure your life would work out the way you want
it to, or have there been more times when you haven't been very sure about it?

_____

J2. Are you the kind of person that plans his life ahead all the time, or do you
live more from day to day?

_____

J3. When you make plans ahead, do you usually get to carry out things the way you
expected, or do things usually come up to make you change your plans?

_____

J4. Would you say you nearly always finish things once you start them, or do you
sometimes have to give up before they are finished?

_____

J5. Do you sometimes feel you don't have enough control over your life, or is
what happens to you your own doing?

_____

SECTION K: EDUCATION

K1. How many grades of school did you (HEAD) finish?

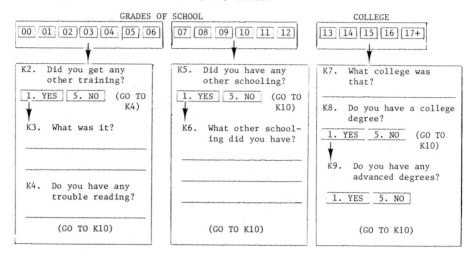

GRADES OF SCHOOL

| 00 | 01 | 02 | 03 | 04 | 05 | 06 | | 07 | 08 | 09 | 10 | 11 | 12 |

COLLEGE

| 13 | 14 | 15 | 16 | 17+ |

K2. Did you get any other training?

1. YES   5. NO   (GO TO K4)

K3. What was it?

_____

_____

K4. Do you have any trouble reading?

_____

(GO TO K10)

K5. Did you have any other schooling?

1. YES   5. NO   (GO TO K10)

K6. What other schooling did you have?

_____

_____

_____

(GO TO K10)

K7. What college was that?

_____

K8. Do you have a college degree?

1. YES   5. NO   (GO TO K10)

K9. Do you have any advanced degrees?

1. YES   5. NO

(GO TO K10)

K10. [ ] YES, WIFE IN FU   [ ] NO WIFE IN FU OR FU HAS FEMALE HEAD (TURN TO PAGE 26, L1)

K11. How many grades of school did your wife finish?

GRADES OF SCHOOL

| 00 | 01 | 02 | 03 | 04 | 05 | 06 | 07 | 08 | 09 | 10 | 11 | 12 |

COLLEGE

| 13 | 14 | 15 | 16 | 17+ |

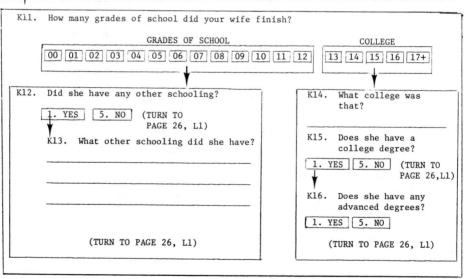

K12. Did she have any other schooling?

1. YES   5. NO   (TURN TO PAGE 26, L1)

K13. What other schooling did she have?

_____

_____

_____

(TURN TO PAGE 26, L1)

K14. What college was that?

_____

K15. Does she have a college degree?

1. YES   5. NO   (TURN TO PAGE 26, L1)

K16. Does she have any advanced degrees?

1. YES   5. NO

(TURN TO PAGE 26, L1)

26

INTERVIEWER: REMEMBER TO FILL OUT "BY OBSERVATION" SECTION FOR ALL INTERVIEWS.

SECTION L: NEW WIFE

L1. INTERVIEWER: REFER TO COVER SHEET AND CHECK ONE:

1. FU HAS NEW WIFE THIS YEAR

5. FU HAS SAME WIFE AS IN 1974 OR FU HAS NO WIFE OR FU HAS FEMALE HEAD
(TURN TO PAGE 27, M1)

L2. How much education did your wife's father have? _____

_____

L3. How much education did your wife's mother have? _____

_____

L4. How many years has your wife worked for money since she was 18? _____

_____

_____ | 00. NONE | (TURN TO PAGE 27, M1)

L5. How many of these years did she work full time for most of the year?

_____

_____ | ALL | (TURN TO PAGE 27, M1)

L6. During the years that she did not work full time, how much of the time did she work?

_____

_____

_____

SECTION M: NEW HEAD

M1. INTERVIEWER: CHECK ONE

| 1. FU HAS A NEW HEAD THIS YEAR | | 5. THIS FU HAS THE SAME HEAD AS IN 1974 |

(TURN TO PAGE 3 OF COVER SHEET)

M2. Now I have some questions about your family and past experiences. Where did your father and mother grow up? (FROM BIRTH TO 18 YEARS OF AGE)

ST, CO- FA

Father: _____   _____
                (State if U.S., Country if foreign)   (COUNTY OR TOWN)

ST, CO- MO

Mother: _____   _____
                (State if U.S., Country if foreign)   (COUNTY OR TOWN)

M3. What was your father's <u>usual</u> occupation when you were growing up?   OCC

_____

_____

M4. Thinking of <u>your</u> (HEAD'S) first full time regular job, what did you do?   OCC

_____ | 0. NEVER WORKED |
                                            (GO TO M6)

M5. Have you had a number of different kinds of jobs, or have you mostly worked in the same occupation you started in, or what?

_____

_____

M6. Do you (HEAD) have any children who don't live with you?

[ ] YES   [ ] NO (GO TO M9)   1st

M7. How many? _____ (NUMBER)   2nd

                                                             3rd

M8. When were they born? _____ _____ _____
                          (YEAR BORN)   (YEAR BORN)   (YEAR BORN) #

M9. Did you (HEAD) have any children who are not now living?   # BY 25

[ ] YES   [ ] NO (TURN TO PAGE 28, M11)

M10. When were they born? _____ _____ _____
                           (YEAR BORN)   (YEAR BORN)   (YEAR BORN)

28

M11. How many brothers and sisters did you (HEAD) have? _____ | 0. NONE |
                                                          (SPECIFY NUMBER)   (GO TO M13)

    M12. Did you have any brothers or sisters older than you?

        | 1. YES | | 5. NO |

M13. Is your religious preference Protestant, Catholic, or Jewish, or what?

    [ ] PROTESTANT | 8. CATHOLIC | | 9. JEWISH | OTHER _____
                                                                         (SPECIFY)

    ↓   (GO TO M15)

    M14. What denomination is that? _____

M15. Did you (HEAD) grow up on a farm, in a small town, in a large city, or what?

    | 1. FARM | | 2. SMALL TOWN | | 3. LARGE CITY | OTHER _____
                                                                  (SPECIFY)

M16. In what state and county was that (EXAMPLE: ILLINOIS, COOK COUNTY)

    ST,   CO- H
    |__|__|__|__|__| _____   _____
                                 (STATE)   (COUNTY)

    (IF DON'T KNOW TO M16) → M17. What was the name of the nearest town?
                                            _____(TOWN)

M18. What other states or <u>countries</u> have you lived in? (Including time spent abroad
      while in the armed forces.)

      _____

M19. Have you (HEAD) ever moved out of a community where you were living in order to
      take a job somewhere else?

    | 1. YES | | 5. NO |
        | ↓
        | M20. Have you ever turned down a job because you did not
        | want to move? | 1. YES | | 5. NO |
        ↓
M21. Were your parents poor when you were growning up, pretty well off, or what?

      _____

M22. How much education did your father have? _____

      (IF LESS THAN 6 GRADES) → M23. Could he read and write? _____

M24. How much education did your (HEAD'S) mother have? _____

M25. Are you (HEAD) a veteran?

    | 1. YES | | 5. NO |

M26. How many years have you (HEAD) worked since you were 18? _____

_____ [00. NONE] (GO TO M29)

M27. How many of these years did you (HEAD) work full time for most of the year?

_____ [ALL] (GO TO M29)

M28. During the years that you (HEAD) were not working full time, how much of the time did you (HEAD) work?

_____

_____

_____

Now I have a few questions about your (HEAD'S) health.

M29. Do you have a physical or nervous condition that limits the type of work, or the amount of work you can do?

[1. YES]   [5. NO] (TURN TO PAGE 3 OF COVER SHEET)

M30. How much does it limit your work? _____

_____

M31. How long have you been limited in this way by your health? _____

_____

M32. Is it getting better, or worse, or staying about the same? _____

_____

_____

(TURN TO PAGE 3 OF COVER SHEET)

30

COMPLETE THIS SECTION FOR ALL INTERVIEWS

SECTION N: BY OBSERVATION ONLY

N1. Who was respondent (relation to head)? _____

N2. Number of calls _____

GLOSSARY

The following is a description of some of the technical terms used in this volume. For more details on the measures used in these analyses see the documentation series entitled <u>A Panel Study of Income Dynamics</u>: Volume I, Study Design, Procedures and Available Data, 1968-72; Volume II, Tape Codes and Indexes, 1968-72; 1973 Supplement (Wave VI); 1974 Supplement (Wave VII); and 1975 Supplement (Wave VIII).

ACHIEVEMENT MOTIVATION - A personality measure from social psychology representing a propensity to derive satisfaction from overcoming obstacles by one's own efforts in situations where the outcome is ambiguous. It is believed to be developed by early independence training, to result in the taking of calculated but not extreme risks and in the raising of goals after success experiences. It was administered in the 1972 interview.

ASPIRATION-AMBITION - A seven-item index of attitudes and plans reflecting attempts to improve economic well-being; see Volume II of the documentation, p. 789. The items include the following:

> Might move on purpose
> Wanted more work, and/or worked more than 2500 hours last year
> Might quit a job if it was not challenging
> Prefers a job with chances for making more money to one more pleasant
> Is dissatisfied with self
> Spends time figuring out how to get more money
> Plans to get a new job, knows what type of job and what it might pay
> (Second and last items neutralized for those for whom they are inappropriate.)

BETA - A measure of the explanatory power of an independent variable when considered in a multivariate context.

BETA WEIGHTS - When the independent and dependent variables in the regression equation $Y = a + b_1X_1 + b_2X_2 + u$ are measured in their "natural" units (e.g., in dollars, years, hours) then the parameters b_1 and b_2 reflect the effect on Y of a one unit change in X_1 and X_2, respectively. If all variables are standardized so that each has a mean of zero and a standard deviation equal to one, then the equation becomes $Y = \beta_1 X_1 + \beta_2 X_2 + v$ and the β's can be interpreted as the fraction of a standard deviation that Y changes as a result of a change of one standard deviation in the X's. The β's are regression coefficients (sometimes called "partial regression coefficients"), the β's are *beta weights* or standardized regression coefficients. The unstandardized and standardized coefficients are related in the following way:

$$\beta_1 = \frac{b_1 \sigma X_1}{\sigma_Y}$$

COGNITIVE ABILITY - See *TEST SCORE*

CONNECTEDNESS (to sources of information and help) - The following eight-item set of reported behaviors measuring the extent to which the respondent has friends or habits likely to keep him informed or provide help; see Volume II of the documentation, p. 793.

> Attended PTA meeting within the year
> Attends church once a month or more
> Watches television more than one hour a day
> Knows several neighbors by name (2 points if 6 or more)
> Has relatives within walking distance
> Goes to organizations once a month or more
> Goes to a bar once a month or more
> Belongs to a labor union and pays dues
> (First item is neutralized for families without children).

COUNTY WAGE RATE for unskilled casual labor - An estimate of the wage rate for unskilled labor in the county where the respondent lives, secured by mail questionnaires sent each year to the state official in charge of unemployment compensation.

COUNTY UNEMPLOYMENT - An estimate of the unemployment rate in the county where the respondent lives, secured by mail questionnaires sent each year to the state official in charge of unemployment compensation.

CRAMER'S V - A measure of association between two nominal scale variables when they have no natural rank order. It is similar to the Chi-square measure except it is adjusted for the number of observations and is constrained to take on values between 0 and 1. The higher Cramer's V, the greater the association between the classification.

DECILE - If all units are arranged in ascending order on some criterion such as income and each tenth marked off and identified, the ten groups formed are called deciles. The actual dividing points of incomes are given in Volumes II and III of the documentation.

DESIGN EFFECT - The effect of departures from simple random sampling in probability samples, defined as the ratio of the actual sampling variance to the variance of a simple random sample of the same size.

ECONOMIES OF SCALE - As the size of a family increases, if the costs do not increase proportionately, then we say there are economies of scale in large families.

ECONOMIZING INDEX - An index of six reported behaviors taken to indicate parsimonious use of money; see Volume II of the documentation, p. 790.

>   Spent less than $150 a year on alcohol
>   Spent less than $150 a year on cigarettes
>   Received more than $100 worth of free help
>   Do not own late model car
>   Eat together most of the time
>   Spent less than $260 a year eating out
>   (The fourth item is neutralized for those not owning cars).

EFFICACY INDEX - An index composed of six self-evaluations which reflect a sense of personal effectiveness, and a propensity to expect one's plans to work out; see Volume II of the documentation, p. 787.

>   Is sure life will work out
>   Plans life ahead
>   Gets to carry out plans
>   Finishes things
>   Would rather save for the future
>   Thinks about things that might happen in future.

ELASTICITY - Refers to the response of the quantity of a good consumed to a change in price or in income. If the percentage change in the quantity of food consumed, for example, is greater than the percentage change in the price, then the demand for food is said to be price-elastic; if it is less than the percentage change in price, it is price-inelastic.

ETA^2 - A measure of the explanatory power of a set of subclass means based on a one-way analysis of variance. It is analogous to the R^2 from regression analysis. Measuring the fraction of variance on the dependent variable which is explained by a single categorical variable.

EXOGENOUS VARIABLE - Variables whose levels and changes are determined by forces independent of those being studied, as contrasted with endogenous variables which are interdependent with variables in the system.

EXPECTED VALUE - When a dependent variable is determined by a combination of systematic and random effects, the expected value is that part which can be predicted from the systematic relationship. In the case of regression, it is the value predicted by the regression equation.

F-TEST - A test of the significance of the proportion of the variance explained by a set of several predictors or several classifications of a single predictor; see *STATISTICAL SIGNIFICANCE*.

FAMILY - All persons living in a household who are related by blood, marriage, or adoption. In occasional cases an unrelated person has been included in the family unit if he or she shares expenses and is apparently a permanent member of the unit. The definition of family used in this study includes single person families. This contrasts with the Census Bureau convention of classifying single persons separately as "unrelated individuals."

FAMILY COMPOSITION CHANGE - Contains several dimensions, most of them related to the family's position in the standard life cycle: marriage, birth of first child, youngest child reaches age six and starts school, children leave home, one spouse dies. The sex and marital status of the head, the number of children, and age of the youngest are the main components.

FAMILY MONEY INCOME - Family income, unless otherwise designated, is the total regular money income of the whole family, including income from labor, capital, and transfers such as pensions, welfare, unemployment compensation, workmen's compensation, and alimony received by all members of the family. It includes neither capital gains (realized or unrealized) nor irregular receipts from insurance settlements.

FAMILY TAPE - A data file containing all the data on that family from all eight interviews. There is one record for each sample family. The final eight-year data tape includes only families interviewed in 1975 so that there are no partial records. Where there are several families derived from an original sample family, the early family information will appear on each of their records.

HEAD OF FAMILY - In nuclear families the husband is defined as the head. In families with a single adult, that adult, regardless of sex, is defined as the head. In ambiguous cases of more than one adult, the head is the major earner or the one who owns the home or pays the rent. Note that the head of the family may change due to marriage, divorce, or death. For splitoff families, the head is similarly defined.

HOUSEHOLD - Probability samples usually sample occupied dwellings, which may contain more than one household, which in turn may contain more than one family. However, the term household is often used loosely to mean family, since the number of individuals living with unrelated adults is very small. A family is a group of individuals related by blood, marriage, adoption.

HUMAN CAPITAL - The economically valued skills which result from the investment in one's self through education or other training.

IMPUTED RENT - A form of nonmoney income and consumption for home owners who can be thought of as in the business of renting a house to themselves. It is estimated by taking 6 percent of the owner's net equity in his house (house value minus remaining mortgage principal).

INCOME - Unless otherwise specified, this means total family money income including regular money transfers. (See *FAMILY MONEY INCOME*.) When a year is given, it is the year of the income, not the (later) year when the interview was taken.

INCOME/NEEDS RATIO - See *NEEDS STANDARD*

INDIVIDUAL TAPE - A data file with one record for each individual as of 1975, containing all the data for that individual over the whole period and all the data for the family that individual was in each of the eight years. The tape contains some individuals who are not in the sample and are thus excluded from the analysis but who are necessary in order to derive family information for those in the sample. Individuals and families have separate weights; see *WEIGHT* and Volume I of the documentation.

INELASTIC - See *ELASTICITY*

INTELLIGENCE - See *TEST SCORE*

LEAST SQUARES ESTIMATION - That method of estimation which minimizes the squared deviations of the actual value from the predicted value of the dependent variable. Such estimators are sensitive to extreme cases and nonnormal distributions.

LINEAR REGRESSION - See *REGRESSION*

MOTIVATION - See *ACHIEVEMENT MOTIVATION*

MULTICOLLINEARITY - A problem arising in estimation if two or more predictors are highly intercorrelated. It thus becomes difficult to estimate the separate effects of these variables.

MULTIPLE REGRESSION - See *REGRESSION*

MONEY EARNINGS ACTS INDEX - An index of behavioral reports that the family is doing things to increase its money income including working long hours, getting to work on time, changing jobs, looking for a better job (see Volume II of the documentation, p. 794).

MTR - Tables and other computer output are indexed by a Machine Tabulation Re-
quest number for checking and filing purposes. The number appears at the bottom
of each table.

NEEDS STANDARD - An estimate of the annual income necessary for a family to meet
basic needs. The standard is generated in the same way as the official federal
poverty line; food needs are determined according to age and sex, as estimated
and priced by the USDA (in <u>Family Economics Review</u>), and food costs are adjusted
for economies of scale; this figure is then multiplied by a factor to allow for
other needs also differentially greater for smaller families. The needs standard, based on the "low-cost" food plan is 1.25 times the official federal poverty standard, which is based on the "economy" food plan.

   The absolute level is to some extent arbitrary and is not adjusted for inflation in later years, but the standard adjusts for differences in family size
and structure so the status of families that differ in composition can be compared.

   The needs standard is corrected for changes in family composition during
the prior year, so that it is legitimate to compare it with the prior year's income. See Volume I of the documentation for further details.

NUMBER OF CASES - The actual number of families or individuals on which the estimate is based. The number does not reflect the proportion of the population represented by that group because of the differences in sampling and response rates.
See *WEIGHT*.

NULL HYPOTHESIS - See *STATISTICAL SIGNIFICANCE*

ORDINARY LEAST SQUARES (OLS) - See *REGRESSION*

QUINTILE - If all cases are arranged in ascending order on some criterion such
as income and each fifth is marked off and identified, these five groups are
called quintiles.

PARTIAL CORRELATION COEFFICIENTS (partial R^2) - The partial correlation coefficient (squared) is a measure of the marginal or added explanatory power of one
predictive variable or set of variables, over and above all the other predictors.
It can be thought of as the correlation of two sets of residuals, after removing
the effects of all other predictors from both the dependent variable and the predictor in question. It is also the fraction of the remaining distance to perfect explanation (1.00) the multiple correlation (squared) is moved by the added
predictor. It is the best measure of the "importance" of a predictor or group
of predictors.

PERCENT OF POPULATION - The fraction of the weight-sum represented by a subgroup is an estimate of the percent of the population (of families or individuals) it represents. Aggregate estimates can be made by ratio-estimating procedures, i.e., multiplying the sample mean by the proportion of the population times an outside estimate of the aggregate number of families or individuals.

PLANNING INDEX - A subset of the efficacy index consisting of the following items:

> Plans ahead
> Prefers to save for future
> Thinks about the future.

REAL EARNING ACTS INDEX - A five-item index, with neutralization of the inapplicable items, reflecting ways of earning nonmoney income or investing in self; see Volume II of the documentation, pp. 789-90.

> Saved more than $75 doing own additions or repairs
> Saved more than $75 growing own food
> Saved more than $75 repairing own car
> Head was taking courses or lessons with economic potential
> Head spent spare time productively.

R^2 - The fraction of variance in the dependent variable which is explained by the set of explanatory variables.

REGRESSION - A statistical technique which estimates the separate, independent effect of each of several predictors on a dependent variable. It minimizes the sum of the squared deviations from predicted values (see *LEAST SQUARE ESTIMATOR*) and assumes that the dependent variable is a linear and additive function of the predictors and a random error term.

REGRESSION COEFFICIENT - The estimated effect of a predictor on the dependent variable obtained from a regression analysis. It shows the expected effect that a unit change in the predictor would have on the dependent variable if all other predictors were held constant.

RESERVATION WAGE - The minimum market wage which will entice a person to seek employment.

RISK AVOIDANCE INDEX - An index of six reported behaviors indicating the avoidance of undue risks; see Volume II of the documentation, p. 791.

> Car (newest if several) in good condition
> All cars are insured
> Uses seat belts (2 points if all the time)
> Has medical insurance or a way to get free care
> Head smokes less than one pack of cigarettes a day
> Have liquid savings (2 points if more than two months income in
>   savings).

SIZE OF LARGEST CITY IN AREA - The primary sampling unit (PSU) is a county or (rarely) cluster of counties and the size of the largest city in that area is intended to reflect the number and variety of jobs, as well as differences in costs and standards of living. When the city is 50,000 or more, the area is a Census Standard Metropolitan Statistical Area.

SPLITOFF - A splitoff is someone who left a sample family and is living in a different household. Most splitoffs are children who left the parental home to set up their own households. When a couple is divorced, one of them is designated as the continuing family and the other is a splitoff.

STANDARD DEVIATION - A measure of the dispersion of a distribution of observations around their average (or predicted) value. If random effects are normally distributed, roughly two-thirds of the observations fall in a range of the mean plus or minus one standard deviation. It is equal to the square root of the variance and is denoted by the symbol σ. The standard deviations presented in the tables should be considered in the context of the design effect.

STATISTICAL SIGNIFICANCE - Traditional statistical inference tests the hypothesis that a finding (e.g., that some effect is greater than zero) is a chance result from the sample not existing in the population. If the probability is sufficiently small (e.g., less than 5 percent), this "null hypothesis" is rejected and it is believed that there is some effect which is "statistically significant."

In most initial searching of data for what matters, and in what form, the assumptions of statistical testing are violated because many alternative models are tried. In addition, there are problems of estimating sampling variance with complex samples.

TARGET POPULATION - Those families who were in the lowest 20 percent of the income/needs distribution in any one of the five years, 1967-1971, or nine years, 1967-1975.

TEST SCORE - A 13-item sentence completion test developed as a culture-free, sex-free, and race-free measure of "intelligence." Of course, like all such measures, it may also test acquired skills or freedom from test anxiety. For further details, see Appendix F, <u>Five Thousand American Families--Patterns of Economic Progress</u>, Vol. I, p. 381-5.

TRUST IN OTHERS - An index composed of five self-evaluating items on trusting others, believing in the fairness of the system; see Volume II of the documentation, p. 788.

Does not get angry easily
It matters what others think
Trusts most other people
Believes the life of the average man is getting better
Believes there are *not* a lot of people who have good things
they don't deserve.

T-TEST - Under certain assumptions, estimated regression coefficients have a frequency distribution known as the t-distribution. This fact can be used to form a test of significance for the coefficients, called the t-test. See also *STATISTICAL SIGNIFICANCE*.

WEIGHT - There are weights both for the file of individuals and families which make the weighted estimates representative of the national non-institutional population of the continental United States. They offset differences in sampling rates and response rates, and the extra probabilities of inclusion of those who married nonsample members. There will be more respondents in lower income and minority groups than the weighted proportions because of oversampling. The oversampling simply makes the estimates for those groups more reliable.

Weighted estimates essentially multiply each case by a number representing the number of households it represents. Each digit of the weight represents 500 households.

YEAR - Interviewing was done in the spring of each year from 1968 through 1975, but the income questions refer to each previous year (1967-1974).

INDEX

514

522